Preservation Education

Preservation Education

Sharing Best Practices and Finding Common Ground

Edited by Barry L. Stiefel and Jeremy C. Wells

University Press of New England
Hanover and London

University Press of New England
www.upne.com

Manufactured in the United States of America
Designed by Christopher Kuntze
Typeset in Warnock Pro, Myriad Pro, Grotesque Condensed, and Empire Display by Westchester Publishing Service

Library of Congress Cataloging-in-Publication Data

Preservation education : sharing best practices and finding common ground / edited by Barry L. Stiefel and Jeremy C. Wells.
pages cm
ISBN 978-1-61168-595-4 (cloth : alk. paper) — ISBN 978-1-61168-596-1 (pbk. : alk. paper) — ISBN 978-1-61168-597-8 (ebook)
1. Historic preservation—Study and teaching. I. Stiefel, Barry, editor. II. Wells, Jeremy C., editor.
CC135.P715 2014
363.6'907—dc23

2014004398

5 4 3 2 1

To Lori, Izzy, and Corinne—the ones who keep things in perspective as to why preservation is so important. B.L.S.

To my beloved wife, Hilary Stevens, whose indefatigable support of my passion for heritage, the built environment, and teaching motivates me each and every day. J.C.W.

CONTENTS

ACKNOWLEDGMENTS

This work was possible through the helpful assistance of several institutions and people. The editors would like to thank the generous support of Roger Williams University as well as the College of Charleston's School of Humanities and Social Sciences in helping to make this publication possible. Furthermore, we are also very grateful to Roger Williams University for hosting the "Preservation Education: Sharing Best Practices and Finding Common Ground" conference that took place September 8–9, 2012 in Providence, Rhode Island. The joint College of Charleston/Clemson University Graduate Program in Historic Preservation, the Cultural Landscape Laboratory at the University of Georgia, and the Historic Preservation Program and Center for World Heritage Research and Stewardship at the University of Florida also gave generous sponsorship for the conference.

Individuals we would like to recognize for their roles in this project, as well as in our lives and respective educations, and in no particular order, include Philip Marshall and Steven White at Roger Williams University, Morris Hylton III at the University of Florida, Cari Goetcheus and Daniel Nadenicek at the University of Georgia, Steven Hoffman from Southeast Missouri State University, and Andréa Livi Smith at the University of Mary Washington. Barry Stiefel would also like to recognize Tom Dodd at Ann Arbor Community High School, Ted Ligibel at Eastern Michigan University, Bob Grese at the University of Michigan, Eugene Cizek at Tulane University, and Robert Russell at Salve Regina University, who have been exceptional mentors and role models.

1 An Introduction to Postsecondary Historic Environment Education

Jeremy C. Wells and Barry L. Stiefel

Higher education is facing greater pressures for reform than perhaps at any other time in its existence. Costs are increasing faster than inflation while the guarantee of a good education seems ever more elusive to students and their parents. As a 2012 article in the *Economist* summarizes, just 57 percent of students complete a bachelor's degree within 6 years and in the process accumulate an average debt of $26,000. Alarmingly, only a quarter of these graduates are judged as having a proficient level of literacy, perhaps due to a rather light average reading load of only forty pages per class.[1] Critics charge that universities are not delivering on their promise, instead focusing on maximizing revenue while ignoring their educational mission, and in the process offering useless or "dumbed down" degrees and producing graduates ill-prepared to enter the workforce.[2] Moreover, while the assessment of student learning is well developed in primary and secondary education, it is far less refined for postsecondary education, so in some respects we do not sufficiently understand to what extent university students are actually learning or not learning.[3] As with many arguments, the reality of the state of higher education is complex with many shades of gray; clearly our anecdotal experiences lead us to believe that universities can and do produce well-qualified graduates, though some would argue that we could do better.

Outcomes-based learning is a concept that has been closely associated with the production of well-qualified graduates since its rise to popularity in the 1990s. This movement is far from new, however, with proposed origins related to the failure of the United States to launch the world's first artificial satellite in 1957. The fact that the Soviet Union beat the United States to this auspicious goal was construed to mean that the American educational system was a failure, and thus needed a complete overhaul.[4] In this charged environment, John Carroll and Benjamin Bloom developed the concept of "mastery learning" in the 1960s that specified certain, fixed behaviors as desirable outcomes of the educational experience while treating the time in which students should achieve these outcomes as a variable.[5] Up until this point, "education" tended to be defined by how long students sat in a specific class rather than expectations of what the students would actually be able to learn. In the late 1970s and early 1980s, William Spady expanded mastery learning into the contemporary idea of "outcomes-based instruction," which required that all aspects of an educational system should be organized around a student's achievement of specific behavioral objectives.[6] By the early 1990s, outcomes-based learning was a driving factor in curriculum development in primary and secondary education and began its rise to prominence within higher education.

Schools are increasingly acknowledging outcomes-based learning, along with its emphasis on accountability, and the importance of exploring diverse pedagogical techniques in an effort to improve teaching as well as to better defend the effectiveness of the academy in producing competent graduates. Across the higher education spectrum, curriculum design is moving "towards an outcomes-based, employment-related and market-oriented" system "increasingly informed by outside interests" with data derived from the assessment of learning outcomes.[7] Not everyone is comfortable with this trend, however; there is significant disagreement that outcomes-based learning is the best or only tool for producing well-qualified graduates. Criticisms include claims that the approach results in "dumbed down" curricula that "indoctrinate" students and discourage independent thought; moreover, the basis of outcomes-based learning is not actually objective, but rather emphasizes the subjective values of its promulgators.[8] While acknowledging the diversity of thought on the necessity of outcomes-based learning, the underlying assumption of the authors of this volume is that outcomes-based learning has sufficiently strong theoretical and empirical bases to have value, even if its implementation may sometimes be flawed.

Curricula, therefore, should be designed to achieve specific learning objectives while the effectiveness of pedagogical techniques should in turn be assessed against how well these objectives have been met. While larger and better known fields, such as the sciences, education, and English, have an abundance of literature on pedagogical techniques and curriculum design, similar resources for heritage conservation simply do not exist and there appears to be little or no evidence of an active discussion on outcomes-based learning in this field, much less pedagogical techniques and curriculum design. Part of this situation may be due to the fragmented, multidisciplinary nature of topics that address the historic environment from disciplines as broad as architecture, landscape architecture, history, construction management, materials science, environmental psychology, and anthropology (among other possibilities) that make a focused approach difficult. Even agreeing on a common term to describe the activities that we, as professionals and academics, do in the historic environment has been difficult. Depending on the geographical location in the Anglophone world, it may be known as historic preservation, heritage conservation, architectural or building conservation, cultural landscape conservation, or conservation of the historic environment. In other languages, words used may be some variation of the English "cultural patrimony" (*patrimonio cultural* [Spanish], *patrimoine culturel* [French]), "cultural property" (*kulturgut* [German]), or "antiquarian" (*antikvarie* [Swedish]).

There is even disagreement as to whether or not our activities in the historic environment can be rightly called a discipline or if other disciplines simply engage in heritage conservation, but this is increasingly becoming a less popular perspective, especially in light of the long-established degree programs specializing in the historic environment at many universities and colleges around the world. These programs were based on the pioneering master's degree programs developed in the 1960s and 1970s at the University of York (U.K.), Columbia University, and Middle East Technical University in Ankara, Turkey.[9] Hundreds of programs have been created following these pioneers, and at all levels: diplomas, certificates, associate's, bachelor's, and doctoral degrees. Unique ontological orientations, epistemological perspectives, and methodological approaches define a discipline,[10] and one could make the argument that heritage conservation as applied to the historic environment satisfies all three requirements. The conservation of the historic environment places a unique meaning on the authenticity of "historic" building and landscape fabric, has a well-developed body of knowledge independent of other disciplines, and its practitioners have created novel methodologies for the assessment of everything from building conditions to stakeholder values. Certainly, there is clear evidence that practitioners label themselves with one of the many terms for the conservation of the historic environment rather than using another disciplinary term, such as "architect," "urban planner," or "architectural historian."

Furthermore, there is also another application of "preservation education" to consider, as used by the library science field.[11] While library and archival materials are important aspects of material culture—indeed, they are artifacts—does the study of the proper treatment of books fall within the scope of "preservation education," as the field of the historic environment perceives it? We do not believe this to be the case.

Last, in the twenty-first century, assumed ideas behind authenticity and significance are increasingly being called into question. The traditional definition of authenticity, which is well documented in national and international doctrine, is defined by the presence of "intact" fabric that has borne witness to past events. While this "fabric-based" definition of authenticity is still widely taught and employed in professional practice, it is now recognized that there are other dimensions of authenticity that are far more ambiguous within historic contexts. When we discuss authenticity it increasingly needs to be qualified, as Peter Howard directs when he asks, "Which authenticity do you mean . . . the authenticity of the material? Of the context? Experience? Function? Site?"[12] The univocal meaning of authenticity, if it ever existed, is becoming increasingly difficult to sustain in the twenty-first century.

In a similar sense, the meanings associated with "significance"—what places have and do not have value—are becoming increasingly diverse. Long associated with historical "facts" and aesthetical value, significance can now encompass social, cultural, and personal (experiential) values.[13] The traditional concept of significance and these more contemporary meanings are often framed as "tangible" versus "intangible" values, respectively, but this dichotomy perpetuates the erroneous assumption that the value human beings associate with objects is somehow contained within the objects themselves.[14] If, as it would indeed seem plausible, all values associated with historical objects are actually contained within the human frame, then all heritage is therefore intangible.[15]

It is not clear, however, how the increasing diversity of meanings associated with authenticity and significance should influence historic environment education, although as a number of chapters in this book suggest, the liberal arts may be particularly useful to better understand these meanings. Assuming that we make students better aware of these issues, how ought a broader definition of significance and authenticity affect practice, even when doctrines and regulatory environments tend to reinforce narrower, traditional interpretations? If authenticity and significance are foundational concepts for all research and practice in the historic environment, then this foundation is far from secure, as it is under attack from multiple perspectives. To meet this challenge, how should historic environment educators therefore address the multidimensional meanings associated with authenticity and significance in their research and teaching, especially in terms of how practice should be affected? This question, perhaps, is one of most significant ones for educators today, yet it has been addressed minimally, if at all, within a pedagogical frame.

The chapters in this volume that explore some of these issues are the result of "Preservation Education: Sharing Best Practices and Finding Common Ground," an international conference held on September 8 and 9, 2012, in Providence, Rhode Island. This conference brought higher education leaders in historic environment programs together from across the globe. Attendees from the United States, Australia, Brazil, Canada, Italy, Israel, Mexico, the Netherlands, Sweden, and the United Kingdom presented their research to explore outcomes-based education in an effort to produce better historic environment specialists and further define educators' roles and responsibilities in the greater professional and public arena. While most attendees were from universities or colleges, vocational programs were also well represented.

The dearth of material on preservation/conservation education in relation to the historic environment was the impetus for both the "Preservation Education" conference and this publication. This book will hopefully provide a better basis for pedagogical methods for individuals responsible for postsecondary instruction at all levels—from the undergraduate to the doctoral—which address the historic environment. As far as the editors of this volume are aware, this is the first work of its kind that *exclusively* addresses historic environment education at the postsecondary (or tertiary) level that is published by an academic press and, as such, has undergone extensive peer review.[16] There is therefore little precedent from which to base the selection and organization of this volume. The chapters herein are therefore representative of a broad range of pedagogical topics in an international context.

A number of similar conferences that have been convened, from the 1960s on, which also addressed historic environment education, but several characteristics make the 2012 "Preservation Education" conference unique. First, it was the first conference of its kind to emphasize learning objectives, assessment, outcomes, and specific pedagogical techniques. Previously, the focus has tended to be on content, topics, and theoretical principles. While these emphases are important, they miss the larger picture of understanding how students, in specific degree programs, should be held accountable in terms of learning outcomes. Second, its international focus is unusual, although not without precedent. The International Council on Monuments and Sites (ICOMOS) International Training Committee has hosted conferences with an international focus, for instance, but most educational conferences have focused on a national scale, such as those from National Council for Preservation Education (NCPE), the Conference on Training and Architectural Conservation (COTAC), and Heritage Canada Foundation's National Roundtable on Heritage Education.

Third, the "Preservation Education" conference is the only one of its kind that has occurred outside of a membership organization, making it more accessible and open to participants from a wider variety of backgrounds. When all three of these characteristics are combined, the "Preservation Education" conference is justifiably unique and will hopefully set a new precedent that others will follow.

Last, the "Preservation Education" conference and this resulting volume were largely inspired by a lack of literature on the subject of historic environment education at the postsecondary level. For instance, NCPE only established the first refereed journal to focus on pedagogical topics in historic environment education in 2008. A literature review on topics related to historic environment education readily shows that there is a chronic lack of focus on pedagogy and curriculum development; specifically, there is little scholarship on assessing outcomes in the context of historic environment programs, defining what a "well-prepared" student is in relation to the job market or continued academic studies (the Ph.D.), and understanding expectations in regard to educating students to advance the discipline. This volume is therefore designed to provide a foundation for these topics and to encourage others to contribute original research and case studies to advance postsecondary level historic environment education.

Preservation Education: Sharing Best Practices and Finding Common Ground is unique within the field of academic study of pedagogical issues specific to preservation/conservation due to its breadth of subject matter, reflecting the growing number of people involved. In many ways it is a product, or an outgrowth, of a long tradition of analysis within preservation that has focused on training, which is sometimes called "best practices."[17] In other words, the subject of the analysis has shifted from "what is the best way to fix a historic building?" to "what are the best ways for teaching people how to preserve historic properties (and why) according to the various standards that have been established?" Additionally, the historic resources are no longer just buildings, but a larger and more nuanced collection of landscapes, districts, sites, and objects. As the questions we ask have become more complex, the resulting analysis of pedagogical issues is increasingly multifaceted, recognizing there may be more than one way to approach the instruction of students through desired outcomes.

One Perspective on the Literature of Historic Environment Education

While acknowledging that historic environment education at the postsecondary level is a global endeavor, it is beyond the scope of this volume to conduct a complete literature review that encompasses aspects of research and practice on six continents representing dozens of languages. Instead, we will offer the perspective from the United States as an example, not because it is necessarily representative of global practice, but because the editors are most familiar with this geographical area. What is discussed here will be applicable to North American practice in general and secondarily to other English-speaking contexts, such as the United Kingdom and Australia. We recognize that Asian, African, and Latin American contexts are not well represented in English-speaking literature and encourage others to more fully explore this area. Additionally, this review is not intended to represent a history of the historic preservation movement in the United States, as this has been done elsewhere.[18] Michael Tomlan and Michael Woodcock have already addressed the history of graduate historic preservation programs in the United States, so this topic will also not be addressed in depth.[19] What this review will accomplish, however, is a focus on seminal publications and events that influenced the development of the educational components of the field.

While any contemporary built environment conservation course would readily acknowledge the foundational nineteenth-century works of John Ruskin[20] and Eugène Viollet-le-Duc,[21] a number of influential publications arose in the twentieth century that were equally influential in creating the basis for accepted preservation/conservation rhetoric, although they are no longer read on a regular basis. By the turn of the twentieth century, preservationists in the United States were increasingly interested in the preservation and restoration work happening in Europe, as evidenced by numerous reports by the American Scenic and Historic Preservation Society on visits to various preservation and restoration projects in many countries, including Great Britain.[22] The Society for the Protection of Ancient Buildings (SPAB), located in England, published some of the earliest examples of educational material on conservation techniques, such as *Notes on the Repair of Ancient Buildings* (1903), Charles Reed Peers's "The Care of Ancient Monuments" published in *The Architectural Review* (1917),[23] and Albert Powys's *Repair of Ancient Buildings* (1929).[24] These widely read materials focused on technical details, emphasizing a scientific approach to practice, including the need for accurate documentation. In essence, they were taking the preservation principles espoused by the 1877 SPAB Manifesto and putting them into action.[25]

While early American preservationists were reading these materials, they did not adopt the strict preservationist mentality of the Europeans, instead opting to restore buildings to a hypothetical period from the past. They did, however, adopt a similar scientific mentality in their efforts as with Joseph Everett Chandler's restoration of Paul Revere's house in Boston from 1907 to 1908. A 1914 article from *The Architectural Record* describes Chandler's work as a process of scientific inference with archaeological overtones.[26] Such an approach achieved its full flower in the restoration and reconstruction of Colonial Williamsburg in the 1930s where any hint of "imagination" or "theatrical" methods was strongly discouraged. Only a "valid" scientific approach could restore the one and only "original reality" of a building, according to Colonial Williamsburg's architects. Fiske Kimball's 1935 assessment of the project was that it "evoked substantial accuracy and perfection."[27] To its inventors, Colonial Williamsburg was the "historic truth" based in "fact."[28] A complete issue of *Architectural Record* in 1935 (vol. 78, no. 6) featured a comprehensive chronicle of the work at Colonial Williamsburg and the principles of its restorers and helped introduce a new generation of architects to a specific philosophy behind the restoration of old buildings.

Not everyone agreed with the restoration philosophy at Colonial Williamsburg, however. William Sumner Appleton, the founder of the Society for the Preservation of New England Antiquities (now called Historic New England), instead emphasized strict preservation over restoration, but, at the same time, was careful to advocate for similar scientifically oriented, archaeological techniques in documentation, and, when justified, restoration.[29] Appleton's publications that outline this approach helped frame the counterpoint to Colonial Williamsburg; eventually Appleton's ideas prevailed, especially with the National Park Service, but it would take many decades for this to be realized.

It was in the 1930s that the National Park Service started to assume an influential role in historic preservation practice, largely through the efforts of Charles E. Peterson. An early, published example of best practice in the United States is the 1935 edition of *Specifications for the Measurement and Recording of Historic American Buildings and Structural Remains.* It was "authored" by the Historic American Building Survey (HABS), which was part of the National Park Service, just two years after the program's creation. It is highly probable Peterson was the sole or contributing author of this publication, as he was responsible for creating HABS.[30] As the title implies, the purpose of this publication (and its subsequent reiterations under various titles to the present, such as the *HABS Field Guide*) is to instruct the reader how to best measure and record historic buildings using accurate, scientific methods.

After World War II, the National Park Service established its official stance on historic preservation, emphasizing "stabilization and preservation" rather than "restoration or reconstruction" and appropriated the words of Diderot, the eighteenth-century French archaeologist: "It is better to preserve than repair, better to repair than restore, and better to restore than to reconstruct."[31] Through its *Preservation Briefs* and *Preservation Tech Notes,* begun in the 1970s, the National Park Service has been responsible for promoting a wide variety of technical recommendations and establishing a philosophical approach to interventions. In a similar sense, the Secretary of the Interior's Standards,[32] a series of documents outlining a doctrinal philosophy of treatment for preservation, restoration, rehabilitation, and reconstruction, and the *National Register Bulletins* have been enormously influential on historic preservation education, justifying the basis for the identification of historic buildings and districts as well as their treatment.

The National Trust for Historic Preservation (NTHP) also played a leading role in the development of preservation education in the United States during the 1960s and 1970s by hosting a series of three conferences in Williamsburg, Virginia, that generated publications that addressed questions concerning the definition and scope of the field as well as the development of training and educational programs. The first of these conferences was the Seminar on Preservation and Restoration, which convened in September 1963 and sought to understand "the history of American preservation (including its European background), to analyze its philosophical basis, examine its present effectiveness, and to discuss ideal ways to shape its future."[33] This conference resulted in the book, *Historic Preservation Today,* which, for the first time, began to codify the boundaries of the discipline of historic preservation, its history, and its philosophy. The appendix of this work contains a page-and-a-half that addresses education, with an emphasis on establishing standards, apprenticeship programs, and reference books on historical building construction.[34] Arguably, Charles E. Peterson was likely the driving force behind these recommendations, emphasizing the need for students to be directly engaged in restoration work.[35]

A year after the publication of *Historic Preservation Today,* in March 1967, the NTHP organized a second conference, "Principles and Guidelines Workshop II," which produced *Historic Preservation Tomorrow,* published in the same year. This book refined the work of the earlier conference, but it is the chapter by Walter Muir Whitehill that is of particular importance, as it describes the need to create a "corps of [preservation] technicians [such as] artisans competent to reproduce the early craft objects in wood, masonry and metal, to architects versed in restoration of individual buildings, to planners and landscape architects skilled in creating proper surroundings for them."[36] Whitehill called on schools of architecture to create these programs at the graduate level and for scholars to research needed reference books on early American construction methods and techniques. He also encouraged institutions to create apprenticeship programs for craftspeople. Whitehill's chapter formed the basis of *The Whitehill Report on Professional and Public Education for Historic Preservation,* a document published by the NTHP in 1968, which formed the foundation of the new degree programs in historic preservation that American colleges and universities would create over the next decades.[37] This report advocated for the immediate creation of university and apprenticeship programs in partnership with the NTHP.

The third, and last, Williamsburg conference was "Preservation and Conservation: Principles and Practices," organized in 1972 in collaboration with the International Centre for Conservation (ICC) in Rome; it produced a publication by the same name in 1976.[38] The material presented at this third conference included a much stronger emphasis on art and materials conservation than in previous conferences, possibly due to the influence of the ICC. This work is particularly important as it presents in clear and unambiguous detail the professional roles of the preservation/restoration architect, historian, materials conservator, and preservation planner. It also includes a series of chapters on historic preservation education, including an analysis by Stephen Jacobs on the inadequacy of most universities to address the growing need to create preservation-specific programs, while lauding the nascent efforts of the preservation programs of Columbia University, Cornell University, the University of Florida at Gainesville, and the University of Virginia at Charlottesville.[39] The art conservation degree program at New York University's Conservation Center, which produced some of the first American architectural conservators, is described in detail, including its curricula and specializations.[40]

At the time, the inclusion of New York University's university-level curriculum in a publication was unusual, and would remain so throughout the 1970s as the major focus on curriculum design was on primary and secondary, not tertiary (postsecondary), education. The first consequential work at the primary and secondary level was *Education Through Historical Preservation* (1979) by Eugene Cizek and Lloyd Sensat, which began as a program two years earlier in select Louisiana public schools.[41] Their premise was "knowing our past helps us to understand the present and see the way toward a more meaningful and environmentally responsible future."[42] In 1981, the Education Through Historic Preservation program was the first preservation education program to be given an Honor Award by the NTHP.[43] Roughly at the same time (1980), Carol D. Holden, Gary L. Olsen, and Michele R. Olsen produced *Historic Preservation Education: Curriculum Materials.* Both publications were lesson plan instruction manuals directed toward teachers of primary education. The manual by Holden, Olsen, and Olsen was funded by several preservation-related organizations, including the Champaign County Historical Museum, the Illinois Humanities Council, the National Endowment of the Humanities, and NTHP. These authors were "deeply concerned by the lack of understanding today's children show for their built environment," and thus went on to guide teachers how to teach the relevance of historic preservation, with an emphasis on architectural history.[44] Both *Education Through Historical Preservation* and *Historic Preservation Education: Curriculum Materials* differed significantly from early publications prevailing at the time, like *Children and Architecture* by Emily A. Barnes and Bess M. Young (1932), where the curriculum was focused on architectural history, design, and nomenclature—not on preservation or repair.[45]

Robert Melnick and Richard Wagner published one of the first guidelines on the creation of postsecondary curricula for historic preservation programs in 1979. Their article identified six guidelines that all such programs should emphasize: there should be clear occupational outcomes, the material must emphasize the interdisciplinary nature of the field, only graduate programs should be created (undergraduate programs were inappropriate), new programs should be a natural outgrowth from related programs, there should be a focus on regional resources, and the programs should remain small to maximize quality.[46] Other, contemporary examples of curricula tended to instead focus on integrating a preservation concentration within an already existing built environment program, such as interior design or landscape architecture.[47]

At the time, Melnick and Wagner's article was a rare example of published material providing guidance in postsecondary historic preservation education. In reaction to this lack of specific guidance on the development of postsecondary educational programs and their curricula, university educators formed NCPE between 1978 and 1980 at the instigation of the NTHP.[48] It was during this time that an understanding was emerging among academics in historic preservation that greater coordination and communication was needed for the purposes of facilitating new and assisting already extant preservation programs, fostering the exchange of ideas (both best practices and pedagogy), and creating better public awareness about the preservation field. Six years later (1986), the nonprofit Historic Preservation Education Foundation was chartered in order to disseminate information on important preservation issues not readily available to the public.

By the late 1980s, a broader academic discussion related to preservation pedagogy and curriculum design had emerged in the form of whitepapers.

Publications from more readily available and peer-reviewed sources, such as refereed journals and university presses, remained rare. Some of these whitepapers are available from the National Center for Preservation Technology and Training (NCPTT), the Getty Research Institute, the International Centre for the Study of the Preservation and Restoration of Cultural Property (ICCROM) (Rome), as well as various research libraries. These papers have been produced by such organizations as the National Park Service, NTHP, and NCPE, among others. Examples include *A Heritage at Risk: A Report on Heritage Education (K–12)* and *Focus on 2000: A Heritage Education Perspective.*[49] A cross-referenced index of repositories as well as their holdings has yet to be developed, so the current extent of these whitepapers is not fully known.

The first historic preservation books that universities and colleges used as textbooks appeared in the 1980s. These works often found a home in the undergraduate and graduate preservation programs across the country, even though many of their authors did not necessarily intend them to be used in this way. James M. Fitch's *Historic Preservation: Curatorial Management of the Built World,* published in 1982, was arguably the first such example.[50] Fitch's books, along with *Keeping Time: The History and Theory of Preservation in America* by William J. Murtagh (1988), were popular because they were written in an easily understood photojournalist format, but their objective was still "formal training" and a basic level of understanding that historic places should be preserved.[51] The great shift here was the intended (or unintentional) audience, which was now an educated person interested in a preservation introduction, in contrast to a technical publication for someone already trained in architecture, city planning, or archaeology, which was common up until this time.

The rise of the book targeted at preservation students took place shortly after two key events within the greater history-heritage umbrella: the bicentennial celebrations of American independence (c. 1975–87) and the formal organization of public history as a discipline (c. 1976–79). The 200th anniversary of the United States fostered people's interest in their historic past, especially in places where significant events had taken place, and so outreach to help foster public understanding of historic preservation needed to be developed. Furthermore, this approach, akin to the public history discipline, had to present the information in a way that was both meaningful and understandable. Previous publications, such as the HABS's *Specifications,* were too technical, targeting professionals in existing, well-established disciplines, rather than assuming their readers originated from a broader background. The new historic preservation textbooks made fewer assumptions about their readers' disciplinary background and were ready tools to engage a broader public in the field.

One area that had broad implications for the public, yet relied on a specific disciplinary background, was law. The regulatory environment figures prominently in the identification and protection of historic resources and has broad impact on property owners and, as such, preservation law has been central to most historic preservation programs since their inception. Robert E. Stipe was an early leader in this area, catalyzing interest with his article, "Preservation Lawyers—Unite," in the July 1970 issue of *Preservation News,* written while he was on a Fulbright Fellowship in England. The NTHP hosted a conference on preservation law in Washington, D.C., the following year.[52] Law journals, such as the *Duke University Law Journal* and the *Wake Forest University Law Review,* published editions devoted to preservation legal topics in 1971 and 1976, respectively.[53] In 1982, the same year that Fitch published his book, Stipe wrote the influential publication *Local Preservation Legislation: Questions and Answers* and *Historic Preservation in Foreign Countries.*[54] These kinds of exchanges in preservation legal approaches between Europe and North America sustain the tradition of exchanging ideas on theory and practice begun by Eugène Emmanuel Viollet-le-Duc and John Ruskin in the nineteenth century.[55]

In the twenty-first century, published articles on preservation education are increasingly focusing on an international context, such as in the Middle East, Latin America, and Asia, and the problems inherent with non-Western concepts of authenticity and intangible heritage,[56] which parallels the growth of new programs that address World Heritage, such as the M.S. in architecture-heritage conservation and preservation at the University of Minnesota. Other emerging themes include techniques to more effectively collaborate with other built environment professionals, even when there are significant differences, such as the mapping, bridging, and integrating model developed at the University of Hong Kong.[57] More is being published on curriculum design and pedagogical techniques, especially those focusing on experiential learning, such as the University of Pennsylvania's graduate "praxis" program[58] and service learning as part of Shepherd University's undergraduate historic preservation program.[59] Unique curricula, such as preservation engineering, are also being explored.[60] Last, there is an increasing focus on the role of liberal arts education in undergraduate programs, "balancing depth and breadth" in the curriculum, and raising questions in terms of the relationship between undergraduate and graduate education.[61]

Perhaps the most promising development in terms of scholarship in historic environment education is NCPE's creation of *Preservation Education and Research* (PER) in 2008, with Anat Geva and Nancy Volkman serving as founding co-editors. This is the first refereed journal in English focusing exclusively on issues of historic environment education.[62] Although the journal is based in the United States, its focus is international and since its inaugural issue has published on a wide variety of pedagogical topics of interest to a global audience. It holds the promise of becoming an influential and essential resource for the historic environment educator.

This publication, as an edited book, is a first—a volume specifically devoted to historic environment education—within the United States, and possibly abroad, to be published by an academic press. The previous efforts, such as by NCPE and Columbia University's Preservation Alumni, were produced by preservation interest groups. Like the publications that came before this, we hope that it becomes a link in a continuously growing chain of understanding on this very important matter, such as a monograph completely devoted to the subject.

The Best Practices Shared and the Ground Found in Common

With the past literature on preservation education behind us what did we—the editors and contributors to this project—find for the present? Moreover, what directions for the future are we going (as well as where are we not)? We begin with Regina Faden's "You Don't Have to Give Up What You Love: Liberal Arts at Work," with her interest in museum studies—an allied field to historic preservation. According to Faden, at a time when Americans are questioning the value of higher education, many parents and students want to be reassured that their significant financial and personal investment toward an undergraduate liberal arts education is not frivolous. Her premise comes from the fact that many undergraduate colleges traditionally fail their students, particularly those in the arts and humanities, by not defining the skills students learn at school and their practical and meaningful application—unless it means graduate school. Liberal arts colleges need to help students identify and apply the skills they learn at college, possibly as part of an internship. Then college graduates will be able to pursue a career without having to forfeit the subjects they love because they do not know how to find a place that values their skills and interests. Robert Russell continues with a similar analysis, expanding it into a comparative study called "First Pete and then Repeat? Fundamental Differences in Intention between Undergraduate and Graduate Preservation Programs." Russell argues that despite the increasing emphasis in undergraduate education across the country on what is essentially job training—the direct (and frequently explicit) correlation between a major and an assumed future employment trajectory—the goal of undergraduate liberal arts education should not be directly related employment. Conversely, the common purpose of graduate training in historic preservation is preparation for a professional career. Few choose academia or some other path. Therefore, even though there might appear to be significant overlap in undergraduate and graduate curriculums, the ultimate goals of the two enterprises are different enough that what may appear to be the same is actually something very distinctive at the graduate level from what is taught to undergraduates.

Robert W. Ogle, in "Thinking and Doing: A Twenty-First Century Pedagogy for Preserving the Historic Architectural Artifact," explores the historical American educational models that were designed to resuscitate the skills requisite of the craft tradition and why they failed. He also reviews the recent revival in heritage preservation and how certain colleges and universities are addressing student and market demand. The preservation integrated learning model (PILM)—which looks at status quo, field school, strategic partnership, and full integration for curriculum design—references the historic craft tradition yet integrates the relational concepts of thinking-doing, head-hand, theory-practice within a framework that recognizes recent advances in preservation technology and the vertiginous variety of contemporary higher education institutional structures in the United States. According to Ogle, PILM serves as a roadmap for administrators, faculty, researchers, practitioners, and stewards of heritage property to see a clearer pathway to reuniting "thinking and doing" in preservation education, especially at the undergraduate level.

Andréa Livi Smith's "The Development of a Preservation Planning Board Game" studies the experience of senior undergraduate historic preservation students as they develop and design a preservation planning educational game at a liberal arts institution as part of their final project prior to graduation. The course included the design and administration of a questionnaire to assess aspects of preservation planning best adapted to game inclusion. The course itself was a valuable learning experience for the students, who had to deepen their mastery of preservation planning concepts and terms as well as work together toward a common goal.

In order to broaden our horizons (referring to the predominantly North American audience reading this book) we also look at international perspectives, beginning with Silvio Mendes Zancheti and the "Challenges and Dilemmas in Heritage Conservation," looking at Brazil and other parts of the world. Zancheti's approach is on using scientific and cultural approaches to conservation. Continuing with the discussion in Latin America is the chapter "Benefits of Using Qualitative Methodologies in the Evaluation of Preservation Training Programs' Performance in Developing Countries: A Case Study of the Northeast Region of Brazil," co-authored by Karla Nunes Penna and Elisabeth Taylor. Within their research they delve into the issue of establishing parameters for evaluating performance of preservation training programs in developing countries, which has (so far) proven challenging to institutions and professionals. Educational programs set within harsh social, economic, and political contexts where heritage preservation is not usually seen as an essential component of the urban development process in the face of poverty and social inequality are confronted with issues affecting the outcomes of evaluations. Considering these issues is essential in order to establish appropriate quality levels for training programs. Evaluations made within this situation demand personal reflections and in-depth understanding of a given context, meaning the evaluation should not depend entirely on quantitative methods. Gathering information through qualitative methods provides new insights into the experiences of individuals, groups, and communities, and highlights "invisible" issues. Their aim is to present some of the benefits of utilizing qualitative ethnographic methods to evaluate the performance of conservation training centers based on "more realistic" standards.

Looking to Europe is the example of Sweden, in "Integrated Conservation of Built Environments: Swedish Reflections from Three Decades of Program Development," co-authored by Bosse Lagerqvist, Ingrid Martins Holmberg, and Ola Wetterberg. Beginning with the bachelor's program in Integrated Conservation of Built Environments at the University of Gothenburg in 1978, and into the mid-1980s, preservation was a local experiment until it was considered acceptable in Sweden's higher education curriculum. As a program that brought together scholarly traditions from the humanities, social sciences, natural sciences, as well as technology, it was gradually accepted due to the growing societal need for professionals mastering the complex problems involved when preserving and developing built environments. Since 1978 the development of content and structure has been balancing three pedagogical perspectives: the subject matter (history of built environments), professional practices, and theoretical perspectives with reflection on subject matter and practices. This chapter discusses the perspectives of the program's pedagogics and challenges that provide useful insights on practice-based higher education, as well as the necessity to generate research that could contextualize coursework with knowledge and meaning.

From the Middle East, the cradle of humanity's earliest built environments and architectural monuments, is a contribution by Shelley-Anne Peleg entitled Saving the Stones—Practical Conservation Training Program: A Case Study of the International Conservation Center, Citt'a di Roma (in Acre, Israel)." According to her research there is a moral responsibility in the way cultural heritage is preserved, entailing an ongoing need for new approaches. It means that conservation must continue to develop and adopt new holistic approaches that address social values as well as the obvious building materials and construction and safety issues. Her case study is that of Acre, Israel, where the heritage there to be preserved includes the Christian Crusaders and Muslim Ottomans, which is administered by the Jewish state's Israel Antiquities Authority and multiple academic institutions. It is within this historic city, built on many layers of civilization, that modern life continues. Ongoing conservation and development procedures present true challenges and questions. Prerequisites for the conservation training programs in Acre include sharing, exchanging, and facilitating students from backgrounds of history, art, archaeology, and architecture as well as law, theology, sociology, and cultural studies.

While international perspectives on preservation education are incredibly valuable and rich, there is also much to be learned from distance learning—education that can take place from *anywhere* (in contrast to somewhere) by means of new technologies and modes of communication. We begin with Henry Russell and Philip Leverton's "Delivering a Changing Conservation Curriculum by Distance Learning in the Twenty-First Century." Russell and Leverton provide a U.K. perspective on the changing shape of university- and college-level education in the field of preservation as the twenty-first century unfolds. Emphasis is placed on the delivery of programs by means of distance learning, enhanced by e-learning capabilities, rather than provision by means of full-time, classroom-based tuition. The evolution of the concept of "heritage" is discussed, with regard to both the range of buildings, structures, and their settings afforded this status, and the growing awareness of the need to understand the significance of such assets from a range of perspectives. The question is asked as to whether our established understanding of what constitutes a "program" is undergoing change as the notion of the traditional "place-based" higher education institution comes under challenge. The emergence of opportunities for learning through massive open online courses (MOOCs) is noted. It is argued that opportunities may emerge for an increasingly more diverse range of students to register from a global pool of online options in order to meet their particular interests in heritage conservation.

In comparison to Russell and Leverton's chapter is "Public History, Adult Students, and the Community: Moving Beyond the Distance-Education Classroom," by Anastasia L. Pratt. Each of the courses brings the theories and methods of public history to the students' local communities. Students visit, analyze, and work with local museums, historical societies, archives, and libraries. They complete oral history interviews of local people. They become part of their community's history. In venturing into the community, local historians, archivists, librarians, teachers, and storytellers are invited to join us in the academic world. Programs ranging from webinars to speaking engagements are a natural outgrowth of this interaction. Of particular interest is the interplay of public history with preservation education.

The origins of preservation education have a strong root in design-related pedagogical studies, such as architecture and interior design, but not exclusively. Paul Hardin Kapp, Lauren Weiss Bricker, and Luis G. Hoyos's study, "Documentation and Design in Association: Historic Preservation Design Using Social History, Advocacy, and Drawing in the Architecture Design Studio," found that historic preservation programs can challenge the traditional curricula offered by schools of architecture. Moreover, historic preservation concentrations offered within larger architectural programs present unique opportunities for the education of designers—whether they are focusing on preservation or not. From the onset, students encounter a building, or a grouping of buildings and spaces; however, they often are not introduced to broader history that both created them or affected them. Moreover, architecture students often lack an understanding of historic context that is embedded in the historic resource. The historic preservation design instructor's primary objective is to introduce to students how to understand and document hierarchical characteristics of historic environments. Their approach explores design pedagogy that incorporates material documentation, understanding, theory, and practice of historic preservation, specifically through the use of social history, advocacy, and graphic presentation in the historic preservation studio. The primary goal in this pedagogical approach is to widen the range of applications of the students' architectural skills while recognizing that architecture has social implications within the patrimony of the city.

Diniz Moreira and Luiz Manuel do Eirado Amorim continue the study of preservation architect pedagogy with "Training in the Conservation of Modern Architecture: A Latin American Experience" and the challenges of preserving modern architecture. Issues pertaining to modern buildings include the use of new materials that were not fully understood in terms of their long-term performance; the use of traditional materials in new ways; the misconception that modern buildings required little maintenance or were maintenance-free; and the misunderstanding of the patina as a dirty stain (and not as a natural sign of aging). In this context, it is necessary to prepare architects and engineers to face the new challenges posed by the conservation of this built heritage. Therefore, they argue that there is a need for specific training in the conservation of modern architecture that differs from the traditional one. By considering these training issues, we also expect to contribute to the discussion of the major challenges faced by the conservation of modern architecture.

Focusing specifically on building interiors is Melissa Santana and Valerie L. Settles's innovative research on "Integrating Historic Preservation into the Undergraduate Interior Design Curriculum." They have found that interior design education most frequently focuses on developing new spaces; however, it is increasingly important for designers to utilize existing buildings in pursuit of more sustainable design strategies. Although many believe that sustainable design addresses only environmental issues, it also encompasses economic and social aspects, as does historic preservation. Consequently, Santana and Settles see historic preservation as a natural choice for inclusion in an interior design curriculum because it is a technique that allows students to integrate sustainable characteristics into a design solution. Due to this natural fit, students are able to understand preservation terminology and apply the standards that are often required for a certified rehabilitation.

Robert Benedict and Cari Goetcheus add to the design-related pedagogical milieu through the real estate profession in "The Critical Role of Preservation in Graduate Real Estate Curricula." Their premise is that preservation curricula have long offered single courses in related fields to broaden the horizons of preservation students, yet a consistent dilemma has been balancing the need to provide preservation-focused skill sets (i.e., preservation theory, historic style identification, preservation law, etc.) with rudimentary exposure to the variety of discipline realms in which preservation resides (i.e., real estate development, public policy, land use planning, etc.). This chapter delves into one of those discipline realms within which preservation resides, real estate development, to address a perceived curricula gap within graduate real estate programs. The perceived weakness in real estate pedagogy is that for real estate development students interested in the adaptive reuse of historic properties and/or taking advantage of historic tax incentives there is little preservation training currently offered, yet a demand exists.

The last two contributing chapters, "Social Science Research Methodologies and Historic Preservation: Broadening the Possibilities for a

Preservation Thesis" by Jeremy C. Wells and "Learning Among Friends: Using Heritage-Based Educational Practices to Improve Preservation Law Pedagogy," by Barry L. Stiefel and Gilbert S. Stiefel, propose that how pedagogical methods are used in preservation programs may need to be reconsidered for qualitative improvement. Each of their approaches has studied others who have questioned the way we learn best. Wells looks at the empirical master's thesis, exploring areas in which social science research methodologies can be applied to specific historic environment research questions. While there is a wide array of social science research methodologies available from grounded theory to phenomenology, many of these approaches can be a poor fit given the limited resources and disciplinary background of a master's student, but a few, such as content analysis, lend themselves more naturally to the pragmatic approach demanded by master's-level research. Wells also discusses ways to more effectively mentor students, especially in the problems encountered with human subject research, such as obtaining appropriate samples along with the importance of creating and sticking with a work plan.

Stiefel and Stiefel propose that historic preservation professionals' perspectives are shaped by educational experiences. Indeed, certain subjects may be learned more efficiently using methods developed by other cultures. This premise is exhibited in the teaching of historic preservation law and legal practice. The traditional Socratic method, as developed by Harvard University's Christopher Columbus Langdell, is compared with the *havruta* method used by the Jewish people, with preservation law used in place of Jewish religious law in a secular academic setting. Therefore, exposure to learning about preservation using methodologies developed by different cultural traditions might facilitate a richer experience, including other subjects besides preservation law.

A final chapter focuses on the outcomes of the scholarship. Here, the editors have analyzed where we appear to be now, the directions we appear to be headed, as well as other directions that should be considered. As mentioned previously, the intention of this scholarship is to be the beginning of a new line of inquiry—not the end all. We not only hope, but also look forward to what lies ahead in the teaching of historic preservation and how it can always be made better. In the words of the late Robert E. Stipe, "basically it [historic preservation] is the saving of people and lives and cities—not just buildings—that is important to all of us. We have before us the unparalleled opportunity, if we are determined, to contribute significantly to upgrading the quality of human existence. If we can achieve this, to some extent at least, the architecture and history [and everything else] will fall into place."[63]

Notes

1. "Not What It Used to Be," *Economist* (1 December 2012), 29–30.

2. See Trevor Hussey and Patrick Smith, *The Trouble with Higher Education: A Critical Examination of Our Universities* (New York: Routledge, 2010).

3. See Richard Arum and Josipa Roksa, *Academically Adrift: Limited Learning on College Campuses* (Chicago: University of Chicago Press, 2011).

4. S. Hodge, "The Origins of Competency-based Learning," *Australian Journal of Adult Learning,* 47:2 (2007), 180.

5. John Carroll, "A Model of School Learning," *Teachers College Record,* 64 (1963), 723–33; Benjamin Bloom, "Learning for Mastery," *Evaluation Comment,* 1:2 (1968), 1–5.

6. William G. Spady, "Competency Based Education: A Bandwagon in Search of a Definition," *Educational Researcher,* 6:1 (1977), 9–14; William G. Spady, *Outcome-Based Instructional Management: A Sociological Perspective* (Washington, DC: National Institute of Education, 1981).

7. Ronald Barnett and Kelly Coate, *Engaging the Curriculum in Higher Education* (Maidenhead: Society for Research into Higher Education, 2005), 38.

8. Kevin Donnelly, *Dumbing Down: Outcomes-based and Politically Correct—the Impact of the Culture Wars on Our Schools* (Prahran, Victoria: Hardie Grant Books, 2007); Phyllis Schlafly, "What's Wrong with Outcome-Based Education?" *The Phyllis Schlafly Report,* 26:10 (1993), 1–4.

9. Michael Tomlan, "Historic Preservation Education: Alongside Architecture in Academia," *Journal of Architectural Education,* 47:4 (1994), 187–96; John H. Stubbs and Emily Gunzburger Makaš, *Architectural Conservation in Europe and the Americas: National Experiences and Practice* (Hoboken, NJ: John Wiley & Sons, 2011), 101.

10. Jack Amariglio, Stephen Resnick, and Richard Wolff, "Division and Difference in the 'Discipline' of Economics," *Critical Inquiry,* 17:1 (1990), 150.

11. See Association of Research Libraries, *Preservation Education in ARL Libraries* (Washington, DC: Association of Research Libraries, 1985); Susan G. Swartzburg, *Preservation Education Directory* (Chicago: American Library Association, 1988); and Michèle Valerie Cloonan, *Global Perspectives on Preservation Education* (Munich: K. G. Saur, 1994).

12. Peter Howard, "Historic Landscapes and the Recent Past: Whose History?" in *Valuing Historic Environments,* ed. Lisanne Gibson and John Pendlebury (Surry: Ashgate Publishing, 2009).

13. Jeremy C. Wells, "Authenticity in More Than One Dimension: Reevaluating a Core Premise of Historic Preservation," *Forum Journal,* 24:3 (2010), 36–40; Randall Mason, "Fixing Historic Preservation: A Constructive Critique of 'Significance,'" *Places,* 16:1 (2003), 64–71.

14. Emma Waterton, Laurajane Smith, and Gary Campbell, "The Utility of Discourse Analysis to Heritage Studies: The Burra Charter and Social Inclusion," *International Journal of Heritage Studies,* 12:4 (2006), 339–55.

15. Laurajane Smith, *The Uses of Heritage* (London: Taylor & Francis, 2006), 54.

16. Since the 1960s, there are examples of individual chapters in broader publications that address historic environment education at the postsecondary level, which are discussed in the section addressing historic environment literature. In addition, the National Council for Preservation Education (NCPE) has released a series of unpublished booklets that address historic preservation education topics.

17. "Best practice" is the improvement of method or technique of a vocational skill applied to preservation practice. This is in contrast to pedagogy (the science of education), which ranges from early childhood development to advance skills acquisition.

18. For instance, see Charles Bridgham Hosmer, *Presence of the Past: A History of the Preservation Movement in the United States Before Williamsburg* (New York: Putnam,

1965); Charles Bridgham Hosmer, *Preservation Comes of Age: From Williamsburg to the National Trust, 1926–1949* (Charlottesville: Preservation Press, 1981); William J. Murtagh, *Keeping Time: The History and Theory of Preservation in America* (New York: John Wiley & Sons, 1997).

19. Michael A. Tomlan, "Observations on an 'Established Discipline': The Continuing Development of Preservation Education at the Graduate Level," in *Historic Preservation: Forging a Discipline: Proceedings of a Symposium in Honor of James Marston Fitch and Twenty Years of Historic Preservation at Columbia University*, ed. Beth Sullebarger (New York: Preservation Alumni, 1989), 57–64; Tomlan, "Historic Preservation Education," 187–96; David G. Woodcock, "Academic Preparation for Preservation Practice," *APT Bulletin*, 40:3/4 (2009), 43–49.

20. John Ruskin, *The Seven Lamps of Architecture* (London: Smith, Elder, and Co., 1849).

21. Eugène-Emmanuel Viollet-le-Duc, *Dictionnaire Raisonne de L'architecture Française* (Paris: B. Bance, 1854).

22. An example of this type of investigation is from the *Twentieth Annual Report, 1915, of the American Scenic and Historic Preservation Society* (Albany: J. B. Lyon Company, 1915), which reported on preservation and restoration work in Great Britain, France, Belgium, the Netherlands, Germany, Russia, Austria-Hungary, Sweden, and Italy.

23. Charles Reed Peers, "The Care of Ancient Monuments," *Architectural Review*, 41 (March 1917), 65–66.

24. A. R. Powys, *Repair of Ancient Buildings* (London: J. M. Dent; New York, E. P. Dutton, 1929).

25. The SPAB Manifesto emphasized the need to preserve old buildings (i.e., keep all layers of change as intact as possible) versus restore them. See http://www.spab.org.uk/what-is-spab-/the-manifesto/.

26. "Restoration of the Paul Revere House, Boston," *Architectural Record*, 36 (July 1914), 80.

27. Fiske Kimball, "The Restoration of Colonial Williamsburg in Virginia," *Architectural Record*, 78:6 (1935), 359.

28. William Graves Perry, "Notes on the Architecture [of Colonial Williamsburg]," *Architectural Record*, 78:6 (1935), 370–77.

29. William Sumner Appleton, "Destruction and Preservation of Old Buildings in New England," *Art and Archaeology*, 8:3 (1919), 131–83.

30. See Historic American Buildings Survey, *Specifications for the Measurement and Recording of Historic American and Structural Remains* (Washington, DC: Historic American Buildings Survey, 1935).

31. Newton B. Drury, "A Symposium on Principles of Historic Restoration: The National Park Service," *Antiques* (July 1950), 30.

32. See http://www.nps.gov/hps/TPS/standguide/. Although originally intended to evaluate federal historic tax credit projects and embedded in a regulatory framework, the Standards have been widely adopted across all levels of practice and education within the United States.

33. National Trust, *Historic Preservation Today* (Charlottesville: University Press of Virginia, 1966), v.

34. Ibid., 254, 255.

35. Ibid., 220.

36. Walter Muir Whitehill, "Education and Training for Restoration Work," in *Historic Preservation Tomorrow* (Washington, DC: National Trust for Historic Preservation, 1967), 32.

37. Walter Muir Whitehill, *The Whitehill Report on Professional and Public Education for Historic Preservation* (National Trust for Historic Preservation, 1968).

38. Sharon Timmons (ed.), *Preservation and Conservation: Principles and Practices* (Washington, DC: Preservation Press, 1976).

39. Stephen Jacobs, "The Education of Architectural Preservation Specialists in the United States," in *Preservation and Conservation: Principles and Practices,* ed. Sharon Timmons (Washington, DC: Preservation Press, 1976), 457. At the time of the conference, in 1972, none of these universities had established a specific degree program in historic preservation. Columbia University and Cornell University would go on to establish master's programs in the 1970s, while the University of Florida continued with its original concept of housing preservation as a concentration within an architectural studies curriculum until it created its first preservation degree program in the 2000s. The University of Virginia still maintains that the best approach to training preservationists/conservationists is to create a specialization within other disciplines.

40. Lawrence Majewski, "The Education of Art Conservators," in *Preservation and Conservation: Principles and Practices,* ed. Sharon Timmons (Washington, DC: Preservation Press, 1976), 481–92.

41. Eugene Cizek and Lloyd Sensat, *Education Through Historical Preservation* (St. Charles Parish, LA: St. Charles Parish Schools, 1979).

42. Will Fellows, *A Passion to Preserve: Gay Men as Keepers of Culture* (Madison: University of Wisconsin Press, 2004), 235.

43. Eugene Cizek, e-mail message to Barry Stiefel, 5 November 2012. We are greatly indebted to Dr. Cizek for the insights he provided with his early, groundbreaking preservation education research.

44. Carol D. Holden, Gary L. Olsen, and Michele R. Olsen, *Historic Preservation Education: Curriculum Materials* (Champaign, IL: The Center for the Study of Art and Architecture, 1980), Introduction (no page number).

45. Emily A. Barnes and Bess M. Young, *Children and Architecture* (New York: Bureau of Publications, Teachers College, Columbia University for Lincoln School of Teachers College, 1932).

46. Robert Melnick and Richard Wagner, "Preservation Education: Guidelines and Implementation of a Program," *Bulletin of the Association for Preservation Technology,* 11:2 (1979), 53–59.

47. Buie Harwood, "A Force for the Future: Preservation Education Case Study: Interior Design, Winedale Institute in Historic Preservation, University of Texas at Austin," *Journal of Interior Design,* 5–6:1 (1979), 23–32; Suzanne L. Turner, "Preservation as a Component in Curricula of Landscape Architecture," in *Research in Landscape Architecture: The Annual Meeting of the Council of Educators in Landscape Architecture, August 20–23, 1980,* ed. Arnold R. Alanan (Madison: University of Wisconsin Press, 1980), 59–60.

48. Michael A. Tomlan, "The Early Years: Founding the National Council for Preservation Education," *Preservation Education & Research,* 3 (2010), 70–71.

49. National Council for Preservation Education, *A Heritage at Risk: A Report on Heritage Education (K–12)* (Burlington: University of Vermont Historic Preservation Program and the National Council for Preservation Education, 1987); and Caneta Skelley Hankins, *Focus on 2000: A Heritage Education Perspective* (Natchitoches, LA: National Center for Preservation Technology and Training, 1997).

50. Fitch was the founder of Columbia University's preservation program, the first in the country. The first editor (Jeremy Wells) used Fitch's book at the University of Pennsylvania while the second editor (Barry Stiefel) used it at Eastern Michigan University.

51. James M. Fitch, *Historic Preservation: Curatorial Management of the Built World* (New York: McGraw-Hill, 1982), i. See also William J. Murtagh, *Keeping Time: The History and Theory of Preservation in America* (Pittstown, NJ: Main Street Press, 1988).

52. "Trust Sponsors 1st Conference on Preservation Law Problems," *Preservation News,* 11:6 (1 June 1971), 1–2.

53. Rufus Edmisten, "Tribute to Robert E. Stipe," *North Carolina Central Law Review,* 11 (1979–80), 201; and "Robert E. Stipe, 1929–2007," *Popular Government,* 73:2 (2008), 46–47.

54. Robert E. Stipe, *Local Preservation Legislation: Questions and Answers* (Albany: Preservation League of New York State, 1982); and Robert E. Stipe, *Historic Preservation in Foreign Countries* (Washington, DC: US/ICOMOS, 1982).

55. Norman Tyler, Ted Ligibel, and Ilene Tyler, *Historic Preservation: An Introduction to its History, Principles, and Practice* (New York: W. W. Norton & Co., 2009), 18–24.

56. Aylin Orbasli, "Training Conservation Professionals in the Middle East," *Built Environment,* 33:3 (2007), 307–22; Mirna Soto Medina and Luis Villacorta Santamato, "Built Heritage Conservation Education: A Reflection from Peru," *Built Environment,* 33:3 (2007), 323–41; Rahul Mehrotra, "Conservation and Change: Questions for Conservation Education in Urban India," *Built Environment,* 33:3 (2007), 342–56; Yongtanit Pimonsathean, "Conservation Education as a Form of Community Service in Thailand," *Built Environment,* 33:3 (2007), 357–70; Robert Garland Thompson, "On-site Conservation Training in Cambodia: A Critical Survey of Activities at Angkor," *Built Environment,* 33:3 (2007), 371–91.

57. Lynne D. DiStefano, Sharif Shams Imon, Ho-yin Lee, and Joseph J. DiStefano, "Bridging Differences: A Model for Effective Communication Between Different Disciplines Through Conservation Training Programs for Professionals," *City and Time,* 1:2 (2005), 1–15.

58. Frank Matero, "All Things Useful and Ornamental: A Praxis-based Model for Conservation Education," *Built Environment,* 33:3 (2007), 287–94.

59. Keith D. Alexander, "Reflections on Eight Semesters of Employing Service Learning in an Undergraduate Historic Preservation Course," *Preservation Education & Research,* 4 (2011), 83–92.

60. John A. Matteo, "Preservation Engineering: Framing a New Curriculum," *Preservation Education & Research,* 4 (2011), 93–106.

61. Andréa Livi Smith, "The Young Preservationists: Findings from the First Undergraduate Historic Preservation Education Symposium," *Preservation Education & Research,* 5 (2012), 87–96.

62. This is in contrast to the *Journal for Education in the Built Environment,* which has primarily focused on pedagogical issues related to the contemporary built environment.

63. Robert E. Stipe, *A Richer Heritage: Historic Preservation in the Twenty-first Century* (Chapel Hill: University of North Carolina Press, 2003), xv.

2 You Don't Have to Give Up What You Love: Liberal Arts at Work

Regina Faden

As a museum professional, I perceived in the past that colleges had an almost guaranteed customer base because of the great demand for a college degree by employers. In contrast, it seemed that informal educational institutions, such as museums, were increasingly challenged for visitors' time and money by amusement parks, beach vacations, and gas prices. That perspective has changed significantly. With the recent downturn and continuing economic strain on families, many Americans have been asking themselves about the value of a college education, particularly in the liberal arts. Parents and students wonder whether a degree will help secure a job for a new graduate.[1] Despite President Barack Obama's call for increased college graduation and the demand by foreign students for a degree in the United States,[2] educational leadership is not helping to make the case for the four-year college. In February 2012, U.S. Secretary of Education Arne Duncan made the pronouncement that he found more and more graduates of four-year universities going to community colleges "to get that technical training to get a real job."[3] This assertion seems to argue against a four-year degree. Given rising tuition, the level of debt that students[4] and their parents[5] currently shoulder, and uncertainty about finding work commensurate with one's education, it is understandable that the cost of earning a degree might seem too high and the returns too uncertain.[6]

Colleges and the "Real World"

One of the most detrimental tropes of the academic world that supports the idea that the liberal arts do not translate into meaningful paid work is that college is not the "real world." Each year at elaborate graduation ceremonies cross the country, students already nostalgically recall their four years at school as they stand on the brink of entering the next phase of their lives: financial independence and self-sufficiency. Yet, what they have heard from many faculty and staff is that where they have been and the liberal arts degree they will pay off over the next five, ten, or fifteen years have no relationship to where they are going—the "real world." What this trope denies is that students are already in the real world. They have competed with other candidates, often from around the world, to secure their place at college. Their choices have been supported or constrained by family finances. They spend four years among highly skilled professionals, faculty and staff, who are already successful in the very competitive field of academia. Students have chosen majors, completed numerous assignments, worked in groups and independently, managed their time, and communicated with peers and professionals in order to arrive at graduation with all required credits and paperwork filed.

Perhaps it would be easier for liberal arts colleges to talk about preparing for a "life's work" rather than job preparation. Today, people will make many changes in their career path; the concept of one engaging in a field that realizes one's potential, supported in the broad understanding of the world shaped by the liberal arts, might be a more palatable way to think about life after graduation. Admittedly, identifying a career path for an English or history major is not always straightforward. An accounting or computer science major, for example, can identify the type of work for which he or she will be qualified after completing college. The same might be said for a nursing or engineering student. Their programs help students understand what their skills are and how they can be marketed in the private sector. Potential employment usually pays well[7] and, therefore, the return on their investment of tens of thousands of dollars and four or five years of work seems tangible.

The problem might be that there is a mismatch between colleges and employers because "higher education and industry speak different languages."[8] Jon Marcus, a higher education correspondent for the *Boston Globe,* explains: "Surveys of company executives find that what they really want in their employees is creative thinking, innovation, and an ability to write and speak well—all products not of technical training, higher education leaders say, but of the liberal arts."[9] This sounds wonderful, but positions remain unfilled and employers frustrated. "While many businesses understand the value of hiring liberal arts graduates . . . many hire business majors and then lament that their new employees lack the most important quality they seek: communications skills."[10] Hiring choices by employers illustrate the lack of understanding of the skills and abilities of the liberal arts grad and the fear of taking a chance on a less obvious candidate. Employers might want someone to develop new markets for business, but they might end up with someone who is better suited to creating flow charts in an office cubicle than engaging with potential clients. People on both sides of the hiring process have to be able to articulate and understand the skills of the potential employee and the actual needs of the company. Rather than categorizing skills that make sense outside of academe, a college will often explain to a student that "you need to know how to think." While this point might be true, it is not usually a persuasive selling point at an interview.

Unfortunately, the current approach launches new graduates with liberal arts degrees into a market where they are more likely to engage in soliloquy than dialogue. They often find themselves without work suitable to their skills and abilities, paying off loans for a degree that seems to have been a frivolous waste of energy and money. And so the cycle continues. Students and parents are deeply in debt and feel betrayed by the educational system. The educational system is not engaged with the non-academic world, and therefore, is of little help to the new graduate. The presumption has been that education is the problem—although Americans know that in the end, one is better off with a degree than without one.[11] If it were easy to secure employment without a degree, there would be no anxiety. Clearly, there has to be an adjustment in the concept and purpose of the liberal arts on the part of the students, parents, administration, faculty, and employers. The perceived disconnection between the needs of the employers and their hiring practices helps sustain the mismatch between education and industry. How can the cycle be broken?

Rather than cast students out into the "real world" seemingly unprepared, while they are in school students can be introduced to a professional world that values them: museums. Museums represent opportunities for work in disciplines that are often considered ill-suited to the "real world." They come in all shapes and sizes and are staffed by experts in anthropology, history, art, biology, architecture, and such technical areas as conservation, preservation, plant operations, and finance. They are dynamic and significant contributors to a community's quality of life and the economy. According to the American Alliance of Museums (formerly the American Association of Museums), there "are over 850 million visits to American museums per year—more than attendees of all major sporting events and theme parks combined. Museums directly contribute more than $21 billion to the national economy. Nearly 400,000 people nationwide are employed by museums."[12] When liberal arts colleges partner with museums or professional organizations, through programs, internships, or field trips, they offer students a glimpse into a profession where they can be successful and still engage with the subjects they love.

A Model Partnership

This essay offers the relationship between Historic St. Mary's City (HSMC) and St. Mary's College of Maryland (SMCM) as an example of a successful partnership in introducing students to the museum field and thereby offering them a greater understanding of the value of their liberal arts degree as they begin their life's work. SMCM is a small liberal arts college and, like many similar institutions, has faced questions about the value of the liberal arts.[13] The museum, located next door, offers students and parents a window into a professional world where the liberal arts are put to work. Once the students gain experience at the museum from an internship or volunteer work, they are excited by possibilities for their future that they had never known existed before. They see that they do not have to give up their love of history or culture; they can direct their intellectual passions into meaningful careers.

Historic St. Mary's City and St. Mary's College of Maryland work together to develop the intellect and skills of undergraduate students. Both institutions are independent but formally affiliated state agencies in rural southern Maryland and both are located on the site of Maryland's first capital, St. Mary's City. HSMC is a history museum whose mission is to preserve, develop, and interpret Maryland's first colonial capital, St. Mary's City. The city was established in 1634, but largely disappeared after the capital moved to Annapolis in 1695. The town-lands were farmed until the 1960s, when the museum was created through legislation passed by the Maryland Assembly. For more than forty years, archaeologists and historians recovered evidence of the city. Over time, staff developed a living history program and reconstructed seventeenth-century buildings in order to create an immersive experience of the first capital. The college was established as a female seminary in the 1840s as a monument to the site and ideals of religious freedom established by the Lords Baltimore. Today, it is Maryland's undergraduate honors college, with 150 faculty members, a student population of approximately 2,000, and one graduate program in teaching.

In 1997, the institutions were formally affiliated by legislation and encouraged to work together at all levels to reduce expenses and better serve the students of Maryland. During the 2000s, the museum and college developed a joint museum studies (MUST) minor program. Representatives of both institutions administer the program through the museum studies steering committee. In the early years, MUST focused on the disciplines that were clearly central to HSMC and SMCM: history, archaeology, and anthropology. More recently, the steering committee has broadened its membership to include faculty from economics and the sciences to better represent the breadth of the museum field. The current program overview explains: "Museum practice is inherently multi-disciplinary and cross-disciplinary, benefiting from knowledge and experience in the fine arts, sciences, history, anthropology, education, computer science, design, marketing, finance, and other fields." Members of the committee have helped solicit and develop courses to support the minor, reach out to faculty of all disciplines, and build enrollment.

Relating Academic Skills to Professional Skills

Members of the steering committee have agreed that even if students never work in a museum, a valuable goal of the program is to educate them in the role of museums in society so they can be visitors and citizens who appreciate the work of cultural institutions. Members of the steering committee have debated how far to develop the curriculum and whether, given the students' interest, there should be a major. Some faculty members believe that a museum studies major would be too focused on career preparation and therefore not appropriate for a liberal arts college. Museum staff have usually advocated for the major and increasing courses that deal specifically with museum topics and operations, such as exhibit development or collections management. Faculty have gradually been developing or encouraging additional courses among themselves, such as curatorship through the Department of Art and Art History. Museum staff and college faculty continually debate whether a college should prepare students only for graduate school or to gain work experience and then attend graduate school. Does a purely academic direction serve the student or the college well? Do students choose graduate school sometimes because they do not know what else to do or cannot identify possible careers for themselves?

At this time, the MUST minor at SMCM requires only one course that focuses exclusively on museums: MUST 200: Introduction to Museum Studies. Since 2010, the course is accepted as part of the core curriculum (general education) and meets a humanities requirement. With that broader applicability, MUST has seen significantly increased enrollment and now offers MUST 200 each semester. The course has been taught by several different steering committee members, most frequently the director of HSMC. Rod Cofield, a former HSMC staff member and executive director at Historic Londontown, has taught the course three times. As of fall 2012, forty-one students were registered for the MUST minor. Demand continues to grow and the committee is contemplating the need for adding additional sections of MUST 200, as well more specific guidelines for course content.

Developing the current guidelines for the MUST curriculum required much discussion as well as multiple drafts. The main question for the steering committee was, "What makes a MUST course different from all other courses?" Ultimately, the committee agreed that a course must include a "public" component. The guidelines state: "a course must involve EITHER: actual public communication or preservation (requiring students to learn how to share information with multiple audiences and demonstrating their *presentation or preservation skills* to an audience outside the course); OR the study of the methods of public communication or preservation (requiring students to learn how to share information with multiple audiences and demonstrating their *understanding of these methods* through standard academic presentation to the instructor and the class)."

In addition to MUST 200, students must complete 12 credit hours (3 4-credit courses), in a related discipline. Eight of the 12 "need to be upper-division, selected from at least two of three primary fields of art history, anthropology, and history." Students may also count courses in computer science, biology, chemistry, education, geology, geography, and religious studies, for example, toward the minor.

Museum staff who hold at least a master's degree have worked with academic departments to create specialized courses. MUST 301: Interpreting History to the Public explores "the theory and techniques of public history and museum education in general and more specifically, at Historic St. Mary's City. A practicum component stresses 'critical and creative' thinking and allows students to develop practical skills." MUST 352 allows for courses on Special Topics. HSMC's historic buildings curator offered a course teaching the history and techniques of timber frame construction known as Post and Beam in an Age Gone Modern. Education staff at the museum's plantation offered a course teaching traditional skills, including sewing and hearth cooking, as preparation for learning techniques for interpreting history for the public. Chesapeake in the Age of Sail is co-taught by one of the museum's education staff and the captain of the museum's replica seventeenth-century wooden sailing ship, the *Maryland Dove.* Scheduling of course offerings by museum staff is dependent on college departmental funding and the specialized knowledge of staff members.

This author has taught Introduction to Museum Studies (MUST 200) three times. From the perspective of an administrator, it makes sense that the course gives students a broad organizational overview of a museum as a nonprofit organization. Many students will likely work for a nonprofit. According to the National Association of Colleges and Employers, only

20 percent of liberal arts graduates seek employment in the private sector. "The liberal arts graduate is equally, if not slightly more inclined to prefer a position with a nonprofit or public sector entity. More than 24% of those graduating in one of the academic fields plan to seek a position either with a nonprofit or state or federal government agency."[14] Thus, an understanding of an organization with a mission, a governance structure, an obligation of public service, a budget, and limited resources are valuable components of the introductory course. Familiarity with these topics enables a student to enter the museum or other nonprofit field with greater understanding of the employee's and the organization's purpose. Frank discussions about the changing nature of education delivery in museums and their challenges to remain relevant make students aware of the current dynamic but sometimes-precarious state of nonprofits.

One of the greatest challenges for museums and other nonprofits is sustainability. Thus, the introduction course also teaches valuable skills, such as budgeting and grant writing, which will transfer to any nonprofit. One student complained in course evaluations that the instructor always talked about money and such a focus on finance could discourage a student from going into the museum field. While finance is not typically the reason one seeks museum work, the important lesson to learn is that the days when museum professionals could ignore budgets or avoid financial matters are long gone. Even in the "ivory tower" of college, faculty and staff members are constrained or empowered by institutional financial decisions. Therefore, it is in a student's best interest to understand this and be prepared to support a museum or other nonprofit through effective management of resources and identification of funding sources, whether earned or donated. Regardless of where students might eventually work, grant writing will be a marketable skill. Using a state humanities grant application as a template, students in MUST 200 develop a program that meets the funder's requirements, including adherence to mission, budget, promotion, Americans with Disabilities Act (ADA) access, and evaluation. Although faculty does not like the word "management" in relation to coursework, students would be ill prepared without the understanding that museums, like colleges, are businesses.

In addition to basic concepts of administration and finance, students need other skills in order to be attractive candidates for paid positions. According to the U.S. Department of Labor, businesses are looking for skills that are developed through a traditional liberal arts curriculum. The Department's 2006 report, "Are They Really Ready to Work? Employers' Perspectives on the Basic Knowledge and Applied Skills of New Entrants to the 21st Century U.S. Workforce," notes that according to 461 business leaders, "employers view 'soft' skills as even more important to work readiness."[15] Unfortunately, employers find "that younger workers frequently lack these skills, which include: [1] Professionalism or work ethic [2] Oral and written communication [3] Teamwork and collaboration skills [4] Critical thinking or problem-solving skills."[16] Colleges might point out that their students graduate with these skills every year, but the problem, again, is the perceived lack of transferability to suitable careers.

Museum professionals can help students bridge the conceptual and practical gap between college and career through experience. For example, students learn about teamwork, professionalism, communication, and problem solving through the museum and college's joint archaeological field school. Each summer for ten weeks, students work together under the direction of Timothy Riordan, director of archaeology, to investigate a site on museum grounds. Over the ten weeks, they will work in the field with Riordan and a field assistant, typically a recent graduate of the field school. They learn a standard set of methods for excavating and recording, identifying artifacts, and describing the provenience (location) of each area they dig. These reports become part of the museum's permanent record. In addition to the field method, each day a student is chosen to engage with visitors who come to the site. The student explains what they are investigating and what they might have found, and responds to any other questions visitors might pose. HSMC pioneered such public archaeology in the 1970s and it is a highlight of every summer (see Figure 2.1).

Riordan explains the broad range of students enrolled in field school and the applicability of their experience from the program. "In recent years, students' majors included art, biology, English, philosophy, and political science. At a minimum the hard science majors have come to see that we use rigorous scientific methods for recording and excavating, while the social science majors learned that our methods include creatively interpreting the facts of excavation."[17] Part of field school is an understanding of how the students' work helps build the historic record. "All students are told on the first day and repeatedly retold that they are part of a larger endeavor for the understanding of Maryland's past. That archaeology destroys what it studies and that they are responsible for making sure the information is not lost."[18] This focus on contribution "helps to build a shared responsibility and foster teamwork and esprit-de-corps. The idea of teamwork is further encouraged by the fact that students work in small groups to excavate a unit or a feature and, as a group, they are responsible for completing the excavation efficiently and with precision."[19]

2.1 Archaeology Field School Student Presents Findings to Museum Visitors. Courtesy of Historic St. Mary's City

In addition to the fieldwork, students also spend time at the archaeology lab, washing, labeling, and preparing artifacts for storage. Curator of Collections Silas Hurry oversees this phase of the field school experience. In the lab, students work together in teams to process collections. Hurry describes their assignment: "working together, the students sort and clean actual artifacts from the current excavations. Students learn why maintaining where the artifacts are from is the most important aspect of laboratory processing. Students are also introduced to problem solving in the lab."[20] Hurry explains: "Students serve as the first line for detecting any problems with the artifacts as they come in from the field . . . They are trained to ask questions if there is anything which seems out of order."[21] Of course, throughout the process students have hands-on experience with collections. "They get to see the artifacts up close and personal which allows them to learn the identification of material culture and reinforces the lectures on artifacts which occur the first week of Field School."[22]

HSMC's field school is unusual in its scope, taking students from the field through the entire curation process. Students also present ongoing work to the public and become part of a team as they uncover artifacts from prehistoric though modern times. From the first day, they know that they

2.2 Field School Students Process Artifacts in the Museum's Lab. Courtesy of Historic St. Mary's City

will leave a legacy of discovery that will be preserved by the museum and used as a basis for further research and museum exhibits. When asked how he would describe his experience at the field school, one student from the 2012 season replied, "Invaluable is certainly one of the best ways to describe how my experiences at Historic St. Mary's City have been . . . a common theme that resonates strongly . . . is interpretation; how the tools that we are using, the work that we are doing, and the spaces we are manipulating, are all part of this living history museum and part of its interpretive goals."[23] This sense of purpose and shared work forges a bond and truly allows the student to make history (see Figure 2.2).

Blending Traditional Skills and Academics

The idea of blending the liberal arts with hands-on training is gaining traction in the academic world. In a recent article in *The Chronicle of Higher Education,* Scott Carlson asserts that liberal arts colleges teach students how to think, "how to be engaged, citizens of the world."[24] At the same time, he also observes the widespread dissatisfaction with the current system of higher education that leads many to believe it might be "broken." Carlson suggests that broadening the college curriculum beyond management skills can be highly valuable and equip students to meet the daunting challenges of the future. "Maybe it's time that instruction—at least at some colleges—included more hands-on, traditional skills. Both the professional sphere and civic life are going to need people who have a sophisticated understanding of the world and its challenges, but also the practical, even old-fashioned know-how to come up with sustainable solutions."[25]

Carlson relates the story of a colleague whose class discussed the weaknesses of and threats posed to our current food system. Although addressing the problem could be as simple as buying locally grown fruits, vegetables, and meat, the instructor was shocked "when the students in the group started talking about the solutions—and found themselves stuck: 'Almost all the students said they didn't know how to cook,' she told me, 'and even the young, single adult employees in the group admitted they lacked both the know-how and motivation.'"[26]

In the increasingly urban world of rich nations, there is an expanding disconnection between production and consumers. People are removed from the agrarian culture that has set the rhythm and focus of human life longer than cities and suburbs. Carlson argues that this is the reason "you see a resurgence of interest in practical skills: Home gardening and raising chickens, for example, have become trendy again in the last few years, perhaps helped by the economic collapse and the embrace of local food."[27] This interest in the way things work can be seen writ large in the political arena. "Even in politics, voters seem to flock to people who consciously project a veneer of authenticity through practical skills. And so we get Sarah Palin, the elk hunter and frontier woman; Joe the Plumber, the straight-talking Everyman; and George W. Bush, the brush-clearing rancher."[28] Outside the realm of politics, one also sees this interest in agriculture, where for the first time since the 1920s, the number of farmers has increased and college graduates are drawn to working the land.[29]

Students are highly aware of their disengagement with the physical, practical world, and they are searching for a different type of experience. They are searching for authenticity. An invaluable part of their experience, and this depends on the skilled people to engage them, can be the traditional handcrafts kept alive in living history museums. HSMC's Historic Buildings Curator Peter Rivers tapped into this longing when he offered Post and Beam in an Age Gone Modern as part of the MUST curriculum (see Figure 2.3). The course first provided students with a context of architectural history and theory. Then the classroom experience was brought to life by learning how to use traditional tools and carrying out a timber-framing project at the museum utilizing these new skills.

During the class in fall 2009, Rivers asked for feedback from the students and they submitted thoughtful and enthusiastic evaluations of the course. One student wrote that the most valuable aspect of the course is the hands-on, practical approach of physically building a timber frame. "The most basic understanding of the labor and energy and physical factors of the actual processes of building these structures can only be taught by experience." Another student observed, "When the academic component is added to the 'hands on' work, things begin to become much more holistic—things that we read in architectural history books come

2.3 Historic Buildings Curator, Peter Rivers. Courtesy of Historic St. Mary's City

alive and we put what we read into context as we feel the tools in our hands."

Students also expressed their appreciation for aspects of their experience that lived beyond the instruction. "It is no longer a class but a project we are invested in that is talked about at parties and at bars and in papers for other classes. We are able to innovate here, which students are truly craving. Where we started as a class is very different from where we are today. The growth of the students in class as a cooperative force is amazing." This focus on teamwork was echoed by another student: "One of the class's strengths has been how each member of the class has been able to carve their own niche. Some of us are better sawing, others enjoy making mallets, while still others measure and draw lines . . . even as we pursued our own individual jobs, we've developed a very strong sense of being a team . . . there is a strong sense that 'we're all in this together.'"

Several themes emerge in these comments. The students are excited to have a tool in their hands and know how to use it so they can produce a tangible product of their labor. They make the connection between the academic classroom work, across disciplines, and the concepts and skills they developed in the timber-framing class. Furthermore, students clearly enjoyed being part of a productive team.

Internships as an Introduction to a Life's Work

Internships with HSMC provide valuable experience for students as they work in an area they might never have considered. At the same time, students can also earn 8 credits to satisfy the SMCM's ELAW (Experiencing the Liberal Arts in the World) requirement. ELAW is part of the new core curriculum developed under the leadership of the former president Maggie O'Brien. SMCM describes the program as a way for students to "bridge the gap between the academy and the world beyond, transcending the theory-praxis divide and giving extra meaning to their academic courses by applying their developing knowledge base to life experiences outside the boundaries of the college campus."[30] All students now fall under the new core curriculum and must meet the requirement through study abroad or an internship.

As interns at HSMC, SMCM students completed internships that produced valuable projects and programs for the museum. At the same time, the students have benefited from their experience working in a variety of supporting positions, from education and marketing to carpentry, event planning, and maintenance of a seventeenth-century sailing ship. The college is appropriately credited with providing real-world experience that enhances the degree. Students and parents are encouraged by their experience and have expressed their appreciation for the opportunities made available for career preparation.

Nat Salzman serves as an example of a student who was influenced by the possibilities museum work has to offer. When a senior at SMCM, Nat enrolled in MUST 200 in fall 2010. The following summer, he worked at the museum as a living history interpreter. During the summer of 2012, he completed an internship with Peter Rivers, restoring an exhibit building, specifically its wattle and daub chimney. Nat now works as a seasonal staff person at HSMC and responded to several questions I posed about his experience at the museum while still a student. "Working at HSMC has helped me greatly with figuring out what I would like to pursue in my life. I have come to the realization that I am interested in both learning history and working with my hands. Before working at HSMC I didn't realize that there were jobs in which both of these skills could be combined."

Having participated in many aspects of museum operations, Nat observed, "I have learned a myriad of hand skills, including colonial carpentry, knots, how to sharpen tools, how to fix broken tools . . . These are all skills which are not only useful to me but give me a greater respect for craftsmanship and also make me a more well-rounded individual, which is one of the goals of a liberal arts program." He also gained an understanding of how to work within a museum. "Though many of these skills may seem esoteric, there are many skills which I have learned such as how to work with co-workers and navigate an organization in order to get things done." While working at a museum might not be the career path for everyone, Nat articulates clearly how the museum experience has been multifaceted, related to his academic work, and applicable to a variety of organizations.

St. Mary's College has taken internships one step further. The college's Career Development Center created a Professional Fellow Program (PFP) that provides paid internships for SMCM at either the college or the museum. The process to secure a fellowship is competitive. College and museum faculty and staff submit requests for a PFP for a specific project. The proposal must describe the work involved as well as the benefit to the student. If a proposal is selected for funding, the position is posted online and students may apply. Each PFP earns $10 an hour and may work up to 120 hours a semester for 2 semesters. Together, the student and supervisor develop a schedule of work.

When a junior in 2011, SMCM student Ken Doutt was hired as a PFP at HSMC's waterfront site, learning about maritime history, ship maintenance, and interpretation for the public (see Figure 2.4). When asked how his experience at the museum helped him think about possibilities for the future, he replied, "Especially for a senior, the question 'What's next?' is very relevant. Without a doubt, I would say that my interest in museums and in pursuing a career within the world of museums has stemmed from my work at Historic St. Mary's City. As a result of this, I am continuing to pursue exhibit creation in other institutions and organizations."[31]

Doutt sees the possibility for other students to gain from experience at the museum. "One of the great things about Historic St. Mary's is its proximity to St. Mary's College of Maryland. Students should realize the importance of how close the museum is and take full advantage of the opportunities that are offered. Strengthening the relationship between these two institutions would help give students invaluable experiences and provide the museum with beneficial help."[32] Doutt is correct in observing that the museum benefits greatly from the students' participation. A student's experience of discovery and excitement is energizing for the museum staff. Doutt's demonstration sail model will be used by museum staff as a teaching aid.

During the summer of 2013, Doutt secured a seasonal internship with American Conservation Experience (ACE), Emerging Professional Intern Corps (EPIC), a nonprofit conservation corps based in Salt Lake City, Utah. He will serve as an education and interpretation intern for the National Park Service (NPS) Tule Lake Unit of WWII Valor in the Pacific National Monument in northeast California. During his internship, he will be

2.4 Working the Sails on *The Maryland Dove* Courtesy of Historic St. Mary's City

"directly assisting the National Park Service interacting with the public as well as leading and creating interpretative programs and exhibits preserving the cultural and historical significance of the monument."[33] Doutt says of his experience with ACE, "I am still enjoying museum work and my interest in interpretation has been increased by being a part of the National Park Service. I certainly hope to continue on this track but as always the market is discouraging!"[34] It is true that gaining employment in museums takes perseverance in a highly competitive field, but the training Doutt has received from the National Park Service will be very attractive to museums.

Prospects for the Future

Colleges and museums face tremendous and similar challenges. They must be vigilant about finances in order to stay solvent and not price themselves out of reach for the people they are meant to serve. They must remain relevant to their constituencies in an increasingly complex social environment. They must keep up with technology, a costly and rapidly changing aspect of communications and operations. Both types of institutions face a far more competitive environment in attracting students and visitors, from online courses or exhibits to the strained finances of families. While partnerships between the two institutions will not solve every problem, there can be great benefit for all involved.

Students, and their parents, find value in their college education because students are empowered to take what they love outside the classroom and begin their life's work. Their academic training and knowledge of and familiarity with the professional realm fortify the students' self-confidence. Those who have learned hand skills have a new confidence in their ability to tackle concrete problems, as well as a greater understanding of both the past and the challenges of the future. Students have also been part of something greater than themselves—members of a cooperative and productive team. At the same time, the college demonstrates its value and graduates enthusiastic alumni. The museum gains from the energy and valuable work of the interns while training the next generations of museum professionals. Finally, the liberal arts are appreciated for all the reasons that colleges explain and are already understood by those who love them and spend years in study—the arts and sciences matter. Through literature, art, history, biology, and so many more subjects, we learn about who we are, how we can appreciate and live peacefully with others on our planet, and, maybe most important, how we can become our best selves.

Notes

1. Marc Fisher and Danile de Vise, "Question in U-Va. Tumult: What Should Premier Public Universities Be?" *Washington Post,* June 23, 2012, accessed August 31, 2012, http://www.washingtonpost.com/local/question-in-u-va-tumult-what-should -premier-public -universities-be; Lynn O'Shaughnessy, "5 Reasons to Attend a Liberal Arts College," *CBSnews.com,* January 21, 2010, accessed September 1, 2012, http:// www.cbsnews.com /8301–505145_162–37241390/5-reasons-to-attend-a-liberal-arts-college/.

2. *Education at a Glance 2012: Highlights,* Organization for Economic Co-operation and Development Publishing, accessed September 27, 2012, http://www.oecd.org/edu /highlights.pdf. p. 24.

3. Jon Marcus, "Putting College Degrees to Work," *Boston Globe,* March 4, 2012, accessed September 21, 2012, http://articles.boston.com/2012–03–04/magazine/31115542 _1_college-degrees-universities-college-study.

4. Tamar Lewin, "Burden of College Loans on Graduates Grows," *New York Times,* April 11, 2011, accessed September 1, 2012, http://www.nytimes.com/2011/04/12/education /12college.html.

5. Ryman Anne, "College Debt Especially Costly for Parents," *Republic,* March 17, 2012, accessed September 1, 2012, http://www.azcentral.com/news/articles/2012/03/17 /20120317college-debt-costly-for-parents.html.

6. "Is College Worth It?: College Presidents, Public Assess Value, Quality and Mission of Higher Education," Pew Research Center, May, 16, 2011, accessed September 16, 2012, http://www.pewsocialtrends.org/files/2011/05/higher-ed-report.pdf.

7. National Association of Colleges and Employers, *Salary Survey: Starting Salaries for New College Graduates,* accessed August 18, 2013, http://www.naceweb.org/uploaded

Files/NACEWeb/Research/Salary_Survey/Reports/salary-survey-april-2013-executive-summary.pdf.

8. Marcus, "Putting College Degrees to Work."

9. Marcus, "Putting College Degrees to Work."

10. Staley and Trinkle, "The Changing Landscape of Higher Education."

11. "Is College Worth It? College Presidents, Public Assess Value, Quality and Mission of Higher Education," *Pew Research Center,* accessed August 18, 2013, http://www.pewsocialtrends.org/value-of-college/.

12. "About Museums," American Alliance of Museums, accessed September 1, 2012, www.aam-us.org/about-museums.

13. Jenna Johnson, "St. Mary's College President Asks Board Not to Renew His Contract," June 4, 2013, *Washington Post,* accessed August 18, 2013, http://failover.washingtonpost.com/local/education/st-marys-college-president-asks-board-not-to-renew-his-contract/2013/06/04/0f050f5a-cd5d-11e2–8845-d970ccb04497_story.html.

14. National Association of Colleges and Employers, *Salary Survey: Starting Salaries for new College Graduates,* accessed August 18, 2013, http://www.naceweb.org/Publications/Journal/2010november/NACE_Research__The_Liberal_Arts_Graduate_and_the_College_Hiring_Market.aspx.

15. "Soft Skills: The Competitive Edge," *Office of Disability Employment Policy, United State Department of Labor,* accessed September 2, 2102, http://www.dol.gov/odep/pubs/fact/softskills.html.

16. "Soft Skills."

17. Timothy Riordan, e-mail message to author, September 24, 2012.

18. Timothy Riordan, e-mail message to author, September 24, 2012.

19. Timothy Riordan, e-mail message to author, September 24, 2012.

20. Silas Hurry, e-mail message to author, September 24, 2012.

21. Silas Hurry, e-mail message to author, September 24, 2012.

22. Silas Hurry, e-mail message to author, September 24, 2012.

23. Ken Doutt, e-mail message to author, September 24, 2012.

24. Scott Carlson, "The Future of American Colleges May Lie, Literally, in Students' Hands," *Chronicle of Higher Education,* February 5, 2012, accessed September 16, 2012, http:// chronicle.com/article/Tools-for-Living/130615/.

25. Carlson, "The Future of American Colleges."

26. Carlson, "The Future of American Colleges."

27. Carlson, "The Future of American Colleges."

28. Carlson, "The Future of American Colleges."

29. Natalie Kitroeff, "After Graduating From College, It's Time to Plow, Plant and Harvest," *New York Times,* September 24, 2012, accessed September 30, 2012, http://www.nytimes.com/2012/09/25/nyregion/the-farm-life-draws-some-students-for-post-graduate-work.html.

30. "Experiencing Liberal Arts in the World," *St. Mary's College of Maryland at Historic St. Mary's City,* accessed September 16, 2012, www.smcm.edu/corecurriculum/ELAW/ELAWOverview.html.

31. Ken Doutt, e-mail message to author, September 24, 2012.

32. Ken Doutt, e-mail message to author, September 24, 2012.

33. Hannah Wendel, e-mail message to author, May 19, 2013.

34. Kenneth Doutt, e-mail message to author, August 16, 2013.

3 First Pete and then Repeat? Fundamental Differences in Intention between Undergraduate and Graduate Preservation Programs in the United States

Robert Russell

The countries in which historic preservation first began in a self-conscious way, France and the United Kingdom, very quickly formalized the processes of preservation and brought them under the purview of the central government. Even though the actual agents of the process—the practitioners—remained at first outside direct government employment, as materials and construction techniques began to change radically at the end of the nineteenth and beginning of the twentieth centuries, and as the techniques of physical preservation became more technical and precise, it became necessary for the governmental ministries to initiate training courses and schools for the men and women who were carrying out conservation work. With the increasing bureaucratization of preservation activities within governmental agencies, the preservation planners, in order to be successful in the competitive world of bureaucracy, perforce increasingly had to become bureaucrats and administer agencies and programs that were part of larger governmental activities. As other European countries recognized the need to conserve their historic patrimonies, the models provided by these two pioneering countries became the ones to follow. As historic preservation (heritage conservation) became more widespread throughout the entire world in the twentieth century other countries, particularly those with strong centralized governments, followed this same path.

Except in the United States. To almost anyone who is not an American, the early—and even recent—history of the training of historic preservationists in the United States makes little sense in that it has no direct

"First Pete and then Repeat" is an old folk phrase, more common a hundred years ago than it is now. It refers to situations where two different people, unknown to one another, arrive at a situation at different times and pose precisely the same question, or respond in exactly the same way.

connection with governmental agencies, funds, or institutions. Virtually everywhere else in the world this training is a function of central government. Even in the United Kingdom, where heritage training is more widely diffused, government money flows to private and quasi-public organizations like English Heritage and the English National Trust, which support and encourage preservation education, but do not directly offer it. In Canada, the national advocacy organization Heritage Canada Foundation (Heritage Canada) is a registered charity, but the actual money for conservation and preservation is public. In the United States, organized preservation education has largely relied on the tried and true American method of the ad hoc: an amalgam of floundering amateurs, private enterprise, and higher education.

A thorough history of preservation education in America has yet to be written. My aim here is much more modest in that I want to examine only one particular aspect of it: the singular way that higher education has moved to fill the void in preservation training and practice caused by the historically minor role that the U.S. government has played in the identification and preservation of the built environment. I want to look at the relationship (more accurately, the lack of relationship) between the study of preservation at the undergraduate and graduate levels of university education. More specifically, I want to look at the teaching of historic preservation in a liberal arts environment.

First Pete: Undergraduate Preservation Studies as Liberal Education

According to the National Council of Preservation Education's (NCPE) Great Chart, there are currently ten American institutions offering undergraduate degrees in historic preservation.[1] Of these ten, the American College of the Building Arts (ACBA) in Charleston, South Carolina, is sui generis: its own thing, admirable and necessary, but unlikely to be replicated.[2] Two others, the Boston Architectural College and the Savannah College of Art and Design, are unabashedly about training for professional careers, and while they grant undergraduate degrees, they make few if any claims about the place of the liberal arts in their institutions. Belmont College—which until recently was called Belmont Technical College—represents the presence of preservation training in American community colleges.[3] The remaining six colleges and universities make explicit claims to offer preservation education more or less within the liberal arts tradition. These range from Roger Williams University's description of itself as a place where "liberal arts education is paired with education for the professions," and Southeast Missouri State University's very reticent statement, tucked deep within its website, that SEMO "provides professional education grounded in the liberal arts and sciences and in practical experience," to the robust claim of the University of Mary Washington in Fredericksburg, Virginia, to be a "public Liberal-Arts university." The institution I know best, the College of Charleston, has become a little less sure of what it is in recent years and has started to call itself a "comprehensive institution . . . honoring the timeless principles of the liberal arts and sciences." The remaining two undergraduate schools—20 percent of the total number of colleges offering degrees in historic preservation—are Catholic institutions: Ursuline College, near Cleveland, Ohio, and Salve Regina University in Newport, Rhode Island. Both of them unabashedly identify themselves as liberal arts colleges.

The point of liberal arts education in the modern world has been to situate the study of any given discipline within the larger matrix of other disciplines and intellectual endeavors to produce, ideally, "the well-rounded individual." This phrase, and the educational ideals behind it, is generally considered terminally quaint within the ivied walls and groves of academe. These ideas have long been left behind by a significant majority of university faculty as evidenced by the abandonment of core curriculums at virtually every level of higher education. In the 1990s it seemed (for a short while at least) that an increasingly important job of academic administrations was going to be the hiding of this fact from the parents of prospective students. That is no longer the case since virtually all parents of current college students have been completely won over to the idea that higher education is job training, pure and simple. In my experience, gathered from many years of talking to prospective students and their parents, as well as (more happily) visiting with the proud mothers and fathers attending graduation functions of their children, very few parents evince any knowledge of—let alone desire for—the well-rounded individual as the primarily valued educational outcome. Almost always their concern is couched in terms of a return on an investment.

Academic training in historic preservation in the United States began, tellingly enough, at the graduate level, at Columbia University in 1964 under James Marston Fitch. I use the word "training" instead of "education" because that is the word Fitch used to describe what he was doing.[4] It also is the most accurate descriptor of what a two-year program must do if it is to take raw recruits and turn them into effective advocates for and practitioners of preservation. Since there were no undergraduate programs in historic preservation that could act as feeders to this new graduate endeavor, the original assumption of American academic preservation programs was that the students would have no formal background in the field. Graduate education at the master's level does not have the luxury of an adequate amount of time to prepare preservationists for their work. It is simply a beginning.[5]

The Undergraduate Ideal

In contrast to this let us turn to a much more recent development in preservation education: undergraduate programs. Note I do not say "undergraduate training." To make the point more forcefully, I will ascend to the empyrean, that realm where everything is as it should be. I will steadfastly attempt to ignore all the realities of American undergraduate life that have been so thoroughly and depressingly catalogued by Arum and Roksa in *Academically Adrift,* the recent exposé of the failures of American higher education, and focus instead on how things ought to be.[6]

Americans have traditionally assumed that college is supposed to be about exploration and broadening one's horizons.[7] This assumption is good for undergraduate preservation programs since it is probably the case that since the inception of the program, only around 5 percent of the historic preservation and community planning students at the College of Charleston—my former institution—have come to the college specifically for that major. I suspect the percentage is about the same elsewhere. Most potential, and even actual, college students do not know that historic preservation exists as an undergraduate major. The majority of our majors come into the program through exposure to historic preservation in the introductory classes, which satisfies a distribution requirement in the college's general education curriculum.[8]

Once students discover preservation and begin to take classes in it, its natural interdisciplinarity frequently becomes a positive feature. Because so many different academic disciplines contribute to the study and practice of preservation, students can almost always find some particular aspect of it they especially respond to. This process of self-discovery takes time, it is true, but time is something that is supposed to be in abundance among undergraduates.[9] Undergraduate education is by and large also supposed to be a process of discovery, with all the excitement and enthusiasm of intellectual voyages to new places. It is perfectly legitimate (however rare in reality) for an undergraduate to say "I didn't know that!" or "I never thought of it that way!" In the same manner, students come to each new class in their preservation major differently and imperfectly formed by their earlier experiences as well as through other courses they are taking alongside their preservation classes, and even the previous preservation classes they have or have not taken (for it is a sad fact that no matter how carefully an undergraduate major is structured, most students take their classes largely in any old order). Perhaps, as John Locke asserted, our minds are blank slates—tabulae rasae—at birth, but by the time students get to college their minds are more like palimpsests, or, even more apt it seems to me, like the Magic Slate toy from the past century: a stylus with which a child could write on a cardboard pad through a piece of cellophane. Then he or she could erase what he had written by a quick lifting of the cellophane and begin again. A close look at the pad would reveal the faint marks of earlier writing on both the cellophane and the backing, but a quick glance showed nothing but fresh emptiness.[10]

But the original idea of a university is that things are connected, hence its very name.[11] At Empyrean University, students have at least the possibility of acquiring a depth of understanding of preservation issues as they work their way through a required curriculum, so that the best of them can really begin to think about *why* preservation is done the way it is, not just learning the way it is done. The introductory class—Preservation 101 or whatever it might be—obviously cannot do this. Its purpose is to pique the students' interest, but no one can seriously start to ask the "why" questions without a sufficient background in the subject, and that comes only through exposure—that is, time—and effort.

This effort has to be on the part of the professor as much as the student. The effort must be always to go beyond the teaching of mere skills to talk about the underlying ideas that make those skills necessary. Learning how to measure a building and turn those measurements into an accurate two-dimensional representation of the building is a fine skill for an aspiring preservationist to acquire, but a discussion of how this exercise can make one look at a building in a qualitatively different way pushes the work from the level of technical training to real education. Likewise, asking a student who is defending a design exercise, "why did you do it this way?" forces a level of self-reflection that many students are uncomfortable with, but that can help to advance them along the road not only to deeper knowledge of their subject, but of themselves as well. This might well be the real dividing point between training and education: training teaches someone how to do something without any concern that the thing, or how it is done, could have some lasting effect on the doer as well as the object being worked on. Education, on the other hand, recognizes that each new thing learned changes irrevocably the person, as well as the object about which something is being learned.[12] If students hear this "why?" asked often enough, they might begin to get the idea that it is an important aspect of what they are learning. Sometimes they even begin to ask it on their own. In this Land of Cockaigne university that is being described here, they would always ask it, just as they would always come to class and always do the reading. Alas, many of them seem to prefer the big rock-candy mountain, where, as the song tells us, they hung the jerk that invented work. Nevertheless, upon reflection it is at the undergraduate level that the possibility best exists for the best students to begin to engage the field of historic preservation at a level that questions and contests the received wisdom of the ancients: their professors.

Since this is a discussion about contemporary academia it would not be complete without recourse to irony. This appears in the fact that historic preservation turns out to be a field of study that is easy to present to concerned parents of potential majors as job training, which is what virtually all of them want their children to be getting, even if they sometimes try not to put it quite so baldly. The single most common question asked by parents of future students is "what can my child do with a degree in historic preservation?" This translates roughly as "how much can I expect my child to make, and will her job land her in the middle class?" Because so many preservation classes result in concrete products—drawings and reports and models—a lot of parents seem to feel instinctively that they are getting their money's worth. This is a case where perception, however inaccurate, can work to the benefit of an academic preservation program.[13]

But let us return to the assertion that it is at the undergraduate level that the possibility best exists for the best students to begin to engage the field of historic preservation at a level that questions and contests the received wisdom of the ancients. On the surface this is clearly counterintuitive: virtually everyone assumes that the function of graduate school is to go beyond anything undergraduate education is capable of. Thinking back on the trajectory of academic preservation training in the United States, however, a different picture starts to emerge. Graduate preservation began in the mid-1960s, as has already been mentioned. It was not until 1980 that the University of Mary Washington began to offer the country's first undergraduate preservation major in the context of a liberal arts university.[14] James Fitch's Columbia University program was not designed to take students who had begun the study of preservation as undergraduates and bring them to a higher place. It took fresh recruits from other disciplines and trained them in the "curatorial management of the built world," as the subtitle of his book has it.[15] Graduate preservation programs still have more than a whiff of midcareer change about them, and it is by no means the norm to major in historic preservation as an undergraduate and continue on to study in a graduate program. In fact, as currently constituted, graduate programs are not equipped to deal with students who have done prior academic work in preservation. Their curriculums are generally rigid, with no clear-cut mechanism to allow students to demonstrate prior mastery of a subject.[16] A single example will have to suffice about how these two groups, undergraduates and graduate students, must necessarily deal differently with the same material.

It is not uncommon for the introductory course in a graduate program—the history and theory of preservation or whatever it might be called—to use as a significant text David Lowenthal's *The Past is a Foreign Country.*[17] These days, most undergraduate intro classes probably use Tyler, Ligibel, and Tyler's *Historic Preservation.*[18] Now it is true these books aim to do different things, but they also operate on completely different levels. The Tyler et al. book aims to be a sort of academic version of one-stop-shopping: it is handy, is relatively cheap, and contains a lot of material suitable for an undergraduate introductory course. It is not a book that a student completing an undergraduate preservation major would think to delve back into; it is a textbook. Lowenthal's book, on the other hand, gets better and better the more often one dips into it. As a text for an undergraduate introduction to historic preservation class it would be incomprehensible, and the students would react to it, most probably, by simply refusing to read it. I suspect most of the graduate students who read it in their first term studying a new field find it equally as mind-numbing and obtuse. The important fact to recognize here is that beginning students in graduate preservation programs are generally every bit as ignorant as beginning undergraduates when it comes to the field they are studying. They might know a little bit about political science, or biology, or construction management, or architecture, but they do not know very much about historic preservation. Having a few additional years of maturity over callow eighteen-year-olds certainly helps, as does the conscious decision to pursue graduate study, placed over against the largely passive acceptance of undergraduate college as some sort of necessary conclusion to a lifetime of "education." But we who are older frequently forget that a book that seems wonderful to us for its depth of thought, its allusions, its multiplicity of references, implied and explicit, in short, its thought-provoking qualities, is that way largely because of the experiences—hard-won over more or less extended lengths of time—we bring to it. To say it is a book that grows on you is to acknowledge that it is a book that needs time to reveal itself. And since the proposition here is that graduate training in preservation is necessarily lacking in a sufficient amount of time, the conclusion is that a first-term graduate student more likely than not will not be able to mine everything that is valuable in Lowenthal's book.

On the other hand, *The Past is a Foreign Country* would be immensely suitable for a senior seminar in an undergraduate program. It would still be a difficult book, but for students coming to the end of four, or six, or eight terms of sustained study of historic preservation, with a range of exposure and experiences, it could provide the basis for a great deal of worthwhile conversation. For students who had begun their study with a textbook like Tyler et al.'s, concluding it with the philosophical loftiness of Lowenthal's book would give them a glimpse of the beauty and complexity of their chosen field almost completely lacking in the textbook.[19]

Then Repeat?: Graduate Training

Graduate students start out as veteran students, having already completed an undergraduate degree in some field. They supposedly know what they want to do with their lives, which is why they are in the graduate program in the first place. They are after one thing and one thing only: training for a profession.[20] This gives them, on the one hand, an admirable sense of purpose, but on the other hand, it tends to make them impatient with theoretical issues and things they do not see as directly applicable to "doing the job." Training is not the same thing as education even though the difference is being increasingly blurred in the early twenty-first century. The traditional American suspicion of theory and abstraction, combined with an equally traditional admiration for practicality and the pragmatic view, join in a particularly emphatic way in academic preservation. Add into the mix the generally unacknowledged but readily evident anti-intellectualism of practicing preservationists and what is produced is an atmosphere at best indifferent to thinking and at times overtly hostile to intellectual activity. Graduate preservation students are looking for professional training. They want to know the Secretary of the Interior's Standards because, they have been told, these are the rules of the game by which preservationists must abide if preservation is to "work" in this country. They are much less interested in knowing how the Standards got to be the way they are, or in having a conversation about what they might actually mean or how they might be changed.[21] They want to learn AutoCAD because it is a marketable skill; they do not want to spend time talking about how that particular software program forces one to think about drawing—which is representation—in ways very different from rendering the same thing by hand. And they absolutely do not want to spend time focusing on theoretical issues connected with preservation.

Now to a certain extent this is understandable. Graduate study is expensive, both because students are bearing not only the cost of tuition and maintenance for two years, but also because they cannot be working full-time while they are studying. The single goal of students in master's-level preservation programs is—or at least ought to be—employment in the field. The danger arises when the preparation for achieving that goal is defined in such a way that most if not all of the purely intellectual aspects of preservation are excluded. As American preservation enters into what might be seen as its "early maturity," there is a growing tendency to formalize and bureaucratize the practice of preservation, which results in an ever-increasing rigidity of interpretation of the "rules," as the discussion of the changes in the Secretary of the Interior's Standards has already demonstrated (see note 21). Among preservation practitioners—and virtually all the graduates of academic programs go on to become practitioners—there is simply no conceivable need to, as Stanley Fish puts it, "academicize" the subject.[22]

It is very important to remember, however, that the academic study of preservation is not the same thing as the practice of preservation, and it is dangerous as well as foolish to try and make the one too much like the other. The regnant anti-intellectualism of the historic preservation business too easily dismisses theoretical and abstract concerns as irrelevant or unnecessary. This attitude is made abundantly clear to graduate students each time they get out in the field for site visits, internships, and other practical experiences.[23]

Having heaped largely undeserved praise on the teaching of preservation to undergraduates (Empyrean University is still to be founded), and equal heaps of warning on graduate programs, it is time to conclude with a relentlessly practical exhortation, a call for job training—of a sort.

A Modest Proposal

A few years ago a colleague of mine attended a conference where he fell into conversation with a representative of a well-known preservation consulting firm. This professional preservationist was bemoaning the quality of his firm's recent hires, and he told my colleague that in his estimation, nine out of every ten people they had to fire were let go because they could not write. To anyone working in the academic side of preservation, this will comes as no real surprise. It is surpassingly easy to find academics who say that the teaching of writing is the job of the English Department, and they only read their students' papers for what they say, not how they say it.[24] It is not really possible to separate form from meaning, and if a student is only vaguely aware of literary form, that student will not be able to communicate effectively. Note well here: I am not talking about literary style when I say form. Language is immensely conventional, but those conventions all too often follow unwritten rules—think of idiomatic expressions in any language. The reality is that vast numbers of students enter college barely able to write sentences, let alone string those sentences together to make an argument. Style is not an issue for these students; for many of them it never will be. They are in immediate need of acquiring a working knowledge of the conventional forms of their language.

The reasons for this state of affairs are numerous, and there is more than enough blame to go around, from inadequate vocabulary acquisition in a child's early years, to the unwillingness of elementary and high school teachers to assign significant amounts of reading, to the infamous five-paragraph essay, which appears to be the dominant form of writing in American high schools. Poverty is also frequently blamed, as a structural and societal problem, and this is no doubt true. But it is also true that students' incapacity to write is scarcely restricted to those who are poor.

This inability of college students to write even marginally comprehensible essays is simply going to get worse as more and more inadequately prepared students are bundled off to college by their hopeful parents, and as colleges themselves, ever eager for students, figure out new ways to accept subpar applicants. These students might be inept, but they are by and large not stupid, and they quickly discover that, while colleges talk a strong literacy and writing game, the reality is often very different. I mentioned above that there are plenty of professors who still believe that it is the job of the English Department to teach composition. English faculty generally despise composition classes, and in most colleges these are taught by overworked adjuncts. English Departments also have lobbied strongly to reduce the number of composition classes students are required to take. The result of all this is that students quickly realize that while everyone professes to believe in the necessity of good writing, very few instructors actually do anything about it. The standard college term paper is due at the end of the term, is perfunctorily read by the professor laboring under a looming deadline of electronic grade submission, is cursorily marked (generally receiving a grade of B), and languishes for a couple of weeks into the next term in a cardboard box in the hall outside the professor's office before it is put into storage for the period required by the institution and then gets thrown out. Students know this, which, I suspect, is why so few of them ever bother to come by and retrieve their papers. They also know that they generally have not earned the B they received.

People who write well know that writing is a process that involves much time and labor. Students who invest minimal time and labor in their writing will never write well. Graduate students in historic preservation programs who are expected to write minimally in their courses, and whose writing consists largely of lab and technical reports, or summaries of other read material, will be weighed and found wanting when it comes to writing a thesis. It is imperative that all students—undergraduate and graduate alike—begin to be confronted with their failures as writers and held accountable for them. As an initial proposal for one way to do this let me suggest that papers be made due in the middle of the term, not at the end. Rather than the cryptic comments occasionally scribbled in the margin, the professor should make the effort to provide a serious and thorough critique of the paper: both its form and its argument, if it has one. The paper should then receive the grade it actually deserves and be returned to the student who now has the opportunity to correct and improve it. This is forced process, it is true, but in my experience it is a novelty to the students, some of whom actually respond to the criticism.

The disadvantage of this is that it requires an enormous amount of time from the professor—time spent doing something that is, in reality, unvalued in academia. That is reason enough to predict that this modest proposal will never see widespread application. Nevertheless, until we insist that writing be done well, it will, by and large, be done poorly. If we are at all serious about both adequate education and competent training, this is where we must begin.

Conclusion

This chapter began by contrasting the much more rigidly formalized structure of preservation education found in most of the rest of the world with what I characterized as the ad hoc nature of this enterprise in the United States. This make-it-up-as-you-go-along quality is probably most evident in the fact that graduate training in historic preservation long antedates any undergraduate programs. A fundamental confusion about preservation education in the United States arises, as I have suggested, from the largely unexamined assumption that all graduate education is "higher" and more "refined" than mere undergraduate work. In more traditional academic programs, this is certainly the case. A student does not normally begin the study of, say, chemistry, or mathematics, or literature, at the master's level with no previous exposure to the subject. But this is precisely the situation of the vast majority of students in graduate preservation programs in the United States. Rather than a trajectory of knowledge rising smoothly from entrance into university to exiting in possession of a master's degree, the reality is almost always much jumpier, with a student following a more or less coherent undergraduate major in virtually anything and then beginning afresh with the concentrated training of a graduate preservation program. In itself this is not necessarily a bad thing, and it can even be admirable in that it maintains at least the dim memory of the time when preservationists were a motley assortment of all sorts and conditions of people, brought together by a common concern for the built environment.

Nevertheless, one result of such a situation is a clear contrast between the hypothetical undergraduate education of Empyrean University sketched out above and the relentlessly practical training in historic preservation forced on graduate students by the twin brutal constraints of time and cost. That the actual quality of undergraduate education falls far short of what it could and should be is glaringly evident in the woeful quality of the writing of so many students in graduate preservation programs. Ultimately students are responsible for what and how they write, but as I surmised above, most students are not stupid and quickly discover that the lip service paid to the importance of writing in American universities is generally mostly that: lip service.

It is now time to return to the question posed in the title of this essay: in America is graduate education in historic preservation simply an extension of an undergraduate program? Is it first Pete and then just Repeat? The answer, I believe, is not just a simple yes or no. Given how graduate programs are organized and the assumptions their faculties make about entering students, it is probably the case that in the majority of programs the answer would be "mostly yes." Graduate preservation programs are built on the assumption that entering students are starting from scratch, not building on an earlier foundation acquired elsewhere. But as I have said, this is because graduate preservation education in the United States came along much before the undergraduate version did. Now that both levels exist and increasingly interact, it is fair to answer the question in the negative: undergraduate preservation programs should not attempt what their graduate cousins undertake; they can do other things better, should their faculties truly desire to.

Notes

1. The "Great Chart" is the unofficial but commonly used term for NCPE's listing of academic programs for historic preservation in America. Until recently it was published annually in the National Trust's *Preservation Magazine,* but it exists solely in the electronic world now.

2. The ACBA began to get off the ground in 2000 when it secured an historic building from the city of Charleston both to restore and to use as its location. The goal of the school is to train preservation craftsmen along the lines of the French Compagnons du devoirs. It began offering college-level classes to students in six building trades areas in

2004. As of this writing it is pursuing accreditation as an institution of higher education. See http://www.buildingartscollege.us/.

3. This is simultaneously curious and sad. Given the terrain of American higher education, community colleges would seem to be the natural place to find programs in preservation education, but almost none exist. Besides Belmont College, there is a certificate program offered at Bucks County Community College in Newtown, Pennsylvania. An attempt in the early years of this century to found preservation training programs at community colleges in Arkansas failed very quickly when it received no support from the central administration of the system.

4. "[This] book . . . is a consequence of my efforts, beginning in the early 1960s, to develop an academic program for formal training in the field of historic preservation." Preface to the first edition, *Historic Preservation Curatorial Management of the Built World* (Charlottesville: University of Virginia Press, 1990), xiii.

5. As an aside, there are perhaps a couple of reasons that preservation first appeared at the graduate level in American education. One of them is the state of higher education in the mid-1960s: college was only beginning its transformation into big business, and the traditional ideas about what was and was not acceptable as an academic subject still held sway. Also, because credentialing had scarcely been thought of as the primary goal of higher education, the community college system had not—and still has not—seen historic preservation training as an area of potential development. Another powerful reason is that preservation is not—and can never be—an academic discipline. It is simply too interdisciplinary.

6. Richard Arum and Josipa Roksa, *Academically Adrift: Limited Learning on College Campuses* (Chicago: University of Chicago Press, 2011).

7. Most Americans have also traditionally assumed that, while this might be a dandy thing, it is not a necessary one: about 2 percent of the college-age population in 1900 actually attended a college. See http://www.publicagenda.org/articles/higher-education.

8. This is a very good reason to have a preservation program situated in a liberal arts context by the way, or at least a liberal arts context in an institution that has not completely abandoned faith in the idea of a "general" or well-rounded education: it is possible actually to spread the preservation gospel to those who never heard it. Absent this minimal distribution structure, academic preservation programs must depend on those already in the know, or else strays, to populate their classes. For a quick, rough and ready look at how America's colleges and universities are faring vis à vis a general education curriculum, see http://www.whatwilltheylearn.com/. It is telling that most of the name-brand institutions earn D or F grades in this admittedly traditionally oriented study.

9. It is clearly the case that students now have more time than they ever have had in the history of higher education. Arum and Roksa report that, on average, college students spend only twelve hours per week preparing for their classes; nearly 40 percent admit to spending less than five hours a week on their schoolwork. Arum and Roksa, *Academically Adrift*, 69.

10. To switch for a minute from how the academic world ought to be to how it really is, this seems to be how too many of our students move through their undergraduate education: beginning afresh with each new class, remembering little to nothing of their earlier studies. This attitude is most concisely represented by the literal—but also symbolic—throwing away of a class's notes on the way out the door of the final exam. Back when books were cheaper, the more aggressive students would sometimes dump their textbooks in the trash along with their notes.

11. And thus the recent conception of the "multiversity," while trendy, is precisely the opposite of the traditional view of higher education.

12. The actual origins of the Greek aphorism γνῶθι σεαυτόν (know thyself) are lost in the mists of time and conflicting reports. Pausanias tells us (10.24.1) that they were

inscribed in the temple of Apollo at Delphi, which would have been a good way to disseminate the sentiment.

13. A thorough discussion of the changes being forced on American higher education would require a book much longer than this one. The point in question, however—what is the purpose of college in America today?—has been largely answered by parents as "getting a job." Academic administrations by and large have been more than willing to agree with this conclusion, which has simply confirmed what the tuition payers already assumed colleges were supposed to do for their children. The enormous amount of questionable information available online regarding the purported earnings differential between those who go to college and those who do not functions essentially as a scare tactic, forcing waffling parents over to the "you must go to college" side of things. The fact too that a college degree is universally accepted as a ticket into the middle class, even for those who subsequently do not ever quite manage to earn enough to qualify financially, is a powerful incentive. President Barack Obama's misguided but understandable campaign-trail assertions that he wanted "everyone" to go to college simply reinforce this unquestioned assumption.

14. Called Mary Washington College from 1938 to 2004.

15. James Marston Fitch, *Historic Preservation: Curatorial Management of the Built World* (New York: McGraw-Hill, 1982; paperback edition, Charlottesville: University of Virginia Press, 1990).

16. An informal, incomplete, and completely unscientific polling of directors of graduate preservation programs reveals that there is no generally agreed-on way to accommodate students with undergraduate preservation degrees. The most common method is to allow students to exempt one or two required classes and substitute electives. Although at times inconsistent, this ad hoc method has so far proved reasonably acceptable. Remember that there are only a handful of undergraduate preservation majors in the country, with graduate programs outnumbering them about three to one.

17. David Lowenthal, *The Past is a Foreign Country* (New York: Cambridge University Press, 1985). Despite what some consider to be its dated coverage of preservation, Lowenthal's book is still one of the most adventurous and intellectually challenging treatments of the field that has ever been written. Clearly the result of many years' worth of thought and reading, as well as having numerous graduate research assistants, the book itself is a stellar example of the necessity of adequate time, in addition to effort, intellect, and imagination, in the production of something worthwhile.

18. Norman Tyler, Ted J. Ligibel, and Ilene R. Tyler, *Historic Preservation: An Introduction to Its History, Principles, and Practice,* 2nd ed. (New York: W. W. Norton & Co., 2004).

19. Undergraduate programs with senior seminar "capstone" courses are supposed to provide a broad, overarching, synthetic experience for their last-term students, something that pulls together as many different strands as possible of what they have been learning in their major. In academic preservation programs that have these culminating courses (not by any means a majority of what is currently available), they tend to have no fixed content, but operate with changing themes and ideas.

The "capstone" concept is, it has to be said, an academic fad, though it is one that has reappeared periodically. It has been traced back at least to the early nineteenth century, most particularly in the United States to Mark Hopkins, the legendary president of Williams College. The idea was revived in the 1970s, but appears to have been short-lived. In the 1990s it came back into fashion, and its current existence can be traced to that period. See Jean M. Henscheid, *Professing the Disciplines: An Analysis of Senior Seminars and Capstone Courses* (Columbia: University of South Carolina, 2000). One of the serious drawbacks of the capstone concept is that it requires almost the opposite approach to a discipline than the one inculcated in contemporary academics: a synthetic rather than a discrete understanding. It is also much more work than a standard course. There is evidence that it is already going out of fashion again.

20. It has to be emphasized here that in speaking of graduate training, I am talking solely of two-year master's degree programs, which is what, to my knowledge, all graduate historic preservation programs are. And while these cannot be officially termed "professional" programs since they do not culminate in licensing exams, most if not all graduate preservation programs emphasize their professional aspect. Ph.D. programs are, of course, very different, but the Ph.D. is, generally speaking, an academic degree, the expectation traditionally being that holders of Ph.D.s will pursue academic careers.

21. This must be particularly frustrating for Brown Morton, who along with Gary Hume was responsible for writing the first iteration of the Secretary of the Interior's Standards in the 1970s. Morton has spoken and written eloquently on numerous occasions about how the Standards were conceived as "a starting point for conversations" about how preservation should proceed, rather than as a series of ironclad rules of practice. Each subsequent revision of the Standards, however, has reinforced the idea that that is exactly what they are. The original "shoulds" have increasingly become "musts," and the "oughts" have become "wills."

22. Stanley Fish, *Save the World on Your Own Time* (Oxford: Oxford University Press, 2008).

23. It is only slightly unfair to single out the field of historic preservation for this criticism. American education in general for most of the twentieth century demonstrated a decided bias against knowledge, particularly abstract knowledge. See almost any of the books by E. D. Hirsch after he published *Cultural Literacy* in 1987. See also Diane Ravitch, *Left Back: A Century of Failed School Reforms* (New York: Simon & Schuster, 2000).

24. What this actually means, all too many times, is that you the reader end up inferring what the student really might have meant, because what was said in the words on paper was largely the opposite of what should have been said.

4 Thinking and Doing: A Twenty-First Century Pedagogy for Preserving the Historic Architectural Artifact

Robert W. Ogle

In colonial urban America, *craftsman* was a badge of hierarchical achievement and status. Following centuries of European tradition, the American master craftsman exercised power over the proliferation of skill and product. He controlled the means of production as well as the ends. The master craftsman was responsible for providing room, board, and training to indentured apprentices and oversight and wages to journeyman-level crafters. He set prices and the quality of finished goods and colluded with fellow master craftsmen to share secrets and to assure barriers to entry to the trade. A moral life was predicated on being useful to the self, the family, and the community. Work was the path to a moral life. The craft work ethic included "moderation, integrity and industry."[1] Craft was generational and the material and moral output of the craftsman class was understood and expected by the community. The craftsman conceived, fabricated, and assembled the architectural artifact that serves as symbol of America's cultural heritage.

During the American revolutionary period, Enlightenment philosophy became laced with the ideology of American republicanism. As Enlightenment humanism took hold in America, the principle of individual freedom deconstructed the traditional class system of apprentice-journeyman-master. Apprentices were free to explore any opportunity, journeymen were released from their traditional career path, and masters were free to shed the costly patriarchal role to perpetuate their craft and hire cheap wage labor. The result was a paradoxical perpetuation of a class system where a new economic structure predicated on self-development replaced the former class system symbols for what development meant.[2] The upward mobility of journeymen (to accumulate capital to become masters) was destroyed in the new system and created a permanent wage-earning class. The master craftsman alternatively sported a new badge of self achievement; "the masters assumed heavy responsibility of reminding both their own craft communities as well as society as a whole of the central place that artisans occupied in the founding and maintenance of freedom and republicanism in America."[3] The journeyman's new badge of self-worth and expression of a moral life became the roots of the organized labor movement during the nineteenth century. Another unintended consequence of the deconstruction of the traditional master-journeyman-apprentice class system was the void in training and education created to perpetuate craft principles and embrace the new learning needs necessary to support complex machine innovation and factory production.

For more than two hundred years the breakdown of this structured education and training system has created tension between the skill sets needed for advancing technology juxtaposed against a burgeoning American sensibility for conservation of the intrinsic and associative values of the historic architectural artifact.[4] Public policy makers and scholars exacerbated the gap in training left by the deconstruction of the former system by continuous debate over the merits of liberal arts versus technical education in meeting American societal needs.

This chapter explores the historical American educational models that were designed to resuscitate the skills requisite of the craft tradition that are critical to preserving the architectural artifact and why they failed. It then reviews the recent revival in interest in historic preservation and how certain colleges and universities are addressing student and market demand. Finally, a conceptual pedagogical and curricular model is offered to demonstrate how educators may connect thinking and doing within their preservation and related disciplines.

Contemporary pedagogical and curricular strategies mirror the panoply of "professional disciplines" that evolved as a result of rationalist theories on the efficiencies gained by the division of conceptualization and execution of work. The more tasks are segmented, the less knowledge and skill are needed to receive or deliver training. This theory can be applied to any profession or discipline, including academia.[5] Unfortunately, the successful preservation of the historic architectural artifact requires a skill set that combines the empiricism of the workplace with visualization of an entire process.

Education Experimentation

The master craftsman was responsible for training the individuals who would perpetuate his skill, trade, and worldview. In nineteenth-century America, two forces disrupted this mechanism. First, American republicanism guaranteed any person the freedom to reap the fruits of individual effort. Second, complex machines and the factory production system required a new paradigm in education.

The Nineteenth Century

The tension between liberal arts and technical curriculum and pedagogy exacerbated the gap in training left by the former system. The public schools failed to respond to the needs of an expanding manufacturing-based economy by continuing to insist on moral and political grounds that alphabetical literacy was the path to worker productivity and economic progress. It was not until the second quarter of the nineteenth century that an institutional mechanism was created to "link the empiricism of the workplace to theoretical foundations in science and mathematics."[6] The linkage required was a pedagogy that included curriculum to address spatial cognition. Courses in drawing, modeling, and geometry became the bridge between the practical and the theoretical. More than one hundred athenaeums and "mechanics' institutes" were formed between 1818 and 1850 to implement the new educational philosophy broadly defined by a loose coalition of reformers. In *The Grammar of the Machine: Technical Literacy and Early Industrial Expansion in the United States,* Edward Stevens claims there were five intentions shared by institutional founders:

> In the early nineteenth century, mechanics' institutes and the educational activities of mechanics' associations served at least five distinct purposes. These included updating technical knowledge, preparing young men for mechanics' positions in manufacturing, increasing the skills of mechanics to a level that would distinguish them from operatives, promoting upward social mobility through liberal education, and building character to increase the chances of success in business.[7]

On the surface, these five purposes herald an egalitarian system grounded in craftsman and republican ideals. For wage workers displaced by the breakdown of the former master-journeyman-apprentice system, the educational programs offered by these organizations represented opportunities to set old wrongs right and give progeny the respectability missing in their own lives. The ideal did not match reality. Most of the institutions discriminated against journeymen by limiting membership to master craftsmen only. During this period, the lexicon of craft also expanded concomitantly with the elites' movement to segment the term "art" into fine art and useful or mechanical arts. By the end of the century the mechanical arts were known as industrial arts. The term "mechanic" generally referred to one who combined creative skills with hand skills. The manufacturer represented an unskilled worker who used machines.

The mechanic-craftsman morphed into the mechanic-entrepreneur who assimilated a fusion of science, craft, and art into a clear vision and "whose virtues linked him to the craft tradition [moral life] but whose business acumen drew him closer to an industrial economy in which vicious competition and capital accumulation were necessary to success."[8]

The mechanics' institutes failed in their mission to create upward mobility for students. The continuous pedagogical experiments to merge liberal and technical learning were outpaced by advances in machine technology, factory production, and Taylorism. Rather, the system supported the further division of rationalized work into the wage classes of mechanic, operative, and laborer. All of these groups would continually struggle for power against the bourgeoning mechanic entrepreneur class. The entrepreneur had no incentive to train personnel, as machine technology had begun to usurp unskilled and skilled functions. The public education system catered to the production of operative automatons trained to work with specific machines and disconnected any efforts to merge liberal and technical learning.

Ironically, the symbolism of the craftsman and the workshop remained a core value of Americans. By 1890, according to the historian David Montgomery, "the shop culture's image of the apprentice is important because it was a compelling social myth."[9] Large industrial firms were promoting "apprenticeships" that included a mandatory night school education and on-the-job training for periods up to four years. Montgomery's research shows that less than 14 percent of the "apprentices" stayed the course. It appears to have been an industrial tactic to attract low-cost operatives without any expectation of developing skill.

Countering the industrialists' scam was a genuine effort by members of the arts and craft movement of the late nineteenth and early twentieth centuries to rebel against modernism and its causes of a collective American nervous breakdown. The advocates for this movement idealized handcraft, promoted authenticity, and revered the American work ethic. They revived the educational model promoted earlier in the nineteenth century of training both the head and the hand. By doing so, immigrants could assimilate into American culture more smoothly, militant workers would be quieted, and the elite would return to productivity. Within their educational model, they advanced a growing class-consciousness by advocating different forms of handcraft (manual) education based on social, economic, and ethnic circumstances. For example, Jane Addams's Hull House manual training model sought to train students of the "lower class" destined to work as machine operatives to understand the history and theory of the factory system because "she believed that by encouraging the spirit of teamwork among factory hands employed on the same product, the fragmenting effects of the division of labor might be overcome altogether."[10] Assembly line and piecework operatives would transcend the menial reality of their lives by becoming happy and proud of their work. Different venues were appropriate for the other classes, such as summer field schools for the elite, hobbies for the upper middle class, and combinations of educational and recreational methods for the middle class. As T. J. Jackson Lears points out in *No Place of Grace: Antimodernism and the Transformation of American Culture, 1880–1920,* the American arts and craft movement was not a protest movement: "what began as a reaction against rationalization ended in therapeutic assimilation to it."[11] By World War I, the arts and craft movement helped American society transition to the twentieth-century system of mass production and foster an even greater sense of class-consciousness among those who aspired to the craftsman ideal.

The Twentieth Century

The nineteenth century saw the transition from the shop culture and form of organization to the factory culture and form of organization. While there were fleeting educational experiments in revival of craft tradition and skill as a means to preserve the historic architectural artifact, the machine and white-collar bureaucracy usurped and redistributed the skills of the former shop culture. The only industry group that remained relatively immune to industrial rationalization was building construction. During the twentieth century, trade unions became the magnets for the former journeyman and apprentice classes. In *Royal Blue: The Culture of Construction Workers,* Herbert Applebaum argues that union construction workers still possess many of the historical craftsman attributes associated with a moral life, that is, being useful to the self, the family, and the community.[12] This self-profiling may be true; however, according to Grace Palladino, organized labor has never become a sustainable power base or training force to advance the upward mobility of the majority of construction trade workers in the United States. She concludes that "although construction remains one of the best-organized private industries in the United States, second only to transportation, according to U.S. Bureau of Labor Statistics, in 2002 building trades unions represented only 17.8 percent of almost seven million workers."[13]

The twentieth century also resulted in an expanding class divide *within* the middle class. As the former apprentice and journeyman organized, the master craftsman internalized his training role and adapted to become craftsman-entrepreneur. According to Charles Sabel, craftsmen take pride in their own culture of skill versus becoming part of the middle class. The master craftsman may be "docile or militant, out for the self or capable of solidarity . . . [he may adopt] a series of remunerative tasks that successfully challenge and require the development of whatever powers one takes as the measure of human worth."

The growing class divides between organized labor and craftsman-entrepreneur further diminished the capacity to educate and train the skills necessary to preserve the historic architectural artifact. It was not until the second half of the twentieth century that American higher education and public policy evolved to support the preservation of the country's collective cultural heritage. The result was the formation of the American community college system and the entry of universities into the formal study of historic preservation.

Twentieth-Century Public Policy and Historic Preservation

Public policy in America has a volatile past regarding the value of preserving the architectural artifact as a symbol of the country's cultural heritage. The Housing Acts of 1949 and 1954 coupled with Eisenhower-era interstate highway public works projects resulted in mass demolition of historic urban neighborhoods. This insensitive form of physical intervention disrupted individuals' abilities to maintain balance between themselves and the external world, resulting in psychiatric disorders collectively called "root shock."[14]

The destructive policies of the post–World War II period were reversed with the passage of the National Historic Preservation Act (NHPA) of 1966 and a series of tax reform acts starting in 1976. The NHPA established professional guidelines for valuing and approaching design and intervention treatments for historic architectural artifacts. The tax acts created significant financial incentives for the rehabilitation of historic buildings.

The formal American preservation education model began to take shape in the 1970s. Despite the recognition that thinking and doing needed to be united in preservation practice, it was difficult for the American educational system to assimilate the concept. A driving force perpetuating the divide were certain recommendations developed by a research committee appointed by the National Trust for Historic Preservation (NTHP) in 1967 to assess the state of preservation education and make recommendations for educational capacity development. *The Report of the Committee on Professional and Public Education for Historic Preservation to the Trustees of the National Trust for Historic Preservation* (the Whitehill report) was presented and approved by the board of trustees in the fall of 1967. One subcommittee charged with review of architecture schools concluded that "specialization in restoration and preservation is most effective at the graduate level." The other subcommittee reviewed traditional building crafts and concluded that "the best method of training a craftsman is the oldest method—apprenticeship—for the hand must be trained as well as the mind." The second group also recommended that the NTHP form a permanent Conservation Council for Traditional Trade Crafts, and that standing members include "the chief professional and craft agencies concerned with preservation *not traditional education*."[15] The American public educational system was dismissed out of hand by the most influential and elitist preservation minds of the day as offering little potential to develop preservation curriculum and pedagogy to meet the acknowledged demand for trained preservation professionals and practitioners.[16]

Twentieth-Century Historic Preservation Education

Since the development of specific preservation coursework during the 1960s at the University of Virginia, Columbia University, and Cornell University, curriculum development has emphasized the interdisciplinary nature of the field and expressed sensitivity to the dynamic discourse among and between professionals, practitioners, policy makers, and scholars to define a universally accepted role for historic preservation in the conservation of the historic architectural artifact. It was not until 1964 that James Marston Fitch at Columbia University developed the first unique curriculum in historic preservation, turning into a master of science degree in 1973, predicated an interdisciplinary foundation that borrowed heavily from the architecture, planning, and history disciplines.[17] Other influential scholars and academicians such as Anthony Vidler echoed this philosophy when speaking of Immanuel Kant's "dare to know" Enlightenment philosophy: "if an architecture school has any place within the university, it is to take up this dare with the confidence that here, as in no other humanities department, the limits of the relationship between knowing and doing are continuously tested."[18]

The National Council for Preservation Education (NCPE) was founded in 1978. This independent group of academics developed academic standards and faculty tenure protocols, and, unlike the Whitehill-led NTHP researchers, recognized the interdisciplinary nature of the field and gave credence to preservation programs housed in Humanities and Social Science Departments in addition to Schools of Architecture. Membership and standards expanded to include associate, baccalaureate, and specialty certificate programs during the 1990s. NCPE became the de facto accrediting body for formal preservation education in the United States and maintains that position today (Table 4.1).[19]

NCPE has proven to be a flexible body adapting standards and membership to the evolving discipline of historic preservation. The organization has had little direct impact, however, on solving what Jeanne Gamble conceptualizes as the "theory-practice conundrum" in education.[20] A small percentage of NCPE-certified programs emphasize or specialize in building craft training or architectural conservation (Table 4.2). I posit that there are three reasons for this situation. First, graduate-level academia, the dominant actor in preservation education, does not have the jurisdiction, traditions, culture, or self-interest to support expansion of the preservation education franchise to other levels and structures of institutionalized education. This is not to say that the members are unwilling and unsupportive, but rather, unable. Second, the majority of current historic preservation scholars and teachers were formally trained in subdisciplines or contributing disciplines to the historic preservation field. They have mastered visualization learning but not actualization learning, creating a gap in the dissemination of knowledge necessary to execute design-build interventions demanded by the market. Christopher Koziol reinforces this position: "The Federal Tax acts of the 1970s and 1980s

Table 4.1 Historic Preservation Programs by Academic Level

	Non-Degree*	2-Year	4-Year	Graduate
# Programs	12	9	10	46
% Schools	2%	9%	16%	74%

Source: NCPE and Ogle, 2012
*Offered In Academic Institutions

Table 4.2 Building Craft or Architecture Conservation Emphasis

	Non-Degree*	2-Year	4-Year	Graduate
# Programs	12	9	10	46
Building Craft or Arch. Conservation	0	9	6	12
% of Level	NA	100%	60%	26%
% of Total	NA	12%	8%	16%

Source: NCPE and Ogle, 2012
*Offered In Academic Institutions

introduced privatist economic policy to the world of preservation, and to this day there remains a certain unease between preservationists trained as essentialists working in privatist influenced government programs."[21] In other words, most formally trained preservationists are comfortable within the discursive theory of the artifact but not a proposed practical intervention.

Community Colleges

The American community college system is unique in the world. No other country combines vocational, pre-baccalaureate, and developmental education within the same postsecondary institution.[22] Despite their similarities in public policy and competitive advantage over other forms of higher educational institutions, community colleges across the United States are subject to idiosyncratic forces that have created an atmosphere of vulnerability and inconsistency, particularly in the face of universal market demand for training, for example, preservation craft. The most significant force responsible for this unlevel playing field has been the change in the mix of funding sources for community colleges over the past one hundred years.

The local community tax base almost exclusively funded the first community colleges at the turn of the twentieth century (Table 4.3). A century later, the sources of funds have changed radically to reflect student and government participation, with state funding becoming the dominant funding source, reaching as high as 45 percent in the aggregate.[23]

As community colleges became more dependent on state funds, the scrutiny of regulators and most significantly methods for allocation of

Table 4.3 **Percentage of Sources of Funds for Community Colleges 1918, 1950, 2000.**

Source	1918	1950	2000
Tuition & Fees	6	9	20
Federal	0	1	6
State	0	26	45
Local	94	49	20
Gifts	0	0	1
Other	0	2	9

Source: Cohen and Brawner, 2008

funds drastically altered approaches to education. The various complex formulas for state allocation of funds can create a paradox between the community college's mission of serving local student, business, and community needs versus the realities of available funds to cover personnel, facilities, and other operating costs.

Cohen and Browner detail four models of state fund allocation. The first is a negotiated budget where the state legislature negotiates an annual budget with the schools. Second is the unit-rate formula where funds are allocated on a per unit measure. Typically this calculation is based on student enrollment. Most states use this formula. The third is a minimum foundation model that is used for colleges with local tax base support, again generally based on some per unit measure. A fourth model, the cost-based approach, allocates funds based on actual costs of an institution, including specific programs, planned benchmarks, or performance criteria.[24]

The unit-rate formula causes the most problems for community colleges, as funds are generally allocated based on full-time equivalent (FTE) student calculations. Unlike secondary school districts, where enrollment is compulsory, enrollments in community colleges can swing drastically. The programs that suffer most under this approach tend to be high cost per student programs. Career and technical programs, including historic preservation trades education, fall in this category. The cost of facilities, equipment, disposables, and instruction on a per student basis generally exceeds the cost of an alternative liberal arts program or large career and technical programs that serve a common public good such as health care and security. The irony for historic preservation trades programs is that there is disconnect between market demand and education supply where market demand far exceeds the supply of trained craftsmen with the skills to preserve the historic architectural artifact.[25]

The Preservation Integrated Learning Model (PILM)

The PILM model conceptualizes four periods of time that are necessary to achieve the goal of fully integrated curriculum design (Figure 4.1). The phases are not mutually exclusive or linear in progression. Some schools will achieve fully integrated learning before others and may still utilize elements of each phase.

Phase I represents the status quo. The characteristics of Phase I are an imbalance between the levels of formal preservation education, credential-

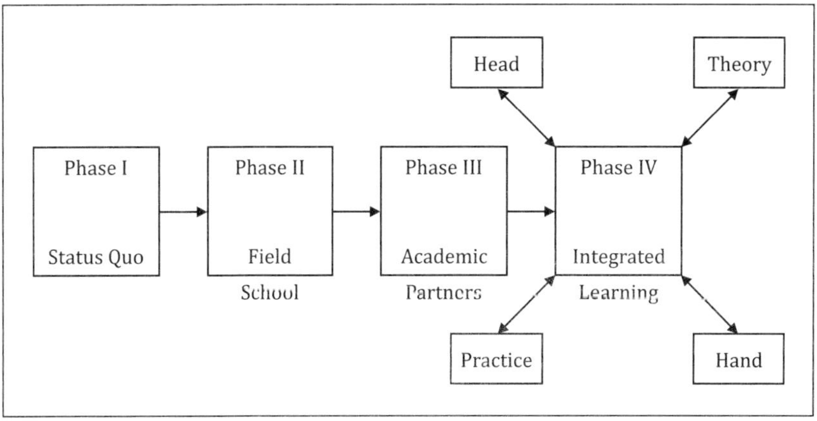

4.1 Preservation Integrated Learning Model (PILM)

ing of faculty, and the lack of curricula offering materials science and craft skills training (Table 4.2).

Phase II is categorized by the evolution of the field school. Field schools are generally offered during the summer months when most formal institutional academic teaching is suspended. Field schools are organized to give students the opportunity to engage in experiential learning associated with physical intervention projects. The student may or may not earn academic credit for participating in these schools. In order to further develop this phase, NCPE could set field school curriculum standards and assist in underwriting the cost through grants and membership school participation.

Phase III evolves through partnerships. Different levels or different institutions may specialize in particular areas of the preservation discipline. In order to offer students an integrated learning experience, partnerships can be formed. For example, a graduate school of design may partner with a four-year or two-year school that specializes in craft and materials science to facilitate faculty and student immersion, and vice versa. Portability of credit and faculty credentials can also be facilitated through this method. Another example could be a two-year school and a four-year school partnering where the two-year school would offer the degree emphasis courses and the four-year school would offer the general education component of the baccalaureate degree. NCPE could also play a significant role in this phase by establishing specific standards for craft and materials science coursework.

Phase IV achieves a fully integrated preservation curriculum design where students and faculty are trained equally in the theory of preservation

Table 4.4 **Percentage Distribution of Coursework in Baccalaureate Degrees**

	Thinking *Liberal Studies*	Thinking & Doing *HP Core, Design Media, Studio*	Doing *Skills Training & Practice*
ACBA	36%	21%	43%
BAC	35%	20%	45%

Source: Ogle, 2012.

but also in practical design, planning, and physical intervention skills. This phase connects thinking and doing.

Case Study

To this point, I have presented how the preservation education system has evolved in the United States and proposed some ideas as to why there is little integration of thinking and doing in curricular design and pedagogy. It is interesting to note that two institutions have achieved Phase IV as conceptualized in the PILM model: the American College of the Building Arts (ACBA) and Boston Architectural College (BAC).

ACBA offers a fully integrated learning system and confers associates and baccalaureate degrees in the building arts. BAC offers baccalaureate and graduate degrees with embedded integration of theory and practice. Since its founding more than a decade ago, ACBA has stood fast to its approach as it strives to demonstrate the validity of this type of student learning to its U.S. Department of Education regional accrediting body. Conversely, BAC is accredited and has been combining academics with professional practice in professional design degree programs for more than 120 years. In the past year, this pedagogical and curricular approach has been expanded to include historic preservation programs.

A comparison of the two colleges' baccalaureate degree programs into courses that represent thinking, thinking and doing, and doing develops an interesting parallel (Table 4.4). Courses that require a practical skill student-learning outcome represent almost two-thirds of the respective curricula.

Conclusion

This chapter has synthesized the evolution of skilled craft training and education in the United States as it directly impacts the potential to preserve the historic architectural artifact. From the literature reviewed, it is clear that the ideal or myth of the craftsman has evolved, adapted, and survived radical changes in the invention and means of production of goods and services over time. I argue that in the second half of the twentieth century, public policy through passage of the NHPA and a series of tax acts has done its part to support the sustainability of demand for education in historic preservation, design, and materials conservation skills. It is the responsibility of the educational community to reinforce this public mandate by moving toward a more balanced curriculum that supports the intellectual and cognitive learning necessary to achieve the desired ends. Further research is called for to achieve the goal of reestablishing thinking and doing in education as it pertains to preserving the historic architectural artifact and America's collective cultural heritage. It is not a new concept. In c. 30–20 B.C.E, Vitruvius wrote, "For neither native talent without learning nor learning without native talent create the master craftsman."[26] The Swedish planner Bent Flyvbjerg revives Aristotle and the concept of phronesis, which "requires an interaction between the general and the concrete."[27] The loss of this integrated learning typology is more analogous to the loss of a historic fabrication or design technique. It can be rediscovered and applied in contemporary interventions as, for example, the rediscovery of lime-based mortars and the energy savings by solar gain-loss orientation in design and site placement.

Preservation education researchers need to step outside their usual design, cultural landscape, and planning research agendas to call on their colleagues from the humanities and the social, behavioral, and physical sciences to collaborate in development of a new integrated learning model pedagogy that recognizes the need for theory and practice to merge in historic preservation intervention. James Marston Fitch was prophetic when he wrote after founding the first formal historic preservation degree program in America, "Perhaps we should visualize an overall educational program with parallel academic and vocational tracks in which crossovers would be permitted to any student who is able and willing to operate at both levels."[28]

Notes

1. Herbert Applebaum, *The American Work Ethic and the Changing Work Force: An Historical Perspective* (Westport, CT: Greenwood Press, 1998), 20.
2. Richard Sennett and Jonathan Cobb, *The Hidden Injuries of Class* (New York: W. W. Norton and Company, 1972).
3. Applebaum, *The American Work Ethic*, 25.
4. Christopher Koziol, "Historic Preservation Ideology: A Critical Mapping of Contemporary Heritage Policy Discourse," *Preservation Education and Research*, 1 (2008), 41–50.

5. Matthew B. Crawford, *Shop Class as Soulcraft: An Inquiry into the Value of Work* (New York: Penguin Press, 2009).

6. Edward R. Stevens, *The Grammar of the Machine: Technical Literacy and Early Industrial Expansion in the United States* (New Haven, CT: Yale University Press, 1995), 50.

7. Stevens, *The Grammar of the Machine*, 108.

8. Stevens, *The Grammar of the Machine*, 110.

9. David Montgomery, *The Fall of the House of Labor: The Workplace, the State, and American Labor Activism 1865–1925* (Cambridge: Cambridge University Press, 1987), 185.

10. T. J. Jackson Lears, *No Place of Grace: Antimodernism and the Transformation of American Culture, 1880–1920* (Chicago: University of Chicago Press, 1994), 80.

11. Lears, *No Place of Grace*, 89.

12. Herbert Applebaum, *Royal Blue: The Culture of Construction Workers* (New York: Holt, Rinehart and Wilson, 1981).

13. Grace Palladino, *Skilled Hands, Strong Spirits: A Century of Building Trades History* (Ithaca, NY: Cornell University Press, 2005), 226.

14. Mindy Fullilove, *Root Shock: How Tearing Up City Neighborhoods Hurts America, and What We Can Do About It* (New York: Random House, 2004).

15. Walter Muir Whitehill et al., "The Report of the Committee on Professional and Public Education for Historic Preservation to the Trustees of the National Trust for Historic Preservation," http://www.iptw.org/whitehill-home.htm (accessed August 20, 2012); emphasis added.

16. Robert W. Ogle, "America's Community Colleges: The Untapped Potential for Preservation Craft Education," in *Finding Common Ground, Papers From the International Trades Education Symposium* (Amherst, MA: Preservation Trades Network Press, 2009), 29–40.

17. Michael Tomlan, "Historic Preservation Education: Alongside Architecture in Academia," *Journal of Architectural Education*, 47 (1994), 187–96.

18. Anthony Vidler, "History, Criticism and Theory," *Lotus International*, 72 (1992), 133.

19. The National Council for Preservation Education is not an accrediting organization; however, membership by academic institutions requires adherence to curriculum standards set by the membership for degree-granting institutions. Many institutions use the standards as part of their external and internal review processes.

20. Jeanne Gamble, "Retrieving the General from the Particular: The Structure of Craft Knowledge," *Journal of Education*, 29 (2003), 73.

21. Koziol, "Historic Preservation Ideology," 48.

22. Arthur M. Cohen and Florence B. Brawer, *The American Community College* (San Francisco: Jossey-Bass, 2008), 27.

23. George B. Vaughn, *The Community College Story* (Washington DC: Community College Press, 2000), 19–22.

24. Cohen and Brawer, *The American Community College*.

25. Robert W. Ogle, *Closing the Gap in Historic Preservation Education* (master's thesis, University of Kentucky, 2005).

26. I. D. Rowland and T. N. Howe, eds., *Vitruvius: The Ten Books of Architecture* (New York: Cambridge University Press, 1999), 21.

27. Bent Flyvbjerg, *Making Social Science Matter: Why Social Inquiry Fails and How it Can Succeed Again* (Cambridge: Cambridge University Press, 2001), 57.

28. James Marston Fitch, *Historic Preservation: Curatorial Management of the Built World* (New York: McGraw-Hill Book Company, 1982), 356.

5 The Development of a Preservation Planning Board Game

Andréa Livi Smith

Educational games are a common sight in classrooms at every level. Urban planners, for example, commonly use *SimCity* to teach concepts of the profession. In addition to using pre-existing games, some organizations have even developed their own. For instance, the U.S. Army developed a game called *The Challenges of the National Historic Preservation Act* to aid in compliance. Unfortunately, the purely educational games tend to suffer in terms of playability. Put simply, they tend not to be fun. Games can be very effective tools, but only when they succeed at being games as well. In this context, a class of senior undergraduate historic preservation students developed and designed a preservation planning educational game. This game focuses on the specifics of preservation planning, including the challenges of balancing growth and preservation, the establishment of historic districts, adaptive reuse, and relationship with sustainability/green space. The goals of the course were to provide a capstone experience, allowing students to apply what they had previously learned in their academic career.

This chapter discusses the development of the game, paying particular attention to the challenges faced in design, balancing of playability and didactic goals, and refinement of the game through play testing. Finally, lessons learned in the design process are discussed. These lessons may be valuable for other preservation educators who want to integrate games into their courses.

Background: Educational Games

Games are nothing new in the context of education. Research abounds regarding the effectiveness of game scenarios in pedagogy. For instance, the *Jeopardy!* format is available as a template and used by teachers of varied disciplines in primary to postsecondary classrooms.[1]

Urban planning has integrated games for decades. Notably, *Monopoly* was introduced a century ago, and has since entered the pantheon of games.[2] While divorced from geography, *Monopoly* is arguably one of the most popular board games in the world and is therefore an entry to urban planning for many children and adults. Maxis's *SimCity* is part of numerous curricula from middle school on,[3] and more advanced versions of the simulation have been in development. Even critics of *SimCity* admit valuable learning opportunities:[4] both what is lacking in the game and what is there can provide the start of meaningful discussion of the different aspects of planning as well as their limitations. Visioning exercises aimed at laypeople and decision makers, such as "Reality Check," have used LEGOS to aid in understanding the effect of growth on the landscape.[5] Recently, there has been renewed and vigorous interest in *gamification.* Gamification adapts game design to other applications such as education or commerce in order to engage subjects. For instance, many businesses have point systems or badges that reward customers for purchases, but also for "liking" on Facebook and e-mailing friends about the product/service. Extremely effective for businesses, as supported by its being adopted by companies such as Coke, Nike, and others,[6] gamification is also becoming omnipresent in didactic applications.

Games whose purpose is more than entertainment are often called *serious games.* They are now used in multiple contexts, including education, military, scientific research, and crisis management.[7] Since games have become a mainstream pedagogical method, integrating them into the preservation planning curriculum seems like a worthwhile effort likely to yield valuable results.

The Preservation Planning Course Format

The University of Mary Washington baccalaureate in historic preservation culminates in a capstone "laboratory" course. Students choose among four tracks—planning, museum studies, archaeology, and building forensics—and complete the appropriate course during their senior year. The preservation planning laboratory is perhaps better described as a studio course. It is fully project-based, and eschews traditional reading/lecture/discussion formats in favor of a problem-solving, team-based approach. The goal is to strengthen and apply skills and knowledge previously acquired and to produce a professional-level report or other document to aid in employment and graduate school opportunities.

Usually, these projects are either purely theoretical—such as a developing a historic ordinance for an area that is not likely to adopt one—or are limited in scope—such as a survey of a tiny village or isolated property. Both of these options are problematic. The first allows for grander plans, but as it is theoretical, it is not very inspiring. It is also challenging to familiarize students with an area in which they are not residents, and which they may have never visited before. The second is challenging for multiple reasons: finding an easily accessible community is itself no small feat, working with stakeholders can be frustrating, and again students can end up disillusioned. While learning the realities of political hurdles is worthwhile, this is perhaps not appropriate for undergraduates. Furthermore, the timeline involved is often untenable. As educators, we have a strict sixteen-week window, which is often ignored outside academia. In my few years teaching this course or others like it at other institutions, I have encountered all of these problems firsthand, with both undergraduate and graduate students. This can result in "teaching moments" for graduate students. For instance, a local historian who was overly critical of students (going so far as to tell them they had "utterly failed") gave me an opportunity to teach students about having a thick skin and being prepared for unreasonable people. Undergraduates cannot be expected to deal well with a situation like this, however, which has led me to be very careful in choosing projects and partners. Consequently, I have concentrated on finding novel projects to supplement the traditional approach.

The idea of developing a board game derived naturally from my personal interests. I have been an avid gamer for many years, and have mulled the possibility of clarifying difficult preservation concepts, like transfer of development rights, by making a game. As there was no pressing local project to take precedence, I thought this past year would be a good time to test out my idea.

Phase One: Research

Though I started from a familiarity with strategic board games, any Internet search would have quickly yielded the same result. *Planetizen,* a popular urban planning website, for instance, lists a half-dozen games related to planning, and the comments section discusses many more.[8] While the dominating urban planning game is *SimCity,* there are many other noncomputerized games used by professionals around the country. For instance, LEGOs are commonly used by planners in visioning exercises, and by architects and designers for a number of educational goals (e.g., the *Place It!* program, accessible at placeit.org). It is no accident that the National Building Museum's LEGO Architecture exhibit was so well attended and long lasting.

Since creating a digital game seemed too technically difficult for students unfamiliar with computer programming, the decision to make a physical game was an easy one. The first phase of this course, as in any other, was to simply undertake research. In this case, this meant finding and playing as many games as possible. The games played as research for this project can broadly be divided into two categories: spatial board games and strategy card games.

Spatial board games include classics such as *Cathedral.* This is a game of control: game pieces of various shapes are placed on a bounded board to control more space than one's opponent. *Blokus* is another example with the same basic goal and gameplay. More recent games, such as *Settlers of Catan,* focus on resource management and growth. *Ticket to Ride* is a similar game but uses the metaphor of rail lines spreading in the United States. Broadly speaking, these games are effective to visualize geographic concepts such as growth, competing interests, and use of limited resources. With already complex gameplay, issues such as funds or resources are distilled to the point of abstraction. In *Settlers,* this means cards to represent building materials (wood, stone, etc.). Considering the need in a preservation planning game to explain concepts that are difficult and varied—such as zoning, taxation, and easements—these games are useful as inspiration but insufficient on their own.

On the opposite end of the spectrum, strategy games such as *Citadels* or *Magic: The Gathering* lack a geographic component but allow for very detailed and complex "action cards." While *Magic,* as its name indicates, is about control of enchantments and beasts, it could really be about anything. In fact, its gameplay has been replicated for games about science fiction, sports, and many other topics. The cards in these kinds of games can and do include extensive information, about both their use in gameplay and "flavor text." Flavor text is a quote, snippet, or definition that enriches the card and makes it more interesting. Using a card-based system like these games would therefore allow for much more detail and complexity. These card games by their very nature, however, lack the geographic component of the board games discussed above.

Early in the course, we listed every game we could think of that could relate to our goal. Students were charged with playing all the games they could find, and taking copious notes while doing so. An interesting issue here was that the students started out completely unfamiliar with strategy games beyond classics such as *Monopoly.* This turned out to be a blessing in disguise. Since they familiarized themselves with varied games—there were too many for everyone to play all of them—each student developed unique expertise, and was subsequently not shy in defending her or his preferred game mechanic in class. Even usually quiet and withdrawn students became engaged.

While neither the spatial board games nor the strategy card games alone were adequate as a model for our game, combining them gave us the building blocks needed to put it together. We appropriated and altered ideas and game dynamics from various sources. Of course, everything was thoroughly documented as we progressed, resulting in a complete rationale and resource list at the end of the semester.

Parallel to familiarizing ourselves with games, we also researched game dynamics in general through *The Kobold Guide to Game Design*.[9] This book, authored by numerous game designers and recipient of the Origins Award that recognizes outstanding work in the game industry, covers every step in game development from concept to design, development, and presentation to potential publishers and distributors. Careful reading of the book, paired with analysis of games we played in class, allowed students to crystallize their thoughts regarding game dynamics.

Beyond game mastery, students also needed an understanding of preservation planning issues and concepts to include in the game, as well as selecting the target audience. Finding the target audience was done with a short web survey questionnaire sent out through social media. The fourteen-question survey focused on an individual's knowledge and interest of preservation planning. The questionnaire was kept purposefully short to increase response rates, and students' social knowhow and networks were used for dissemination. Of the 194 people surveyed, 67.4 percent had no background in historic preservation and urban planning, but 47.9 percent responded "somewhat likely" to playing a game to learn more about the topic. The survey also yielded concepts that would interest potential players (such as historic districts and eminent domain). The survey results clearly pointed to a lay audience generally unfamiliar with preservation but more likely to know general planning concepts who would be interested in furthering their knowledge.

With the results of the survey, students were given the direction they needed to focus on specific preservation planning terms and issues. They delved into their old class notes, textbooks, and web references to find the definitions and implementations of these terms and concepts. I asked them to develop a spreadsheet, housed online for easy collaboration, to list all relevant terms and concepts. Common concepts in preservation planning, as well as particularly difficult ones, were emphasized. For instance, the class decided as a whole that Section 106 had to appear in the game in some way. Other tools/ordinances such as preservation easements, historic districts, transfer of development rights, revolving funds, and others were also noted as must-haves.

Phase Two: Brainstorming

Once we all familiarized ourselves with game mechanics and the game audience, the course became a series of brainstorms. This was perhaps the most challenging part of the semester. This kind of open-ended, nebulous work is particularly difficult for undergraduates, who are usually given specific tasks and direction. As the instructor, I had to alternate between cheerleader and brakeman: sometimes they became intimidated and needed a new idea to inspire them, while at other times their plans became too ambitious or veered off topic, and needed to be reined in. The brainstorms yielded many ideas, and eventually consensus was reached on an overall game concept. This was followed by slow progress with details of game dynamics.

A particular breakthrough was settling on characters/roles for each player rather than stand-alone goals. This had a twofold benefit. On the game side, using characters meant more varied gameplay: each character is different, and works with/against others in a dynamic way. As we eventually designed seven characters and the game is meant for four players, the game is different every time as the combination of characters will vary. On the didactic side, settling on characters made the game much more realistic. Only one of the seven characters is an overt preservationist. The others have goals ranging from allied to preservation to outright

5.1 Two of the *Plunked!* characters. Photograph by the author

anti-preservation, as shown in Figure 5.1. For instance, the "small business" developer is generally pro-preservation, as is the environmentalist, but these are not their final goals. Furthermore, the character system meant that at least one of each character's three goals requires collaboration with at least one other player. This subtle lesson is applicable to all planning efforts.

Game dynamics were borrowed from many games, melding the card-based and geographical approaches. Multiple game board permutations were discussed before settling on the eventual design. Similarly, the action card system went through a few iterations before functional game dynamics were settled on. Once that was done, the more "fun" parts of the game creation could take place.

Phase Three: The Game Takes Shape

With major game dynamics in place, we still needed hundreds of action cards. These had to simultaneously (1) cover all major preservation planning concepts realistically; (2) be balanced so as to avoid lopsided games; and (3) allow for deck-manipulation to make gameplay interesting. In other words, some action cards had to allow for cards to change hands, or to be used twice, or the deck to be shuffled, and the like. What followed were more brainstorms and lists. Students had to come up with card ideas, which were then discussed in class and tailored to the game. Levity was also injected into the course at this point: some cards were given silly names, illustrations, or flavor text.

In a parallel effort, the seven game characters had to be developed so their goals were approximately equivalent in terms of difficulty, while making sure they retained their characteristics. At first, this led to drastically uneven games. Extensive debates took place to develop realistic and feasible goals for the various characters. Students became advocates for their favorite characters and gave them backstories and more depth.

One felicitous asset in the course was a talented artist among the students. She drew all characters as well as the game logo and game board. While this added welcome polish to the game, this was not strictly necessary. The class also ably took on the other design tasks. Fonts, colors, and other design decisions were made democratically. Students brought multiple ideas/mockups to each session, which were improved in an iterative process. The class chose the name of the game, like everything else, democratically. While *Plunked!* was not my first choice, the democratic approach kept everyone engaged and enfranchised.

Phase Four: Play Testing and the Mad Dash

As the semester progressed, the game took shape but was still untested. To balance gameplay and finalize ideas, extensive game testing was implemented. At first, only the class participants played the game. The first game took close to three hours. The second took barely more than fifteen minutes because of poor recalibration. After each playing of the game, we engaged in extensive discussion of things that worked and things that did not, and made changes accordingly. Tax amounts, income, and the point system all had to be changed multiple times to achieve balance. Similarly, action cards were periodically culled, changed, and added. At this point in testing, these were just handwritten slips of paper in card sleeves, as shown in Figure 5.2.

After weeks of this iterative process, action cards were slowly finalized. Only then were they printed in color on card stock. Once the game was presentable, players from outside class were brought in. These consisted mainly of students' friends and significant others. They were asked their thoughts both during and after each game. Further polishing was completed according to their comments. Their feedback also informed the rules: while formal rules were written from the start, they were clarified and illustrations were added to make them easy to follow even for beginners. This polishing process took another two to three weeks of daily games. An extremely encouraging byproduct of this process was that most of the outside game testers asked how they could purchase the game.

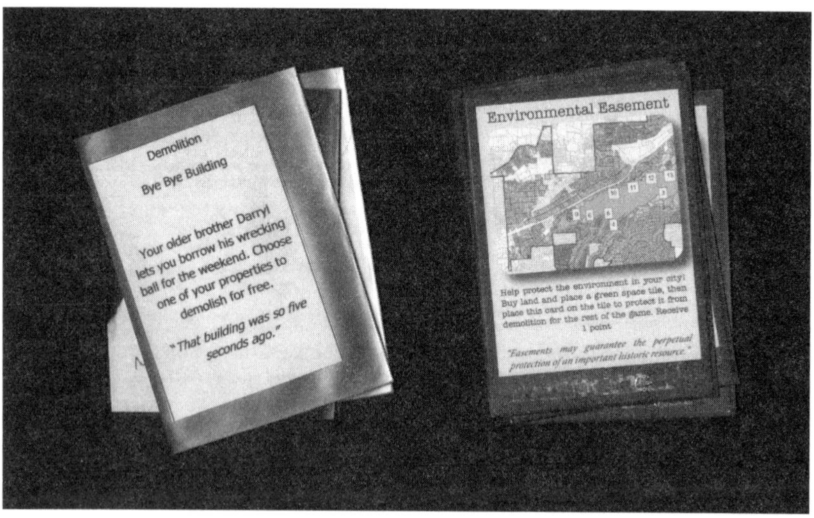

5.2 Development of action cards from paper slips to complete design. Photograph by the author

As the semester ended, the focus shifted to finalizing and printing the game rules and presenting our product to the larger university community. This was again an exciting and positive experience, as all feedback from students and faculty alike expressed enthusiasm for the game. Nonetheless, by necessity the students' attention moved away from developing the game to the practical needs of the end of the semester. More game testing was certainly desirable—from my limited experience, there can never be enough game testing—but time simply ran out. The final result was a complete prototype, including game board, game pieces, character and action cards, property tiles, illustrated rules, and rationale, all enclosed in a decorated box.

Lessons Learned

No project is completely successful, but this risky endeavor certainly went beyond my expectations. The usual goals of the preservation planning laboratory were met: students meaningfully deepened their knowledge and skills, engaged in extensive teamwork, and produced a project that should help them in their future career and educational goals. This course was also thoroughly enjoyed by both students and faculty. Far from trivial, this enjoyment entailed intense engagement from all the students. Even students who had been uninterested in previous courses were active participants. It was extremely gratifying for me to see them work longer and harder than I had expected them to, to volunteer for tasks, and to follow up rather than relying on reminders and deadlines. Half the class has since contacted me and specifically asked about the game and what the next steps are going to be.

By necessity, the syllabus for this course was vague to the extreme. I thought of the tasks to be completed and assigned what I thought would be sufficient time while allowing for spillover at the end. In retrospect, I still believe this was the only way to go, and feel lucky that it mostly worked. Familiarity with the topic at hand and therefore a vague idea of the time needed for each step was crucially helpful. My main challenge, once the semester started, was to keep all the tasks moving forward. This was no small feat, as any part of the process—game dynamics, card development, design, rules, game pieces—could create a bottleneck for every other task. Furthermore, many tasks overlapped in terms of timing, especially later in the semester, as shown in Figure 5.3. This therefore required good time management and multitasking from all of us. This was achieved by giving leadership roles to each student: while each student worked on multiple aspects of the game, he or she was responsible for at least one of them. This resulted in self-imposed pressure to be on top of tasks.

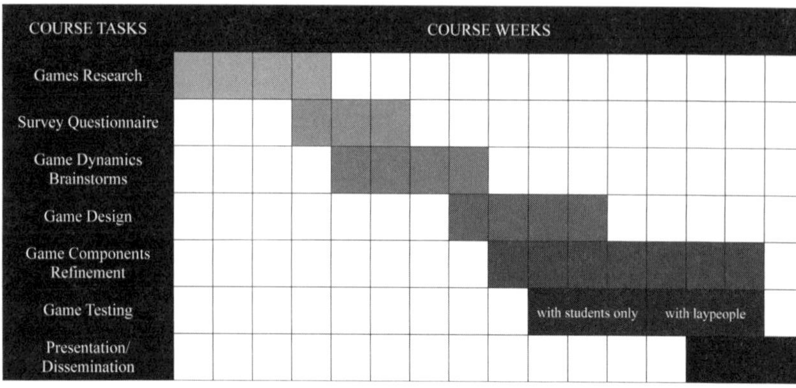

5.3 Course timeline. Image by the author

One note should be made as to the potential cost of the course. As implemented, the course was very inexpensive: we found game pieces online for less than one penny per piece. I bought card sleeves for less than \$20 and the final game was placed in a pizza box donated by a local store. Other than extensive use of a color printer and card stock, the game was all but free. This presupposes access to Adobe InDesign (as well as students who know how to use it) and to all the board games necessary for research, however. An avid gamer, I already owned more than a dozen games. Students owned the rest. Purchasing all these games, and having them available at the start of the semester, would be costly and require advance planning. Nonetheless, many game stores now offer rentals, and there are often gaming groups in colleges who may be wiling to lend their collection. This kind of project I believe compares positively to more traditional studio courses in terms of costs.

Overall, my biggest satisfaction with this course is the problem solving that the students were able to achieve. In terms of preservation planning content, students more than once surprised me with the depth of their understanding and the connections they made between different issues. Working with fourteen divergent opinions (including my own) was continually challenging but ultimately rewarding. Students were able to work independently and together to resolve the problems they encountered. Often, these were solutions I would not have thought of on my own. Class was always raucous and energized, sometimes edging into conflict and chaos, but always engaged.

As this project was essentially insular in nature, students did not have to interact with professionals or the public at large beyond the survey respondents and game testers. This is a notable weakness, and for a graduate course might have been problematic. As these students will have subsequent studio course(s) in graduate school with these kinds of experiences, however, I think this was an acceptable loss in this case. Gamification in general also presents the risk of oversimplification and distorting students' perceptions of decision making and the consequences thereof. While a game by definition will simplify reality, a good game will do so overtly and in a thoughtful manner. This was the topic of a great deal of discussion in this course, which may not have otherwise taken place. As for taking decision making and consequences lightly, this is again a risk of all games. It should be said, however, that the safe and lighthearted environment of a game allows beginners to experiment and take risks. This, in my view, is a benefit.

Next Steps

The sixteen-week semester left us with a mostly finished product. The game prototype is fully playable and documentation, including rules and rationale, is complete. There was simply no time to go further, however. The thirteen students in the course are now scattered around the country, complicating further steps. Thankfully, this is something we discussed as a class before graduation. It is my hope that this game can fulfill its second goal: to reach a broad lay audience and teach them about preservation planning.

The one task that remained incomplete at the end of the semester was the game website. We acquired two likely URLs and are keeping them as placeholders. The ubiquitous Internet makes it possible—if unlikely—that our game will be found and interest can be stoked by word-of-mouth. Many practical decisions remain unmade. For instance, while the prototype is functional, it is imperfect. The board and cards were all handmade. We used game pieces bought from the Internet, but it would be nice to have custom-pieces. The board, at present, is almost four feet square. While it folds to a more manageable size, a few more rounds of design could reduce its size significantly without adversely affecting gameplay.

Trying to sell the game as-is would be challenging. Making and assembling everything would be very time consuming and there is no clear person to take that responsibility. One other option would be to make the game components available free of charge online. While this may be the altruistic solution, I balk at using the students' work without reward.

The only other way to disseminate the game would be to have a gaming company take over, complete the design, and produce it for sale. This is perhaps a long shot, but I hope that a game developer will take interest in our game. From the class's extensive research over the course of the semester, nothing quite like it currently exists, and it is a fun and effective way to learn about preservation planning.

Should technological hurdles become more manageable, I would also consider making the game digital. Currently, digital versions of many games explored in this course exist. Some, like *Carcassonne* and *Ticket to Ride,* are playable on smartphones and tablets as well. Collaboration with the Computer Science Department may also be worth exploring. This kind of solution would be in the long term, however. Perhaps a future preservation planning laboratory could be involved in adapting the game to this format.

Whatever the dissemination plan turns out to be, my students and I have every intention of following through on making *Plunked!* accessible. Playing the game is almost as enjoyable as the process of developing it.

Notes

1. Lee Revere, "Classroom Jeopardy: A Winning Approach for Improving Student Assessment, Performance, and Satisfaction," *Decision Line,* 23 (2004), 26; and Tina Bayer-Hummel, "The Effects of Jeopardy as a Test Preparation Strategy for Nursing Students," *Teaching and Learning in Nursing* (2010), 12.

2. Mary Pilon, "How a Fight Over a Board Game Monopolized an Economist's Life," *The Wall Street Journal* (2009), accessed June 19, 2013, http://online.wsj.com/article/SB125599860004295449.html?mod=rss_US_News.

3. Kathleen Bridgewater, "Almost the Real World: Teaching City Living with Simulation Software," *Voices from the Field* (1999), accessed September 18, 2012, http://www.alliance.brown.edu/pubs/voices/4qrt1999/almost.shtml.

4. Daniel Lobo, "A City is Not a Toy: How SimCity Plays with Urbanism," London School of Economics and Political Science (2004), accessed September 17, 2012, http://www.daquellamanera.org/files/Lobo_CityToy05LSE.pdf.

5. Chris Steins, "Planning With Legos," *Planetizen,* February 28, 2006, accessed September 18, 2012, http://www.planetizen.com/node/18929.

6. Adam Swann, "Gamification Comes of Age," *Forbes,* July 16, 2012, accessed September 12, 2012, http://www.forbes.com/sites/gyro/2012/07/16/gamification-comes-of-age/.

7. Anne Derryberry, "Serious Games: Online Games for Learning," Adobe whitepaper, accessed September 18, 2012, http://www.adobe.com/products/director/pdfs/serious_games_wp_1107.pdf.

8. Mark Ferrall, "Board Games for Urban Planners," *Planetizen,* September 8, 2011, accessed December 29, 2011, http://www.planetizen.com/node/51243.

9. Mike Selinker, *The Kobold Guide to Board Game Design* (Kirkland, WA: Open Design, 2011).

6 Challenges and Dilemmas in Heritage Conservation

Silvio Mendes Zancheti

Heritage conservation has become a big issue in global society. More and more people are involved and consequently there is a growing interest in training activities in this field. Some decades ago there were few conservation training programs in universities and higher education institutions. Professionals were normally trained in their practical activities with the support of some short-term programs. The International Centre for the Study of the Preservation and Restoration of Cultural Property (ICCROM) was a pioneer institution in offering many types of programs in various fields of specialization.

Today it is different. There are many training activities in all specializations of heritage conservation and at all levels of academia and professional expertise. Educational programs in conservation have also spread to all continents and, with the exception of only a few countries, it is possible to find groups of professionals, with different fields of expertise, capable of setting up graduate-level specialization courses. Certainly, the World Heritage Centre of UNESCO was one of the main organizations responsible for promoting and providing the start-up resources for these programs, as was the case in Brazil and some other Latin American countries.

The complexity of the training activities has also increased. Using again the experience of ICCROM, we may take a quick glance of what has happened in the past two or three decades. Initially, ICCROM provided courses in architectural conservation and specialized courses on the restoration of building materials, such as its stone and wood conservation programs. These courses aimed to train specialists in many countries, who are today leading experts in their local settings. With the spread of architectural conservation programs all over the world, ICCROM has changed its scope to include the conservation of collections of objects, other materials (such as paper and textiles), and entire cities and territories. Today, one of the most important programs run by ICCROM is Sharing Conservation

Decisions, which is focused on the process of conservation with many stakeholders involved in decisions regarding what to do when restoring/conserving any type of material or nonmaterial object.

My purpose in this chapter is not to provide an account of how conservation training has evolved recently, but to present the hypothesis that conservation education is facing a big challenge due to a shift in the conservation/restoration paradigm.

The Big Shift

Since the 1980s, what is understood to be an object worthy of conservation has shifted from architectural monuments and sites to cultural and urban landscapes. The scale of urban conservation areas may contain many thousands of buildings, public spaces, and even a wider natural or built environment. The enlargement of the field of action of conservation is the result of the social inclusion of different kinds of people in the planning and decision processes relating to cultural policy. It is the outcome of the enlargement of the political participation process of social groups that are gaining self-confidence regarding the importance for society of their cultural representation. A new concept of culture is being formed as a network of symbolic systems that make sense to groups of people belonging to many generations. Thus, culture and heritage are seen in a more pluralistic and diverse perspective that goes beyond the narrow scope of high culture.

Part of this movement is the recognition that development is always culturally oriented. There is no culturally neutral development, as Amartia Sen has argued,[1] and the links between heritage, memory, and social practice make conservation and development an inseparable pair in cultural, social, economic, and environmental policies. This does not mean that the dynamics of conservation and development may not differ during certain periods of time, however. When they do differ, the consequences may be disastrous.

Culture and heritage are part of people's daily lives. Those involved with conservation policies, plans, and projects are not only professionals, but may come from a broad spectrum of society. The challenge is to establish what heritage is and who defines it in this new context. Conservation policies and regulations rule over large urban areas and territories as is, for example, the case of the city of Rio de Janeiro, recently inscribed in the UNESCO World Heritage List. With a population of more than six million, Rio de Janeiro is one of the most dynamic cities in the world and the second most important economic pole of Brazil. The urban area of the city will be under a conservation regulation since it was considered a buffer zone for protected areas.

The Challenges

The big shift in the social importance of heritage conservation has led to a change in the scientific scope of the discipline and the requirements for academic and professional education. The conceptual and theoretical framework of the conservation discipline is being revised due to problems that came directly from the application of policies and regulations for new objects, especially large urban areas and cultural landscapes. At least three main challenges have been identified regarding these issues:

1. The change in the *scientific paradigm* of the discipline from a scientific objective to a postmodern cultural standpoint
2. The decision process involving many stakeholders and the search for a balance between the use of *new and traditional knowledge, techniques, and materials* in diverse cultural contexts
3. The renewed importance of a *conservation ethic* for professional practice

The Change in the Scientific Paradigm

Since the 1980s, the long and sound tradition of conservation theory (Ruskin, Viollet-le-Duc, Boito, Giovannoni, and Brandi) has been revised according to the postmodern standpoint.[2] The Burra Charter's concept of "significance" was used in the interpretation of "different individuals or groups."[3] This was well explained and contextualized by Salvador Muñoz Viñas,[4] when he advanced the following: (1) the uses of objects are necessarily a concern for conservation; (2) the new approach to the discipline is no longer attached to the ideas of truth and objectivity; (3) there is a shift from objects to subjects (people or stakeholders); and (4) conservation is conditioned by expressivity and interpretation of the meanings of objects.

The conservation of cultural heritage is an activity involved with the maintenance of past and present cultural significances. To achieve sustainable conservation, managers of urban areas and other stakeholders act on the attributes of the heritage objects that convey cultural meanings identified throughout *intersubjective* processes. These attributes may be of a material (tangible) or a nonmaterial (intangible) nature. The social agents involved in conservation may retain, change, restore, reshape, or replace attributes or even objects. They may also engage in activities that help to foster meanings as part of the collective memory of society, through educational and cultural activities. The actions of managers and other stakeholders should be guided in such a way that the meanings, the integrity, and the authenticity of the objects' attributes are maintained over time.

This means that sustainable conservation seeks to maintain the condition for the interpretation of the relation of attributes-meanings between generations because it should (1) carry forward the present meanings of heritage to future generations; (2) maintain records of meanings given by past generations for the use of present and future generations; and (3) leave open to future generations the possibility of interpreting and associating new meanings with past and present heritage. But in order to do this, it is fundamental for sustainable heritage conservation to maintain the integrity and the authenticity of material or nonmaterial attributes of objects. So conservation has to deal with the relation between objects and subjects. I explore this point in some detail below.

The Use of New and Traditional Knowledge

The conservation of heritage is an activity that walks a razor's edge between new and traditional material and construction techniques. This is a question that will certainly never be solved because there will always be room for both. What I discuss here is the need for conservators to judge the use of traditional materials and construction techniques since they have already been trained in the use of modern materials and techniques.

The problem is very difficult since contemporary conservation practice is still strongly attached to the material fetishism of scientific conservation.[5] Hard sciences, such as chemistry and physics, came to dominate the thinking of conservators as the answer to practical questions. After many years of research and application of scientific principles, however, fundamental questions have still not been answered: Are the new materials more efficient than the traditional ones? How can the choice of materials and techniques be made in relation to the conservation of the significance of objects?

It is quite difficult to find conservators of monuments and sites who have this knowledge to a sufficient degree to allow them to decide which way to choose. Traditional techniques are not normally considered at universities, at least not in Latin American countries like Brazil. This knowledge is held by a restricted number of artisans, artists and master craftsmen who are rarely involved in the education system. What I am identifying as a challenge is the capability of conservators to understand the local contexts in which decisions are made since the choice of materials and techniques is not culturally neutral. Their choices reflect the training background of the specialist, their commitment to the criteria of authenticity, and the availability of master craftsmen with traditional knowledge, among other factors.

Nowadays, it seems that these questions are important because we will soon face the problem of preserving the built heritage of the twentieth century. This heritage was built under the umbrella of scientific knowledge and innovation as cultural values in themselves since the use of modern techniques and materials formed the strongest part of the ideology of the modern movement.

The Renewed Importance of Conservation Ethics

The challenges outlined above are associated with moral judgments. Since ethics involves decisions related to social values, such as "good or bad" or "right or wrong," it is an important subject in the discipline of heritage conservation, as shown by Mirian Clavir.[6] It may be defined as "any and all sets of moral principles and values that govern individual and group behavior."[7] John Ruskin formulated his ideas based on ethical principles. He advocated that we did not have the right to touch historical monuments because they belonged to the past generations and the future generations have the right to receive them as we did.[8] His ideas were very close to the present definition of sustainable development, which is certainly based on a moral stance. Since Ruskin, the ethics of conservation has been associated with the idea of truth, which was later associated with the concept of authenticity. Cesare Brandi, who was concerned with the signs of the passage of time on objects, said that restoration activity should not produce something that is artistically or historically a fake.[9]

From Viollet-le-Duc to Brandi, the responsibility of specialist conservators for the definition of what a heritage object is and how to conserve or restore it went unquestioned. But this is no longer the case. The role of science is not accepted as completely determining conservation action and the opinion of the common people has been brought into the field so far as conservation decisions are concerned. For example, what we perceive as damaged is completely different from what it was understood to be some time ago. Nowadays, damage is associated with "those changes that we regard [as] undesirable"[10] so it is seen throughout subjective evaluations. On the other hand, the conservation of complex heritage objects, such as urban areas or the cultural landscape, may impact the lives of thousands of people. Therefore, ethical principles require that the conservators should evaluate the consequences associated with the transmission of heritage from generation to generation, as was the case with Ruskin's or Brandi's approach, and with the present use and the way people evaluate heritage.

Conservation is a set of actions involving identification, analysis, judgments, and decision making. For the new paradigm of conservation, critical judgment is a double act of synthesis and choices that, first, seeks out knowledge so as to be able to interpret the value of the heritage and, second, decides which material and physical attributes will be chosen and how they will be used, depending on how their conditions of integrity and authenticity are judged. The contemporary theory of conservation recognizes its dependence on subjective evaluations.

This theory does not interpret the conservator as an enlightened rational human being, as imagined by Brandi, but as a social agent who works in a context of intersubjective interpretations and decisions. His or her role is to work with intersubjectivity, recognizing that individuals and groups value heritage differently and thus seek to identify the maximum social consensus that can be reached on conservation decisions.[11]

It is on these plural bases that decisions as to what and how to conserve are taken, supported by practical knowledge, common sense, and prudence; that is, on *phronesis,* the Aristotelian concept for defining the capacity of individuals to form judgments regarding conflicting values in different situations or contexts.[12] Viñas expresses the new role of the conservator very well when he states that the "contemporary theory of conservation calls for 'common sense,' for gentle decisions, for sensible actions. What determines this? Not truth or science, but rather the uses, values and meanings that an object has for people. This is determined by the people."[13]

The cultural relativism of today makes it difficult to apprehend what is common. The conservator must support decisions and actions on ethical principles that may help him or her to define professional conduct in three senses: (1) in relation to objects; (2) in relation to the people involved with objects; and (3) in the relation of people with objects. This is certainly a new form of engagement in society that goes beyond the role of the scientist or the artist.

The Dilemmas

The dilemmas for educational systems are framed by these challenges. These systems must train specialists in "positive" knowledge and technical expertise, the capacity to participate in decision making, openness to the opinion and participation of social agents, and the capacity to act according to clear ethical principles. But, where should the emphasis be placed? Should heritage conservators be specialists, generalists, or facilitators?

Certainly the answer is multifaceted and associated with improving the critical capacity of heritage conservators to promote continuity of meanings and values across generations in changing cultural contexts. Communities across the world, which are seeking new and innovative solutions, active project participation, and sustainability, will define these meanings and values. In the words of the Institute of Conservation's "Positive Future in an Uncertain World" conference of 2013, "Rather than being suspicious of this paradigm shift conservators need to develop their communication skills to respond to the intricacies of community engagement."[14] Professionals see heritage as belonging to broad communities, but it may retain meaning and value if it is recognized by local people as their heritage.

As social contexts are so fundamental for designing conservation training strategies it is difficult for me to present an opinion about training challenges in the United States. Certainly, for the United States the challenges are different from those in most Latin American countries. So what follows is my brief evaluation of what is happening in Brazil and other Latin American countries.

Conservation can only be an effective concept in the development of Latin American countries if it is well understood and accepted by large sectors of the population, politicians, administrators, intellectuals, and, in particular, development decision makers. Today, in Latin America, there are some training institutions dealing in heritage conservation. They cover only a small part of the spectrum of the educational structure needed to raise the conservation awareness of the population, however. In general, conservation courses are in the graduate programs of some universities. The conservation institutions of the area are also largely dependent on professionals trained in foreign universities, with the exception of Mexico and Brazil, which have their own professional training centers.[15]

In two surveys, conducted some years ago by Paulo Ormindo and me, respectively, it was found that most of the training programs in Latin America are architecture-oriented and lack interdisciplinary work as well as a management context. In addition, architecture undergraduate programs generally do not deal with conservation issues. Again, Mexico and Brazil are the exceptions.

Recently, there have been some initiatives to create graduate programs in heritage conservation and its relation to the sustainable development process. These programs are quite new, however, and they have not had the time to increase the number of professionals with multidisciplinary training. Therefore, the capacity of these people to influence the decision-making process is limited. There is a need to expand training activities to other levels of the educational system and to include conservation principles in different subjects of the general curricula of the educational system.

One of the main tasks is to integrate heritage conservation within the environmental conservation training programs that have been introduced at all levels of the educational system, especially at the undergraduate level, with the younger generation. The environmental movement is very successful in propagating conservation principles and this experience may be very helpful. This strategy may have a very important long-term impact because it involves the younger generation in the process.

Some Experiences

The education and training developed at the Center for Advanced Studies in Integrated Conservation (CECI) provides a better approach to the challenges in bringing together conservation and development. CECI began with a group of researchers and professors at the graduate program in urban development of the Federal University of Pernambuco, located in Recife, Brazil. It started its activities in 1997, launching the graduate program in Integrated Territorial and Urban Conservation, the ITUC/BR, in partnership with the World Heritage Centre and ICCROM.

In 2003, CECI became an independent nonprofit institution devoted to the promotion of the scientific field of integrated conservation. From the outset CECI has acted as a training, research, publishing, and community service institution, working in partnership with many Brazilian and international institutions. All the activities of CECI are self-financed since it does not receive any grants for its functioning. Today CECI has a record of more than 300 trained graduated students, 17 published books, a series of research articles with more than 100,000 downloads in 3 years, the scientific journal *City and Time,* and innumerous research, restoration, and urban planning projects undertaken for many institutions and for the community at large.

The three graduate training programs developed by CECI are:

- Integrated Territorial and Urban Conservation (ITUC/BR) program

- Management of Architectural Restoration Site program
- Modern Architecture Conservation (MARC/AL) program

In spite of the differences between the three programs in terms of objectives, concepts, and methods, they share common ground in their approach and the way that they deal with the challenges explained above. These programs start from the following premises:

- Objects, monuments, and sites are heritage because they are culturally meaningful to different groups of people in a society.
- The assessment of the values of this heritage is made through a long and continuous intersubjective process of comparing the relative values of the meanings of objects, monuments, and sites.
- The conservation process of heritage is not scientifically defined. It is a matter of searching for partial consensus among the stakeholders involved with the heritage in question, taking into account their objectives/expectations and available resources.
- The management of the conservation process of heritage requires an interdisciplinary and conflict management approach.

The ITUC/BR Program

The ITUC/BR program was designed as an urban conservation management course intended mainly for public officials working in local urban administrations. It was inspired by MBA programs and focused on training managers of heritage conservation. CECI has made an effort to define a clear theoretical line for its actions on training for urban conservation. This effort was based on the definition of usual concepts associated with the discipline of heritage conservation: the management of heritage conservation and integrated conservation.

Urban management is understood as the part of the public management of cities that comprises the management of the public and semipublic goods and the supply of public services. Training in urban management is normally based on theories of public management and government.

The city as a public good poses a challenge for these theories because of its conflicting facets: it is a source of innovation and development and also the source of dispute and conflict among its stakeholders. The action of the public/government management is thus considered essential on an everyday basis to mediate disputes and conflicts. The heritage of urban areas is an exemplary case of the need for a differentiated public management for the following reasons:

- The multifaceted character of public heritage, which comprises private and semiprivate assets depending on the perspective of the management action
- The irreversibility of the heritage assets
- The criteria for assessment and evaluation of the values of the heritage public assets, which are based on ethical principles as well as relative cultural perspectives
- The absence of clear definitions as to what it means to conserve, to restore, or to protect, which are essential concepts for the practice of heritage conservation management

All the uncertainties contribute to making the process of urban heritage management open ended, non-teleological, contingent, and conflictive. The ITUC/BR program defines urban heritage conservation as "the public process of decision making on the management of urban areas and the allocation of resources for urban conservation in a context of dispute between multiple public and private actors with differentiated capacities, perceptions and objectives relative to the political mobilization to define the use of public goods and other resources."

The second concept, integrated conservation, is widely used in the field of conservation in general. Since its initial formulation in the Declaration of Amsterdam (1975),[16] however, it has not been precisely defined. This was not a problem since it was in continuous elaboration and flexible enough to be adapted to new ideas regarding heritage conservation, urban planning, and sustainable development. In the ITUC/BR program it was the central concept for the development of the theoretical and practical parts of the program and it was defined as follows:

> Integrated conservation is part of the general process of planning and management of cities and territories, according to a multi-referential perspective (economic, political, social, cultural, environmental and spatial);

It centers on (but does not limit itself to) the physical and spatial aspects of consolidated urban areas that are socially recognized as of cultural value and seeks to maintain the integrity, authenticity and continuity of the urban areas of cultural value for present and future generations;

It emphasizes the conservation of the physical and spatial aspects within the development/transformation process of the city, while seeking sustainable development by treating the cultural values of the city as assets that aggregate value in all dimensions of the development process (economic, political, social, cultural, environmental and spatial).

These two concepts were used to formulate a management approach that guided the development of the content and the syllabus of the training program. The approach is defined by a structure of four groups of management activities performed simultaneously by the public manager responsible for the conservation process of an urban site. The activities are:

- Analysis and evaluations
- Negotiation
- Proposals
- Monitoring and control

These tasks are directly entwined with the management of conservation measures and indirectly linked to action taken by agencies in other sectors of public administration. The relationships between tasks and implementing bodies will depend on the style of the public administration in charge of urban conservation.

The ITUC/BR program is composed of seven modules:

- One theoretical and conceptual module
- Four modules corresponding to the activities of the management approach
- One practical module for designing and developing a management plan for an urban heritage site
- One individual research module

The first five modules use distance-learning methods and the sixth is a group work done in situ.

The Management of Architectural Restoration Site Program

This program is one of the most successful initiatives of CECI. It is aimed at managers working in situ on architectural restoration work. Its target group is made up of mid-career architects and engineers with some previous experience in conservation/restoration of architecture. This program places a strong emphasis on introducing traditional materials and construction techniques to managers to improve their capacity to judge and make decisions in the field. It requires the improvement of the communication skills of the participants since it brings together very different groups of professionals. The students are, in general, architects and engineers and many of the instructors are artisans or master craftsmen specializing in traditional crafts such as wood carving and carpentry, stone cutting and carving, mortar and plaster, stucco, wrought iron, lime painting, reinforced concrete, and others. The program is divided into three modules:

- Management of construction sites and services
- Theory and practice of building systems
- Practice of traditional crafts, fieldwork, and in situ case studies

The final work of the students is the development of a management plan of a specific restoration site chosen by the individual participant.

The MARC/AL Program

The MARC/AL program was designed to answer some questions such as the following: "Is specific training for the conservation of modern architecture necessary, and does it need to be different from traditional approaches? What sorts of disciplines are necessary? What is the best balance between theory and practice? How is it possible to unite different professional viewpoints (practicing architects, architectural historians, conservationists, engineers) into a single approach?"[17]

The conservation of the modern architecture has raised many questions about the relevance of the contemporary theory of conservation to answer specific problems related to this type of architecture. The development of the MARC/AL and its application in 2009 has shown that there is need for specific training in the conservation of modern architecture but there is no need to search for another conservation theory. What is necessary is to deal with three main questions related to: (1) the identification of the values of this architecture among the different social groups and individuals; (2) the aging process of building material used experimentally in this architecture; and (3) a better understanding of the main concepts of the conservation theory applied to the conservation practice of the modern buildings, specifically those that are not socially recognized as possessing outstanding cultural values.

Final Remarks

Heritage conservation is certainly a field where many changes are occurring in terms of theory, practice, and the involvement of people and institutions. The challenges faced by educators in developing training programs are also considerable and there is certainly no clear path to follow. There is an open horizon with a great diversity of prospects. In my opinion the great challenge today is to organize training activities that respond to the new theoretical challenges posed by the shift in the conservation paradigm.

Notes

1. See Amartia Sen, *Development as Freedom* (New York: Knopf, 1999).

2. "Postmodernism is largely a reaction to the assumed certainty of scientific, or objective, efforts to explain reality. In essence, it stems from a recognition that reality is not simply mirrored in human understanding of it, but rather, is constructed as the mind tries to understand its own particular and personal reality. For this reason, postmodernism is highly skeptical of explanations which claim to be valid for all groups, cultures, traditions, or races, and instead focuses on the relative truths of each person. In the postmodern understanding, interpretation is everything; reality only comes into being through our interpretations of what the world means to us individually. Postmodernism relies on concrete experience over abstract principles, knowing always that the outcome of one's own experience will necessarily be fallible and relative, rather than certain and universal" (http://www.pbs.org/faithandreason/gengloss/index-frame.html).

3. ICOMOS Australia, Burra Charter, 1999, http://australia.icomos.org/publications/charters, accessed 12 December 2012.

4. See Salvador Muñoz Vin~as, *Contemporary Theory of Conservation* (Oxford: Elsevier Butterworth-Heinemann, 2005).

5. Viñas, *Contemporary Theory of Conservation*, 86.

6. Mirian Clavir, *Preserving What is Valued: Museums, Conservation and First Nations* (Vancouver: University of British Columbia Press, 2002), 26–66.

7. Clavir, *Preserving What is Valued*, 26.

8. John Ruskin, *The Seven Lamps of Architecture* (New York: Dover Publications, 1989), 185–86.

9. Cesare Brandi, *Teoria del Restauro* (Turin: Einaudi, 1977), 6.

10. Sarah Staniforth, "Group Report: What are Appropriate Strategies to Evaluate Change and Sustain Cultural Heritage?" in *Durability and Change: The Science,*

Responsibility, and Cost of Sustaining Cultural Heritage, ed. W. E. Krumblein, P. Briblecombe, D. E. Cosgrove, and S. Staniforth (New York: John Wiley and Sons, 1994), 218.

11. Clavir, *Preserving What is Valued,* 43.

12. Bent Flyvbjerg, "Phronetic Planning Research: Theoretical and Methodological Reflections," *Planning Theory & Practice,* 5:3 (2004), 283–306.

13. Viñas, *Contemporary Theory of Conservation,* 212.

14. Institute of Conservation, *Positive Future in an Uncertain World 2013,* conference preliminary program, 2012, http://www.iconpf13.com/uploads/1/3/7/6/13769325/programme_draft_01_november__2012.pdf.

15. Heritage conservation programs can also be found in Argentina, Bolivia, Chile, Colombia, Ecuador, Peru, and Venezuela, but without the robust professional training centers that Mexico and Brazil have developed.

16. Congress on the European Architectural Heritage, Declaration of Amsterdam, 1975, http://www.icomos.org/en/charters-and-texts/179-articles-en-francais/ressources/charters-and-standards/169-the-declaration-of-amsterdam.

17. Diniz Moreira and Luiz Manuel do Eirado Amorim, "Capacitação em conservação da arquitetura moderna: a experiência do CECI e do MDU-UFPE," in Proceedings of the *9° Seminário Docomomo Brasil: Interdisciplinaridade e experiências em documentação e preservação do patrimônio recente* (Brasilia: DOCOMOMO Brasil, 2011), http://www.docomomo.org.br/seminario%209%20pdfs/000_M12-CapacitacaoEmConservacao-ART_fernando_moreira.pdf, accessed 3 January 2013.

7 Benefits of Using Qualitative Ethnographic Methodology in the Evaluation of Preservation Training Programs' Performance in Developing Countries: A Case Study of the Northeast Region of Brazil

Karla Nunes Penna and Elisabeth Taylor

Many problems need to be overcome in developing countries in order to be able to envision a sustainable context for cultural heritage. In many regions and countries key issues of daily life involve basic health care, poverty reduction, education, and civil and political rights. These may be assessed by considering the number of hospitals and clinics, the amount of government assistance for food and clothing, school and university access, and active judicial and civil enforcement. When people are faced with poverty, heritage preservation is not generally seen as an essential component of the social urban or rural development process.

When conducting an exploratory ethnographic case study of training centers located in northeastern Brazil between 2010 and 2011, we noticed two principal issues: (1) the difficulty in managing the training centers, which may be attributed to the strong influence of the harsh, poverty-related context; and (2) the extent to which these contexts impact the performance of training centers as well as the quality of conservation works. This socioeconomic and political background appears to have a strong effect on the provision of sustainable preservation processes, making impracticable initiatives of development promotion and consequently affecting negatively the outcomes of programs.

A commonly shared perception of interviewees in the study was that program outcomes did not meet local communities' and market demands. Identifying reasons for this situation was not an easy task as there is a lack of documentation indicating social, economic, and cultural impacts of the programs on local communities and preservation systems. A review of pertinent literature in the field identified that program evaluators seem to adopt almost exclusively quantitative rather than qualitative evaluation methods for cultural heritage training programs. While quantitative data are undoubtedly useful for measuring the successful execution of goals, context-specific qualitative aspects affecting training programs have so far been largely ignored in the existing official reports. The aim of this chapter is therefore to discuss the potential of utilizing ethnographic methodology in naturalistic settings to evaluate the performance of conservation training centers, which seems essential for ensuring successful conservation practices and initiatives that promote sustainable development. Furthermore, we investigate the influence of the local contexts on the establishment of indicators for program evaluation.

Conservation Training Programs and the Importance of Evaluations

According to the *Guidelines for Education and Training for the Conservation of Monuments, Ensembles and Sites* (International Council on Monuments and Sites, 1993, par. 1), conservation is a cultural, artistic, technical, and craft activity based on humanistic and scientific studies and systematic research. Conservation practices demand well-trained people with appropriate skills to lead interventions and to deal with decision-making processes that take into account the complexities of the field. Thus, training for conservation is a fundamental part of the preservation system.

The International Centre for the Study of the Preservation and Restoration of Cultural Property (ICCROM) states in the document "Training Strategy in the Conservation of Cultural Sites" that the aim of training is to

> guarantee that conservation management is applied to heritage resources taking into consideration the qualities and values of each heritage site, as well as their specific condition, the cultural, social, and economic context, and the risks that each site may meet. Training should provide the skills that are required by the professionals, crafts, or administrations involved; training should also facilitate collaboration between different disciplines, and the communication with the general public. While training should be understood in relation to specific needs in each area, the response may be obtained in different forms, at the international, regional, national, or local level.[1]

Based on Jukka Jokilehto's[2] and UNESCO's[3] statements it can be concluded that conservation and preservation training programs are vital since these programs are responsible for preparing specialized professionals who will develop and implement preservation initiatives, lead efforts, and teach others how to operate within the heritage processes. There are international recommendations such as the Convention Concerning the Protection of the World Cultural and Natural Heritage's, in article 5,[4] which suggested that to ensure effective and active measures for the protection, conservation, and presentation of the cultural and natural heritage, each government should foster the establishment and development of national and regional centers for training in the protection, conservation, and presentation of the cultural and natural heritage. The quality of these training centers depends on regular evaluations.

Program evaluation has gained importance within the preservation field given that institutions, sponsors, and stakeholders are progressively more interested in adequate and convincing data as a means to attain public recognition and support.[5] Evaluating and monitoring are important processes within the strategic planning.[6] While analyzing official documents produced in the past two decades by training centers situated in cities considered World Heritage Sites in Brazil, however, we observed that these tasks are often neglected by training centers. During the fieldwork for this research, we identified a growing concern among professionals involved with training programs in Brazil regarding the ways preservation education is being conducted. From their point of view, the effectiveness of training courses seemed particularly affected by political and economic pressure, resulting in the deviation between current goals and the sociocultural purposes of preservation education initiatives. It appears, therefore, that when developing training programs in poor areas utmost efforts must be employed to establish appropriate quality levels as problems not directly related to heritage issues also require attention and action so as to overcome them.

The *Guidelines for Education and Training in Conservation of Cultural Heritage*[7] indicated that there is still a considerable gap between the stated importance of developmental or monitoring assessment and its actual deployment, mainly caused by the prevalent beliefs and culture in organizations with respect to assessment. The need to evaluate conservation training centers' performance is timely, principally since it provides feedback relating to processes and effects on program participants. [8] Designing and gathering information involves appropriate evaluation strategies taking into consideration the particular context, including all related stakeholders, as training and education in cultural heritage matters requires social involvement and integration into national systems of education at all levels.[9] The challenge for evaluators is obtaining the best and most useful information possible for the people who need it for monitoring, controlling, improving, and decision making. In addition, evaluations need to be readable and accessible for interested parties; otherwise they are useless.

Influence of the Local Context on Conservation Training Program Evaluations

Silvio Zancheti and Katriina Similä stress that one of the greatest challenges for heritage institutions has been the development of instruments for assessing the performance of conservation actions.[10] The performance and their impacts on training centers must be assessed based on objective parameters, as they have to comply with legal and technical frameworks. At the same time, there is a need to develop a holistic approach to program evaluation based on social practices and cultural pluralism, as conservation must respect the complexities of local contexts.[11] Thus, it is essential to take into consideration issues affecting the outcomes of evaluations that are not only based on statistics but also include qualitative indicators. Factors such as the effects of the economic context on preservation training, the interrelationship between programs and political and institutional systems, as well as the social impact of training programs on target populations must be considered while developing training program evaluations.

Regarding the economic context, the scarcity and instability of resources is generally reported as a cause for not implementing evaluation mechanisms. There is an ever-present lack of resources, especially money, in developing countries. Financial obstacles prevent poor nations from implementing solutions to various problems caused by fiscal and financial difficulties in a timely fashion.[12] Obtaining resources for heritage preservation initiatives demands strong political articulation and institutional efforts. It can therefore be concluded that for training centers, the provision of resources is a constant concern. Many countries lack specific governmental programs that provide finance for heritage training programs. Resources required for implementation and maintenance often come from private and public stakeholders, both national and international. Often these resources prove insufficient when it comes to management tasks such as monitoring and evaluating the programs and keeping track of graduate students.

Local political attitudes strongly impact the implementation of conservation evaluation mechanisms based on qualitative parameters since transparency is not a common practice in heritage policies in developing countries.[13] While analyzing data generated from the research fieldtrip, we noted a discrepancy when comparing official reports and evaluations with interview comments made by insiders: while quantitative data indicated that conservation training centers had relative success in preparing graduates through practical programs, research participants' interview comments revealed that in reality the courses did not provide the necessary training and skills for graduates to properly operate in the job market. On the one hand, programs face sociocultural challenges affecting their performance and interfering with the overall quality of the professional training; on the other hand, there seems to be a lack of interest from governments in quality assessment, resulting in resistance by institutions to the reporting of qualitative data.

What institutions officially report is strongly affected by political pressure. Particularly in northeastern Brazil and in other regions with a similar socioeconomic status, people feel pressured by the government as local politicians expect positive quantitative results, even if their validity and reliability are questionable. In that sense, institutions and stakeholders in general are groups put at potential risk by evaluations. Egon G. Guba and Yvonna S. Lincoln identified stakeholders' tendency "to act to protect" their interests when they feel their stakes may be jeopardized by an evaluation should there be negative findings.[14] Thus, evaluation reports often suppress relevant qualitative information, thereby leading to unrealistic assessments.

A detailed review of literature (such as training centers' annual reports and financial sponsors' reports) conducted during this research found that current reports and evaluations lack detailed investigations of the interactions of training centers and local people, although evaluating the impact of training centers' performance on local communities' social development is known to be fundamental for the preservation process. It is a gap to be filled as planning and conservation management strategies in theory have to be developed in relation to the perceived quality and value of a heritage resource based on a consensus of the population.[15] Evaluations should be useful for indicating to what extent the programs are attending to communities' needs.

Our goal in emphasizing qualitative evaluation methodologies in this chapter is not to be critical of quantitative approaches; rather, we are concerned about which methodology is more likely to yield meaningful, realistic, and useful information for supporting preservation training efforts. Conducting evaluations of preservation training centers that draw on information provided directly by instructors, students, stakeholders, and sponsors is likely to provide a comprehensive, in-depth, and relevant account for those with an interest in improving the training programs' performance.

Monitoring and evaluating programs is an important management task to be carried out at all stages of training program development as recommended by the *Guidelines for Education and Training for the Conservation of Monuments, Ensembles and Sites*[16]; regular evaluation of conservation training programs by peers is also a necessity. According to the training strategy in the conservation of cultural sites,[17] it is important to conduct continuous monitoring and assessment involving both students and teaching staff in forward planning and continuous improvement. Indicators are essential tools for evaluations and cannot be developed in an isolated manner. Efficient indicators should always be defined within a managerial context and conceived as tools designed to orientate and improve specific procedures of training courses.[18] The effective use of indicators requires cautionary attention to what these indicators represent and should focus on a training program's role within the heritage system. Regarding the challenges to be overcome for evaluations of heritage programs, Jeremy Wells raised an important discussion about the need "to understand what should be measured in order to define the nature of heritage conservation performance."[19] The difficulty is how to define relevant, proper indicators. Indicators for heritage training program evaluations depend on the context in which they are applied and are influenced by how associated persons deal with key issues. Purpose and expectations of evaluations define what kind of information is needed and what the level of writing should be.[20]

The Potential Benefits of Employing Ethnography in Preservation Training Program Evaluations

Qualitative methodologies are derived from the field study traditions of anthropology—specifically from the methodological tradition of ethnography.[21] The philosophical roots of ethnographic methods emphasize the importance of understanding the meanings of human behavior and the sociocultural context of social interaction, which sits well within the context of the critical constructivist and social constructionist paradigms.[22] These paradigms promote the development of empathetic understanding based on subjective experience, and understanding the connections between personal perceptions and behavior.[23] Ethnographic approaches take into consideration the interdisciplinary character of cultural studies, which is helpful for understanding social relations and cultural practices through critical analysis. Gaining knowledge from the context and understanding phenomena through the meanings local people ascribe to them is an essential feature of high-quality evaluations. Field techniques such as participant observation, in-depth interviewing, detailed description, and case studies typically include portrayals of the world as understood by the people studied, as well as the researcher's own understanding.[24] For the development of training program evaluations based on qualitative methodologies, some concepts are important as these evaluations demand more sensibility to deal with the multidisciplinary aspects of local contexts.

The Link Between "Responsive Evaluation" and Ethnography

"Responsive evaluation" is an approach that emphasizes the importance of personalizing and humanizing the evaluation process. In their seminal work *Fourth Generation Evaluation* Guba and Lincoln integrated ethnographic inquiry and responsive evaluation into an overall framework for improving the usefulness of evaluation results.[25] For the purpose of evaluating preservation training programs, the depth of the ethnographic inquiry permits the evaluator to be especially sensitive to the differing perspectives of all related stakeholders. This sensitivity allows the evaluator to gather data and report findings based on those differences. Including responsiveness in ethnographic evaluations allows strong stakeholder involvement.[26] Responsive evaluations include identifying issues and concerns; observing and gathering information straight from participants through direct, personal contact; and portraying realities that are easily understandable and rich with description.[27] In that sense, findings in ethnographic responsive evaluations are created, not discovered.[28] This creation is an emergent construction, resulting from a joint effort among all stakeholders. It is not merely about investigating the context, but also about contributing to the empowerment of stakeholders involved and the possible transformation of the studied reality.[29]

Ethnography—Everything Starts in the Field

Fieldwork is a central activity of ethnographic evaluation methods.[30] It allows direct and personal contact with people and programs in their own environments. It is a naturalistic methodology,[31] which means that data are generated in naturalistic contexts without trying to "control variables." Getting close to people and local situations permits us to make sense of social facts. Fieldwork allows for firsthand information and helps develop a holistic perspective. In the field of naturalistic evaluation, ethnography is a qualitative methodology that aims for a cultural interpretation based on understanding a cultural group from an insider's perspective, intending to explore and provide a detailed, in-depth description of everyday values, behaviors, perceptions, and practices (thick description) as an attempt to explain the webs of meaning of a specific community.[32] Ethnographic studies have the following characteristics:[33]

- Observations take place in a natural setting (naturalistic approach).
- Evaluators aim at understanding how an event is perceived and interpreted by the people in a specific community, trying to interpret the situation from the perspective of the participants (constructivist approach).
- Evaluators rely on observations of interactions and interviews with participants in naturally occurring situations.

- Studies are "holistic" and "hermeneutic" whereby the researcher moves between seeing the data as a whole in order to get a basis for understanding the parts, and vice versa.
- Evaluators do not formulate hypotheses prior to conducting the evaluation. The theory emerges concurrently with the data collection—the theory is grounded in the data (grounded theory).

An ethnographer's goal is not just to report events and experiences: he or she documents people's beliefs and practices from the participants' own perspectives.[34] The emphasis in this representation is to allow critical categories and meanings to emerge from the ethnographic encounter rather than through imposing existing models.[35] According to Martin Hammersley and Paul Atkinson, ethnographic studies investigate a small number of cases, perhaps just one case, yet study them in detail. There is a strong emphasis on exploring the nature of particular social phenomena rather than setting out to test hypotheses about them. They are primarily unstructured, uncoded data at the time of collection. The analysis of data involves explicit interpretation of the meanings and functions of human actions.[36]

Research Strategies Used in Ethnography

The aim for evaluators undertaking ethnographic evaluations is to use qualitative methods and techniques when conducting a relevant, meaningful, understandable, useful, reliable, and believable evaluation. The goal in qualitative data gathering and analysis is constructing a comprehensive, holistic portrayal of the social and cultural dimensions of a particular context.[37] Qualitative methods include collection and analysis of a variety of empirical materials, such as personal experiences explored through in-depth interviews, grounded theory practices, and observations.

- Interviews: An interview can be described as a conversation with a purpose.[38] Interviews are helpful for understanding and putting into a larger context the interpersonal, social, and cultural aspects of the environment. A common practice in qualitative research is the use of semi-structured interviews, guided by a set of basic questions and issues to be explored. Data from open-ended interviews consist of direct references from people concerning their experiences, opinions, feelings, and knowledge.

- Grounded theory practices: In preservation training program evaluations, it is important that the evaluator generates theories from holistic data gathered through ethnographic inquiry. The purpose is helping program staff and decision makers to understand how the program functions, why it functions as it does, and the way in which the impacts/consequences/outcomes of the program flow from program activities, providing relevant information useful to their efforts to improve their program.[39]
- Observations: The data from observations encompass detailed descriptions of program activities, participants' behaviors, staff actions, and the full range of human interactions that can be part of program experiences.[40] Observational data (direct or participant observation) portray the big picture of the context where the program is set. Despite being a relatively time-consuming and expensive evaluation strategy, it provides depth and detailed data. Also, qualitative evaluators must be skilled observers, able to read nonverbal messages, sensitive to how the interview setting can affect what is said, and carefully attuned to the nuances of the interviewer-interviewee interaction and relationship.[41]

Qualitative evaluation reports seek to generate useful and credible information. This may include detailed descriptions of program implementation; analysis of major program processes; description of different types of participants and different kinds of participation; descriptions of how the program has affected participants; observed changes (or lack thereof), outcomes, and impacts; and strengths and weaknesses of programs as reported by related people.[42] It must also be written in a highly descriptive way, sufficiently for interested readers to understand it—thick description provides a level of detail that allows readers to draw informed conclusions and compare one context to others. Narrative writing styles make the text accessible and understandable.

Challenges to Overcome in Developing Ethnographic Evaluations

As Guba and Lincoln state, evaluation is a form of inquiry whose end product is information.[43] During this research experience we faced several challenges that qualitative-ethnographic evaluations impose on evaluators. For a large and significant set of data and evidences the researcher needs to spend enough time (how long is "enough"?) interacting with the studied object for obtaining data that allow the development of rigorous and strong analysis. Thick description demands original analysis and specific conclusions, demanding prolonged engagement, which can involve much time and costs.[44] Qualitative approaches also demand a certain level of involvement with the context. This is a subjective and tenuous line, easily traversable. As Harry Wolcott states, "with too much distance and perspective, one is labeled aloof, remote, insensitive, superficial; with too much familiarity, empathy, and identification, one is suspected of having 'gone native.'"[45]

In developing qualitative-ethnographic evaluations from the researcher's own interpretive standpoint, we have the huge moral responsibility of not only investigating and writing about an issue, but also of interpreting and representing "real" people. This is a delicate position, as representation has ethical implications.[46] Even with the best of intentions, representing others is always complicated and can be contentious. We can help or we can harm, depending on the way we express our position as researchers.

According to Wolcott, the ethnographer's purpose is to learn, record, and portray the culture of the other group.[47] But what does culture mean? Besides being a highly subjective concept, the meaning of culture for a group can be very different from the researcher's interpretation. In our experience two situations can compromise a study. First, during this investigation, we observed that participants sometimes behaved in contradictory ways; what people actually did could be different from what they said they were doing in the interviews, what they said they should be doing, and what meaning they assigned to such behavior.[48] Second, results also depend on the fieldworker's interpretation, which is always imbued and influenced by her own background. Given the high degree of subjectivity that qualitative evaluations demands, the methodology strongly reflects our own life stories. Finally, qualitative evaluators need to be mindful when observing, recording, and analyzing the data, so as to allow them to identify potential errors.

Case Study—Evaluating a Conservation Training Program in Northeastern Brazil

Conducting an ethnographic study of training centers in northeastern Brazil was helpful for understanding the particular situation in that area. Qualitative data were generated through exploratory research and fieldwork investigating in-depth conservation training centers located in World Heritage Sites in the target region. The evaluation captured individual differences and unique variations in depth, in context, and holistically.[49] Ethnographic strategies involved semi-structured interviews, collection and review of specific document analysis, and direct observations. Feedback from technicians and governmental heritage institutions was also regarded as important input. For the interviews, recorded by audiotape, a semi-structured approach was used to investigate local beliefs and perceptions. The sample consisted of twenty-eight participants located in six training centers in five historical cities in the northeast region of Brazil; all were knowledgeable and key informants involved in the training centers' activities and the local communities.

The adoption of ethnographic methods such as observational techniques and in-depth interviews allowed recording events as they occurred. Interviewing and observation mutually reinforced the findings, as they were a bridge to understanding the major themes involved in the evaluation. The many histories that surround the context were revealed in its complexity. For each participant the reality seemed different and was interpreted differently depending on his or her level of involvement.

An ethnographic approach demanded a higher degree of concern from the evaluator, not only with the technical aspects, but also with the deeper implications, such as the theories that are the foundation of the research, the level of the researcher's reflection, and the required perspective of historicity of the studied phenomena.[50] The aim was to reach the essence of phenomena and comprehend them in their entirety, even if a relative entirety, as this research approach demands immersion in the research field, a long presence in this area, as well as an expanded analysis time.

While current reports demonstrated mostly qualitative data related to the number of resources invested and certificates afforded, data analysis generated by this investigation demonstrated important insights about the impact of political, economical, educational, and social issues on the training centers' performance. It is not possible, within the scope of this chapter, to discuss all the factors that impact the performance of training centers; however, some factors familiar to professionals working in developing countries can be cited:

- The influence of the political context on the management of training centers: It was possible to identify a common notion from all interviewees of this investigation that there is a lack of political interest in preservation. Preservation is a long and costly work where the correlation between invested resources and the results achieved are not politically advantageous. Moreover, political discontinuity is another important issue affecting the centers' performance. Programs and projects discussed, developed, and executed by an administration are impacted by political leadership changes. With the common change of a political leader at every new election (every four years), there is always a change of staff that follows. The new staff generally does not necessarily continue projects or plans that were discussed and developed in the previous administration. This discontinuity generates a tendency for governmental departments to develop short-term projects that can be implemented and start generating results within a maximum of four years from their inception. In contrast, preservation training is a long, systematic, and continuous process. The training of apprentices demands time for involvement with the work environment, from sensitization and appropriation of their culture to the learning of specific technical procedures.

- The training centers' interactions with local communities: We have observed that there is low interaction between the training centers and the local communities in which they are located. In interviewing professionals, it was clear they recognize the importance of social participation in training processes but stated how difficult it is to include local community representatives in these processes in developing countries. This is usually caused by political decisions and lack of understanding or interest from the local people. Yet the local community affected by the interventions is the main stakeholder of the preservation system. According to Juarez de Paula, any preservation strategy needs to allow local communities to participate, in order to render people "capable of identifying potentialities, opportunities, comparative and competitive advantages, problems, limits and obstacles to their development, from which they can choose vocations, establish goals, determine strategies and priorities, monitor and evaluate results, in order to gain the required capacity to plan and manage, in a shared manner [with governments], the process of local development."[51]
- The lack of preparation of the faculty body, technicians, and managers: The lack of knowledge by administrators, managers, technicians, and teachers about the methodological, technical, and legal framework that governs preservation

practices also affects the training. We observed in the training centers under investigation teachers and craftsmen teaching without the appropriate method and approach to preservation as well as administrators, managers, and technicians who demonstrated a lack of knowledge of technical procedures, legislation, project management, and budgeting. Many are engaged in training programs based on the political positions they hold, and not on merit or knowledge of the craft. Without expertise, teaching efficacy is harmed and the training is under serious threat of providing inconsistent information. It is not possible to lead conservation training without such knowledge; otherwise, people are being qualified as trainers who are alienated from the local and global contexts that dictate conservation practice.

- The training centers' technical and theoretical efficacy: Currently, the Brazilian government is focused on certifying the largest number of people possible within the shortest period of time feasible. Thus, there is a strong tendency to implement training courses that are significantly shorter than traditional ones. This may be affecting the quality of learning and teaching, as well as placing graduates in the job market who are not sufficiently prepared for preservation practices. This tendency also leads to the development of scopes focused mainly on technical procedures and practices, while preservation training demands a much deeper understanding of theoretical, cultural, social, and historical matters.
- The lack of follow-up of graduates: Another issue identified in the research is that there has been no monitoring of students after their graduation. Without it, there is no feedback for the process. It is not possible to know if the students are applying their knowledge in the market, if the knowledge received is adequate or sufficient, or whether they as professionals meet the requirements of the market. This highlights the importance of establishing qualitative analysis and evaluation of training programs based on socioeconomic impacts and effective changes in cultural values and practices. There is also a need to develop more effective mechanisms for monitoring, taking into consideration the practical, educational, and social level of the programs.

- Management issues: The context in which training programs are inserted impacts their management. This scenario is composed of a collection of disarticulate and fragmented departments and actions. Such a situation compromises the comprehensiveness of interventions, the legitimacy of attributions, and institutional responsibilities. During this research, we observed that the most successful programs were the ones developed and managed under a shared management system. In these programs various institutional partners sought incremental integration of preservation policies, the active participation of all related stakeholders, social participation in formulating goals, and financial cooperation of public and private, national and international, partners.

Applying qualitative methods for evaluating performance of the preservation training programs was useful to produce knowledge based on specific contexts. Constructing interpretations based on insider heritage professionals' experiences provided important insights and brought to the fore issues initially invisible to the outsider. Since through this research experience we could identify that quantitative data were not portraying accurately all aspects of the context, generating qualitative data allowed for gathering high-quality information directly from people's experiences, activities, perspectives, perceived impacts, and other subjective information from the point of view of participants, staff, and others involved in and knowledgeable about the training programs being evaluated. Data generation was not constrained by predetermined categories of analysis, which contributed to the depth and detailed qualitative description of programs' situations, events, people, interactions, and observed behaviors. Taking into consideration the qualitative results of the research it is possible to assert development guidelines for improving the management and effectiveness of the teaching/learning process of conservation training centers in the given context.

Conclusions

As powerful instruments, qualitative evaluations go beyond traditional and potentially meaningless measurements.[52] Ethnographic methodology allows for evaluations to be situated within a holistic approach, to give nuance, and to illuminate complex issues by presenting the situation as a whole. This systematic understanding is vital for overall and systemic understanding, identifying the interdependence of different subsystems involved. It is helpful for better understanding of how training programs behave in a larger context and indicates how they could be managed.[53]

Despite being founded on subjective aspects of the context, evaluations based on qualitative methodologies allow for more "realistic" results and deep and detailed understanding of the complexities of the field through multiple perspectives and different viewpoints. This information provides new insights into the experiences of individuals, groups, and communities and highlights otherwise "invisible" issues.

Good evaluations demonstrate in-depth understanding of the context in which the conservation training programs are being developed, meaning the evaluation should not be dependent entirely on formal quantitative methods. It is understandable that quantitative data are politically important as the relationship between invested resources and the number of graduates is commonly used for indicating social and economic development of local communities. It is also important, however, to establish indicators that show the quality of teaching, learning effectiveness, and the application of knowledge in the "real world." It is necessary to establish valid ways to assess whether training programs' goals have been achieved or not. Otherwise, figures grow but where is the quality?

Notes

1. International Centre for the Study of the Preservation and Restoration of Cultural Property (ICCROM), *Training Strategy in the Conservation of Cultural Sites (revision)* (Rome: ICCROM, 2010), 5, accessed 8 October 2010, http://cif.icomos.org/pdf_docs/Documents%20on %20line/Training%20strategy%201995.pdf.

2. Jukka Jokilehto, "Built Heritage Conservation Education: An International Perspective to Conservation Education" (ICOMOS, CIF—International Training Committee, 2006), accessed 21 January 2010, http://cif.icomos.org/pdf_docs/Documents%20on%20 line/Built%20Heritage%20Jokilehto.pdf.

3. United Nations Educational, Scientific and Cultural Organization (UNESCO), *Convention Concerning the Protection of the World Cultural and Natural Heritage* (Paris: UNESCO, 1972), 3, accessed 10 October 2009, http://whc.unesco.org/archive/convention-en.pdf.

4. UNESCO, *Convention.*

5. Isabel V. Alonso and Valerie M. Meurs, "Assessing the Performance of Conservation Activities," in *Measuring Heritage Conservation Performance,* ed. Silvio Zancheti and Katriina Similä (Rome: ICCROM, 2012), 1.

6. Fatima Furtado, "O Processo de Monitoramento, Avaliação e Controle de Projetos," in *Gestão do Patrimônio Cultural Integrado,* ed. Silvio Zancheti (Recife, Brazil: Ed. Universitária da UFPE, 2002), 164.

7. International Council on Monuments and Sites (ICOMOS), *Guidelines for Education and Training in Conservation of Cultural Heritage* (draft document/under revision), International Training Committee (CIF)/ICOMOS (Rome: ICOMOS, 2011), 9, accessed 3 April 2011, http://cif.icomos.org/pdf_docs/CIF%20Meetings/Guidelines/Guidelines%20training%20english_Paris%202011.pdf.

8. Michael Q. Patton, *Qualitative Research and Evaluation Methods* (London: Sage, 2002).

9. International Council on Monuments and Sites (ICOMOS), *Krakow Charter: Principles for Conservation and Restoration of Built Heritage* (Rome: ICOMOS, 2000), accessed 24 October 2011, http://lecce-workshop.unile.it/Downloads/The%20Charter%20of%20Krakow%202000.pdf.

10. Silvio Zancheti and Katriina Similä, eds., *Measuring Heritage Conservation Performance* (Rome: ICCROM, 2012), v.

11. International Council on Monuments and Sites (ICOMOS), *Guidelines for Education and Training in the Conservation of Monuments, Ensembles and Sites* (Rome: ICOMOS, 1993), accessed 19 August 2009, http://www.icomos.org/charters/education-e.pdf.

12. Dora A. Guzmán, "Processo de Financiamento de Projetos de Conservação Urbana," in *Gestão do Patrimônio Cultural Integrado,* ed. Silvio Zancheti (Recife, Brazil: Ed. Universitária da UFPE, 2002), 273–78.

13. Zancheti and Similä, eds., *Measuring Heritage Conservation Performance,* 1–14.

14. Egon G. Guba and Yvonna S. Lincoln, *Fourth Generation Evaluation* (Newbury Park, CA: Sage, 1989), 51.

15. ICCROM, *Training Strategy.*

16. ICOMOS, *Guidelines for Education and Training.*

17. ICOMOS, *Multi-disciplinary Collaboration in Conservation Projects in the UK Based on ICOMOS Guidelines for Education and Training in the Conservation of Monuments, Ensembles and Sites* (Rome: ICOMOS, 2010), accessed 13 November 2011, http://cif.icomos.org/pdf_docs/Documents%20on%20line/cotac.pdf.

18. Herb Stovel, "Monitoramento para o Gerenciamento e Conservação do Patrimônio Cultural," in *Gestão do Patrimônio Cultural Integrado,* ed. Silvio Zancheti (Recife, Brazil: Ed. Universitária da UFPE, 2002).

19. Jeremy Wells, "Using Sequential Mixed Social Science Methods to Define and Measure Heritage Conservation Performance," in *Measuring Heritage Conservation Performance,* ed. Silvio Zancheti and Katriina Similä (Rome: ICCROM, 2012), 165.

20. Patton, *Qualitative Research.*

21. Patton, *Qualitative Research.*

22. Peter C. Taylor, Elisabeth Settelmaier, and Bal C. Luitel, "Multi-paradigmatic Transformative Research as/for Teacher Education: An Integral Perspective," in *International Handbook of Science Education,* ed. K. Tobin, B. Fraser, and C. McRobbie (Dordrecht, Netherlands: Springer, 2012), 373–87.

23. Peter C. Taylor and Milton Medina, "Educational Research Paradigms: From Positivism to Pluralism," *College Research Journal,* 1:1 (2011), 1–16.

24. David A. Erlandson, Edward L. Harris, Barbara L. Skipper, and Steven D. Allen, *Doing Naturalistic Inquiry: A Guide to Methods* (Newbury Park, CA: Sage, 1993).

25. Egon G. Guba and Yvonna S. Lincoln, *Effective Evaluation: Improving the Usefulness of Evaluation Results Through Responsive and Naturalistic Approaches* (San Francisco: Jossey-Bass, 1981).

26. Egon G. Guba and Yvonna S. Lincoln, *Guidelines and Checklist for Constructivist (a.k.a. Fourth Generation) Evaluation,* 2001, accessed 23 January 2012, http://www.wmich.edu/evalctr/archive_checklists/constructivisteval.pdf.

27. Guba and Lincoln, *Fourth Generation Evaluation.*

28. Erlandson et al., *Doing Naturalistic Research.*

29. Taylor, Settelmaier, and Luitel, "Multi-paradigmatic Transformative Research," 373–87.

30. Patton, *Qualitative Research.*

31. Erlandson et al., *Doing Naturalistic Research.*

32. Brian A. Hoey, *What is Ethnography?* accessed 12 March 2012, http://www.brianhoey.com/General%20Site/general_defn-ethnography.htm.

33. Lusia M. Nurani, "Critical Review of Ethnographical Approach," *Jurnal Sosioteknologi,* 14(7) (August 2008), accessed 1 May 2012, http://www.fsrd.itb.ac.id/wpcontent/uploads/5%20Lusi%20Ethnography%20 Approach.pdf.

34. Francis J. Riemer, "Ethnography Research," in *Qualitative Research: An Introduction to Methods and Designs,* ed. Stephen D. Lapan, Marylinn T. Quartaroli, and Francis Riemer (San Francisco: Jossey-Bass, 2008).

35. Hoey, *What is Ethnography?*

36. Martin Hammersley and Paul Atkinson, *Ethnography: Principles in Practice* (New York: Routledge, 2007), 248.

37. Erlandson et al., *Doing Naturalistic Research.*

38. Erlandson et al., *Doing Naturalistic Research.*

39. Patton, *Qualitative Research.*

40. Erlandson et al., *Doing Naturalistic Research.*

41. Furtado, "O Processo de Monitoramento."

42. Guba and Lincoln, *Fourth Generation Evaluation.*

43. Guba and Lincoln, *Fourth Generation Evaluation,* 52.

44. Furtado, "O Processo de Monitoramento."

45. Harry Wolcott, "Ethnographic Research in Education," in *Complementary Methods for Research in Education,* ed. Richard Jaeger (Washington, DC: American Educational Research Association, 1997), 56.

46. Soyini Madison, *Critical Ethnography: Method, Ethics, and Performance* (Thousand Oaks, CA: Sage, 2005).

47. Wolcott, *Ethnographic Research in Education.*

48. Wolcott, *Ethnographic Research in Education.*

49. Patton, *Qualitative Research.*

50. Jefferson Mainardes and Maria Ines Marcondes, "Reflexões sobre Etnografia Crítica e suas Implicações para Pesquisa em Educação," *Educação e Realidade,* 36 (2011): 425–46, accessed 20 April 2012, http://www.ufrgs.br/edu_realidade.

51. Juarez de Paula, *Desenvolvimento e Gestão Compartilhada* (2005) accessed 12 February 2013, http://www.biblioteca.sebrae.com.br/bds/BDS.nsf/3093035CA1CC0D4C83257640006A272E/$File/NT00042956.pdf.

52. Patton, *Qualitative Research.*

53. Neil Ne Browne and Stuart M. Keeley, *Asking the Right Questions: A Guide to Critical Thinking,* 6th ed. (Upper Saddle River, NJ: Prentice-Hall, 2001).

8 Integrated Conservation of Built Environments: Swedish Reflections from Three Decades of Program Development

Bosse Lagerqvist, Ingrid Martins Holmberg, and Ola Wetterberg

In 1978, the bachelor's program in integrated conservation of built environments was launched at the University of Gothenburg. In the regulations that governed higher education in Sweden at the time, it was designed initially as a local experiment since it was not formulated on the governmental level.[1] Instead, it was created in response to a number of dysfunctions in societal management of qualities in architecture and built environments, as perceived by a group of scholars at the University of Gothenburg. In its early years it was regarded with some skepticism by neighboring academic disciplines due to its distinctive orientation on professionalism—toward a profession not yet defined—as well as its novel multidisciplinary ambition set in the academic context of the humanities. Today the program is one of five bachelor's programs that, together with a master's and a Ph.D. program, represents a department that has a strong focus on material culture and its intangible qualities and how this heritage can be described, interpreted, valued, preserved, developed, and used as an asset in the continued development of society.

In addition to the program in integrated conservation of built environments, which is the focus of this chapter, the department runs bachelor's programs in objects conservation, building crafts, garden and landscape crafts, and leadership in handicraft. The research is organized in three subareas: built environments, objects conservation, and craft. Through the third subarea in craft a unique melding is constituted between what is normally perceived as tacit knowledge on the one hand and general scientific requirements on the development of knowledge on the other, posing questions and problems that to some degree correspond to issues related to artistic research and inquiry. To improve the methodological development within craft research, the department has set up a craft laboratory together with some key players in applying craft in restoration or preservation of buildings or built environments—the National Heritage Board, the National

Property Board, the Swedish Church, the Swedish National Handicraft Council, the Association of Local History Societies, the Västra Götaland region, and the city of Mariestad. The departmental coverage of the heritage field therefore is substantial and the bachelor's program in integrated conservation of built environments has constituted the backbone of this educational development for the past three decades.

Background

The background to the initiative in Gothenburg in 1978 can be found on three levels: the local, the national, and the European. On the *national* level, a number of radical transformations in city cores had raised general awareness of the historic qualities that were represented in the built environment,[2] especially when such qualities were replaced by new construction that the majority of people had difficulty appreciating in terms of its architecture and aesthetics. Critique and resistance were widespread. For example, in Stockholm, the renowned architectural historian Frederic Bedoire had a column entitled "Today's Demolition" in the major morning paper *Dagens Nyheter*,[3] and the general resistance became apparent in the so-called elm fight.[4] The latter was a protest against the decision to cut down a number of trees to make room for a subway entrance in the central part of Stockholm. Thousands of people gathered on the premises to climb the trees or form human chains and refused to leave. Eventually, the plans were changed and the trees are still standing.[5] The elm fight became the best known of a number of similar clashes between preservation and new development, which took place not only in city cores but also in large infrastructural developments in the countryside. These conflicts could also be interpreted as public representations of a growing formally recognized understanding of the need for better knowledge of heritage preservation and values and how to improve methods within the heritage practice area for gathering information that could lead to such knowledge. For some this also implied an increased interest in the usability of the built heritage[6] and the concept of "heritage" as an integrated part of societal development.[7]

Locally in Gothenburg a number of older city districts like Landala, Annedal, and Masthugget were knocked down during the late 1960s and 1970s to make room for modern housing areas, while at the same time, interest in preservation was growing, specifically represented by the historical museum and the staff and students in the architectural section at the Chalmers University of Technology in Gothenburg.[8] In 1976 an investigation was launched by the humanities faculty at the University of Gothenburg, studying the possibilities for students from archaeology, ethnology, and art history to pursue career opportunities outside their respective academic areas.[9] The investigation specifically focused on the need to increase the number of heritage professionals on different societal levels in order to gauge heritage resources in connection with urban and land use planning. This was especially relevant since heritage protection had become part of the governmental county boards in 1976 with increased demands in that respect on the regional museums to produce accurate knowledge bases.[10] The university report, written with the collaboration of specialists in the concerned areas and linked closely to the faculty in architecture at Chalmers University, concluded that more targeted professional training was needed, preferably in comprehensive bachelor's degree programs.[11]

At the final congress in Amsterdam of the European Architectural Heritage in 1975, the conservation of the architectural heritage was recognized as one of the major objectives of urban and regional planning. The declaration from the congress states:[12]

> The conservation of the architectural heritage should become an integral part of urban and regional planning, instead of being treated as a secondary consideration or one requiring only incidental action as has so often been the case in the recent past. A permanent dialogue between conservationists and those responsible for planning is thus indispensable.
>
> There is a fundamental need for better training programmes to produce qualified personnel. These programmes should be flexible, multi-disciplinary and should include courses where on-site practical experience can be gained.

As an apt reply to this, molded in the local context of Gothenburg and addressing the perceived demands on a national level for better-trained heritage professionals, the program in integrated conservation of built environments was initiated in the fall semester of 1978. Between twenty and twenty-five persons have been accepted every year since then, and within each group between fifteen and twenty students have finalized their education. The departmental experience thus covers classes from thirty-two graduation years, which has affected the professional field and the role of the heritage practitioner as well through a steadily growing number of alumni who go on to become external lecturers and experts, and who through continuous valuable dialogue have influenced program revisions.

Program-Establishment Phase

During the first years the program had an additive character formed by successive blocks of principally two subject matters—art history and ethnology—interlinked with courses that broadly framed the history of the built environment divided into traditional historical epochs. Art history and ethnology provided the students with methodological tools to form a tentative heritage practice, while the history of the built environment was not a discipline of its own but rather an emerging cross-disciplinary area not yet defined at the time. Apart from the history of the built environment as a new academic field of study, the program focused on recording and survey techniques, rehabilitation of buildings, and the societal processes for urban and land use planning as well as the formal position of the heritage field in relation to such processes. During the first years the students thus understood the program as a kind of "hopscotch," where the responsibility for merging all into a consistent whole rested in large part on the students. This merging was primarily intended to take place through different fieldwork assignments and in students' thesis work, and in most cases was successfully concluded.

Students who graduated from the program ended up in regional or local museums or local community administrations, working mostly with inventories of built environments and related materials. Such inventories could be undertaken due to the possible designation of older buildings as listed buildings or the definition of certain areas of built environment as of national heritage interest, following the opportunities given by the Swedish law and executed on a governmental level at the county boards.[13] More normally, however, the inventories aimed at formulating preservation plans and programs for different planning contexts on a local community level, but without strong government support. This imbalance between the communities on one hand and the governmental level on the other was severely disturbing for successful architectural preservation, due to the fact that local authorities through their planning monopoly have owned all issues related to urban and land use planning since 1959. Thus, questions related to exploitations and transformations of built environments were, and are, activities managed by local administrations. Heritage preservation—listed buildings—was up to the 1980s still predominantly considered a governmental responsibility.[14]

The ambition of the bachelor's program was to promote the notion of heritage practitioners positioned within local public authorities to work closely with other planning officials. Due to this understanding of how the practice ought to be positioned, the architectural and built heritage was from the beginning understood by the program designers not as properties that should be identified and saved from societal development, but rather as qualities that needed to be integrated with ongoing transformation processes.[15]

In 1988, the new Planning and Building Act was launched and it provided the local level with instruments for improved management of historical properties in the built environment: buildings considered specifically valuable from an architectural and/or historical viewpoint could be protected through urban plans; and when renovating or transforming any existing building, regardless of age, its existing qualities and properties are required to be dealt with in a sensitive and careful manner throughout the rebuilding process.[16] These heritage-oriented instruments were refined in the new Planning and Building Act and were the consequence of a twenty-year overview of the older Building Act. During that period of overview the old act had been amended with components pointing in the direction of providing the local authorities with better ways to safeguard existing buildings and built environments. The new act also confirmed a development during the 1980s where a majority of the program students after graduation worked predominantly on a local level, either through commissions hosted by regional museums or within local public authorities.

Program-Settling Phase

In the mid-1980s, the program achieved regular status and together with a new bachelor's program in cultural objects conservation, a new department was formed. Following the changing nature of the practice field and an internal ongoing discussion on how to form a more consistent educational structure, the program was during the latter half of the 1990s composed of three main areas:

- *Expert knowledge,* which represents the heritage content in terms of material and intangible qualities and properties, that is, the history of built environments going from antiquity to the present day with a certain focus on the Nordic context during the past two hundred years
- *Communication and processes* in different operative contexts within the heritage area, that is, recording techniques, survey methods, urban and land use planning practices, and internship periods
- *Critical reflection* on professional practices, valuations, and how content and meaning can be interpreted, that is, theory and history of conservation, research overview, research methodology, and individual thesis work

In this program development the problems addressed were at least twofold. First, the need to increase the students' preparedness to enter Ph.D. programs required continued development of courses in research methodology. This concerned the ability to enter Ph.D. programs in general, but particularly regarding the departmental Ph.D. program in conservation that started in the fall semester of 1992. The Ph.D. program was long needed for formulating a theoretical context of the subject matter of conservation that at the same time became the departmental name. In 1986, the department co-hosted, together with the Swedish Institute in Rome, the conference "Air Pollution and Conservation," held in Rome. At the conference, Sir Bernard Feilden defined "conservation": "Conservation may be defined as the dynamic management of change in order to reduce the rate of decay."[17] This definition became significant in the continuing departmental evolution, implying on a broader scale the need for integrating conservation practice with societal transformation processes in a context where "heritage" becomes an asset for development.

Second, the program needed to strengthen the students' professional training by balancing two perspectives on conservation practice—the first with a focus on restoration of buildings and the second perspective oriented toward urban and land use planning practices that involve heritage interests. Of the two perspectives, a certain focus was, and still is, put on the latter since the main direction of the program is toward planning procedures and how heritage perspectives can be prioritized on a local level in the transformation of the built environment.

One base for the department's development of the conservation area was, apart from Feilden's definition, perceived dysfunctions of conservation practices within a broadly understood heritage area. Principally, natural and cultural heritage practices are performed through a wide range of activities that comprise a number of operative measures but also the formulation of different strategies, regulations, organizational forms, occupational groups, and so on that in many situations operate independently within their own field. These practices have in several cases been developed depending on what sort of object constituted the focus of the activities. In a very general sense, the field can be divided into different activity systems, or contexts, according to "typical" cultural or natural heritage objects, as exemplified by the boxes in Figure 8.1. Within every such system one could find specific professions, regulations, economies, rationales, and the like. The activities within one box, however, might have positive or negative effects in the other boxes. From a general conservation viewpoint one could argue that the success of performed activities within

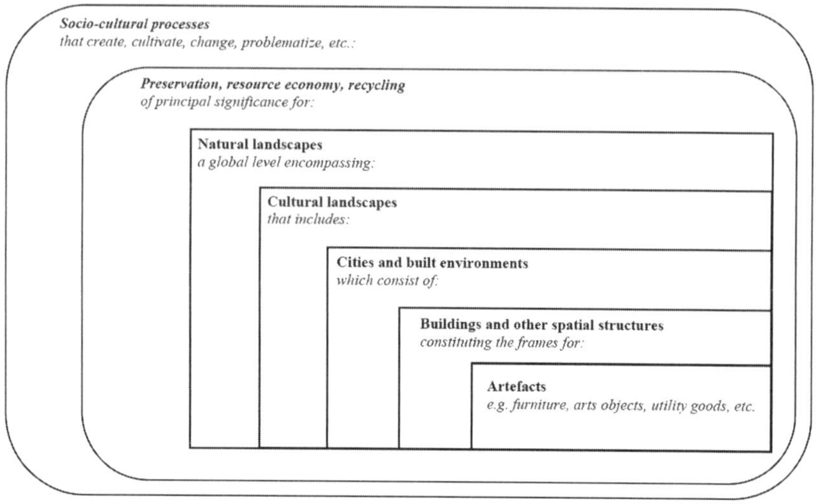

8.1 Heritage practice as traditionally object-oriented sub-systems. After van Gigch, Rosvall and Lagerqvist, 1996. Drawing by the author (Lagerqvist)

these boxes of practices is dependent in a broader societal context on more general attitudes toward concepts such as preservation, recycling, or resource economizing, and these attitudes are in turn the consequences of ongoing sociocultural processes in society. To reach sustainable preservation solutions, these boxes need to be understood as an interlinked system. Following this the subject matter of the department was defined broadly and conservation of built environments thus incorporated such diverse areas as architectural conservation, urban restoration and renewal, and landscape protection, but also on a departmental level moveable artifacts due to the program in objects conservation that was started in 1985.

The profession was gradually established during the 1980s. The professional title in Swedish is *antikvarie,* which is the same word as "antiquarian" in English but without the same meaning. An *antikvarie* could be an architectural restorer, or someone working with heritage perspectives on urban renewal or landscape development, or anything in between. During the 1990s, the professional title became more diversified with different prefixes added to *antikvarie,* such as building-, industrial-, landscape-, church-, and planning-, indicating a general acceptance of the profession and enabling an in-depth orientation toward a specific specialty. In spite of this specialization in the professional area, the program's ambition was to maintain as broad an approach as possible toward the built environment, thus covering all professional perspectives but without the in-depth orientations reflected within the practice. The in-depth approach of the program was rather turned toward how the built environment could be understood as a whole and the value systems of the practice that dictated the outcome of the field's activities. "Conservation" in this respect aims in a general sense to use cultural heritage without misusing it in order to respect its authenticity and embedded meanings. Cultural heritage is understood as the traditions and values that consciously or unconsciously are inherited from previous generations, and are both material and intangible. Its content is dynamic and constantly affected by temporally and socially changing values.

"Preservation" in this context is a collective term for the management of the cultural heritage in the form of conservation, restoration, maintenance, modification, and development and thus also the cultural environment's integration into a broader societal context—in this way defining the meaning of "integrated conservation" in the program name. Research and education in conservation aims at developing skills and insights needed for qualified preservation performance, meaning that not only the "hows" are important but also, and in some cases even more so, the "whys."

Heritage as a field of activity extends in principle over the society's entire operating environment. The departmental research during this phase was grouped into four areas of importance for the performance of such heritage activities: *objects conservation, the built environment, the cultural landscape,* and *theoretical development and societal impact.* Knowledge of relevance to these fields of activity was and is found in many traditional academic disciplines, implying the necessity of multidisciplinary research. History of buildings and built environments has a strategic position in this context, combining research on urban history and societal development with studies on individual consciously designed monuments, and incorporating perspectives on economic and legal control instruments as well as methods and theories for preservation, in a way not found in other disciplines. Based on this research area a natural synergy could be established with other disciplines but also with the surrounding society, thus providing an important frame for continued program development.

Program-Development Phase

The past twelve to fifteen years have been marked by rather big steps in the continued development of the program. An early change during this period was adding a fourth year, providing a master's degree following the Swedish regulations of the time. The motivation behind this was to enable a choice between two tracks in the final year: one with more focus on the context of architectural conservation and the other directed more toward urban and land use planning. Roughly, at the same time, discussions started with a local education institution in the city of Mariestad, some 180 kilometers northeast of Gothenburg. The institution offered a qualified professional training program in building crafts, and was part of a national system of programs that in cooperation with the concerned professional fields defined and provided education and training in needed areas of expertise. The programs gave academic credits, but not academic degrees, and each program initiative could run for five years. After its fifth year the program in Mariestad was scheduled for closing, although the need for qualified craftsmen in sensitive restoration projects was (and still is) an issue. Being part of an ordinary university's activities was a certain road to continuation of the program, and thus a relationship was established with the Department of Conservation. The eventual result in 2004 was three more bachelor's programs within the department, one in building crafts and two in crafts and management issues related to green heritage—gardens/parks and landscapes. With the increased number of programs the department became geographically positioned apart from Gothenburg in Mariestad.

In 1995, the Planning and Building Act was revised with one effect that changed the prerequisites for architectural heritage practitioners who wished to enter professional careers outside public bodies and instead work for architects in private practice. Previously the act had stated that officials at local planning and building authorities should make inspections during new constructions as well as restoration and rebuilding projects. With the revision this responsibility was transferred to contractors, meaning that they had to define a schedule for inspections and who should be inspectors, which then had to be approved by the local authorities. Historical and architectural values in existing buildings, clarified in the act of 1988 to be considered when rebuilding, was still a possible instrument for preservation in the revised act. Together with a general shift toward a more approving recognition of such values in the built environment, real estate owners, contractors, and architects became gradually more interested in incorporating relevant competence for securing these values in transformation processes. Specifically, this was the case in Stockholm, where the City Museum had produced a map together with the local planning and building authority in which all buildings were coded in different colors, giving information on heritage-based limitations for building transformation and the possible need to involve heritage competence in such transformations. Persons who could be involved as heritage professionals in these cases needed to prove their competence (in the rules and practices of the heritage field and in the history of the built environment) to be approved by the City Museum, thus implementing a de facto certifying system. Partly inspired by this the National Board of Housing, Building, and Planning, together with the National Heritage Board, organized a series of workshops and seminars for a couple of years where representatives of the concerned practice and academia discussed the need for a more general nationwide regulation. Finally, in 2006, the National Board of Housing, Building, and Planning implemented a regulation stipulating that architectural heritage practitioners need to be certified when working in a contractor's organization with the objective to inspect—following the revised Planning and Building Act of 1995—how historical and architectural values are secured through a transformation process. The program in integrated conservation of built environments was one of two programs that automatically provided a person with the full educational competence needed to be certified, although a couple of years of professional experience had to be acquired before applying for certification. The departmental involvement in the discussions leading to the implementation of the certification system increased the internally felt demand to provide the students with a flexible and diverse employability. The possible future employment areas for most students were represented by local, regional, and national authorities, museums, architectural consultants, and engineering and contractor firms, but private practice was also an attractive opportunity for some students. Several students have passed through most of these areas in their professional careers, implying high demands on the department to balance the curriculum. Parallel to this expansion of how the practice was perceived, both by the students and by the faculty, the organization for higher education in Sweden underwent substantial changes.

In 1999 in Bologna, the European ministers of education made a joint nonbinding declaration of the European higher education area, known as the Bologna Declaration. The motive was to strengthen the competitiveness of European universities on a global level by a number of measures. The need to develop comparable degrees was identified as an important objective, including the formulation of a standardized supplement to accompany a student's diploma clarifying the details of courses taken. The declaration further identified the need to develop a system based on two main cycles—undergraduate and graduate—where course length would be defined through a comparable credit system. To secure the quality of courses and programs throughout the participating states, comparable criteria and methodologies in quality assurance were to be developed. Finally, the mobility of students, teachers, researchers, and administrative staff promoted as well as facilitated the intended processes.[18] The Eurocentric motives for the agreement were later revised in favor of possibilities for cooperation within higher education with other regions on a global scale.[19]

Twenty-nine countries signed the declaration in 1999 and by 2005 a process—the Bologna process—was running in each country. By 2010, when the Bologna objectives were fulfilled the European Higher Education Area (EHEA) was launched with the number of countries increased to forty-six.[20] In Sweden the process started in 2005 with a transformation to a model similar to that of most countries, namely, an undergraduate level of three years leading to a bachelor's degree, a graduate level of two years leading to a master's degree—and in Sweden also a master's degree after one year of studies—and a doctoral level of four years leading to a doctoral degree, but also with the possibility of achieving a licentiate degree after two years of study at an intermediate level within a Ph.D. program. With the Bologna process a stronger focus was put on how curricula were formulated in regards to learning outcomes. The need to clarify the progression during the first cycle studies leading to the bachelor's degree and the advanced components in courses in the second cycle became the main task for faculties involved in education during the years after 2005.

At the Department of Conservation the Bologna process meant an intense period of defining which of the learning objectives should remain at the undergraduate level and which should be moved to and developed for the graduate level, and how the learning outcomes could be defined. During this process, the department was running five programs: integrated conservation of built environments and objects conservation, both leading to a master's degree, and building crafts, garden and parks, and landscape, all leading to a bachelor's degree.[21] They were transformed into five new bachelor's programs and one new master's program. Today they share some common courses; a five-week introductory course, a five-week course during the second year on the theory and history of conservation, and a five-week course during the third year on theory and methodologies for thesis work in conservation.

Within this process the program in integrated conservation of built environments underwent an intense critical examination and evaluation by the concerned colleagues of the faculty at the department. The result is an educational structure where all courses were adapted to 7.5-credit slots (60 credits equal an academic year), and grouped into 3 areas: History of Built Environments with 7 courses, The Professional Field—Rules and Practices with 7 courses, and Tools and Applications (transferable skills) with 8 courses, and with the final bachelor's thesis of 15 credits completing the program. The last area on tools and applications combines practical hands-on courses such as methodologies and techniques for recording buildings, with critical reflections and scientific requirements on how architecture and built environments can be described, analyzed, interpreted, and valued. In the two other areas there are also practice-related components as well as theoretical discussions and critical reflection, thus differing from the previous program layout where there was a more distinctive division between practices on the one hand and theory and critical reflection on the other.

The choice made on course contents and learning outcomes to be placed on either the undergraduate level or the graduate level was guided by the principle that students leaving with a bachelor's degree should be fully employable in public agencies as well as in the private sector. The master's level, on the other hand, provides opportunities for in-depth studies based on individual interest with an application of critical perspectives on societal heritage and memory processes, such as conflicting interests within the preservation area, or studies on methodologies for analyzing built environments, or subject areas like industrial heritage or churches.

Cooperation with Practitioners

From the early program years to the present the continuous dialogue with practitioners has been of vital importance—not only for providing input to the development of the program content, but even more for their function as adjunct teachers with expert knowledge from the practice, as well as suggesting real-life problems and situations for student projects and individual thesis work. Combined with an internship-based course in the program curriculum, the students become relatively well prepared for understanding the professional routines of the practice. The internship involves individual placements at public agencies within heritage or urban and land use planning, on national, regional, or local levels, but also at private architecture and engineering enterprises.

Since 1981, when the first group of students finalized their education, around 480 students have graduated from the program. A large majority of these are working within the area of heritage preservation and are valuable alumni who facilitate the ongoing cooperation between the department and the practice. This is not only giving the program a competitive edge, but also provides the departmental research activities with a good base for discussing and defining research and development projects that aim at both methodological development and critical reflection on how the practice functions and how it might face challenges ahead.

Challenges

Since the program started in 1978 the heritage field has witnessed an increased enlargement, not only concerning the application of practice on a yet broader span of objects, but also concerning a shifting focus on subjects for heritage practices. As exemplified by Gregory J. Ashworth in Figure 8.2, it can be understood as a paradigm shift from physical preservation toward cultural heritage.

The challenge for the program is balancing and integrating these two concepts on how the practice should or might direct students' attention. One crucial aspect is understanding how different interests and groups of people relate to history and memory and how these are or could be inten-

	Preservation	*Heritage*
Focus	Object	Message
Goal	Keep	Use
Justification	Value	Utility
Time	Past	Present/Future
Past	Real	Imagined
Authenticity	Object	Experience
Change	Immutable	Flexible
Creators	Experts	Users

8.2 The differences between the paradigms of physical preservation and cultural heritage, defined through some key concepts, as identified by Gregory J. Ashworth's keynote lecture at the Cultural Heritage Seminar Start-up Conference, University of Gothenburg, 20 May 2010, Gothenburg, Sweden

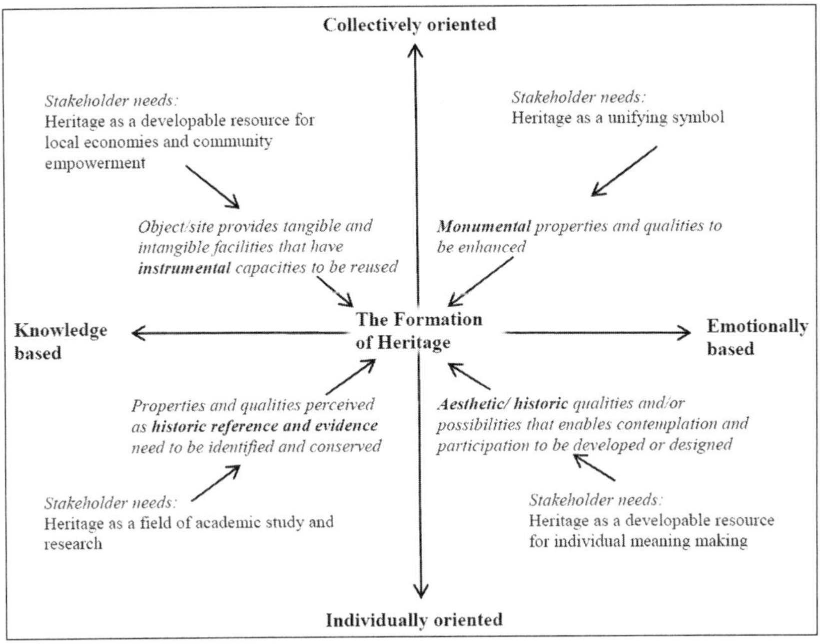

8.3 A generalized framework for interpretation of stakeholder interests. The production of heritage could be interpreted as the locus of the intersection of two differing types of tensions—one representing the dynamics between knowledge-based and emotionally experienced heritage, the other illustrating the relation of heritage to individually or collectively oriented needs. Different processes, possibilities, and conflicts could be discussed by placing stakeholder needs in and between the four activity areas of this structure. Drawing by the author (Lagerqvist)

tionally used for the definition of heritage. This indicates the necessity to train students in dialoguing with different stakeholder interests, as exemplified in Figure 8.3.

Another challenge in the continued program development, besides balancing the two principal directions of practice following the scheme in Figure 8.2, is how to formulate training situations where students have to negotiate citizen participation, which is a growing concern for the practice. Situations where interaction with other professionals—such as engineers, architects, real estate developers, economists, and the like—in time-limited project phases are representative of how the heritage professional to a large degree works. These situations and processes are difficult to prepare the students for or to recreate within the framework of the classroom. So far it has been possible to train students how to communicate with nonprofessionals, but it is still situated in a context that reflects how the academe rather than the heritage profession interacts with the community.

As a consequence of the continued expansion of the department and the increased number of bachelor's programs covering a yet broader perspective of the heritage area, the faculty represents a broad diversity of discipline-based as well as professional backgrounds. The need for various in-depth orientations both in education and in research is constantly challenging the same kind of need for a more overarching set of activities promoting the conceptual development of conservation/heritage studies.

The disposition of the bachelor's programs in relation to course contents on the master's level also needs to be reviewed more closely. Today most of the particular program-wise in-depth focuses rest within each bachelor's program, while the master's levels content is composed of more general courses on a theoretical advanced level. One perspective on future revisions of the education structure at the department would be to move some of the in-depth components from the bachelor's level to the master's level while at the same time developing them to promote advanced course content.

Concluding Remarks

The program in integrated conservation of built environments has provided the heritage practice in Sweden with an independent profession that is not a track within the curriculum of architectural training, geography, or urban and land use planning. The program has thus been instrumental in the forming of the Swedish heritage profession. From the start in 1978 the contacts with the practice have been important and since then they have grown closer, providing valuable input to continuous program revisions. The duality of these links has also affected how the practice has transformed, due to the relatively small application area Sweden represents in this case.

The program structure within the department broadly covers the heritage field and enables possibilities of creative meetings between student groups that eventually will represent different professions and tasks. The combined effect of the programs provides simultaneously a critical mass with respect to the understanding of *conservation* as the main overarching subject matter.

Although there is a strong focus on professional training, the sustainability of the program in integrated conservation of built environments is dependent on the necessity of a Ph.D. program and ongoing faculty-based research to provide theoretical and methodological discussions and inputs to the program. The establishment of the Ph.D. program in 1992 can also be understood as the academic acceptance of the department as a full-grown academic body, ultimately finalized by the installation of the chair in conservation in the early 2000s.

Managing a program and course structure as exemplified by the Department of Conservation requires a constant critical reflective monitoring of learning goals and outcomes in dialogue with practitioners. An ability to implement changes and adjustments as well as seeking the competitive edge, the long-term objectives, and the independent academic role of a university department is crucial for success.

Notes

1. See Nanne Engelbrektsson and Jan Rosvall, "Förslag till inrättande av byggnadsantikvarisk utbildning som lokal utbildningslinje vid Göteborgs universitet," *Meddelanden från Avd för Etnologi* (Gothenburg: University of Gothenburg, 1978); and Nanne Engelbrektsson and Jan Rosvall, *Conservation of Building Areas: Short Presentation of a Three-year Education Programme* (Gothenburg: University of Gothenburg, 1979).

2. See Göran Lindahl, *Saneringsfrågan—en kritisk översikt* (Stockholm, 1969); and Göran Lindahl, *Trästad och stenstad: Tradition och förändring i nordiskt stadsbyggande* (Oslo: Föreningen till Norske Fortidsminnesmerkers Bevaring, 1972).

3. Thordis Arrhenius, "Preservation and Protest: Counterculture and Heritage in 1970s Sweden," *Future Anterior,* 7:2 (Winter 2010), 118.

4. Arrhenius, "Preservation and Protest," 108.

5. Arrhenius, "Preservation and Protest," 108.

6. Jonas Grundberg, *Kulturarvsförvaltningens samhällsuppdrag: En introduktion till kulturarvsförvaltningens teori och praktik* (Gothenburg: GOTARC, Serie C. Arkeologiska skrifter no. 30, 1999), 68–69.

7. Sverker Janson, *Kulturvård och samhällsbildning* (Stockholm: Nordiska Museet, 1974).

8. See Stina Ejderoth-Linden and Gudrun Lönnroth, "Vad ska det bli av Haga? Kommunens engagemang i Hagas förnyelse," *Varför revs inte hela Haga? Om bevarandet av en stadsdel i Göteborg* (Gothenburg: Länsstyrelsen Västra Götalands län, 2009); Ingrid Holmberg, *På stadens yta: Om historiseringen av Haga* (Gothenburg: Makadam förlag, 2006), 238–43; and Ingrid Holmberg, "'Where the Past is Still Alive': Variation Over the Identity of Haga in Göteborg," in *The Construction of Built Heritage: A North European Perspective on Policies, Practices and Outcomes,* ed. Angela Phelps, G. J. Ashworth, and Bengt O. H. Johansson (Aldershot, UK: Ashgate Publishing Ltd, 2002), 64–65.

9. Nanne Engelbrektsson et al., *A-E-K Arkeologi, Etnologi, Konstvetenskap* (Gothenburg: University of Gothenburg, 1976).

10. Vägledning för kulturhistorisk bebyggelseinventering, *Riksantikvarieämbetet Rapport 1976 D 12* (Stockholm: Riksantikvarieämbetet, 1976).

11. Vägledning för kulturhistorisk bebyggelseinventering, *Riksantikvarieämbetet Rapport 1976 D 12.*

12. Declaration of Amsterdam, Congress of the European Architectural Heritage, 21–25 October 1975, http://www.fcpcrv.com/images/pdf2011/english/4 The Declaration of Amsterdam (1975).pdf (accessed August 20, 2012).

13. Bengt O. H. Johansson, "The Conservation of the Built Environment in Sweden," in *The Construction of Built Heritage: A North European Perspectives on Policies, Practices and Outcomes,* ed. Angela Phelps, G. J. Ashworth, and Bengt O. H. Johansson (Aldershot, UK: Ashgate Publishing Ltd, 2002), 39–42.

14. Johansson, "The Conservation of the Built Environment in Sweden," 40–41.

15. See Nanne Engelbrektsson, "Integrated Conservation: Research and Student Projects in Swedish Communities," in *Planning and Conservation: Third International Congress on Architectural Conservation and Town-Planning* (London: Heritage Trust, 1987).

16. Ingela Blomberg, *Varsam ombyggnad: Hinder och möjligheter* (Stockholm: Statens råd för byggnadsforskning, 1991); Planning and Building Act, SFS 1987:10. 3rd Chapter, 10§. http://www.notisum.se/pub/Doc.aspx?url=/rnp/sls/lag/19870010.htm (August 20, 2012).

17. Jan Rosvall and Stig Aleby, eds., *Air Pollution and Conservation: Safeguarding Our Architectural Heritage* (Amsterdam: Elsevier Science Publishers B.V., 1988), 23.

18. The Bologna Declaration on the European Space for Higher Education: An Explanation, http://ec.europa.eu/education/policies/educ/bologna/bologna.pdf (August 20, 2012).

19. Pavel Zgaga, *Looking Out: The Bologna Process in a Global Setting: On the "External Dimension" of the Bologna Process* (Norwegian Ministry of Education and Research, 2006), 34–36.

20. EHEA, Bologna Process—European Higher Education Area Official website, http://www.ehea.info/ (August 15, 2012).

21. A master's degree at this time implied four years of full-time studies; this was changed with the implementation of the Bologna process to two years of full-time studies on top of a bachelor's degree.

9 Saving the Stones—Practical Conservation Training Program: A Case Study of the International Conservation Center, Citt'a di Roma (in Acre, Israel)

Shelley-Anne Peleg

In the past few decades, study programs in conservation of the built environment have become an important topic in Israel. To date, the term "heritage conservation" is used in Israel when referring to the equivalent of the American term "historic preservation." Ongoing debates within the Israeli conservation community have lately revealed that this term also refers to archaeological object conservation, artistic conservation, and architectural site conservation, with little differentiation. Although there are many shared philosophies among conservators in each domain, basic practical approaches and needs are different. Without recognizing these different requirements, it remains difficult to address diverse training needs in academic programs. Currently Israel has four academic programs related to heritage conservation: a bachelor's degree program in conservation of sites and monuments at Western Galilee College; a master's degree program in the Archaeological Department at the University of Haifa; a master's degree program in preservation and development of cultural landscape and cultural heritage in the Geography Department at Bar-Ilan University; and a master's degree program in architectural conservation for architects at the Technion—Israel Institute of Technology. In addition, various departments in other academic institutions offer heritage conservation courses. But these programs and courses focus on architectural site conservation, which can be compared to American historic preservation. These programs have not yet managed to influence the professional market and do not yet offer actual solutions to ongoing challenges embedded in heritage management and the heritage conservation process.

The Holistic Approach to Active Conservation Studies

It is not the intent of this chapter to discuss the definition of "heritage" or to discuss what heritage management is, as these are ongoing issues all over the world. Any discussion on heritage conservation studies and training needs to begin with an understanding of current best practices to these topics. The idea that the conservation community has taken upon itself to bequeath the past to future generations suggests that heritage conservation is not "just another job," but rather a mission, a state of mind, a responsibility, and an approach. It is becoming widely accepted by the international community that heritage conservation represents many things, and has become a continuing search for cultural values that are important to a society.[1] These values are embedded in the built environment, in archaeological historical monuments and objects, as well as in intangible heritage. Conservation entails an understanding that heritage is much more than building remains. It also includes material artifacts, knowledge, behaviors, customs, arts, history, experience, languages, legacies, beliefs, values, institutions, philosophical systems, social relations, and other aspects of culture handed down from the past.[2] Bequeathed to us by previous generations, heritage is a valuable resource that cannot be replaced or reproduced; hence the moral responsibilities to safeguard, preserve, conserve, and restore it for the benefit of future generations.[3] This is a moral responsibility, entailing an ongoing need for new approaches to assume this responsibility. It means that heritage conservation must continue to develop and adopt new holistic approaches that address social values as well as the obvious building materials, construction, and safety issues. With this in mind, it becomes clearer that heritage conservation is a multidiscipline field and that those involved in these processes come from a wide variety of backgrounds. It is quite common to find on a heritage conservation project a diversity of professionals that includes architects, urban planners, engineers, building contractors, masons, carpenters, archaeologists, lawyers, and chemists, among others.

But a deeper look into heritage conservation practice demonstrates significant gaps between these professionals. It is common to find a situation in which each professional is an expert in a specific field but has little knowledge of the supplemental fields that are essential to the entire process. More often than not, architects and urban planners lack an understanding of materials, application methods, and implementation skills. Engineers may not appreciate heritage values and the evaluation process. Material specialists are not fully aware of documentation procedures and are usually only involved in the implementation stages of conservation measures. Tourist developers lack an understanding of other stakeholders that are not part of their industry. Technical practitioners and property developers are often oblivious to social needs, as well as the knowhow of community participatory procedures.

Thus it is not surprising to find that the end product of a heritage conservation project can result in an incomplete monument, unsolved technical problems with materials that are incompatible with environmental surroundings, or unhappy residents who remain alien to the sites or feel neglected and forgotten by the development organizations.[4] It is becoming important to recognize that a place of significance embraces certain qualities, for which it has become a focus of spiritual, political, national, or other cultural sentiments for the inhabitants.[5] This alone requires greater stakeholder engagement and engaging constituents who have not always been considered part of the conservation process. For instance, sociologists and social workers who have the ability, qualities, and know-how to initiate community engagement and involvement are not always invited to participate in the heritage planning process.

It therefore seems only natural that if heritage conservation includes various professionals, and that they all lack knowledge of the expertise that falls outside of their respective subfield, that the appropriate action would be to connect these professionals and create a more interdisciplinary profession with a common ground, an accepted language, and a code of conduct. A change in methods of heritage conservation education is an appropriate response. At this stage, in which young professionals are still flexible and can be molded into adopting a new type of professional thinking and action, it is easier to begin with new codes of conduct. This means connecting the various specialty backgrounds into a single profession, which could be called a *holistic* heritage conservation profession. The Merriam-Webster dictionary defines "holistic" as "complete systems rather than the analysis of, treatment of or dissection into parts."[6] This is certainly true of heritage conservation procedures and should be true of heritage conservation education. A holistic approach to heritage conservation studies and training means:

1. Heritage conservation training programs that include students from history, art, archaeology, and architecture as well as law, theology, sociology, and cultural studies as a prerequisite for conservation and historic preservation studies. This multidisciplinary approach enables the sharing and exchanging of ideas, and serves as a model for future multidiscipline dialogue between different heritage

conservation stakeholders—both formal institutions as well as community residents.

2. Training programs that follow a general order of conservation procedures, beginning with initial surveys and recording procedures, continuing on to value identification, preparation of conservation plans, and implementation, and concluding with a heritage conservation report (describing materials, implementation, results, recommendations, etc.).
3. Teaching theory through a methodology of case studies, field trips, and discussions with leading experts. This enables young professionals to relate to and understand different issues in heritage conservation practices.

If this is to be a new foundation for heritage conservation education, it means that academic heritage conservation studies should address practical issues, and that practical heritage conservation training should address academic-theoretical topics. Thus, a common language is necessary for the professional international heritage conservation community. But this basic approach alone is not enough. An additional and essential component for heritage conservation education is *active heritage conservation training,* defined as:

1. Combining heritage theoretical studies with hands-on practical conservation work
2. Using living historic cities and archaeological sites as training laboratories
3. Involving students on real heritage conservation projects, so as to develop their craftsman skills and decision-making abilities

Thus in-depth heritage conservation training through hands-on experience in the context of an actual conservation process becomes an integral part of the learning experience. It enables understanding the complexity of implementing heritage conservation practices. Without this, years pass until young professionals are able to make heritage conservation decisions based on accepted theoretical practices and act on them with a full understanding of the implications and dilemmas that could arise in the future. Since moving to its new grand home, the International Conservation Center—Citt'a di Roma in Old Acre has become a focal point for national and international heritage conservation training and study programs applying this theory.

In recent years the archaeological, historical, and tourist site of Acre has been the subject of national and international conservation and intensive tourist development.[7] The nomination of Acre onto the World Heritage List in 2001 was the result of a long process that concentrated on the preservation of the historic fabric of the city. This approach began under the British Mandate administration (1923–48), during which a new master plan for Acre was compiled in 1946. According to this plan, tourism was regarded as key for the future development of the city. Since then local residents have been regarded as part of the city's economy, contributing to tourist development. This approach has been generally adopted by Israel for the development of Acre. Much can be said about tourism as a tool for conservation and (re)development in historic cities. It is a concept that can impair the balance between a vibrant city that has multiple functions versus a place with a singular touristic use. Therefore, it becomes essential to manage the pressures that result from tourism-related development through a sound governance structure that puts people and community front and center with heritage conservation (see Figure 9.1).

9.1 Students training in the Historical Caravan Serei Khan esh-Shewarda in Acre. Photograph provided by Shelley-Anne Peleg and International Conservation Center, Citt'a di Roma. Photograph by Alison Goren

Recognizing this, the heritage values of the city were identified in the new master plan in 1993, and again during the nomination process of Acre for the World Heritage List. Acre is an exceptional historic port city that preserves substantial remains of its medieval Crusader buildings that date from the twelfth and thirteenth centuries. These lie beneath the existing Ottoman fortifications constructed in the eighteenth and nineteenth centuries. It is due to this that the cultural values identified during the nomination procedure relate to the built heritage of Acre and include aesthetic, historic, and scientific values. The Antiquities Law officially protects these Ottoman buildings.

The nomination of Acre as a World Heritage Site has brought international recognition to the importance of the city. As a result intensive excavations have uncovered massive Crusader remains of the Hospitaller compound and the Templar quarters. Together with the traditional Turkish bathhouse and other buildings, these have been conserved, restored, and turned into international tourist sites attracting thousands of visitors from all over the world each year. Although the infrastructure of the city has been replaced and housing in the central residential quarter has undergone restoration procedures, social rehabilitation has not yet accompanied these developments.

Today, Acre is a vibrant city. Local residents live within Ottoman buildings that are at least 300-year-old. Most of them are Muslim Arabs who moved into Acre after Israel's War of Independence (1948) and are generally of low socioeconomic status. Thus the contrast in the city is enormous: beautiful restored tourist sites on the one hand and, on the other, old buildings inhabited by the local residents who have few resources to update homes to meet modern everyday needs. It is due to these features that the Israeli training center for practical heritage conservation is situated in the Old City of Acre.

Heritage conservation procedures, taught in the city as an apprentice profession, ensure the applicability of ethical theory in conservation procedures. This entails an understanding that cultural heritage is much more than building remains. Important to understand but hard to grasp are ideas laid out by the Venice Charter.[8] This charter recognized that any replacements that occur during a conservation process must be integrated harmoniously with the whole, but at the same time be distinguishable from the original. Another basic principle for conservation is that all interventions should be minimal and reversible. A cautious conservation approach means respecting the existing fabric of all periods, changing only what is necessary. This prioritization of reversibility, compatibility, and maintenance are important goals of all conservation treatments and stems from the recognition that future actions could take advantage of progress in scientific knowledge and techniques. Therefore, a basic conservation requirement is the ability to undo a process with no or minimal changes to a place or object. By adopting these ethical principles, conservators recognize that they work within the limitations and values of their own specific era and context.

Designating specific parts of the Center's building for student training has turned the structure itself into a laboratory, enabling the practice of these principles rather than teaching them in a classroom setting. Situated in the courtyard of the building, the exterior staircase is one such example.[9] It is built with a local stone, called *kurkar*, and can be accessed through an alley leading into the building. It consists of thirteen steps that lead up to the second level of the building and is supported by a small barrel vault. In April 2011 the staircase was partially cleaned from cement/concrete mortar and vegetation by students in the Saving the Stones—Practical Conservation Training Program as an object of practice in developing documentation skills. After removing the cement from the staircase the stone joints were opened and several stones broke or became detached. Additional intervention was urgently needed in order to prevent further deterioration. Student research enabled a better understanding of the staircase's weaknesses and the application of appropriate conservation interventions. After consulting with experts, the students established methods of treatment and identified materials to be used. Stabilization began with a first layer of mortar and continued with mortar injections into the facade of the vault. The students developed a lime-based mortar that matched reversibility requirements, protected the stones' surfaces, and covered uneven surfaces so as to aesthetically fit. Additional procedures included removal of the metal insertions, fastening unsecure stones, and replacement of deteriorated stones. The final report prepared by the students includes recommendations for these procedures. Specifically stated are regular inspections and reapplying mortar when necessary. Such a project planned, documented, and implemented entirely by students under the guidance of heritage conservation experts demonstrates the possibility of applying theoretical knowledge of conservation principles in a professional manner (see Figure 9.2).

Acre itself, as a historic living city, serves as a laboratory for training, studying, and practicing heritage conservation work with unconventional stakeholders. Training programs introduce local residents as party stakeholders in any conservation or development project. What is the true nature of the city's heritage? Who has the right to decide on conservation procedures of this heritage? What are the means of preserving this heritage? These many dilemmas and issues enable students of heritage conservation to combine the process of acquiring knowledge with working on structures and objects of considerable historical significance while dealing with matters of great community concern that can arise at historic and archaeological sites.

The Hammam al-Pasha is one of the most visited tourist attractions in the Old City of Akko—the historic center of Acre.[10] Discussion of the site can be found in almost any tourist guidebook on Israel.[11] In order to better understand the historical and cultural significance of this site, students conducted research to analyze the interpretation of the Turkish bathhouse. An outcome of this project was a thorough record of the tourist perspective of the Hammam al-Pasha during a specific moment in

9.2 Student practicing stone carving at the International Conservation Center, Citt'a di Roma. Photo provided by Shelley-Anne Peleg and International Conservation Center, Citt'a di Roma. Photograph by Alison Goren

time (June 2011). It combines interviews of locals, surveys of tourists, and content analysis of tourist advertisements. The recent history behind this building revealed many tensions between the importance of saving buildings and the significance of social function. The head of the Old Acre Development Company admitted to the students that restoring the Hammam al-Pasha as a functioning Turkish bath was a wonderful idea. In fact, the Old Acre Development Company even explored the possibility of returning the Hammam al-Pasha to its original use. A physical survey of the building, however, revealed an extensive amount of structural damage to the heating and water systems supporting the hammam. Repairing these problems would necessitate the physical destruction of the building. The Old Acre Development Company, in accordance with the Law of Antiquities for Akko, decided to protect the building's authenticity at the expense of its original use.

During the process of conserving the Hammam al-Pasha, the biggest challenges were primarily architectural: restoring the glass in the ceiling, the tiles on the walls, and the marble floors. According to the head of the Old Acre Development Company, locals were involved in each step of the conservation process and made up 50 percent of the workforce responsible for conserving the hammam. Nonetheless, the local Arab residents with whom the students had a dialogue expressed frustration at the direction of tourism development in Akko, as exemplified through the Hammam al-Pasha tourist attraction. These residents highlighted the role of the stakeholders of the city (the municipal government, the Old Acre Development Company, and the Israel Antiquities Authority), who manage the tourism and conservation planning of Old Akko under an implicit policy of prioritizing stones before people. This management has facilitated the development of a cultural landscape that symbolizes a "nonfunctioning" community, a society frozen in the past. For example, using the motto that "a museum designer should be a storyteller," the exhibit designer of the Hammam al-Pasha tourist attraction aimed to tell the history of Acre in the Ottoman period as the walls of the bathhouse would have heard it from the bathers. As the Hammam al-Pasha presents a chapter of Ottoman history through the story of an imaginary line of bath attendants, the attraction freezes the Hammam al-Pasha at a specific moment in time through the narrative presented and the placement of aluminum-cast statues of traditional Ottoman bathers. Thus, the Hammam al-Pasha tourist attraction is not simply conserving the physical building. It is also portraying—as its primary cultural value—a glimpse of historic Ottoman life, rather than a functioning Turkish bathhouse of cultural and social importance for contemporary residents.

In many ways the conservation of Old Akko through the development of Ottoman-era themed tourism creates a self-fulfilling prophecy: each decade the Turkish bathhouse remains nonoperational, another generation of Old Akko residents become distanced from the Turkish bathing traditions of their Ottoman ancestors. This project work can demonstrate to students the tension between development organizations and economic, political, and social issues. While community leaders in Old Akko work to organize the residents in ways they can actively engage with the power institutions of Akko, the students found a general consensus that change in the city will not occur unless instigated by the Old Acre Development Company, the municipal government, and the Israel Antiquities Authority. If these powerful organizations are able to listen, the residents of Old Akko have many innovative ideas about the development of tourism in Old Akko. These residents have a direct stake in preventing the "preservation-of-buildings-before-cultures" policy, which could transform Acre into an outdoor museum of buildings with no living soul.[12]

Students of architectural conservation are taught the principles of conservation ethics in the early stages of their training. A professional ethics code is a result of connecting values with conduct. Therefore, any discussion about conservation ethics must address conservation values. What are the values that guide conservation procedures? How are they defined? To what extent do they take into consideration social values of indigenous peoples, minorities, and local inhabitants living around or within archaeological sites or historic cities? Does the commemoration of the past facilitate the coexistence of current cultures, or emphasize the historical and cultural boundaries with them?

But can these questions be addressed in a classroom and simply taught through the Burra Charter?[13] Better practice could be conducted with an evaluation process. For example, there is the Burj el Kashla ruin overlooking the sea located in southwestern Acre. This site used to be the

Templar compound during the Crusader period.[14] The current structure is part of the Ottoman city wall, an important military monument of Acre dating to the late eighteenth and early nineteenth centuries. The city wall of Acre represents well-preserved Ottoman fortification work of the Arab Sheikh Daher el Omar (c. 1690–1775), of succeeding Turkish pashas, and of the Egyptian conqueror Ibrahim Pasha (1789–1848). Later the structure was reinforced and reused during the British Mandate. In accordance with a request from the Akko Economic Company, Burj el Kashla became a location for site evaluation training, which resulted in a full documentation report. Values identified by the students serve as actual recommendations for future development of the site. Within the guided evaluation process, students conducted a full architectural documentation of the site with photos and sketches, examined the current ruined architecture and space, categorized the building materials used, and identified on-site problems, among other issues. The urban analysis discusses problems of the monument's conditions, transportation and access to the site, integrating the site with the surroundings, physical and visual features, and public perception. This study led the students to a new appreciation for the site and a better understanding of age value for the ruins. The Burj el Kashla expresses a romantic beauty of its own due to its antiquity. The old sandstones, the empty vaults, the fallen pieces of masonry, the complex arches, and the vivid skyline evoke peoples' memory of the past and a sense of nostalgia. Thus the ruins have crystallized into a new form for our own time. This transcendent feeling of immortality is also embedded in the age value of the ruins. The notion of a site as a ruin, in a state of arrested decay, is innovative as it contradicts the proposed economic development plans for the site.

This procedure can demonstrate the way students confront questions, dilemmas, and issues that contemporary heritage conservators are often required to address. Although the Burj el Kashla is just one architectural monument in the city, it is an excellent case study. It was a life learning experience that enabled the students to undergo the actual procedure of site evaluation, understand the recurrent contradictions between development and heritage conservation, appreciate the complexity of conservation work, and understand the value of a place. As future professionals, they are going to find themselves in many such situations. Without defining site value, it could have been quite easy to make a poor decision, which in this instance would have resulted in a new building replacing the old ruins.

Addressing real-life dilemmas enables students to understand the full responsibility of a conservator as a protector of all aspects of cultural heritage—tangible as well as intangible. It is this that conveys the understanding of and appreciation for the "spirit of a place," as well as the basic principles of conservation. From this can come the foundation for the proper attitude needed by heritage conservationists, changing from "just another profession" to a mission, a state of mind, a responsibility, and an approach. Understanding that social values should also be respected, for which a place has become a focus of spiritual, political, national, and other cultural sentiment for a local population, requires greater stakeholder engagement and constituents that have not always been part of the conservation process. Examples include sociologists and community workers. More complex is community engagement and participation. Hands-on conservation training programs can introduce the local community as a party stakeholder in any conservation or development project.

Final Thoughts

Gustavo Giovanni, an architect-planner who worked in Rome during the early twentieth century, perceived that "it is essential that architects should have an integrated training, one from which they would be as conversant with traditional building techniques as well as technical innovations, masters of historical architecture and urban form, attuned to contemporary social needs, and respectful towards context when designing new structures."[15] This is a "holistic" approach to heritage conservation, an approach forgotten within the development of specialized expertise, but one that should be revived in heritage conservation education.

With this concept in mind, I offer some final conclusions about heritage conservation training. First, heritage conservation is about preserving a site's cultural values by finding ways to prolong the life of the fabric that embodies these values. This includes dealing with the physical decay of buildings and their everyday maintenance, as well as readapting redundant buildings for sustainable new uses.[16] Basic research and evaluation of a site is therefore the first phase of any heritage conservation procedure. This phase entails many aspects: physical and intangible, economic and social. Although architects and planners are needed, they often lack the skills and knowhow to fully complete this phase. They have the ability to address aesthetic and architectural issues and can identify, survey, and record sources relating to the historical development of sites and analyze these sources in relation to the site's historical significance. Specialists can recognize architectural qualities in buildings and structures in terms of its design, spatial relationship, mass, form and proportion, influence of light, color and texture, and details and use of materials, and assess how these compare to other structures of the same age and type.

But specialists like architects and conservators lack a point of view and skills necessary to enhance social issues and community needs. They are often unable to fully identify and quantify cultural, social, and emotional attachments that connect a community to a place. Thus, the cultural significance created by living people is lost forever. It is easy to transform this understanding for heritage conservation education. It requires absorbing into our programs young professionals from supplementary fields, thus enriching the profession with new expertise and skills. This is how a true change can be made, transforming the dialogue into a multidisciplinary one. Thus education can produce pluralistic perspectives for heritage site conservation and interpretation, so much needed for a more holistic approach.

Second, education should take place on real-life projects in the form of apprentice training. Medicine is an appropriate example of on-the-job, apprentice training. Young medical professionals obtain basic surgery skills and develop them by performing actual procedures. Medical theory and academic knowledge are gained as they participate in live decision-making scenarios, headed frequently by leading specialists from various fields. It is also a requirement that students rotate through basic medical fields. Thus a common "medical language" and a full understanding of all disciplines are obtained through this long training period. Heritage conservation education has much to learn and duplicate from this training method. It means that heritage conservation needs to define basic practical skills and include them in education programs, thus ensuring a common language for all heritage conservation practitioners. Basic practical skills involve much more than just measuring buildings, architectural drawing, field surveys, historical research, or exercises in planning. This means understanding material and technological pathologies, planning interventions, conducting implementation procedures, and utilizing ancient building technologies. It entails acquiring many talents such as the ability to repair, maintain, and perform a diversity of applied skills. In order to make a critical analysis of possible solutions for technical or functional problems on sites, practitioners need to be able to consider the implications of decisions on the existing cultural resource and choose solutions that satisfy the technical, functional, and cost requirements of the project. Therefore, it is not only a notion of training through actual ongoing conservation projects and heritage decision-making discussions, but also the idea that heritage conservators can only understand practical issues by doing them. Practicing skills alone is not enough! It is a prerequisite to ensure that these skills are obtained according to the appropriate process of the heritage conservation curriculum. This means that training and education experiences of this order should follow a prescribed set of procedures that includes basic surveying, continuing with documentation and recording procedures, evolving into the preparation of an intervention plan, and concluding with the implementation of plan recommendations and a full report.

Training programs need to introduce traditional building techniques, as well as technical innovations, attuned to contemporary social needs that are respectful to the context of sites. This is the true meaning of integrated training, one that can be considered a holistic approach to conservation studies. But basic training alone is not enough. Continuing education is needed for all conservators to make them better professionals. Even a talented dancer needs to practice and repeat again and again basic steps grasped in initial dance classes. Various European countries have created accreditation and certification systems that identify professional conservators and their continuing education needs. The fact that the heritage conservation field in Israel has finally come to this realization, alongside academic education, is a sign of maturity. Israel's heritage conservation field is now confronting a new challenge. It is time to question previously accepted means of identifying heritage conservation professionals and create a new means to monitor their long-term capabilities.

Notes

1. Faro Convention on the Value of Cultural Heritage for Society, last modified by the Council of Europe in 2005, http://conventions.coe.int/Treaty/EN/Treaties/Html/199.htm.

2. Getty Institute, *Art & Architecture Thesaurus Online*, http://www.getty.edu/vow/AATFullDisplay?find=cultural+heritage&logic=AND&note=&english=N&prev_page=1&subjectid=300265422.

3. Convention concerning the Protection of the World Cultural and Natural Heritage, last modified in 1972, http://portal.unesco.org/en/ev.php-URL_ID=13055&URL_DO=DO_TOPIC&URL_SECTION=201.html.

4. Shelley-Anne Peleg, *The Interaction and Relationship between the Local Population and the Development and Conservation Procedures in Old Acre* (master's thesis, University of Haifa, 2010).

5. Quebec City Declaration on the Preservation of the Spirit of Place, last modified in 2008, http://www.international.icomos.org/quebec2008/quebec_declaration/pdf/GA16_Quebec_Declaration_Final_EN.pdf.

6. "Holistic," *Merriam-Webster Online Dictionary*, http://www.merriam-webster.com/dictionary/holistic.

7. Yoel Mansfeld, Noga Collins, Eran Ketter, and Shelley-Anne Peleg, *Optimizing Community Benefits in and around Culture-based World Heritage Sites (WHSs)—The Case of Akko, Israel* (Haifa: University of Haifa, 2011).

8. The International Charter for the Conservation and Restoration of Monuments and Sites (Venice Charter), adopted by ICOMOS in 1964, http://www.icomos.org/charters/venice_e.pdf.

9. Caitlin M. Davis and Ashley Norman, *Presenting the Hammam al-Pasha: Conserving Heritage by Creating an Attraction, Israel Antiquities Authority—Conservation Department* (2011), http://www.iaa-conservation.org.il/article_Item_eng.asp?id=153&subject_id=36.

10. "Hammam al-Pasha" translates into Arabic as the Governor's Bath, or Lord's Bath.

11. Davis and Norman, *Presenting the Hammam al-Pasha.*

12. In other words, a "Disneyfication," which so commonly plagues successful heritage sites overly devoted to tourism.

13. Burra Charter—The Australia Charter for Places of Cultural Significance (modified by ICOMOS-Australia in 1999), Article 1.1—1.2, pp 2 http://australia.icomos.org/wp-content/uploads/BURRA_CHARTER.pdf.

14. Igor Demchenko, Bin Li, and Judy Zheng Jia, *Documentation Report of BURJ EL-KASHLA, Old City of Akko, Israel Antiquities Authority—Conservation Department* (2011), http://www.iaa-conservation.org.il/article_Item_eng.asp?subject_id=36&id=146.

15. Dennis Rodwell, *Conservation and Sustainability in Historic Cities* (Malden, MA: Blackwell Printing, 2007), 35.

16. *A framework description of competence for a shared approach to built environment conservation accreditation schemes in the UK*, commissioned by Historic Scotland in cooperation with the Department of Building Engineering & Surveying, Heriot-Watt University, and the School of Architecture, Edinburgh College of Art (2002).

10 Delivering a Changing Conservation Curriculum by Distance Learning in the Twenty-First Century

Henry Russell and Philip Leverton

This chapter explores the implications of a changing conservation curriculum for delivery through distance learning. Note that in the United Kingdom (as in some other countries) the term "conservation" is regularly used rather than "preservation." The latter has a rather different meaning in U.K. practice, representing a resistance to any change to a building or structure, whereas conservation is seen as being concerned with the management of change in a manner that is consistent with the character and significance of the building concerned. Some aspects of what we label conservation may, indeed, constitute preservation (in the U.K. sense), but the process also allows for appropriate and sympathetic alteration and adaptive re-use.

The College of Estate Management

Based in the United Kingdom, the College of Estate Management was established in Lincoln's Inn Fields, London, in 1919, gaining its royal charter in 1922, with the principal objective of training surveyors.[1] Although the college had offered University of London external degrees for more than thirty years, in 1967 it became associated with the University of Reading. The college's body of full-time students was transferred to the university, leaving the college to focus on delivery by distance learning—or postal courses, as they were then known. The college moved to the university's campus in 1973, and it remains an independent educational institution. The college's distance-learning master's program in conservation of the historic environment has been running since 1990 and is accredited by the University of Reading. When it was established the focus was principally on conservation of the built heritage fabric, and the teaching of conservation philosophy, international charters, and heritage law underpinned this.

Teaching Conservation in 1990

In 1990, conservation teaching at the college and elsewhere was strongly based on an understanding of philosophy rooted in the Venice Charter.[2] The course was strongly orientated toward the analysis and repair of historic fabric, based on an understanding of historic buildings and their history. The International Council on Monuments and Sites' (ICOMOS) *Education and Training Guidelines* had not been published, but their approach broadly mirrored that of the course at the time.[3] As far as U.K. students were concerned, this body of philosophical and technical knowledge and understanding was applied within a framework of national legislation dealing with the protection of the most ancient monuments and the conservation of buildings (individually and in groups) and whole areas of architectural and historic significance.

In the intervening period since then the landscape of conservation education has been subject to three significant changes—first, changing ideas about the identity of heritage and the way in which this impacts the curriculum; second, the consequent change in the skill set and range of practitioners involved in conservation; and third, changing ideas about the appropriate content of programs to provide for the more diverse range of requirements that flow from the first two changes—to which we might link a fourth change, to our understanding of what constitutes a program.

Responding to the Changing World of Conservation

The historic environment in Europe and North America is changing in two main ways. First, there is a legacy of heavy industry and infrastructure that is now redundant, and second, the perception of what constitutes heritage is changing. In the United Kingdom, this is manifested most notably by the demise of the coal and steel industries over the past thirty years. The effect of this has been to leave a legacy of large sites with buildings and machinery—and industrial processes are important in understanding the way in which these sites were operated. Not all such large sites can be retained, but in many cases nineteenth- or early twentieth-century industrial buildings can be successfully converted to other uses while respecting their heritage values.

Finding new uses has a social dimension because the loss of heavy industry means loss of employment for communities. Those communities may live in late nineteenth-century terraced housing that has a heritage and community value. The last British (Labour) government (in power from 1997 to 2010) had proposals to demolish large areas of such housing on the basis that it had little or no market value where communities were declining. This produced a backlash from those communities that sought to save them.[4]

This leads to the second point, which is the changing perceptions of heritage, in that people regard it as being not only the traditional perceptions of heritage as country houses and cathedrals, but also the local and vernacular. This was highlighted by the English *Power of Place* report as long ago as 2000 where a poll prepared for the report indicated that people thought the historic environment "represents the place in which they live." [5] This was backed up by a Market and Opinion Research Institute (MORI) opinion poll conducted for English Heritage in 2003.[6] It showed that 91 percent of people in Cornwall (a rural county in the southwest of England), 85 percent of people in Bradford (a large city in the West Yorkshire conurbation in the north of England), and 82 percent of people in London agreed with the statement that "heritage in my local area is worth saving." Furthermore, 90 percent of those polled considered their local area to be "heritage" just as much as castles and stately homes.

The same poll mentioned that heritage should celebrate the roles of different communities, and this points to an important aspect of heritage: it helps to define our identity, whether on a national or a local scale. There is a problem in some communities, where heritage is seen as elitist and speaking only to a privileged few. In the past few decades, open-air museums of vernacular buildings that have been collected on one site show the life and habitations of the ordinary people. An example is the Weald and Downland Museum in the south of England, which has a collection of timber-framed buildings. The Welsh National History Museum at St. Fagans near Cardiff also has a collection of Welsh farmhouses and cottages and other structures that, as at Weald and Downland, have been dismantled on their original sites and re-erected at the museum. The study of vernacular buildings is in some senses relatively recent in that it began in earnest in the past sixty-five to seventy years with such studies as Iorwerth C. Peate, Cyril Fox and Lord Raglan, and Raymond Wood Jones.[7] These studies are nonetheless academic and therefore restricted in their wider public appeal, so the challenge remains to make understanding of the vernacular heritage more accessible to a wider range of the community.

In recent years, English Heritage has had programs to investigate the development of suburbs in the 1920s and 1930s.[8] This involves a study not of individual buildings, but of groups of buildings, and therefore the area-based study based on characterization techniques is developing. The English National Trust has acquired and opened small houses such as the childhood homes of John Lennon and Paul McCartney in Liverpool and

Mr. Straw's House in Workshop, Nottinghamshire. These small properties present difficult problems in accommodating visitors, and the Trust runs pre-booked tours. The houses of the former Beatles evidently have an appeal above that of the ordinary suburban house, but when the Trust acquired them, it marked a major change in the type of property that they opened to the public.

We are now dealing with a range of heritage assets that twenty to thirty years ago received only limited consideration—witness the eclectic mixture of both recently inscribed and tentative World Heritage Sites. In the United Kingdom, the idea that modernist public residential blocks (in London and Sheffield), a fading art deco resort hotel (Morecambe), a fairground ride (Margate), a Cold War local command bunker (York), and the suburban childhood homes of the Beatles in Liverpool (and the crosswalk in London that they featured on the Abbey Road album sleeve) could be regarded as "heritage" would have merited little serious attention, as would the idea of converting the Victorian-era prison in Oxford into a hotel. This change of emphasis is evidenced by recent themes adopted by English Heritage's biannual *Conservation Bulletin;* Gemma Abercrombie commented in her editorial to the summer 2012 edition dealing with sporting heritage (taking its cue from the London Olympic and Paralympic games) that "the narrow focus of listing, with its concentration on special architectural and historic interest, doesn't allow us to recognize the huge value of sporting sites as repositories of shared memories, the emotional connection that spectators and participants have with particular places and traditions."[9]

Historic environment conservation needs to become more holistic by embracing wider notions of landscape and nature conservation. It also needs to be more aware of the social and economic contexts in which it is working. Changes are already being made in this direction within the United Kingdom in new national land use planning policy for England.[10] Policies for the natural and historic environment are grouped together in the "Achieving Sustainable Development," "Requiring Good Design," and the "Conserving and Enhancing the Historic Environment" chapters, so this is becoming more common. The historic and natural environment sectors are working more closely together on matters of common interest. For instance, the Heritage Alliance, which is an English organization working on heritage public policy, has in its membership the Campaign to Protect Rural England and Greenspace (supporting local parks). Another example of closer working relationships is the present U.K. government's Department for Transport's recent meetings with representatives of different interest groups in the environment sector to discuss the proposed new London to Birmingham rail line, High Speed 2 (HS2). If it is constructed, this line will cross through open country and villages, as it is an entirely new route. The environmental groups that attend these meetings come from both the natural and historic environment sectors.

The ICOMOS/UNESCO principles of outstanding universal value already embrace natural and cultural values for inscribing World Heritage Sites, and the *Operational Guidelines* make provisions for sites of mixed cultural and natural value, as well as recognizing cultural and natural as separate categories.[11] UNESCO seeks to maintain a balance between sites of cultural and natural value, and perhaps one way of achieving that will be to encourage more sites to recognize both sets of values where this is possible. As a result of these developments skills in reuse and adaptation of historic buildings will become more necessary. Traditional heritage, which is usually characterized by domestic construction, has been adapted and reused for centuries. But the new industrial and commercial heritage requires new skills. These will be architectural, engineering, and construction skills, but also urban design and place-making skills (including project management) when large areas are being dealt with.

Finally, the sustainability agenda affects us all. There is a temptation to see it in terms of energy efficiency in historic buildings. It is important to reduce energy consumption, whether through technical measures or changed behavior, and in the United Kingdom, policies such as the Green Deal whereby the energy companies finance the installation of insulation are being implemented. Since historic buildings tend to be of low carbon construction, this is a strong argument in favor of their retention.[12]

The Changing Conservation Curriculum—The Challenge

During the past dozen years there has been a shift toward heritage values and significance of places. The Australian Burra Charter was the international spur for this while the principal driver in the United Kingdom was the publication of *Power of Place,* the English Heritage paper looking at the public's perceptions of their heritage.[13] The first edition of the Burra Charter was published in 1979, but its effect on the mainstream of conservation has been slow to develop. It introduced the conservation plan methodology, which has provided the tools for identifying and measuring a wide set of values, including values to the local community. The U.K. Heritage Lottery Fund has played a major role in embedding conservation planning into the system, with its core elements of assessing values and significance. This has had an effect on the course curriculum. Teaching of heritage values has become much more important, and it forms the backdrop to making much more widely informed decisions on conservation of the historic environment, be this basic maintenance and fabric repair, or larger changes and interventions.

The ICOMOS *Education and Training Guidelines* of 1993 have a basis in fabric repair.[14] The *Guidelines* are currently being revised and there have been differences of opinion about the extent to which they should reflect the expansion of curriculum to include aspects of significance and heritage management, the latter including financial appraisal, funding, marketing, and interpretation. This apparent tension between a narrower, more traditional curriculum that focuses on methods of investigation and repair and on materials and techniques and a broader curriculum, which embraces knowledge, understanding, and application of this range of contextual subject matter, reflects a growing awareness of the importance of the relationship between conservation and sustainability, as mentioned previously. Donovan Rypkema suggests that "if we go back to the graphic representation of sustainable development . . . heritage conservation is, in fact, the only strategy that is simultaneously environmental responsibility, economic responsibility and social/cultural responsibility."[15] The consequence of this is the expansion of the curriculum, as conservation becomes a more complex and multidisciplinary subject. Various research studies in the United Kingdom have explored this, including:

- The study *Towards More Sustainable Places* undertaken by the University of Aberdeen and Kelvin Murray Associates for the RICS (Royal Institution of Chartered Surveyors) Foundation that addresses, inter alia, urban regeneration skills[16]

- A chapter in the edited volume *Education and the Heritage Environment* by Peter Lassey that, although it deals primarily with archaeology, provides an exploration of issues that are relevant to vocational training in the heritage sector generally[17]

- The report entitled *Higher Education, Professionalism and Skills in the Built Environment: The Impact of the New Urban Agenda on Teaching and Learning* published by the Centre for Education in the Built Environment (CEBE) at Cardiff University[18]

- Research sponsored by the Attingham Trust on the intellectual and practical education potential of historic properties and sites, published under the title *Opening Doors: Learning in the Historic Environment*[19]

- The Egan Review of Skills for Sustainable Communities, commissioned by the, then, U.K. government, particularly the chapter that concerns itself with "The Right Skills for the Job"[20]

Although the scope of some of these is more extensive than the specific teaching and learning agenda for heritage education, many of the issues raised further the understanding of the processes of heritage conservation in terms of their relationship to urban renewal and regeneration and the development of sustainable communities. As such they provide a range of relevant and valuable insights to help in understanding this agenda. This includes evidence of a shortage of both students and subsequently qualified practitioners in heritage conservation and several other allied disciplines. Additionally, historically there has been lack of provision of the means to enable the (usually highly detailed and technical) professional toolkit to be used in enabling the gap to be crossed between vision and reality—that is, in developing competence.

The work undertaken by Sir John Egan and his colleagues of behalf of the, then, U.K. government to review the skills required to secure the creation of sustainable communities argues for the development of certain competencies that transcend discipline-centered knowledge and understanding. These may sometimes get referred to as "soft" or generic skills, but they are anything but soft in terms of their complexity and importance and in developing ability to do the job—to facilitate the crossing between vision and reality. Indeed, they may not be teachable in the conventional sense. Competence and aptitude are likely to be developed through experience—which highlights the familiar catch-22 situation that such experience is difficult to acquire without already having the skills.

Egan put forward a menu of sought-after generic skills required to enable:

- Inclusive visioning
- Project management
- Leadership
- Breakthrough thinking/brokerage
- Team/partnership working

- Making it happen given constraints
- Process management/change management

It might be argued that the use of this heritage "management-speak" terminology risks obscuring the essence of the message—that practitioners with good discipline-specific knowledge and understanding also need expertise in a range of strategic and operational implementation tools. This includes the ability to work with the other professionals and agencies that may be involved in the design and implementation of heritage conservation projects, and with the individuals and communities whose lives are affected by these proposals.

The question inevitably is how best to accommodate this subject matter within the timeframe of a typical program of study without discarding important content. For those involved in education and training, however, the very concept of "a typical program of study" is being challenged by a combination of economic, professional, and technological forces that are having an impact on the cost, pace, and mode of study. These are as significant as the forces for change that are influencing the scope and content of the subject material with which we are concerned about in this volume. As mentioned previously, throughout its ninety-three-year existence the College of Estate Management has always provided a significant proportion of its academic offerings by means of distance learning—entirely so for the last forty years. Thus, for CEM a particular challenge in addition to seeking to establish the right balance of content (e.g., between core and elective modules) is how to enhance delivery of the outcome within a dedicated distance-learning environment within which capabilities for e-learning have been steadily developed over the last decade.

This is a challenge that is being faced by a growing proportion of predominantly campus-based universities and colleges. The concept is, of course, not new, either within the United Kingdom or internationally, particularly at the postgraduate level. It is where distance learning might take us, however, that is the interesting area to explore. Bill Gates suggested at a conference in 2010 that what he called "place-based" institutions could become less important over the following five years due to the rise of online options.[21] Since then, Massachusetts Institute of Technology (MIT) and Harvard University have formed an alliance to deliver courses online (edX, building on MIT's earlier MITX initiative), as has Stanford University in setting up the Coursera online platform, with input so far from university partners in the United States, Canada, the United Kingdom, Israel, and Hong Kong.[22] In the United Kingdom the changing landscape for higher education, including the consequences of the U.K. government's whitepaper "Higher Education: Students at the Heart of the System," is prompting closer exploration of alternatives to the classroom-based model of delivery.[23]

The College of Estate Management's own New Academic Offer (NAO) project is allowing the college to significantly redesign its suite of courses to incorporate greater web-based content aimed at a more international student population, which currently represents around 40 percent of the approximately 3,500 students whom the college has actively pursuing courses. Emerging technologies allow the upgrading of study materials and learning activities and the securing of interaction between tutors and students through the Moodle and Blackboard Collaborate platforms (tools used by colleagues in many other U.K. institutions, although other platforms may be adopted elsewhere). As far as the curriculum of the postgraduate program in conservation of the historic environment is concerned, the changing scope of the subject area, referred to previously, is being addressed through the provision of elective modules in the second year of study. A further solution may be to leave significant exploration and reflection relating to the heritage management topics to a second phase of postgraduate/post-qualification study—for example, as a specialist pathway within the college's construction and real estate-focused MBA program.

This is very much a hands-on discipline, however, and some skills can only be shown by site visits and craft demonstrations. Indeed, it is questionable whether a true conservation program can exist without these opportunities. Online demonstrations and guided tours may be technologically impressive, but they cannot easily replicate the experiential aspects of learning. What these can do, however, is to provide a more inclusive approach to these aspects of a program for students who may not be able to attend in person—either in real time or on demand online.

The college's solution is a more blended learning approach. Joanna Poon has concluded from her research that "the general consensus is that blended learning is a combination of face-to-face experiences . . . and online learning experiences."[24] At the college this incorporates elements from a toolkit of teaching and learning components—a schedule of site visits alongside online delivery and periodic face-to-face classroom tuition. Issues of assessment remain; online assessment opportunities (e.g., automated marking of tests) have increasing use for formative assessment, but their acceptance by the academic and professional communities to support summative assessment presently remains open to resolution on grounds of rigor and security.

This may be only a staging post. If Bill Gates's anticipated future for place-based universities and colleges is a rational prediction, the place of distance-learning education in the field of heritage conservation may assume greater significance. If the likes of MIT and Harvard University, and Stanford University, Brown University, University College London, University of Edinburgh, and University of British Columbia are already prepared to collaborate, others inevitably will follow. So far, this collaboration in what have been termed MOOCs (mass open online courses) is not geared predominantly to formal academic or professional qualifications (other than certificated completion), but circumstances are likely to change as momentum for providing credit-bearing programs increases.[25] During 2012 it was announced that Pearson, the world's largest specialist education company, through its subsidiary VUE, would be making its network of 450 test centers in 110 countries (and a means of authenticating the identity of candidates) available to edX. This will build formal invigilation and credibility into the assessment process. VUE has already contracted to offer similar facilities to learners following courses available through the privately run Udacity platform. While the courses themselves currently remain freely available, however, a charge will be levied to those learners wishing to use this facility.[26]

Present funding challenges and changing patterns of demand in college and university education make expansion into blended and distance learning an attractive option, but provision of high quality in learning materials and mechanisms for delivery do not come cheaply (and it follows that if such cost is to be recouped, free access to non-credit-bearing study may give way to paid-for access to credit-bearing courses). Equally, higher education institutions with a stake in this field of study are unlikely to be able to provide modules devoted to every possible aspect of a changing curriculum. Thus, since we are imagining conservation education as it might evolve during the twenty-first century, the possibility emerges of a "mini-MOOC"—a discipline-specific, international collective of colleges and universities offering shared access to modules in which there may be individual institutional specialism and/or mode of delivery. Issues of quality assurance, cost and credit accumulation, and transfer (plus inevitable, but hopefully diminishing, skepticism on the part of academic and professional institutions) remain to be resolved, as well as how to design and agree on the most appropriate means of tracking and managing a body of students who may pursue their program through several different modes of study and across more than a single continent. Despite these operational challenges, however, the opportunities that such an arrangement would afford would be attractive to (what we suspect will be) a primarily graduate body of students looking to marry both their existing academic background with a new set of knowledge and skills and work experience with study, "earning while they are learning."

In summary, conservation has evolved from being an essentially fabric-based repair discipline to a much wider study of the impact of change on the historic environment, which itself is seen as more holistic and all-embracing. This does not diminish the role of traditional conservation and repair, but sets it in a bigger context of understanding, valuing, and managing heritage. Delivering courses by distance learning may become mainstream as higher education responds to a different funding climate and new technologies develop. The challenge for the future is how to utilize the potential of distance learning and the blended learning toolkit, while retaining the appropriate intellectual and practical characteristics of heritage conservation; and at the same time in catering to a more internationally and culturally diverse student body with a broader range of career backgrounds and aspirations.

Notes

1. College of Estate Management, *Our History* (Reading, UK: College of Estate Management), http://www.cem.ac.uk/aboutus/ourhistory.aspx (accessed 23 June 2012).

2. International Council on Monuments and Sites, *International Charter for the Conservation and Restoration of Monuments and Sites: The Venice Charter* (Paris: ICOMOS, 1964).

3. ICOMOS, *Education and Training Guidelines* (Paris: ICOMOS, 1993).

4. SAVE Britain's Heritage, *Pathfinder's Shameful Legacy Exposed in Devastating New SAVE Report* (2011), http://www.savebritainsheritage.org/news/campaign.php?id=193 (accessed 17 August 2012).

5. English Heritage, *Power of Place* (London: English Heritage, 2000), http://www.english-heritage.org.uk/publications/power-of-place/ (accessed 13 March 2012).

6. English Heritage, *Heritage Counts 2003* (London: English Heritage, 2003), 2, http://www.helm.org.uk/upload/pdf/Heritage%20Counts%20summary.pdf?1347876182 (accessed 20 September 2012).

7. See Iorwerth C. Peate, *The Welsh House* (Liverpool: Brython Press, 1944); Cyril Fox and Lord Raglan, *Monmouthshire Houses* (Cardiff: National Museum of Wales 1951–54); and Raymond Wood Jones, *Traditional Domestic Architecture in the Banbury Region* (Manchester: Manchester University Press, 1963).

8. English Heritage, *The Heritage of Suburbs* (London: English Heritage, 2007), http://www.helm.org.uk/server/show/nav.19602 (accessed 20 September 2012).

9. Gemma Abercrombie, "Editorial: Repositories of Memory," *Conservation Bulletin 68* (London: English Heritage, 2012), 2.

10. Department for Communities and Local Government, *National Planning Policy Framework* (London: DCLG, 2012).

11. ICOMOS, *Operational Guidelines for the Implementation of the World Heritage Convention* (Paris: ICOMOS, 2012), 14–15.

12. Department for Energy and Climate Change, *Green Deal and Older Property Workshops,* http://www.decc.gov.uk/en/content/cms/tackling/green_deal/gd_stakeholder/olderbuildings/olderbuildings.aspx (accessed 14 August 2012).

13. Australia ICOMOS, *Charter for the Conservation of Places of Cultural Significance (Burra Charter)* (Burwood, Australia: Australia ICOMOS, 1979 and later eds.). See also English Heritage, *Power of Place.*

14. ICOMOS, *Education and Training Guidelines.*

15. Donovan Rypkema, "Heritage Conservation as Sustainable Economic Development," paper to colloquium to launch *Heritage and Beyond* relating to the contribution of the Faro Convention, Lisbon, Portugal, 20 November 2009, http://www.coe.int/t/dg4/cultureheritage/heritage/identities/SpeechesLisbon/LisbonpresentationRypkema_EN.pdf (accessed 29 September 2012).

16. University of Aberdeen / Kelvin Murray Associates, *Towards More Sustainable Places* (London: RICS Foundation, 2004).

17. Peter Lassey, "Vocational Training in Archaeology," in *Education and the Historic Environment,* ed. Don Henson, Peter Stone, and Mike Corbishley (London: Routledge, 2004), 101–9.

18. Sarah McIntosh and Nick Bailey, "Higher Education," in *Professionalism and Skills in the Built Environment: The Impact of the New Urban Agenda on Teaching and Learning* (Cardiff: The Centre for Education in the Built Environment, 2004).

19. Giles Waterfield (ed.), *Opening Doors, Learning in the Built Environment* (Hampton, UK: The Attingham Trust, 2004).

20. Office of the Deputy Prime Minister, *Skills for Sustainable Communities* (The Egan Review) (London: ODPM, 2004).

21. Jeffry R. Young, "A Conversation with Bill Gates about the Future of Higher Education," *The Chronicle of Higher Education,* 25 June 2012, http://chronicle.com/article/A-Conversation-With-Bill-Gates/132591/ (accessed 28 June 2012).

22. Sean Coughlan, "Top US Universities Put their Reputations Online," *BBC Business News,* http://www.bbc.co.uk/news/business-18191589 (accessed 27 June 2012); and Sean Coughlan, "London Joins US-based Online University Coursera," *BBC Education & Family News,* http://www.bbc.co.uk/news/education-19647938 (accessed 19 September 2012).

23. Department for Business, Innovation, and Skills, *Higher Education: Students at the Heart of the System* (London: DBIS, 2011).

24. Joanna Poon, "Use of Blended Learning to Enhance the Student Learning Experience and Engagement in Property Education," *Property Management,* 30:2 (2012), 131.

25. Mike Sharples et al., *Innovating Pedagogy* (Milton Keynes, UK: The Open University, 2012), 19–20; and Bonnie Stewart, "Is MOOC More than Just a Buzzword?" *The Guardian Higher Education Network,* http://www.guardian.co.uk/higher-education-network/higher-education-network-blog/2012/sep/13/mooc-buzzword-meaning-higher-education (accessed 17 September 2012).

26. Sean Coughlan, "Harvard and MIT Online Courses Get 'Real World' Exams," *BBC Education & Family News,* http://www.bbc.co.uk/news/education-19505776 (accessed 19 September 2012); and Sharples et al., *Innovating Pedagogy,* 19.

11 Public History, Adult Students, and the Community: Moving Beyond the Distance-Education Classroom

Anastasia L. Pratt

According to David Vanderstel's 2003 essay for the *Public History Review*, public historians are "those [trained in but] engaged in work outside the halls of the academy and those within the academy who prepare students for careers in government agencies, museums, libraries, historic preservation, and in private business enterprises."[1] Though a conservative definition, this explanation of the field shows that scholars must actively engage with museums, archives, and community groups. Thus, public history programs regularly ask students to go out into the community. In colleges with brick and mortar campuses, that pursuit is relatively easy to manage. When the study of public history involves adult students working a distance through an online or hybrid platform, however, the need to look outward becomes more important, even as it simultaneously becomes more complicated. Whereas students attending traditional institutions can go out into the same communities as their instructors—even *with* their instructors—adult students working at a distance must look to their own communities, oftentimes hundreds of miles away from the instructor's location. Yet, work within the community remains essential: how can the tenets of public history be fully explored if students only look to an online classroom, with its members only known as virtual entities? How can students come to practice public history fully and effectively if they have only encountered online instructors and digital resources?

SUNY (State University of New York) Empire State College's Advanced Certificate in Public History, a program that is unique among graduate-level public history programs because it is entirely online, seeks to answer this dilemma by sending its graduate students in public history out into their own communities, regardless of their geographic location and proximity to the course instructors. In so doing, the program asks its students to learn more about the role of history in local and regional settings, to probe the boundaries of public history as a discipline and as a practice.

That focus requires that a set of predetermined criteria be in place. First, students must work within the boundaries of accepted theory and methodology, explored and explained within the structure of the courses. Second, course instructors must establish the appropriate support for the experiences that occur outside of the online classroom. Last, instructors must work to understand the host institutions, their staffs, and the learning opportunities they can provide for students. When those criteria are in place, students benefit greatly from the opportunity to work with museums, archives, historical societies, and other public historians within their own communities.

This movement toward using the community as a learning space is supported by recent trends in distance and open learning. In fact, it recalls Ross A. Perkins's explanation that "the primary goals of open universities, unlike their brick and mortar counterparts, have been and continue to be focused on providing educational opportunities to all, no matter their background, and doing so in a way that overcomes limitations of time and space."[2] On a practical level, the integration of online classrooms and community involvement requires the creation of supports throughout the program. Empire State College, characterized by its mission and its public history program, offers a chance to explore those real-life meanings as one public history program within the larger contexts of other public history and preservation programs and a program within the different contexts of distance learning and open education. This chapter explores the intersections of college and community, showing the manner in which the community as classroom fits within current public history and preservation pedagogy.

SUNY Empire State College—A Brief History

Established in 1971 to serve nontraditional students, Empire State College has long been committed to the idea that learning happens throughout one's life, in and out of the classroom. As a faculty member at Empire State College, I have a special love for that commitment to lifelong learning, in all its forms. The School for Graduate Studies, which is the home of the Advanced Certificate in Public History, is selective, with a significantly lower acceptance rate than that of the undergraduate program, which accepts more than 98 percent of applicants to the college. The advanced certificates, however, require only a completed application (with a fee) and documentation of the completion of a bachelor's degree.[3] Thus the public history program was designed to be more accessible, more open, than many other, similar programs.

The college's definitions support that openness. Empire State College's mission statement, which was revised in 2010, just in advance of its fortieth anniversary, is clear: "SUNY Empire State College's dedicated faculty and staff use innovative, alternative and flexible approaches to higher education that transform people and communities by providing rigorous programs that connect individuals' unique and diverse lives to their personal learning goals." The college's commitments, revised and reaffirmed at the same time, also support that mission, affirming, among other things, "a collaborative mentoring environment."[4]

These guiding principles infuse Empire State with a determination to offer innovative, adaptive, and collaborative learning opportunities. Accepting a general definition of open education as accessible, student-centered, and community-based, faculty at Empire State college strive to create learning experiences and to define learning objectives that require students to use resources within their own communities to become knowledgeable and skilled in the field of public history, even while pushing for rigorous standards, proposing a 15-credit certificate program instead of the usual 12-credit sequence of courses for a certificate.

A History of the Certificate Program

In a practical sense, the certificate was designed to offer the strongest open education possibilities for the target audience. Many of the groups on whom attention was focused were already drawn to Empire State College's Master of Arts in Liberal Studies (MALS) program, the specific home of the Advanced Certificate in Public History. The certificate is designed so that it may form a disciplinary specialty within an MALS, should a student wish to continue on to a degree. Public history institutional employees who occupy professional and semiprofessional positions and who look to certificate programs and a MALS degree to advance in their organizations were among this intended audience. Middle and high school social studies teachers looking for content-based degrees instead of master of teaching degrees form another of these natural constituencies. For these teachers, public history offers strong possibilities for classroom experiences and curriculum design. Similarly, community college instructors without master's degrees can engage in this program as a means of earning the credentials necessary for their continued employment.

Informed by work in various communities, we further wanted to offer opportunities for museum docents who want to learn more about public history so that they can engage in a more sophisticated way in the work of the places to which they are already devoted. Staff members of nonprofit organizations and local unions also fell into this intended target audience, as their work often requires the preservation and archiving of records for use in internal and external education campaigns.

More specifically, we sought to focus on the members of the Association of Public Historians of New York State (APHNYS). Since 1914, the state of New York has required all municipalities to have an official historian. APHNYS works with the 1,600 municipal historians in New York, and seeks ways to credential its members, many of whom come to their positions from beyond the world of formal or academic history. Although it does sponsor conferences and meetings, APHNYS does not offer formal educational programs. This means that many New York municipal historians are in need of more formal training in the theories and methodologies of public history.

Finally, we expected to attract students from other professional organizations similarly focused on public history. Among these the Museum Association of New York State (MANY), the Upstate History Alliance, the American Association of Museums, the Society of American Archivists, the New England Museum Association, the Mid-Atlantic Museum Association, the American Association for State and Local Historians, the National Council on Public History (NCPH), and the Oral History Association were especially significant. Not only do these groups have active members throughout New York State, but they also regularly point to a need for continuing education. With this certificate, we could provide a place for that continued education, online and within the various regional locations of the students.[5] Importantly, the program expects students to begin with much of the historic knowledge taught within more traditional programs. Rather than requiring content, reading, and seminar courses, which are the norm in most master of public history programs, Empire State College's certificate strives to begin where the students are and to help them capitalize on their local and regional knowledge.

Serving those students required us to look beyond traditional and nontraditional classrooms and to find educational opportunities within the students' own communities. Further, as much as possible, the Best Practices for Master of Arts Work in Public History developed by the NCPH should be adhered to.[6] The course descriptions included in our proposal attest to our primary goal, which is to get students into the community and to get community organizations involved in the education of our students. This led us to a certificate composed of five courses:

> Museums and Public History: Theory and Practices, a 3-credit, web-supported course designed to use historical and cultural

theory in the interdisciplinary examination of museums and their role in co-creating history and public memory with communities.

Archival Theory and Practice, a 3-credit, web-supported course developed to introduce students to the history, theories, and practices of archives and manuscript collections; included in this course are examinations and discussions of the public dimension of archives and their use in research, outreach programs, and historic editing and publishing.

Exhibition: Planning and Interpretation, a 3-credit, web-supported course that builds on the theory and practice learned in Museums and Public History and asks students to work within a history museum (or equivalent collection) to produce an exhibition.

Oral History: Theory and Methods, a 3-credit, web-supported course that introduces students to various theories, derived from a variety of academic disciplines, underlying the practice of oral history. Students read secondary sources, review primary sources, and identify subjects to interview, as well as learn to develop questions, learn the techniques of interviewing, transcribe interviews, and present an analytical interpretation of the interview.

Internship, a 3-credit internship, developed according to the recommendations of the NCPH: "Internships are an important part of public history education that allow students to gain new insights into the nature of public history practice by engaging in meaningful work under the mentorship of experienced and knowledgeable public history professionals. Successful internships provide students with work experience combined with structured opportunities to reflect on their activities and connect their practical experience with the skills and knowledge gained in their public history training."[7]

Now, two years into the program, we have served students from all of our intended audiences and have developed supportive experiences that bring public historians into virtual classrooms and face-to-face college events. These courses, which have undergone some slight revisions, and the other activities, represent our best practices as we strive to serve adult students in a distance-learning environment.

A Review of Public History and Preservation Programs

The requirements of SUNY Empire State College's Advanced Certificate in Public History are in line with those of most public history and historic preservation programs in the United States. The NCPH offers seven recommendations for best practices in public history certificates. Beginning with the notion that 15 credit hours is the minimum number necessary for an effective program, the recommendations call for programs to emphasize the significance of gaining a contextual and theoretical background for the study of public history; combine certificate training with a degree, to include an introductory course "where students learn the theoretical and methodological basis for their field of study"; offer skills-based courses including, but "not limited to: archival practices, museum and archive management, exhibit design, oral history, and museum methods"; gain hands-on experience; provide students "with access to professionals practicing in the field of public history, above and beyond the contacts they establish through internships"; and "use the resources that are available in the surrounding area to guide their program development."[8] Those guidelines refer to hands-on or skills-based learning no fewer than seven times, emphasizing the importance of moving beyond the classroom to engage fully in the pursuit of public history.

Most, if not all, public history and historic preservation graduate programs in the United States take the advice to heart. A survey of the public history programs listed by the NCPH and of the preservation programs catalogued by the National Council for Preservation Education (NCPE) illustrates the great value assigned to the application of theories and methods learned in the classroom. Virtually every public history and preservation program provides field and hands-on experiences as part of standard coursework and as part of an internship or practicum experience. Some programs, like that at Ball State University, explain, "Preservation students also learn outside the classroom, taking trips to significant historic communities and places, attending conferences, and participating in field study programs."[9] For other programs, like those of Boston University, the College of Charleston, and Eastern Michigan University, internships form a vital part of the educational process. Boston University describes both field experiences and internships as "critical" to the program,[10] while Delaware State University explains that "in addition to cultivating skills that translate directly to the workplace, students gain professional contacts via their internships, which may lead (directly or indirectly) to future employment."[11] Roger Williams University bridges the gap, with this mission statement:

> The program couples a multi-disciplinary approach with a rigorous core of field-based professional offerings. Students gain an understanding of the preservation field through coursework in preservation history and philosophy, documentation and research, architectural conservation, community planning, law and regulation, design and economics. Students are placed into practice through field-based workshops and an internship—all in partnership with regional, national and international organizations and firms.[12]

Internships are thus common among public history and preservation programs.

Many preservation and public history programs also point to their unique ability to provide fieldwork and internships because of their locations and their existing community collaborations. Columbia University explains that "the program's renowned faculty uses the architectural and historic riches of New York City as its laboratory, while encouraging study throughout the United States and the world,"[13] while the School of the Art Institute of Chicago asserts, "Chicago, a world center for modern architecture, provides the ideal environment for the program. The city is a living laboratory for the study of late-nineteenth- and twentieth-century architecture, urban design, landscapes, and interiors."[14] Tulane University, SUNY Albany, Ursuline College, the University of Minnesota, the joint College of Charleston/Clemson University program, the University of Southern California, and Auburn University are also among those who point to the unique geographic and regional attributes that allow them to work within a vital preservation and public history tradition.

Still other programs underscore the significance of community collaboration and service to public history and preservation education. The University of Vermont, for example, states, "The Historic Preservation Program offers students an intensive practical, community-oriented, professional experience. Strong emphasis is placed on community-based projects through linkages with local, state and federal groups, organizations, and agencies."[15] The University of Colorado at Denver lists a goal to "serve the community by promoting Historic Preservation as a means to build broad cross-cultural understanding. Be involved in local, national and international service and educational activities with stakeholders in academia, government and civil society."[16] These programs, like many others, point out the importance of tying public history and preservation programs to the communities in which they are housed. That work becomes increasingly difficult, of course, when a program is not housed in one geographic region. Goucher College addresses that dilemma through low residency requirements (two-week summer sessions on campus), while the Savannah College of Art and Design uses e-learning to reach students across the United States and beyond.[17]

Much like public history and preservation colleagues across the United States, the focus at SUNY Empire State College has decidedly been on the integration of students and community, through application of knowledge, fieldwork, and internships. Students visit, analyze, and work with local museums, historical societies, archives, and libraries. They complete oral history interviews of local people. They become part of their community's history. Within the public history program, then, is reaffirmed the idea that courses need to be accessible (in this case, upon payment of tuition), student-centered, and community-based. In so doing, we also reaffirm the relevance of distance and online learning as a means to provide that open education.

Collaborative Distance-Education Practices and Open Education

Distance education has a long history. Beginning with correspondence courses, the idea of "various forms of study at all levels which are not under the continuous, immediate supervision of tutors present with their students in lecture rooms or on the same premises, but which, nevertheless, benefit from the planning, guidance and tuition of a tutorial organization"[18] has taken root in American society and provided a plethora of distance technologies and online learning options. Those options, which include course management software used to supplement face-to-face coursework as well as information and communication technologies designed to create collaborative learning experiences for students at a distance from each other and from the instructor, have served to limit the barriers to continued education. That potential to reach "the needs of special clienteles that for a variety of reasons cannot attend a face-to-face gathering, a school or a conventional campus" is a distinctive characteristic of distance learning according to Sarah Guri-Rosenblit, professor of education at the Open University of Israel.[19]

To be successful, distance education requires students to interact both with content and with others (students and instructors) about the content.[20] Whether that interaction is asynchronous or occurs in real time, the purpose is the same: "the mutual engagement of learners in the learning process."[21] This collaboration echoes John Dewey's belief that effective learning requires a "shift from the memorization of a body of knowledge to a process of inquisition, knowing and understanding."[22] Instructors help to create that effective learning environment in several ways. One of these is the "organization of learning activities that enable the student to reach certain learning outcomes."[23] Independent learning can be buoyed through the creation of a study guide that establishes clear descriptions and directions, the use of traditional textbooks, the inclusion of online examples, and the assignment of "student tasks (projects, assignments) that constitute the learning experiences that the students will engage in, either independently or collaboratively, in order for them to master the objectives of the course."[24] Regular and timely feedback is necessary, as are various types of communication, including asynchronous and synchronous exchanges within the course space and e-mail messages or phone calls outside of that space.[25]

This ideal online classroom can include experiential and service learning activities. According to Mary Alice Ball, senior program officer at the Institute of Museum and Library Services, service learning is a collaborative venture, in which students contribute to the needs of a local organization while also being involved in a rich learning experience in which they can tie their service to learning objectives.[26] Like service learning, experiential learning moves away from classroom-based study to become "a process through which a learner constructs knowledge, skills, and value from direct experiences."[27] In both of these ideas, the adult student is the agent of his or her own education, a scholar in training. Within the realm of public history this is particularly true, as "community-based projects heighten student awareness of the local impact of broader historical events . . . [, increase] the opportunities for cooperative and experiential learning inside *and outside* the classroom . . . [, and] bring the community together."[28]

The idea of student as active agent of learning is essential to this vision of distance education. In part the creation of Ernest L. Boyer, an advocate for wider definitions of scholarship, Empire State College embraces the idea of placing "responsibility for learning on the student in return for his freedom to pursue his education according to his individual needs and interests."[29] The realm of distance education allows students to take on the role of scholar, as "the convergence of interest in technological innovation and the visibility of online pedagogical practices and materials can help educators to constitute communities where teaching is both a joint effort and a subject of collegial inquiry."[30]

This focus ties distance learning to open education. The Cape Town Open Education Declaration, on its Frequently Asked Questions page, asserts that open education, regardless of specific definition, expects "a greater focus on the learner as an arbiter of his or her educational needs and desires. In addition, the openness that is promoted necessarily leads to a need for more responsive and adaptive teaching tools in order to accommodate the diversity of learning styles and motivations, both in and out of formal educational contexts."[31] With increased access to online technologies, more adults are able to return to the classroom, regardless of their work schedules and hectic personal lives. That increased access helps to address inequalities related to class, gender, and race, as well as those created by limitations of time and space.[32]

Community Involvement—Planned Interactions for the Benefit of the College Community

At its heart this public history project is open. Issues of access for adult students who cannot physically attend college courses are addressed through the course offerings, which are organized so that students may become active learners in an online realm, and through collaborations with other students and with their instructors. We encourage further collaborations as well, operating in a service and/or experiential learning environment and invite local historians, archivists, librarians, teachers, and storytellers to join us in the academic world. Programs ranging from webinars to speaking engagements are a natural outgrowth of this interaction. So, too, are the exhibitions that public history students complete for and with local historical sites and the internship projects they develop as a capstone of their certificate program.

Over the past two years, those interactions have been quite varied. Speakers and panelists have visited our graduate studies residencies, held once each term for students enrolled in master's degree programs in liberal studies, labor policy, social policy, and business administration. Faculty members and students have visited local museums and archives and have presented and/or published in various scholarly venues. The college has made connections—both formal and informal—with wide-ranging organizations, working to expand open education resources and the ability to accredit various college-level learning opportunities. Making use of courses offered through museums, like the Metropolitan Museum of Art, as components of individualized learning contracts is one way that Empire State College has made these connections. Other, more personal connections are forged every time a student works with an archivist, curator, or museum professional. Public history faculty have networked with professionals in the field and worked to become better practitioners of public history. And, all the while, the college has tried to bring students along for the journey, introducing them to public historians in their locales, opening doors for their continued studies, and exposing them to the varied faces of public history. Through these activities are provided the support necessary to send students into their communities to experience how public history works.

To illustrate and model public history in action, public history faculty and students participate in a variety of activities. Though their forms differ, each is designed to showcase the interplay between community and college and between community and public history, modeling the work of public history for students near and far. In addition, since most of the physical interactions occur during residencies, the activities attempt to bring Empire State's students—who come to the residencies from all across New York State and, indeed, from all across the world—into the communities that host the college. They allow us to use the community as a classroom.

Presentations offer real-life advice and point out the many and varied ways that public historians interact with members of their communities. More to the point, presentations by faculty and professionals in the field demonstrate that public historians are part of their communities. Similarly, exhibits by various local museums and libraries offer a working model of how exhibitions can be tailored for specific purposes and of how exhibitions can be incorporated into events outside of the traditional realms of history and art museums.

Faculty members have also displayed various facets of public history. Through individual research and collaborative endeavors (including poster sessions and research projects), we have sought to model public history in action. As well, it is recognized that the virtual world in the pursuit of public history is important. Beyond encouraging students to explore the websites, web galleries, networking sites, and listservs used by museums and archives in their own regional locations, the public history program has created a website and blog, as well as a Twitter account to feed that website and profiles on the college's internal social networking site, "The Alumni Community." Our virtual presence serves to highlight community connections and to offer steady reminders of the theories and methods of the academic discipline that is public history.

All of these projects, though interesting and compelling in a broader public historical sense, have not served to let us be as open and innovative as we wish to become. As a result, public history faculty members are working on several other projects. Among these are webinars, which allow us to engage with public historians across New York State (and beyond) in a more systematic and regular way. In addition to providing a service to public historians, this series allows students to engage in the field and extend their learning beyond the virtual classroom.

Another project that is actively being worked on is the creation of a digital college archive that will preserve the materials currently in the college archives and make them available to a wider audience. In addition to serving various research purposes, the creation of a digital archive would allow some students in the Archival Theory and Practice course to work on every step of the archiving process, from collecting and organizing hard materials to scanning, indexing, and evaluating the digital quality of those materials, to maintaining the physical and digital documents and website access after digitization.

Community as Classroom

All of these opportunities help to engage students in the world of public history. They offer a glimpse behind the scenes of work that is undertaken around the world, in libraries and museums, in archives and historical societies. The reality, however, is that not all students attend residencies, and not all can participate in public history projects centered around Saratoga, where Empire State College's main offices are located. Work and family commitments often compete even with virtual and online experiences, with students finding that they are unable to participate in events designed to occur across New York State. With those difficulties and conflicting demands, then, how can this public history program provide learning opportunities, through practical fieldwork, for those students, understanding the realities of the life of a working adult student?

Our solution has been to encourage students to work with museums, archives, and historical societies in their own communities. Students are asked to find learning opportunities, to schedule their own interactions, and to commit to local projects and activities. Building on Carl Rogers's idea that "we cannot teach another person directly; we can only facilitate his learning,"[33] our required courses build learning opportunities that entail finding local public historians and doing the work of public history within local communities. We do not stop with that community action, though. While students are exploring public history resources in their own communities, they are simultaneously reading, discussing, and engaging with texts that explore the theoretical and methodological underpinnings of the academic discipline of public history. Through successful completion of the certificate courses, students are actively tying together didactic and theoretical work in the discipline with practical experience in public institutions.

In the Archival Practice and Theory course, for example, students are asked to visit and analyze several archives within their communities. Ranging from traditional document repositories housed in libraries and historical societies to archives attached to specific museums and their collections, these local archives serve as vivid examples of the theoretical works covered in the class. Assigned readings address various theoretical and methodological issues and are tied to required online discussions. Although each discussion forum contains specific questions (for an introductory unit these include "What is a document?" and "What are archives?"), students are encouraged to branch out, to pose and answer questions of their own, to probe the readings.

Students also create an individual but identifiable frame of reference for their discussions by visiting and describing two local archives. A later assignment asks them to describe two local museums and their archival holdings. In both cases, once they have completed the initial visits and descriptions, students are required to critically evaluate the manner in which the repositories treat finding aids, the tools offered for determining holdings, the manner in which the values of the records are described, and other relevant aspects of the archives. Thus the students are able to make use of a local resource to understand the theoretical work of the course.[34]

Recently, students have visited a wide variety of archives, some very small and narrowly focused and others large and seemingly all-encompassing. Included among these archives are the Putnam County Historian's Office in Brewster, New York, and the Westchester County Archives in Elmsford, New York. These archives, relatively close to each other geographically, represent opposite extremes of the archival spectrum. Putnam County is small, with a population of just under 100,000, yet its Historian's Office is staffed by a historian, a deputy historian, three research/clerical assistants, and an archivist, as well as several volunteers.[35] Conversely, Westchester County, with its population of more than 950,000, contracts with the Westchester Historical Society to maintain its archives and provide research support.[36]

Students have also made use of our existing, informal partnerships by visiting the archives at The Center for Folklife, History and Cultural Programs at Crandall Public Library in Glens Falls and the Brookside Museum in Ballston Spa. Other students have used their local resources, visiting Cortland's Living History Center, Saranac Lake's Adirondack Research Center, and Manhattan's Theater on Film and Tape archive (part of the New York Public Library's archival collection). It seems clear, then, that the course assignments allow students the variety and flexibility that they need, while holding them accountable for understanding the theories and practices of archives.

Similarly, in Exhibition: Planning and Interpretation, students are asked to step into their communities to contextualize and complete the work of the course. This third course in the certificate sequence requires students to plan and mount an exhibition. Coursework, including assigned readings, lays the groundwork for that pursuit. Students are asked to identify five history museums or collections within their communities and then to write short descriptions of each, taking care to respond to each museum's mission, collection, and directorship, as well as one exhibition currently on view. Following this introduction to local museums, students write a formal proposal requesting the opportunity to work within one of the history museums or to create a virtual exhibit for Empire State College that explores a facet of public history. By dividing these steps into this sequence, the course instructor has a chance to verify that the selected museums will fit the student's needs and that the student will be more actively involved in the exhibition process than as an unpaid laborer. The final assignment for the course is a portfolio, detailing the student's experience at the museum and analyzing the effectiveness of a particular exhibition. Students are asked to include each of the following elements within this portfolio:

- A description of the exhibition on which the student worked, including the museum's holdings used in the exhibition and the objects and images that needed to be acquired
- The plan for the exhibition, including the timeline for action, the overarching theme, a list of necessary materials, and a budget for the project
- An annotated bibliography of sources for the exhibit, including both primary and secondary sources
- A map of the exhibition, including any changes made over time and also including views of the exhibition as it fits within the larger space of the museum and of individual portions of the displays within the exhibition itself
- Descriptions of each artifact and image displayed in the exhibition, including the historic value of the artifact/image, the local value of the artifact/image, and the value of the artifact/image within the exhibition
- The text for labels and signs used within the exhibition
- A training guide for docents who will work within the exhibition OR an information sheet/guide to the exhibition for museum visitors

- A journal (written and photographic) of the installation process
- A brief analysis of the effectiveness of the exhibition, including commentary on the educational value of the exhibition, the historic significance of the exhibition, and the effectiveness of the experience for the public historian (a description of what could be done differently in the future and a summary of visitor and museum staff responses to the exhibit is also required as part of this analysis)[37]

Again, this experience allows students the chance to put their theoretical and methodological learning immediately into practice. Although the lack of face-to-face contact between the instructor and the museums can be difficult, the process of helping students connect with local museums and public historians and the carefully specified sequence of events for proposing and working on an exhibition allow for a great deal of interaction between the instructor and students. More important, the process allows students to use their communities as their classrooms.

A sampling of the exhibitions on which students worked during the 2011–12 academic year showcases the variety of their interests and the geographic distance between their locations. One student completed a digital exhibition for the Adirondack Research Center entitled "Cure Cottages of Saranac Lake: Cottage Row 1897–1959." Another student, a member of the Actors' Equity Association, created an exhibit entitled "The Presidents of the Actors' Equity Association" for the Association's New York City office. A third student, unable to work with a local museum because of time and budget constraints, created an online exhibition "American Woman Suffrage: Dueling Images" for Empire State College.

Conclusion

In creating these community-learning experiences the Advanced Certificate in Public History and Empire State College hope to create richer, more vibrant learning experiences for students operating within a distance-learning system. Although the format is not always ideal, when the appropriate supporting structures are in place, using community museums, archives, historical societies, and public historians as resources has proven quite successful. As a result of our looking outward, students are able to put their learning to more immediate use, which helps them to cement their understanding of the academic discipline, its theories, and its methodologies.

For adult students working at a distance through e-learning technologies, these forays into the community offer a chance to fulfill the recommendations of both the NCPH and NCPE to apply the theories and methodologies of public history to hands-on projects. Although the geographic distance between students and instructors poses some issues, clear course objectives, respected reading materials, regular and timely feedback, and various forms of communications can help to overcome the difficulties of distance.

In looking to a variety of local communities for collaboration, the classroom is expanded from the virtual to the face-to-face. Whether through formal agreements with specific organizations or informal associations based on individual students' interests, public history courses can support the necessity of experiential and service learning. Furthermore, in bringing students to the community and members of the community to virtual classrooms and college activities, some of the barriers to continuing education can be removed, creating a more open institution.

While this model of public history education will not replace more traditional programs, it does help to establish the promise of distance learning for public history and preservation programs. A field that asks practitioners to collect, preserve, and disseminate information about the past to the general public demands a variety of educational modalities and methodologies. SUNY Empire State College's Advanced Certificate in Public History offers one such alternative to the traditional classroom-based model of education.

Notes

1. David Vanderstel, quoted in Paul Ashton, "Introduction: Going Public," *Public History Review*, 17 (2010), 2.

2. Ross A. Perkins, "A Walling Out of Open and Distance Learning," *Tech Trends* 55:2 (March/April 2011), 25.

3. "Graduate Admissions Policy," SUNY Empire State College, accessed 6 September 2012, http://www.esc.edu/policies/?search=cid%3D35553.

4. "College Mission," SUNY Empire State College, accessed 6 September 2012, http://www.esc.edu/about-esc/college-mission/.

5. Adele Anderson, Dan Katz, Anastasia Pratt, and Mark Soderstrom, "Abbreviated Proposal for Advanced (Graduate) Certificate, Proposed Certificate Title: Public History" (proposal presented at the SUNY Empire State College Senate meeting, Saratoga Springs, New York, 19 May 2010).

6. Prepared by that group's Curriculum and Training Committee in April 2008 and adopted by the board of directors in October 2008; "Best Practices for Public History Training," National Council on Public History, accessed 6 September 2012, http://ncph.org/cms/education/graduate-and-undergraduate/.

7. "Best Practices for Public History Training."

8. "Best Practices for Public History Training."

9. "Ball State University—Master of Science in Historic Preservation (MSHP)," Ball State University, accessed 10 December 2012, http://cms.bsu.edu/Academics/CollegesandDepartments/CAP/Programs/Architecture/Programs/Masters/MSHP.aspx.

10. "Preservation Studies Introduction," Boston University, accessed 10 December 2012, http://www.bu.edu/amnesp/ma/preservation-studies-introduction/.

11. "Historic Preservation M.A./D.S.U.," Delaware State University, accessed 10 December 2012, http://www.desu.edu/arts-humanities-and-social-sciences/historical-preservation-ma.

12. "Historic Preservation, Roger Williams University," Roger Williams University, accessed 10 December 2012, http://www.rwu.edu/academics/schools-colleges/saahp/degree-offerings/historic-preservation.

13. "Historic Preservation Mission," Columbia University, accessed 10 December 2012, http://www.arch.columbia.edu/programs/historic-preservation#historic–preservation/mission?_suid=13551541708480014869392783788015.

14. "SAIC—Master of Science in Historic Preservation—School of the Art Institute of Chicago," School of the Art Institute of Chicago, accessed 10 December 2012, http://www.saic.edu/academics/graduatedegrees/mshp/.

15. "Historic Preservation Program: University of Vermont," University of Vermont, accessed 10 December 2012, http://www.uvm.edu/histpres/.

16. "College of Architecture and Planning, University of Colorado at Denver," University of Colorado at Denver, accessed 10 December 2012, http://www.ucdenver.edu/academics/colleges/ArchitecturePlanning/ExplorerPrograms/masters/HistoricPreservation/Pages/default.aspx.

17. "Master of Arts in Historic Preservation: Goucher College," Goucher College, accessed 10 December 2012, http://www.goucher.edu/graduate-programs/ma-in-historic-preservation; "SCA > Programs > Historic Preservation > About," Savannah College of Arts and Design, accessed 10 December 2012, http://www.scad.edu/historic-preservation/index.cfm.

18. B. Holmberg, quoted in Jorge Larreamendy-Joerns and Gaea Leinhardt, "Going the Distance With Online Education," *Review of Educational Research,* 76:4 (Winter 2006), 568.

19. Sarah Guri-Rosenblit, "'Distance Education' and 'e-learning': Not the Same Thing," *Higher Education,* 45 (2005), 472.

20. For fuller discussions of this idea, see Pamela A. Havice and Catherine Y. Chang, "Fostering Community Through the Use of Technology in a Distributed Learning Environment," *College Student Affairs Journal,* 22:1 (Fall 2002), 74–82; Lisa A. Petrides, "Web-based Technologies for Distributed (or Distance) Learning: Creating Learning-Centered Educational Experiences in the Higher Education Classroom," *International Journal of Instructional Media,* 20:1 (2002), 69–77; Anna Espasa and Julia Meneses, "Analysing Feedback Processes in an Online Teaching and Learning Environment: An Exploratory Study," *Higher Education,* 59 (2010): 277–92; Sydney R. Castle and Chad J. McGuire, "An Analysis of Student Self-Assessment of Online, Blended, and Sustainable Education Delivery," *International Education Studies,* 3:3 (August 2010), 36–40; and Robert M. Bernard, Beatriz Rojo de Rubalcava, and Denise St-Pierre, "Collaborative Online Distance Learning: Issues for Future Practice and Research," *Distance Education,* 21:2 (2000), 260–77.

21. Bernard et al., "Collaborative Online Distance Learning," 262.

22. Tarah Sharon Alexandra Wright, "No More Pencils . . . No More Books? Arguing For the Use of Experiential Learning in Post Secondary Environmental Studies Classroom," *Electronic Green Journal,* 1:13 (2000), 2.

23. Alison Carr-Chellman and Philip Duchastel, "The Ideal Online Course," *Library Trends,* 50:1 (Summer 2001), 149.

24. Carr-Chellman and Duchastel, "The Ideal Online Course," 151.

25. Carr-Chellman and Duchastel, "The Ideal Online Course," 151–54.

26. Mary Alice Ball, "Practicums and Service Learning in LIS Education," *Journal of Education for Library and Information Science,* 49:1 (Winter 2008), 72–73.

27. Wright, "No More Pencils . . . ," 2.

28. A. Glenn Crothers, "'Bringing History to Life': Oral History, Community Research, and Multiple Levels of Learning," *The Journal of American History,* 88:4 (March 2002), 1447.

29. *Prospectus for a New University College: Objectives, Process, Structure, and Establishment* (1971), quoted in Richard F. Bonnabeau, *The Promise Continues: Empire State College: The First Twenty-Five Years* (Virginia Beach: The Donning Company, 1996), 19.

30. Larreamendy-Joerns and Leinhardt, "Going the Distance With Online Education," 568.

31. "The Cape Town Open Education Declaration," accessed 6 September 2012, http://www.capetowndeclaration.org/faq.

32. "A Radical Definition of Open Education," Graham Atwell, Bridge to Learning, accessed 6 September 2012, www.pontydysgu.org/2010/01/a-radical-definition-of-open-education.

33. Carl Rogers, quoted in Michael Peters, "The History and Emergent Paradigm of Open Education," in *Open Education and Education for Openness*, ed. Michael A. Peters and Ricardo G. Britez (Rotterdam, Netherlands: Sense Publishers, 2003), 3.

34. Anastasia Pratt, "Archival Practice and Theory," fall 2012 course, accessed 27 September 2012, https://esc.angellearning.com/section/default.asp?id=EMPU-8VDTEL.

35. "About Historian," accessed 27 September 2012, http://www.putnamcountyny.com/index.php/historian/about-us/.

36. "Community Historians," accessed 27 September 2012, http://www.westchesterhistory.com/index.php/historians/overview.

37. Anastasia Pratt, "Exhibition: Planning and Interpretation," fall 2012 course, accessed 27 September 2012, https://esc.angellearning.com/section/default.asp?id=EMPU-8VDTEN.

12 Documentation and Design in Association: Historic Preservation Design Using Social History, Advocacy, and Drawing in the Architecture Design Studio

Paul Hardin Kapp, Lauren Weiss Bricker, and Luis Hoyos

Historic preservation presents different challenges in the architecture design studio than other design studios that focus on theory, sustainability, and fabrication. Unlike faculty teaching within an autonomous historic preservation program, historic preservation faculty are embedded along with scholars and professional architects in a professional architecture school. The goal is simple: provide students with the basic educational foundation for the architecture profession. In the past, historic preservation has been viewed as a specialization or a secondary objective in architectural pedagogy; but as the shift from focusing on building new buildings to adapting existing ones gains momentum in the next decade, this attitude will change. This is clearly evident in the new *2009 NAAB Conditions for Accreditation.* In it, historic preservation in the architecture curriculum is clearly stipulated both in "Realm B: Integrated Building Practices, Technical Skills and Knowledge" and in "Realm C: Leadership and Practice." These Student Performance Criteria (SPCs) bring historic preservation not only at the technical level but also at the legal and community levels in architectural education. Programs will now be required to specifically address the built patrimony of communities and instill an ethic in the students' education foundation that respects the cultures of all peoples in a community.[1]

Pedagogy has been debated within historic preservation programs and at numerous conferences, both in the academy and in the profession, for the past thirty years; however, historic preservation pedagogy in architecture programs has not been debated at a similar level of intensity. Throughout the past decade, the American Institute of Architects (AIA) Historic Resources Committee sponsored a series of conferences, where they recommended the need for historic preservation content to be part of the architecture curriculum. Their advocacy is now reflected in the National Architectural Accrediting Board's (NAAB) revised Student Performance

Criteria, which now stipulate an understanding of historic resources by students. Although the need for historic preservation in architecture education has been addressed, very little has been discussed on how historic preservation should be taught in architecture programs. The three authors of this chapter (two of whom are in one institution and a third from a separate institution) have developed a three-step approach to teaching historic preservation in the design studio. This approach builds on fundamentals commonly used in historic preservation programs but is often unique in architecture programs. The authors propose pedagogy that implements social and oral history, preservation advocacy and ethics, and accurate building documentation to teach historic preservation in the architecture design studio. By implementing historical research, preservation ethics through advocacy, and a rigorous approach to graphical representation, a new and more structured approach to historic preservation in the design studio is presented as a model for implementing historic preservation in architecture programs. This chapter presents each facet of this pedagogical approach in the same manner that the content should be presented in the studio. Case studies of specific projects in the authors' design studio will be used to illustrate how this design approach has worked and where it could be improved. With this approach, two common themes emerge in a historic preservation design studio—the students work with real sites and buildings, and students work with people who are real clients. The authors' concluding remarks address the new paradigm in both architecture education and historic preservation education: as society reuses more of its built patrimony, architecture and historic preservation will become a more collaborative enterprise that will require professional architects well versed in historical research, advocacy, and accurate graphical representation.

Using Social and Oral History as a Design Tool in the Design Curriculum

Courses on architectural history and documentation techniques are standard fare in historic preservation programs. Classes in both areas must be offered for preservation programs to qualify for membership in the National Council for Preservation Education (NCPE).[2] As noted in the Standards, the "objective of such instruction will vary in response to the goals of the individual program and may extend from awareness of the issues in a particular topic, through understanding, to the development of expertise." When the academic context is architectural, how does that affect the ways history and documentation are taught? Conversely, how might knowledge of these subjects impact the development of young designers? Might there be broader implications for the field of historic preservation historic if preservation practices became standard within architectural education?

Architectural history has been something of an ideological football in American architectural education. At one extreme, under the influence of France's École des Beaux-Arts, dependence on precedent defined much of the curriculum—only to be superseded by Walter Gropius and followers who sought to expunge history from the curriculum in the name of pure design.[3] Current attitudes seem to be swinging somewhere between these poles. Postmodern *theory*—especially its espousal of context and human scale in architecture and urban design certainly—has been influential on current attitudes to history; however, the specter of postmodern *design* lurks behind the cautionary attitude toward making history too explicit in the design process if the 2009 NAAB conditions for accreditation is any indicator. NAAB provides that "the student must have an *ability* [NAAB's higher standard] to examine and comprehend the fundamental principles present in relevant precedents and to make choices regarding the incorporation of such principles into architecture and urban design projects,[4] and they must have an *understanding* [a lower level of comprehension] of parallel and divergent canons and traditions in architecture."[5] So how does the instructor bridge this seeming artificial divide between the role of history in architectural practice and historic preservation in architectural education? One response is to ignore it. At Cal Poly Pomona, the introduction to the theory and practice of historic preservation is called Architecture and Historic Preservation. A central premise of the course is that there is a long and deep connection between architecture and historic preservation and that the preservation of historic buildings has been and continues to be an important aspect of the architecture profession.

At Cal Poly Pomona, the preservation theory and practice course includes a "real project." This is selected based on several criteria: (1) learning outcomes—it presents an opportunity for students to learn basic preservation skills—field survey methodology, assessment of historic value of resources usually based on the application of National Register of Historic Places criteria; (2) opportunity to work with a client—the client is usually a public agency; the selected project typically helps them meet their environmental compliance, and, occasionally, assists in future treatment of historic properties; (3) scale of project—its goals should be attainable within the context of a ten-week quarter.

Trading Community Services

At Cal Poly Pomona, Luis Hoyos and Lauren Weiss Bricker have been active participants in Southern California's "Garden Apartment Wars" waged since the early 2000s. The bucolic appearance of these sites, as well as their history as places designed to promote community, belies the effects of California's current highly charged real estate market, where efforts to preserve low-density housing set within an expansive landscape are grounds for unbridled legal challenges, and in one case ultimately destroyed a community.

The conditions are different with publicly owned garden apartment housing though no less critical. The Los Angeles County Housing Authority owns Harbor Hills and Carmelitos, among the most important examples of garden apartments in Southern California. The agency is faced with the difficult challenge of increasing the number of units in its properties to meet the needs of the 120,000-person waiting list—and in an economic climate with reduced support from the federal government. Initially, the goal for the preservation theory course term project was to have the students evaluate the properties for National Register eligibility. In exchange for access to the sites, the county staff requested that the students develop design solutions that would respect the historic architectural character of the sites and begin to meet their need for more units and alternative sources of financial support. Using a survey methodology that was grounded in the practices of cultural landscape, the students conducted field surveys. The size of each site—253 housing units on 69.14 acres at Harbor Hills and 500 units on 64.5 acres at Carmelitos—as well as the repetitive nature of the units led them to use a field method that focused on building types rather than to survey each building. These were assessed within the context of the site plans and landscape features (Figure 12.1).

There was a wealth of primary and secondary documentation on the two housing developments. The Housing Authority borrowed funds from the U.S. Housing Authority in 1938–40 to build the units. Because they were sited within the Los Angeles Harbor District, it was anticipated that they would house low-income harbor workers and their families; during World War II the units were converted to defense housing. An impressive roster of designers was involved with each project. The architect Clarence Stein, of Sunnyside Gardens and Radburn fame, whose design concepts were promulgated through the federal government's housing programs of the 1930s and 1940s, led the teams. Following the British garden city ethic, the extensively landscaped, low-density complexes were planned as environments conducive to community building. Located on a sloped

12.1 Camelitos, Long Beach, California. Photograph by the author (Bricker)

site divided into two parcels by a major road, Harbor Hills was planned as a series of cul-de-sacs; the narrow units had dual access from the paved parking lots and grassy pedestrian walkways. The site plan is a modification of Stein's earlier concept of the superblock, and the notion of separation of pedestrian and vehicular traffic certainly informs the design. The buildings were constructed to last: reinforced brick walls sheathed with cement plaster and a reinforced concrete slab roof.

Carmelitos has a large "V" or chevron plan sited on a flat plane. Two major streets run through the development with units grouped around parking lots. Emphasis was placed on the connection between the lots and units; kitchens were placed at the rear of the units so that children playing in the semiprivate spaces at the rear of the units or in the parking lots could be observed. Wide lawns stretched between the more formal "front" facades. Again, the units were built to last: monolithic 6″ reinforced concrete slab walls and reinforced concrete roof framing with timber trusses.

In order to better understand the sense of community within each development, and assess where there might be some flexibility in the new units, the students conducted interviews with long-term residents in each complex. These proved to be extremely informative. The students were organized into teams according to each development. The Carmelitos team presented the most thorough analysis of the site, in part because they were also in Luis Hoyos's studio that quarter and had learned strategies about how to craft realistic options for garden apartments. The students studied the pattern of development in Carmelitos and developed three major approaches: (1) create a historic district that followed the boundaries of the original development, but treat the southwest corner as a noncontributing area: (2) develop new housing blocks following the cul-de-sac pattern used elsewhere on the site: and (3) create a vertical farm in the southwest corner replacing the current community garden and build commercial units along the perimeter street. A review was held at the end of the term with county staff members, preservation architects, and faculty members in attendance.

The students worked closely with the clients during the course of the quarter. In this way, they gained some knowledge of the associations architects must develop when working with existing sites. The students learned firsthand the impact of their work on government agencies and property owners. In the case of these public housing developments, the students hoped their projects would suggest strategies that would meet the current needs of the Los Angeles County Housing Authority. Whether these ideas ever get implemented, the projects may be a reminder for these future architects that historic preservation need not be antithetical to current requirements.

Introducing Advocacy for Historic Preservation in the Design Studio

Studios devoted to the training of architects in historic preservation tend to fall into two broad categories: one is the "let's give you technical skills" category that deals with the Secretary of the Interior's Standards for Rehabilitation, Historic American Building Survey (HABS), and perhaps training in materials conservation. These are good skills to have if you want to be a responsible practitioner in the field. The second category is a much more active type of studio, one that has the purpose of examining preservation advocacy through a current example. This approach is a worthwhile educational experience that enriches the studio and gives the student a sense of the real, possibly resulting in new recruits to the preservation movement. When city departments and historic preservation organizations are given an opportunity to partner with schools, this often results in a long-term relationship based on a shared experience. The demands on the faculty are considerable. One must gain the trust of public agencies, elected officials, local preservation groups, and, in rare instances, developers. Of these actors, the local preservation groups are by far the most important as they allow the studio to access the process of what happens behind closed doors. By acting in the public interest, preservation groups have the motivation and the legal wherewithal to engage in oppositional actions benefiting the retention of historic buildings and landscapes. These nonprofit groups welcome the participation of academics, as it is usually free of charge. Students are useful as they have time to try out ideas and at a conceptual level verify the feasibility of a certain project concept, physical layout, or design feature. Property owners obviously have different motivations in dealing with a historic resource than preservation groups. They acquire a building with the aim of implementing a project that returns a profit. Often, they undergo environmental review at the local level and naturally they have an interest in reducing the number of variables in the process. In short, they want certainty, so they are reluctant to engage in an open debate involving academics.

Issue: The Environment Where Advocacy Actions Take Place Is Intimidating

The Wyvern Wood Apartments in the Boyle Heights district of Los Angeles (1938, Wittmer and Watson, architects) is a nearly intact eight hundred-unit garden apartment project, one of the first and biggest. The project is conceptually and physically reminiscent of the Baldwin Hills Village (a.k.a. the "Village Green") as a large, shared park-like space with connected lesser open spaces that serve as settings for clustered housing groups. The property owners want to demolish the project and replace it with a much denser New Urbanist perimeter block solution. Design is at the center of the controversy, as the large central park space is credited with creating a generations-long series of associations by friendship, church, and marriage among the resident families. Put another way: the site plan was effective; the hundreds of families making up the resident population have formed a cohesive, integrated community. The proposed plan would chop up and constrain the green space to allow for the construction of a series of mid-rise and high-rise buildings that would quadruple the density from 15 dwellings per acre to 57. To implement the plan, all buildings would have to be demolished (Figure 12.2).

The Cal Poly Pomona design studio began with the pragmatic position of saving most of the project while allowing some new denser development. This created a hybrid preservation and urban studio. Students met with residents and the local preservation group. Intense discussion ensued centered on the rights of developers and the rights of residents in the context of privately held projects. What is the public good? How might a preservation group argue for listing a project over the objections of a property owner? The student teams had to discuss their preservation

12.2 Wyvern Wood, Los Angeles, California, (A) historic aerial view rendering, (B) existing units, (C) proposed site design, by Fariba Mostajer, Jennifer Guerra, and Sabrina Blackman, B.Arch Program, Cal Poly Pomona, Spring 2011, (D) proposed unit design, Letica Recinos, B.Arch Program, Cal-Poly Pomona, (E) project illustrative sketches by Fairba Mostajer, Jennifer Guerra, and Sabrina Blackman, B.Arch Program, Cal-Poly Pomona

plans that, while retaining more than half of the project in all cases, also proposed significant areas of demolition. As could be expected, heated, sincere, and direct exchanges with the residents occurred.

The Los Angeles Conservancy mounted a well-organized campaign to save the complex. Local residents were already organized and exerted considerable political pressure on elected officials to reject the project. Direct community pressure tactics included massive tenant attendance of community consultation meetings and digital and print media, among others. Inner-city advocacy cases often involve minority populations that have occupied historic areas undergoing rapid demographic change. This was an excellent chance to talk about the environmental review process and the political aspects of development. Under the California Environmental Quality Act (CEQA), the proponent must offer a range of development alternatives, including a no-project alternative. The assessment of the alternatives often lands both sides in court, delaying the project.

Students, working in teams, developed defensible positions as preservation designers even though the local community often did not agree with the plans and defended Wyvern Wood at a distinctly emotional level. Understandably, students were afraid of speaking their minds for fear of making a mistake, being acutely aware of the fact people's homes or jobs were on the line as an outcome of their designs. Providing a real-life project where the students witness the actual dynamics of opposing views, public hearings, the press, and local residents is an invaluable experience that enriches the studio, but it comes at a certain price. The final review was a pivotal moment as the stakeholders had hardened their positions. The developer wanted to implement the plan. The city councilman was now backing preservation in the face of mounting community opposition. The residents did not want to endorse any student plan that proposed even minimal demolition, a very extreme position.

The proposed site plans varied in approach and amount of retained original buildings. Most teams retained the signature Wyvern Wood greensward and placed new development at the edges. Some proposed modest insertions to be scattered among the historic courtyards. All of the student teams recognized the value of the shared open space and modified it only slightly if at all. It is fair to say all proposed plans were met with respect, but also with skepticism from a community that had dug in its heels and was not inclined to compromise. The public hearing, while severely underattended due to the possibility of a media presence, was seen as successful and sparked discussion at school for some days. The replacement project remains unbuilt and the environmental review process halted.

The inclusion of preservation advocacy in the studio is a worthwhile experience, which enables both faculty and students to encounter real-world situations where the positions must be argued in public, where the demands for research are heightened, and where the outcomes are design-based and tangible. The advocacy-oriented design studio may be in a position to alter the course of events and make a contribution to the preservation of a community. The service learning orientation is beneficial for the academic institution. Finally, preservation advocacy in the studio presents a career path worth exploring for certain students.

Incorporating HABS Standards and Documentation in the Design Studio

Unlike other design studios, historic preservation directly encounters the real, whether it is tangible or intangible. The tangible is the historic resource; it could be a historic building, a historic district, a landscape, or an object. As a tangible object, it has both attributes and deficiencies. These real aspects determine the historic resource and they must be accurately documented and understood by the student. The resource also has intangible aspects—its history—as well, which have been discussed earlier in this chapter. More often than not, both the tangible and intangible are threatened with development; in order to appreciate the significance of a historic resource and then advocate for its preservation, it is necessary to understand it through careful documentation. Along with historical research using social history, accurate graphical depiction of both the existing conditions and proposed design solution is necessary in teaching an effective historic preservation design studio.

Historic buildings provide an alternative to what has now become the predominant building design experience in architecture education: virtual design. What was once considered a primary objective in architecture schools—a computer workstation for every student—is now a reality. Today, entry-level graduate students are expected to be proficient in BIM (Building Information Modeling). BIM is not just a new computer-generated graphic tool; it is the database facet of an entirely new way of designing and building called integrated practice, which is the construction industry's response to the mandate for buildings to be completed faster and cost less to design and build. The premise behind BIM is a calibration between the "virtual" building and the built object. This idea is fairly straightforward in new building design but becomes more problematic in designing with an existing building, as is always the case in historic preservation.

Digital media also tends to engage design in a parametric form-based graphical manner. Shapes and forms, which were once considered arduous to depict or build, can now be done effortlessly. Moreover, with the use of digital tools such as Photoshop, students can assemble images in a collage-like manner that can depict a sense of reality to the casual observer. All of this has allowed today's architecture students to depict a dynamic reality for their design ideas. When one looks at these drawings in greater detail, however, discrepancies are always brought to the critic's attention, especially when depicting actual existing buildings. Unlike the digital world, where parabolic forms can seamlessly engage other forms, planes and masses in real buildings have distinct and separate surfaces. Planes abut each other and this often requires careful attention to design connections such as roof and parapet flashing. Structural systems in historic buildings also do not work in ways one might expect in a computer model. Reality sometimes defies logic, which is often the case in examining historic buildings. Factual and accurate documentation is required in order to fully understand the challenges in a historic building design problem.

At the graduate-level design faculty, graphics are not always prescribed. Not every instructor explicitly states that students present their solutions in plan, section, and elevation. In most architectural programs, the use of digital media has gradually evolved into an ad hoc way of presenting student work. Images generated through various BIM software programs are imported into Photoshop, where students then assemble a presentation in a poster-like manner. Often this entails a flashy three-dimensional rendering (known in the studio vernacular as the "the Money Shot"), large title graphics, and several diagrams. Floor plans and building sections drawings are often small and, sometimes, they are not plotted at any scale at all. Students tend to focus on the three-dimensional rendering, which during the design review or jury quickly becomes extraneous. From 2008 to 2011, the Historic Preservation Studio at the University of Illinois did not mandate graphical representation. It was the students' prerogative to use whatever digital platform they were comfortable using. In evaluating the final designs of a proposed project to adapt an abandoned Sheriff's Residence and Jail in Crown Point, Indiana, it was evident that graphics had become an impediment to the learning process. Students were not demonstrating an understanding in designing with historic buildings. More often than not, they were struggling with the development of their digital models and not on the architecture problem assigned to them. In order to focus on the preservation issues of the project, limits had to be set for using parametric media and graphic deliverables had to be specified at the outset of the project. The decisions for specifying literally what pen to use was based on the primary objective of the studio experience—a foundational understanding of how to design for a historic resource (Figure 12.3).

"You Can Have Any Color You Want as Long as It Is Black"

By paraphrasing Henry Ford ("any customer can have a car painted any color that he wants so long as it is black"), the Historic Preservation Studio at the University of Illinois departed from the normal graphical expectations in the school; the new graphic standard for the studio became black lines on white paper. Digital platforms, such as Revit and Rhino, were prohibited in the studio. Only AutoCAD could be used for producing measured drawings in the studio. Line weights and fonts that conformed to the HABS standards developed by the National Park Service

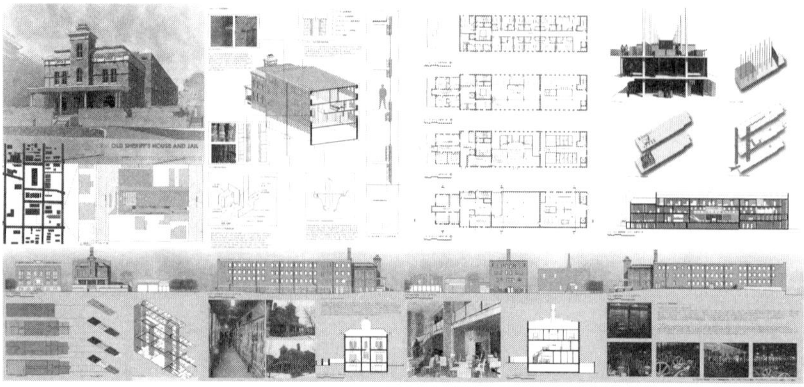

12.3 Proposed design for a new hotel in the Old Sherriff's Residence and Jail by Zach Helfer and Meghan Robertson, M.Arch Program, University of Illinois School of Architecture, Spring 2011

were also mandated. Even the size of the drawing sheets and the sheet format were specified for all presentations; the "plate" format, similar to drawings produced by the iconic architects/delineators Carl Fredrick Schinkel and Paul Letarouilly, was specified as the sole means for depicting design solutions. These decisions may appear arbitrary and tetchy; however, it accomplished the primary objective in the studio—forcing students to consider every aspect of the historic building in their design work. Students could no longer hide underdeveloped aspects of their design using Photoshop. They also did not waste valuable time at the end of the semester composing their boards in the poster-like manner that has become the accepted norm in most architecture programs, Illinois being no exception.

The plate format for presentation also yielded desirable outcomes. Plans, sections, and elevations were now only featured in the design reviews; secondary diagrams (usually found on the Internet) were prohibited. Moreover, design solutions were drawn at a recognizable scale and finishes and assemblies were not merely pasted into the drawings. In this studio experience, students were forced to actually consider how buildings were put together. The better they understood historic construction, the more compelling the drawings became. Last, the mandated plate format brought back typical graphical conventions that have been discarded by most students and instructors during the past decade. North arrows were required for plans, rooms and spaces were labeled, and graphic scales were featured on drawings plotted at an architecture scale, ¼″=1′-0″, ½″=1′-0″, and so on. Such fundamental requirements for graphic presentations seem

12.4 Lemp Brewery, St. Louis, Missouri, proposed design for the Lemp Brewery Perspective Rendering, proposed facade by David Fortino, M.Arch Program, University of Illinois School of Architecture, Fall 2011

trivial, but they have a tremendous impact on how historic building technology and students comprehended design (Figure 12.4).

The Lemp Brewery Adaptive Use Project

The new graphic format for the University of Illinois Historic Preservation Studio was introduced in the fall 2011 semester for a single term project, the adaptive use of the historic Lemp Brewery in St. Louis, Missouri. Lemp is an impressive artifact of the industrial era, built between 1870 and 1950. It is composed of twenty-nine buildings with more than one million square feet of usable space that is set on thirteen acres located five blocks south of downtown St. Louis. At the beginning of the twentieth century, it was the third largest beer brewery in the United States. Prohibition led to Lemp's demise as a beer-making company, and the complex was later sold and converted into the International Shoe Company in the 1930s. The Lemp complex was abandoned after 1980 when the International Shoe Company closed its operation in St. Louis. In 1991 it was listed on the National Register of Historic Places. Architecturally, Lemp embodies the rich German-influenced building tradition of expressive brick masonry architecture that defines St. Louis architecturally. Existing drawings are necessary in order to understand and design for a historic resource. Fortunately for the studio all of the as-built and designed documentation developed by the Physical Plant Offices Lemp Brewery and International Shoe survived and had been scanned by HOK Architects in 2005.[6] During the first weeks of the semester, the students analyzed the changes that occurred in all of the buildings over time, as they were converted from bottling plants to shoe factories. Patterns of changes throughout the buildings such as in-filled masonry openings, closed arched openings, and trabeated openings had acquired historic significance.[7] These features were noted and evaluated by the studio. By the third week of the studio, students were assigned a specific building to adapt for a future use, which included live-work units, office space, retail space, and small batch manufacturing, all of which was determined through a program analysis of the site and the historic district adjacent to the complex.

Digital media and methods were not dismissed in the studio; instead, they were strategically employed in order to produce specific educational content that was pertinent to the objectives of the studio. During the initial weeks of the design studio, an exercise, first developed in the mid-1980s by Val Warke, associate professor of architecture at Cornell University, was assigned.[8] Warke's exercise consisted of a series of facade analyses of Renaissance buildings, which followed the ideas of visual structure and phenomenal perception of facades formally introduced by Colin Rowe in his writings such as *The Mathematics of the Ideal Villa and Other Essays* and *Transparency: Literal and Phenomenal.* But instead of analyzing great works of Renaissance architecture, the students were assigned a specific facade in the Lemp complex and implemented Warke's methods for understanding facade composition. The Lemp buildings, with their complex and architecturally rich facades, provided similar challenges encountered by Warke's students during their analyses of notable Renaissance buildings. Students were required to present a series of facade analysis diagrams and two bas-relief models that explained the inherent structure of the facade's composition. In the 1980s the Warke exercise was an arduous one, consisting of hours of hand cutting multiple layers of Strathmore board in order to correctly convey the layering qualities of the facade. The sheer repetition of drawing the facade was also time-consuming. But today, with the assistance of the laser cutter and AutoCAD, the exercise is not as daunting. In fact, the very nature of the laser cutter, in which the technician divides the model into "laser files," is ideal for the exercise. In this example, the attributes of the digital tool were considered in planning the design exercise.

At the beginning of the studio, students struggled with the HABS graphic standards. Most of them had not worked with line weights for drawings since their sophomore introductory courses; some of them had never worked in AutoCAD due to the fact that their prior studios fully utilized parametric-based graphical software. They also had little or no previous experience drawing traditional building technology or historic architectural ornament. The Warke exercise provided a good introduction, but the documentation processes had to be streamlined in order to allow enough time for development of student design work. Once the existing as-built documentation was reworked in a HABS format, students were asked to analyze existing conditions and building deficiencies. Specified graphic standards compelled the students to recognize the inherent nature of the historic resource, both its attributes and its challenges. As is typical in historic buildings, floor elevations in the Lemp complex did not line up, grade changes were significant, and accessibility design solutions were required in all of the buildings with deliberate precision. Not only did the students' solutions meet historic preservation objectives, specifically, the Secretary of the Interior's Standards for Preservation, but also performance metrics specified by NAAB under the Student Performance Criterion, "Comprehensive Design." In this criterion, students are expected to have an ability to implement their understanding of design thinking, technical documentation, historical traditions and global culture, life safety, accessibility, and site design, to name a few. Mandating the use of HABS standards in the historic preservation studio enabled the students to understand the nuances of the historic resource and to produce an understandable and technically competent design solution.

The Historic Preservation Studio also provided opportunities for the students to be introduced to other issues that are now required for NAAB accreditation: community and social responsibility, technical documentation, historical traditions and global culture, collaboration, investigative skills, and applied research.[9] This was accomplished through the exploration of adapting a historic building, while simultaneously incorporating NCPE curriculum standards for historic preservation, specifically, design issues, technical issues, and planning issues.[10] Historic preservation in the architectural design studio provides a different and more focused way to teach design than architectural design studios that have an emphasis on new buildings, in either sustainability or critical design. Through the use of an actual building as the focus of the studio experience, more often than not, students are introduced to actual building conditions and are required to address deficiencies. Moreover, by also introducing students to issues of appropriateness, adverse effect, and historic preservation standards for best practice, students are also introduced to a level of rigor more often found in architectural practice and not necessarily in the academy. Finally, historic preservation design studios allow students to develop technical documentation skills, which are necessary for the successful student to become a successful professional architect.

Conclusion

The new NAAB SPCs, which address historic preservation in the architecture program, is a good start to what is hoped to become a continuing trend in allowing historic preservation to have a more prominent role in architectural curricula in U.S. architecture programs. The changes in the 2009 NAAB Conditions, which included historic preservation, were the response to industry conditions and professional demands on the architecture academy. Throughout the past decade, adaptive use and historic rehabilitations of historic (and not-so-historic) buildings have dramatically increased. For example, in 2007, the city of Chicago issued 55,000 building permits, 5,000 of which were for building new buildings.[11] Professional architects have responded to this demand and have expressed their concern that recent architecture graduates should have a better educational foundation in historic preservation. Throughout the past decade the Historic Resources Committee of the AIA examined how historic preservation was being taught in the academy. Their findings are what led to the inclusion of SPCs such as C.7-Legal Responsibilities and C.9-Community and Social Responsibility.[12] It remains to be seen how architecture programs will respond to this new criterion.

Teaching historic preservation in the design studio not only presents different challenges than in other types of design studio experiences such as theoretical-based design, fabrication, or sustainability. It requires much more rigor and a high demand for accuracy than new conceptual design; it also requires intense historic and archival research and an understanding of historic building technology. Horizontal coordination between design instructor and history instructor, as demonstrated by Lauren Weiss Bricker and Luis Hoyos, is the key to successful historic preservation design instruction. Through this collaborative dialogue several issues, from historical research to design thinking, can be presented in a fluid manner that will lead inevitably to advocacy for preserving a historic resources. Students begin to see the value of oral and archival historical research methods for investigation and how it can enable them to play a more prominent role as leaders in the civic realm. These are skills that both the academy and the profession wish to see in future architects. As design continues to utilize different digital graphic platforms, it is important to acknowledge that more traditional orthographic graphical standards are the most appropriate means of representing a traditional or historic building.

Historic preservation design instills an ethical approach that not only addresses environmental issues but also a responsibility to protect the cultural values of a people and their imprint on an environment. The pedagogical approach presented in this chapter is built around the ethical approach to historic preservation and how patrimony can continue to best serve the people who use it. In the 1993 Conference on Historic Preservation Ethics, Richard Striner best summed up the ethical objective in historic preservation and architecture design in citing Edmund Burke's observation that society is a "partnership between those who are living, those who are dead, and those who are to be born."[13] Through the development of an integrated design studio curricula incorporating social history, preservation advocacy, and accurate drawing, the fundamental ethic to preserve the societal partnership that exists throughout time and across generations should be instilled in future architects.

Notes

1. National Architectural Accrediting Board, Inc. (NAAB), *NAAB 2009 Conditions of Accreditation* (Washington, D.C.: National Accrediting Board, Inc.), 20–26. http://www.naab.org/accreditation/2009_Conditions.aspx (accessed 23 September 2012).

2. National Council for Preservation Education, *Membership Standards*, 3.1.1 and 3.1.3, http://www.ncpe.us/about-ncpe/standards/#.UGRiVo7ZXww (accessed 23 September 2012).

3. Jill Pearlman, *Inventing American Modernism: Joseph Hudnut, Walter Gropius, and the Bauhaus Legacy at Harvard* (Charlottesville: University of Virginia Press, 2007), 209–12.

4. *NAAB 2009 Conditions of Accreditation*, 20–25.

5. *NAAB 2009 Conditions of Accreditation*, 22.

6. HOK Architects collaborated with Red Real Estate Developers of Kansas City, Missouri, on a commercial real estate venture to convert parts of the Lemp complex into a hotel and entertainment complex. The project was abandoned in the 2009 recession.

7. National Park Service, Secretary of the Interior Standards for Preservation and Rehabilitation, Standard #4, retrieved http://www.nps.gov/hps/tps/standguide/rehab/rehab_standards.htm [accessed 19 September 2012].

8. Val Warke, "Façade Explorations," unpublished manuscript, 1984.

9. *NAAB 2009 Conditions for Accreditation*, 20–25.

10. NCPE, *Membership. Standards*, 3.2.

11. Illinois Historic Preservation Agency, Springfield, IL, whitepaper, 2009.

12. *NAAB 2009 Conditions for Accreditation*, 23.

13. Richard Striner, "Historic Preservation and the Challenge of Ethical Coherence," in *Ethics in Preservation Conference Papers*, NCPE, 1993. http://www.ncpe.us/reports.html (accessed 15 August 2012).

13 Training in the Conservation of Modern Architecture: A Latin American Experience

Fernando Diniz Moreira and Luiz Manuel do Eirado Amorim

The field of conservation has experienced many transformations in recent years. It has expanded to include distinct professionals and laypeople in the decision-making processes. The idea of an expert, an experienced professional with academic high standards, with the exclusive authority to interpret and to dictate measures and actions to conserve heritage is no longer valid. The conservator also needs to develop communication skills in order to facilitate the process among the many stakeholders involved in the conservation process. Likewise, training activities have also expanded their target audience from specialized restoration expertise toward training specialists from many countries, including non-specialists. The field of conservation also saw a great expansion in the number of objects to be conserved. The objects of architectural conservation are no longer regarded as recognized monuments of the past but as entire cultural and urban landscapes, even containing modern sections of cities, with many buildings and public spaces. The modern built environment has been increasingly considered a focus of conservationists.

Modern heritage poses many challenges for conservationists. In the past fifteen or twenty years, many modern buildings have been restored or renovated. Some of these restorations were successful but others affected negatively and irreversibly the value of this heritage. These experiences, in addition to the weathering of modern buildings, pose a series of challenges, which require more careful reflection. These challenges include: (1) the rapid functional obsolescence of these buildings—caused not only by rapid changes in social demand, but also by the careful attention modern architects have paid to functional aspects in the definition of spatial arrangements, which requires particular attention to the introduction of new uses; (2) the material dimension of the building, which poses problems due to the use of new materials without previous knowledge of their long-term performance, as well as the use of traditional materials in new ways, construction faults, poor detailing, and the use of prefabricated materials; (3) the need to replace service systems in order to keep the building in use; (4) the lack of a maintenance culture, which directly affects modern buildings that were once considered to be maintenance-free; (5) the understanding of the patina as a dirty stain in modern buildings, and not as a natural sign of aging; and (6) the general lack of recognition of modern buildings, sites, and districts by larger sectors of society.[1]

Although these issues challenge the conservation theoretical background, we do not believe that the conservation of modern architecture should be different from the conservation of architectural works from the distant past. These challenges raise new issues regarding the training of conservationists, however. It is necessary to train specialists to face these transformations in the field. These specialists need to better understand community demands, stakeholders' aims, and the intricate process according to which decisions are made in order to participate effectively in decision processes and properly develop communication skills for broad communities.[2] These specialists should also be able to understand a broader sphere of objects to be conserved, particularly those of modern heritage.

To meet these challenges there is a strong need to train qualified professionals who are able to identify the values of modern architecture and the problems related to its conservation, in addition to being able to intervene without compromising its integrity and authenticity and to manage change in buildings and districts. Thus, it is necessary to prepare architects and engineers to face the new challenges posed by the conservation of modern built heritage. For this reason, the Center for Advanced Studies in Integrated Conservation (CECI) and ICCROM ran the 1st Latin American Modern Architecture Conservation Course (MARC-AL), in association with DOCOMOMO Brazil and the Federal University of Pernambuco (UFPE). The course was an intensive program combining theory and practice through traditional lectures, distance learning, group work, and study tours. It was held between March 2009 and March 2010, with eight months in an online format and one intensive full-time month in November 2009, in which the participants were fully involved in a conservation project in Recife with field trips to Belo Horizonte and Brasilia. This experience was reproduced in a graduate seminar course format at the UFPE, which was offered twice, in 2010 and in 2011. This chapter presents the reflections provoked by the authors' experience running the MARC-AL and its graduate counterpart. By presenting this experience we are trying to address some questions that may contribute to future similar courses.

On the Pedagogical Structure

The MARC-AL was developed primarily by CECI, in partnership with ICCROM. CECI is an independent nonprofit institution dedicated to the promotion of the scientific field of integrated conservation and has acted as a training, researching, publishing, and community service institution, working in partnership with many Brazilian and international institutions. The MARC-AL followed other CECI courses, which are based on the following principles: (1) buildings, sites, and districts have cultural meaning for social groups; (2) the assessment of the value of this heritage is made through a long and continuous intersubjective process involving the community and stakeholders, considering their aims and expectations to reach a broad consensus; (3) conservation is an interdisciplinary process involving different professional and nonprofessional viewpoints; and (4) the conservation process should be managed by a maintenance and monitoring system, aiming for long-term conservation and sustainability.

MARC-AL set out to provide professionals with the skills they need to recognize the value of modern building and sites, to identify their value, and to understand the problems and propose solutions for conserving them. It was structured into an initial distance-learning stage that took place between March and October 2009, comprising 24 classes, totaling 240 hours, and a final in situ 120-hour phase during the month of November. The course thus comprised a total of 360 hours. This concluding phase consisted of one period spent in Recife that focused on developing a conservation plan for a building, and a second consisting of field trips to Belo Horizonte and Brasilia to visit important intervention works that had already been completed or were still being implemented. The course involved two years of preparation.

The teaching staff included twenty-two instructors, twenty Brazilians and two from abroad, Joseph King (ICCROM) and Tommi Lindh (Finnish National Board of Antiquities), who participated in the traditional lecture module of the course.[3] The first MARC-AL class had twenty candidates: a dozen from Brazil, four from Guatemala, and one candidate each from Cuba, Mexico, Portugal, and Chile, all of whom were architects.[4] The purpose of offering a mixed-learning format was to ensure interaction between instructors and students on a digital platform throughout the seven-month course and to foster the mastering of the core content of the course and the discussion of its central issues, prior to the traditional lecture module. The online distance learning ran in parallel with the drawing up of a conservation plan for the site that the participants had selected in their cities. The online learning format also enabled participants living in other states and countries to take part in the course without having to move from their hometowns.

Modules one to four contained twenty-three lessons, each lasting a week. Each lesson consisted of a text written by the professor with required additional reading. The professor coordinated a forum discussing the content of the lesson. During each lesson, the participants were evaluated by their responses to questions provided by the professor. In addition to these questions, the participants were required to present one paper per module in which the theoretical content of each module found practical application in a building selected by the participant in his or her city. Shortly thereafter, the participant drew up an approach to the conservation of his or her building. Each module covered a set of theoretical and practical skills needed to deal with the conservation of modern heritage:

- Module 1, entitled Values of Modern Architecture, introduced the major issues of the conservation of modern architecture, its values, and the characteristics of the Latin American listings; forms of inventory; and preparing a statement of significance. As a final product of the module, the participants were asked to draw up the inventory and identify the main values of the works that were the subject of their study and to draft a statement of significance.
- Module 2, Theory of Restoration and of the Conservation of Modern Architecture, discussed the theories of restoration and conservation since the mid-nineteenth century, including contemporary conservation theory and its implications for conserving modern architecture, international recommendations, and international conservation frameworks. Participants presented an analysis of the building they had chosen to discuss in their monograph by recounting the different phases through which it may have passed, taking into account the forms of occupation and changes it had undergone, and discussed the main theoretical implications to be tackled as to its conservation.
- Module 3, Modern Architecture Built Materials and Technics, dealt with the material aspect of modern architecture.

It provided an understanding of the nature of building materials and techniques most used in modern architecture. It also studied the process of degradation and the conservation solutions for each material. One of the classes was dedicated to conserving the modern garden. The last class sought to identify the relationships of the various pathologies referred to by means of case studies. The students were asked to draw up a map of damage to the buildings studied.

- Module 4, Conservation Interventions and Modern Architecture, was devoted to theoretical and methodological procedures focusing on a conservation project for a modern building. The participants defined guidelines for conservation and analyzed to what extent these buildings could withstand future transformations, taking into account the bases laid out in theories of conservation and restoration, appropriate procedures regarding the scale of intervention necessary, and ways of monitoring and controlling these after undertaking the proposed interventions.
- Module 5, In Situ Module, consisted of the group of students developing, with assistance from the professors and lecturers, an intervention project in a modern building in the city of Recife. The module also included lectures by faculty and guest speakers, guided tours, and a study trip to the cities of Belo Horizonte and Brasilia.

Finally, the end-of-course monograph consisted of drawing up a conservation plan for the example selected by the student, in accordance with the principles, procedures, and guidelines built up over the course.

On the Traditional Lecture, or the In Situ Module

The traditional lecture module, sometimes called the in situ module, synthesizes the contents and procedures taught throughout the entire course. A group of fourteen students and nearly all instructors involved in the course took part in this module. The first three weeks were devoted to developing a conservation plan for the former Institute of Mycology of the University of Recife (now UFPE), currently occupied by the Hotel Trade and Tourism Unit,[5] built on the João Amazonas Campus, in Recife. The Institute of Mycology was one of the first buildings to be designed and constructed on the university campus, work on which began in 1950. It

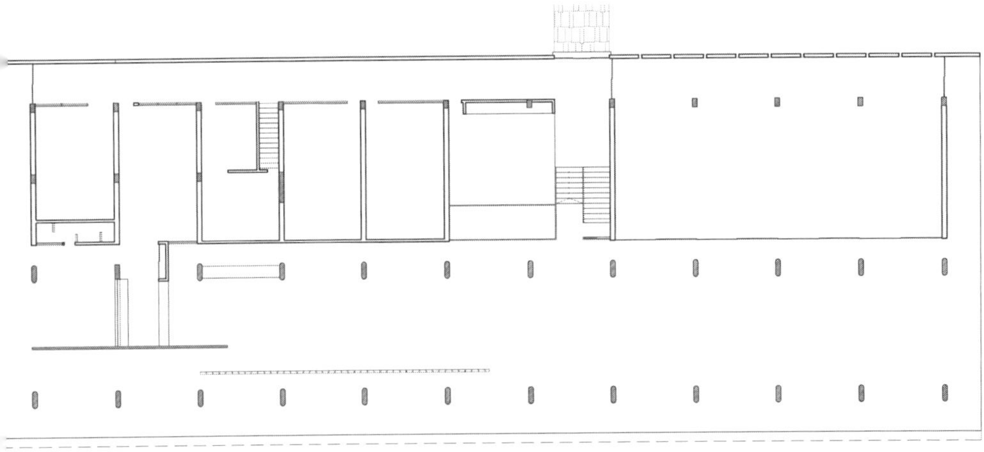

3.1 Ground floor plan of the Mycology Building in 1956. Drawing by the author (Amorim)

was designed by the then recent graduate in architecture Reginaldo Esteves, in 1956, an official of the Technical Office of the Cidade Universitária (ETCU), coordinated by the architect Mario Russo.[6] The building was part of the complex designed for the School of Chemistry, which comprised the main building of the institution and the institutes of antibiotics, of Russo himself, and of mycology.[7]

The building is arranged in three levels: an intermediate floor that provides access and distributes movement, the unobstructed ground floor, and the upper floor occupied by laboratory units (Figure 13.1). The intermediate level occupies the western portion of the building, while the other two, which overlap it, occupy its eastern side. It is on the intermediate floor that the main access, via the central span, is located and consists of a hall and staircase access to the other floors. The awkward orientation is countered with the provision of circulation along the facade and double veneer masonry, which seeks to ensure that the interior is not overheated by the sun. The laboratories and health units are located on the upper floor. The organization of space follows the same design as the Institute of Antibiotics, with the provision of public and private circulation through all floors of the building.

The plans are integrated under a single roof, as a sloping slab with trim toward the western side. Part of the plan is interrupted by the insertion of a shed skylight for the purpose of illuminating and ventilating the spaces located on the intermediate floor. The compositional treatment of the building seeks to bring together under one volume the three levels described by using a few artifices that are typical of modern architecture in

Brazil, particularly that designed by architects belonging to the Carioca School, such as the continuity of the limits of the gable sides as the frame of the plans for opening other facades and the use of inclined planes on the facades themselves.[8] The tile panel and the hollow elements in glass are noteworthy elements of the building.

Regrettably, there are few documents and data concerning the building, especially with regard to changes throughout its useful life. The few documents identified are incomplete and do not provide a clear understanding of how the original internal spaces, levels, uses, and cladding materials and colors were linked. In fact, the original floor plans were not preserved or have not yet been located, nor are there any precise pieces of information or records regarding the process of constructing the building. All that has been found in the archives of the Town Hall at the Cidade Universitária are cross sections and facades dating from 1956, a 1962 floor plan with a cross section, a 1964 floor plan with facades and cross sections, and a 1965 cross section (see Figure 13.2). Photographic documentation is also sparse and does not contribute to understanding changes made to the building.

The building, however, never came to house the Institute of Mycology, which continued to occupy a building outside the campus for many years. The School of Chemistry occupied it for decades until being transferred to its own building in the 1980s. The property lay vacant for a few years, and then, in the mid-1990s, was set aside to house the Hotel Trade and Tourism Unit, after being adapted to meet the demands of this specific use. In short, it was adapted to a hotel-like structure in order to train students. During this stage, the property underwent its deepest transformations: (1) the open ground floor colonnade was occupied, reducing its integration with the surrounding garden and the access to the building; (2) the

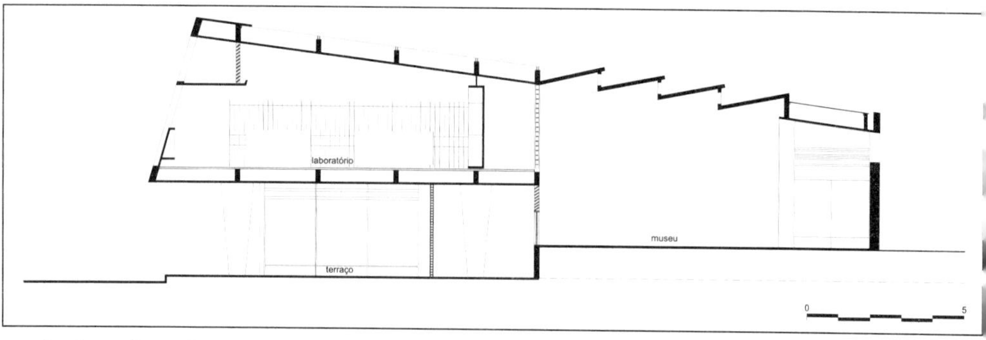

13.2 Institute of Mycology, cross section showing original conditions in 1956

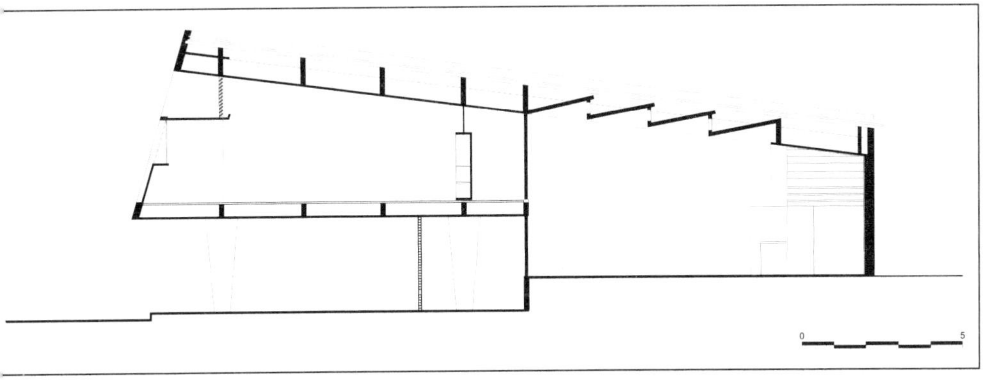

3.3 Institute of Mycology, cross section showing transformations as of 1964

original cladding in small squares of ceramic in soft tones (a mass-produced material that was no longer available for replacement) was replaced with brightly colored 10 × 10 cm ceramic tiles; (3) the laboratories on the first floor were transformed into classrooms with varying dimensions without regard for the existing modulation; (4) the new partition walls were raised to the east facade, thus modifying the original rhythm and continuity of the inclined plane of this facade; and (5) the frames on the east facade were removed, without a record made of how this was technically solved. The building was also neglected by the campus community, evident in the wear of its patina, and was not recognized for its quality or as an example of the pioneering buildings of the campus. Thus, the building experienced typical problems that affect modern buildings in general: poor maintenance, change of use, unavailability of original materials, and renovations and updating operations that disregarded any possible value the building might carry (Figure 13.3).

The architectural qualities of the original proposal, the difficulties of accessing documentation regarding the property, and the degree of loss of character were important matters as to the choice of the property as an object of study because this corresponded to the most likely scenario the participants would encounter in their own states or countries, in a Latin American context. In other words, the majority of participants will not be faced with indisputable masterworks, but with buildings without proper documentation, threatened or under severe risk of loss of character, and undervalued by local communities. This is important for the conservation of our modern heritage because it involves not only masterworks but also the everyday modern buildings that lie around every corner.

In the first week (November 2–6) participants made a thorough investigation of the pathologies of the building and a study to identify its main characteristics and value. The group also had the opportunity to attend lectures on various topics related to the building (the history of the university campus, Pernambuco's architecture during the period, the way the building came about and the records regarding it, the current challenges of administering the campus, etc.). The professionals involved with the management of the building, the campus, and the users also made their voices heard. The week's work led to the production of two documents: a brief map of damage and a declaration of significance.

The map of damage revealed some mistakes in the original design, even though it involved ETCU experience and technical support. It is an example of the innovations sought by modern architects that have not found a parallel in the materials and techniques available at the time and place of construction. The solution of a roof with a shed skylight presented problems and was redesigned during 1964, supposedly to correct a mistake in sizing rainwater run-off gutters. This alteration obstructed the shed skylights, which adversely affected the ventilation and lighting of the building, thus impairing its efficiency and comfort. Because the alteration lengthened the upper part of the facade, interfering with the total height of the building, it thus changed the building's original composition—the ratio of the proportion of its constituent elements. The map also revealed that the cladding applied to the alterations made in the 1990s facilitated the infiltration of rainwater because it was inadequately applied. Moreover, the transformation of the private access corridor to the laboratories into verandahs caused sealing problems and run-off of rainwater, which caused serious infiltration of water inside the building and damage to the slab flooring.

In terms of the significance of the building, it was concluded, after discussions within the group, that the building is important because it has cultural value (since it represents the optimism of Latin American nations, expressed in the creation of a higher education system and the construction of the physical structure necessary and the idea of progress widely taken on board by modern architecture); social value (because it represents the efforts of the local intellectual elites to transform Pernambuco society through education); aesthetic value (because of the spatial experience produced by visual integration and because of the mix of levels of its floors; the ratio between the masses and the voids; the inclined plane of the front facade; the integration with the gardens; the recesses and framing of the facade and its integrated elements: hollow glass elements and tiled paneling); technical and scientific value (since it is the result of the research and experimentation with technical, scientific, and methodological criteria carried out while drawing up the blueprint); and, finally, documentary value (as it bears witness to experimentation with new construction techniques in the public works of Pernambuco, such as shed skylights and sloping frames).

In the second week (November 9–13) the participants were divided into three teams. Each team developed a different proposal for intervention, while being supervised by the instructors. The proposals contained a variety of conservation attitudes of greater and lesser extent. Proposal 1 included the recovery of the original design of the facade, proposed a solution for the construction problems encountered, and retained the existing spatial features. Proposal 2 adopted the idea of expanding the Institute of Antibiotics, next to it, so as to strengthen the link between the two buildings, by means of reopening the colonnade and transforming it into a space devoted to socializing. Finally, Proposal 3 adopted the posture of minimal intervention and respect for previous interventions, but also freed the colonnade and integrated it into the front garden. The proposals were discussed at the end of the second week during a critical review in which several instructors took part. The group of participants reached a consensus using guidelines for the final blueprint developed by the entire team.

The third week (November 16–13) was dedicated to drawing up and presenting the conservation plan, including the proposed intervention in the building studied (Figure 13.4). The conception of the intervention was based on the purpose of housing the teaching and research activities of the Institute of Antibiotics. The program was to contain a library, a mini-auditorium, reading and study rooms, and spaces where instructors and students could socialize. The intention is not to return the building to its original state but rather to intervene on the basis of its current state by seeking to recover crucial points for understanding and giving value to its architecture. Regarding the original structure and spatiality, it was proposed: (1) to clear the obstructions from most pillars as a way of revealing the structural solution, (2) to recover the original internal circulations on the upper floor and on the rear facade of the ground floor, and (3) to remove the partition walls added in the 1990s that changed the modulation of the east facade and the plasterboard panel that internally covers the hollow glass element of the panel. Consequently, it was possible to restore the size of the laboratories, as originally conceived by Reginaldo Esteves, by recovering the modulation corresponding to the structural system. The purpose of enhancing the central hall was to facilitate fluidity between the floors and to denote the main entrance and its relationship with the external space.

13.4 Conservation problems at the Institute of Mycology. East facade and the plasterboards covering the glass breeze-blocks. Photograph by the author (Moreira)

Regarding the roofing, it was proposed to re-open the shed skylights and to reverse the increase in the roof to recover natural lighting and ventilation, which will require technical solutions that enable it to function adequately. Consequently, it was proposed to remove the plasterboard that obstructed the view of the panel of hollow elements and the shed skylights. With regard to the facades, the proposal was premised on recovering the sloping front facade, one of the main features of the building. The solution proposed was to place new aluminum profiles on the balcony of the main facade of the upper floor, thus keeping the modulation of three elements by spacing them between pillars, in an allusion to the original frames. This measure will provide guidance and the visual continuity of the original inclination of the facade without obstructing it from view and this will maintain the peripheral circulation, which looks out onto the garden. It was proposed that the current ceramic cladding be removed and replaced with a vitreous mosaic, in colors in accordance with the chromatic survey to be performed. On the lateral surfaces the proposal is to replace the sandstone cladding lining of the original design, which is still produced commercially and easily acquired. It was also proposed that an investigation be undertaken to identify the original color of the pillars, thus enabling the primary tonality to be recovered.

In regard to external areas, an attempt was made to recover and strengthen the relationship with the Institute of Antibiotics in front, by giving attention to the flowerbeds and paving. The external flowerbeds, placed along the front facade, should be replaced by vegetation of low height so as not to interfere with the view of the facade and to integrate the building with the square. As for the integrated elements, the proposal is to map and identify the specific pathologies so as to recover the tile pieces, which comprise the existing panel on the *pilotis*/colonnade. The replacement of damaged parts, when necessary, is feasible because these are industrially produced elements that can be acquired. The floor cladding, originally a bed of granite (granulated marble and granite called *granilite*), was covered with plastic flooring (Paviflex), and, therefore, the proposal includes its removal in order to recover the original flooring on the ground floor and to complement it where parts are missing. The proposal also includes the renovation of the electrical installation systems and the adaptation of the building to recent accessibility, safety, and fire regulation standards.

Study Visit

The in situ stage was brought to a close with a study tour on the fourth and last week. Two cities were chosen—Brasilia and Belo Horizonte—because of their collection of paradigmatic examples of modern architecture in Brazil and the opportunity to observe in situ works of restoration recently completed or under completion. In Brasilia, technical visits were made to the Alvorada Palace (the official residence of the president of Brazil), Brasilia Cathedral, the National Congress, projects by Oscar Niemeyer, and the Three Powers Square, which was designed by the town planner Lucio Costa, as part of a program organized by Docomomo-Brasília and the Faculty of Architecture and Town Planning of the University of Brasilia, on November 23 and 24. During the visit, there were lectures on the history of the city, and especially on the challenges of conserving it. The stay in Belo Horizonte was on November 26 and 27. The interest of the technical visits was concentrated on the Pampulha complex, by Oscar Niemeyer, with special emphasis on the restoration of the St. Francis of Assisi Church of Pampulha. The visits were preceded by lectures organized by the School of Architecture, Federal University of Minas Gerais.

On the Assessment

The process of evaluating the course activities was drawn up first with the participation of students, lecturers, conservators, and professors as one of the conditions necessary for improving the course. The authors of this chapter further elaborated these findings in order to assess the strengths and weaknesses of the course. The strengths of the course included: (1) applying the taught content to case studies chosen by the students, thus enabling its immediate application in practice, which was of particular interest and, in some cases, with direct implications for drawing up a conservation plan by a municipal, state, or federal body; (2) the digital resources that enabled, in the online phase, familiarity with the course content and instructors to be obtained; (3) the introduction and methodology applied in the present module since this integrated and applied the knowledge delivered and gave direction to the visit to restored buildings or those being restored; and (4) the validity of adopting descriptive and analytical methods suitable for assessing the impacts caused by changes of use throughout the history of the buildings, such as the DRAPI-Conservation methodology, drawn up by the instructors Luiz Amorim and Claudia Loureiro,[9] which proved to be very adequate for these purposes.

The weaknesses of the course included the intense workload, particularly during the in situ phase, the need for the module 3 lessons (dealing with the materials) to establish more connections with the modern buildings through examples, the need for more cases for illustration purposes, and the short time allotted to each city for the visits. The experience of the MARC-AL brought some outcomes we believe would be helpful to conservation educators in implementing similar courses. These outcomes also address recent shifts and the theory of conservation:

a) The promotion of greater understanding of the value of modern buildings and more sensitivity in identifying what is of value, especially in those buildings considered ordinary. Thus, in addition to a better understanding of the history and theories of modern architecture, we need to understand that the value assessment is carried out by way of a long and continuous intersubjective process, involving not only specialists but also those involved with the building and the local community. The conservator is a social agent who works in a context of intersubjective interpretations and decisions, striving for maximum social consensus.[10]

b) The encouragement of a better process for involving users and communities associated with the building and sites. Conservation can only be effective if it involves users and communities and if it is well understood and approved by large sectors of the population, public officials, intellectuals, and decision makers. Teaching methods should also address the development of the students' communication skills, as they will probably play the role of facilitators among the many stakeholders involved in the process of conservation. These outcomes also include issues related to the structure of the course and the strategy for intervention in the chosen building.

c) The attention to the need for greater dialogue between the various professionals involved with conservation (architects, architectural historians, conservationists, engineers, specialists in materials, and the like). These different professional viewpoints need to coexist in order to achieve a better and more thoughtful approach to the conservation of modern building and sites. We need to encourage these professionals to overcome the strict limits of their professional outlooks: architects dedicated to the theory and history of architecture tend to favor a return to an ideal state, which sometimes never existed; experts in restoration materials and techniques tend to emphasize the technical solution and disregard broader questions about the building and its users; conservationists tend to favor certain theoretical conservation positions arising from reflections targeting architectures of periods prior to the modern era, while modern buildings bring new problems for these theoretical positions; and finally, architects responsible for refurbishment projects or for inserting new uses very often tend to consider certain characteristics of the buildings as obstacles rather than as elements to be highlighted or recovered in their interventions.

d) The need to achieve a better balance between theory and practice and attention to current demands, as already suggested by John Allan,[11] so that the buildings remain in use, particularly those that do not yet have such recognition. The process of conserving heritage should not be rigidly defined by science. It is a matter of seeking consensus among the stakeholders involved with the building. Consequently, we should understand that the project should respect the authenticity of the materials, but it should not overestimate their value. This is a difficult topic for the discipline of conservation because the ethics of conservation, from the outset, has been associated with the idea of truth, which was later associated with the concept of authenticity. We agree with contemporary authors when they state that materials by themselves do not define the essence of modern architecture, but the way they are arranged and the space they create.[12] The approach to modern buildings and sites should not be guided only by ideas of truth and objectivity or extremist approaches to authenticity.[13] The current material fetishism of scientific conservation should be balanced with the inclusion of space and design intention. The approach to modern buildings and sites should also take into account that modern architecture brings problems in term of materials (such as the use of new techniques and traditional materials), which requires a more comprehensive and sensible approach.

e) The need to adopt case studies, such as the restoration works of the Ville Savoye, the Zonestraal Sanatorium, the Cathedral of Notre-Dame du Raincy, the Van Nelle factory, and the TWA Terminal, and so forth, as well as to study long-term master plans (e.g., Sydney Opera House) and listings dossiers (e.g., the Barragán House). In the study of cases like this, the student encounters the new and unexpected problems that conservators had to face.

f) The need for greater expertise regarding the properties, degradation, and recovery of materials and to disseminate this appropriately among architects. Although this is a lifetime experience, Latin American conservators need to improve their knowledge of the performance of modern materials.

g) The need to study long-term master plans as alternatives to the practice of restoring a building every fifteen or twenty years, which puts the authenticity of a building at risk. Thus, long-term master plans should be promoted and adopted because these are able to establish a framework that links future restoration interventions and establishes the practice of continuous maintenance.

Findings

The MARC-AL experience showed us that, although there is no new theoretical approach for dealing with modern architecture, there is a need for specific training in the conservation of modern architecture. These outcomes are also related to major shifts in the recent theory of conservation. MARC-AL attempted to encourage professionals to recognize the value of modern buildings and sites, identify their values, understand problems, communicate and achieve consensus among those involved, and propose solutions for their conservation. For this, there is a need not only for practical and scientific knowledge, but prudence and sensibility.

Notes

1. Theodore H. M. Prudon, *Preservation of Modern Architecture* (New York: John Wiley, 2008); S. Macdonald, "20th Century Heritage: Recognition, Protection and Practical Challenges," in *ICOMOS World Report 2002–2003 on Monuments and Sites in Danger* (Paris: ICOMOS, 2003); Diniz Moreira, "Os desafios postos pela conservação da arquitetura moderna," *Revista CPC*, 11 (2010–11), 154–59; and Susan Macdonald, Kyle C. Normandin, and Bob Kindred, eds., *Conservation of Modern Architecture* (Shaftesbury: Donhead, 2007).

2. Salvador Muñoz-Viñas, *Contemporary Theory of Conservation* (Oxford: Elsevier Butterworth-Heinemann, 2005).

3. The following were all members of the teaching staff: Andrey Rosenthal Schlee (Universidade de Brasília - UnB), Ana Rita Sá Carneiro (Universidade Federal de Pernambuco - UFPE and Centro de Estudos Avançados da Conservação Integrada - CECI), Antônio Alves Júnior (Votorantin), Arnaldo Manoel Carneiro (Universidade Federal de Pernambuco - UFPE), Carlos Eduardo Comas (Universidade Federal do Rio Grande do Sul - UFRGS), Danilo Matoso Macedo (Chamber of Congressmen, Brasília), Fernando Diniz Moreira. (Universidade Federal de Pernambuco - UFPE and Centro de Estudos Avançados da Conservação Integrada - CECI), Flaviana Lira (Centro de Estudos Avançados da Conservação Integrada - CECI), Flavio Carsarlade (Universidade Federal de Minas Gerais - UFMG), Lucia Hidaka (Universidade Federal de Alagoas - UFAL), Luiz Amorim (Universidade Federal de Pernambuco - UFPE), Guilah Naslavsky (Universidade Federal da Paraíba - UFPB), Jorge Tinoco (Centro de Estudos Avançados da Conservação Integrada - CECI), Joseph King (The International Centre for the Study of the Preservation and Restoration of Cultural Property - ICCROM, Italy), Leonardo Miranda (Universidade Federal de Pernambuco - UFPE), Monica Harchambois (Centro de Estudos Avançados da Conservação Integrada - CECI), Natália Vieira (Universidade Federal do Rio Grande do Norte - UFRN), Renata Cabral (Centro de Estudos Avançados da Conservação Integrada - CECI), Roberto Araújo (Centro de Estudos Avançados da Conservação Integrada - CECI), Silvio Zancheti (Universidade Federal de Pernambuco - UFPE and Centro de Estudos Avançados da Conservação Integrada - CECI), and Tommi Lindh (National Board of Antiquities, Finland).

4. The students were: Alcione Sarkis Simão (Federal District, Brazil), Barbara Cortizo de Aguiar (Pernambuco, Brazil), Daniel Lopes Moreira (Rio de Janeiro, Brazil), Fernanda Chitto Rosa (São Paulo, Brazil), Gabriela Nagoya Tamari (São Paulo, Brazil), Márcia Silva dos Reis (Bahia, Brazil), Marilia Brasileiro Vale (Minas Gerais, Brazil), Noêmia Barradas (Rio de Janeiro, Brazil), Pricylla Amorim Girão (Pernambuco, Brazil), Rodrigo Pontes Lucas (Pernambuco, Brazil), Sergio Ricardo dos Santos (São Paulo, Brazil), Silvia Denardi Roveroni (São Paulo, Brazil), Edwin Rodolfo Saraiva Tablas (Guatemala), Rafael Aycinena (Guatemala), Raúl Monterrosso (Guatemala), Sonia Fuentes Padilla (Guatemala), Josel Saap Nuño (Cuba), Carolina Llanos Ulloa (Chile), Maria Mestre Martí (Mexico), and Lisandra Franco de Mendonça (Portugal).

5. The information on the history of the building was obtained from *The Space of Architecture as an Object of Heritage Interest (in Portuguese)*, coordinated by Prof. Luiz

Amorim and funded by CNPq. On Mario Russo's career, see Renata Campello Cabral, *Mario Russo: Um Arquiteto Racionalista Italiano em Recife* (Recife, Brazil: UFPE, 2006).

6. The ETCU, headed from 1949 to 1956 by the Italian architect Mário Russo, was the unit responsible for the planning, works, and projects of the university campus and its first buildings. Russo was invited to institute the architecture course of the University of Recife (which arose from the School of Fine Arts, founded in 1932), which was anchored on the principles of modernism. Together with Acácio Gil Borsoi (a native of Rio de Janeiro who arrived in 1950) and the Portuguese Delfim Amorim (who arrived in 1951), Russo laid down the bases of modernist architecture produced in the state of Pernambuco.

7. L. Amorim, C. Brasileiro, and R. Ludermir, "Da restauração do espaço da arquitetura: o Instituto de Antibióticos," in *Anais do 8° Seminário Docomomo Brasil* (Rio de Janeiro: Docomomo-Rio, 2009); Universidade do Recife, *Instituto de Antibióticos* (Recife, Brazil: Escritório Técnico da Universidade do Recife, 1955).

8. H. Segawa, *Arquiteturas no Brasil, 1900–1990* (São Paulo: Edusp, 1998); Y. Bruand, *Arquitetura Contemporânea no Brasil* (São Paulo: Perspectiva, 1981).

9. L. Amorim, C. Loureiro, I. Figueirôa, and R. Canuto, *DRAPI uma metodologia de intervenção em edificaç ões recentes,* unpublished research report (Recife: Laboratório do Estudos Avançados em Arquitetura, 2011); and C. Loureiro, L. Amorim, F. Almeida, and C. Nascimento, "Metodologia de avaliação de mudança de uso," in *Anais do II Congresso Internacional na Recuperação, Manutenção e Restauração de Edifícios* (Rio de Janeiro: UFRJ, 2006).

10. Miriam Clavir, *Preserving What is Valued: Museums, Conservation and First Nations* (Vancouver: University of British Columbia Press, 2002), 42–43.

11. John Allan, "Conservation of Modern Buildings: A Practitioner's View," in *Modern Matters,* ed. Susan Macdonald (London: Donhead, 1996), 127.

12. Allan, "Conservation of Modern Buildings," 126. Also Andrew Saint, "Philosophical Principles of Modern Conservation," in *Modern Matters,* ed. Susan Macdonald (London: Donhead, 1996), 20–22; W. Zonestraal De Jonge, "Sanatorium, Hilversum," in *Modern Movement Heritage,* ed. Allen Cunningham (London: E&FN Spon, 1998), 155.

13. Muñoz Viñas, *Contemporary Theory of Conservation,* 86.

14 Integrating Historic Preservation into the Undergraduate Interior Design Curriculum

Melissa Santana and Valerie L. Settles

Interior design education often focuses on developing new spaces; however, it is increasingly important for designers to utilize existing buildings in pursuit of more sustainable design strategies. Due to the economic constraints of recent years, society has come to realize the benefit (and necessity) of adapting what is already existing rather than relying on new construction to meet contemporary demands. The relationship between interior designers and historic preservation is often overlooked; however, they can play an integral role in preservation efforts as a result of their training in the historical use of space as well as today's functional requirements. Similarly, their experience in integrating all types of sustainable strategies into the built environment makes them valuable contributing members of project teams for the rehabilitation or continued use of older buildings. Unfortunately, if interior design students are not exposed to the value of historic preservation in their undergraduate degree program, they may be unprepared for the type of work they are likely to see during their professional practice.

Interior design education is regulated by the Council for Interior Design Accreditation (CIDA), which requires programs to meet a comprehensive set of standards in a variety of areas. While these do not specifically address historic preservation, a number of standards relate directly to many aspects of the field, including an extensive understanding and application of historical movements and styles, along with the significant level of sustainability evident in the profession. The importance of sustainability and various strategies for achieving it are often emphasized in design education, and this content could serve as a logical connection between preservation and interior design if highlighted by faculty. The purpose of this chapter is to demonstrate that there is a need to integrate historic preservation into interior design curriculums in Oklahoma; an example of a project is included to demonstrate one technique for doing so. To accomplish this, a literature review provides an understanding of the connection between interior design and preservation as well as an overview of what is currently being taught in the universities. This is followed by a survey that assesses the knowledge and interest in preservation of Oklahoma undergraduate interior design students. The chapter concludes with an example of how a historic preservation project can be integrated into an interior design curriculum.

Literature Review

Since the first structures were built by early civilizations there has been a concern for the design of the interiors. Over time the interior design profession has transitioned from a home economics perspective to a social science perspective, with practitioners evolving from "society decorators" into the more contemporary roles of designers and researchers. Today, the definition of interior design provided by the National Council for Interior Design Qualification (NCIDQ) asserts that design solutions acknowledge the social context of the project and must be "functional, enhance the quality of life and culture of the occupants, and aesthetically pleasing," and that interior designers "protect and enhance the health, life safety, and welfare of the public" while integrating research and analysis into the design process.[1] While the profession of interior design continues to grow, the emphasis has shifted from aesthetics to the social responsibility designers have in providing spaces that create a positive impact on people, the environment, and the economy.

The American Society of Interior Designers (ASID) notes in "Health and Safety" that "the issue of public welfare, within the realm of professional interior design, includes the responsibility of considering the greater whole."[2] The spaces interior designers create should ultimately allow the users to access their full potential, whatever that may be, and ensure that the design solutions are functional, accessible, and aesthetically pleasing.[3] In a similar vein, the International Interior Design Association's (IIDA) mission statement on sustainability promotes the use of materials and space plans that reduce the negative impacts on the natural environment and improve the health and well-being of all people.[4] The inclusion of well-being is imperative because it is often an overlooked aspect of social responsibility. IIDA's stance on the profession is that the goal of the interior designer's plan should be beneficial to everyone and not just those who use the space. To meet that goal it asserts that using socially responsible materials and construction methods is one way of providing a benefit to everyone involved in the project.[5] Last, the International Federation of Interior Architects/Designers (IFIA/D) believes that utilizing interior design improves the overall quality of life and upholds human dignity for all.[6]

It is evident that the responsibility often falls on interior designers to carefully consider the implications of their projects and their impact on how people live and conduct day-to-day activities.[7] Barbara Anderson, Peggy Honey, and Michael Dudek believe that the primary social value of the interior design profession is to design physiologically and sociologically supportive interiors.[8] While Nadia Nieves and Catherine Anderson agree, they add that a design should enhance the quality of life for the occupant.[9] A study conducted by David Philips, Oi-ling Siu, Anthony Yeh, and Kevin Cheng concluded that interior environments have a greater effect on well-being than exterior environments, proving that interior design is essential to social responsibility.[10]

In order to educate the public on social responsibility in design, some architects and interior designers are now adapting the corporate social responsibility model because it fits so closely to the definition of their profession. As designers, they realize they are responsible for creating buildings that affect the environment, the well-being of society, and the prosperity of the economy.[11] Ayman Othman describes how overall responsibility is directly linked to the individual factors of environmental responsibility, social responsibility, and economic sustainability.[12] Donovan D. Rypkema, a historic preservation expert, takes the links between social, economic, and environmental responsibility further by describing the connection of all three and how they relate to total sustainability. In a 2005 lecture he stated: "For a community to be viable there needs to be a link between environmental responsibility and economic responsibility; for a community to be livable there needs to be a link between environmental responsibility and social responsibility; and for a community to be equitable there needs to be a link between economic responsibility and social responsibility."[13] In essence, it can then be concluded that if designers are incorporating all forms of social responsibility into their solutions they are ultimately trying to achieve a sustainable design.

Sustainability is sometimes a buzzword for the "green" movement, which emphasizes the environmental impact on the earth. The term encompasses more than just the environmental aspect, however. The World Commission on Environment and Development (WCED), also known as the Brundtland Commission, published a report in 1987 that first defined sustainable development as "development which meets the needs of current generations without compromising the ability of future generations to meet their own needs."[14] The idea was that the support of strong economic and social developments is not possible when they destroy natural resources. The term "sustainability" has long been debated because it is quite broad in its definition. In an effort to clarify this, three "pillars" of sustainability were developed at the European Union's Copenhagen Summit with the Treaty of Amsterdam of 1997. Pascal Bader, head of the Policy Department of the Ministry of the Environment of Baden-Württemberg, argued that it takes the "three-pillar model of sustainability"—social, economic, and environmental equity—to support sustainability.[15]

As the well-known preservationist Carl Elefante stated, "the greenest building ever . . . is the one that is already built,"[16] and one viable form of sustainable development is to rehabilitate or reuse an existing historic building. A study by Beser Oktay Vehbi and Sebnem Onal Hoskara emphasizes that the Declaration of Amsterdam recognizes the protection and enhancement of architectural heritage as a part of the economic, social, and cultural factors that shape the environment.[17] Similarly, design solutions created by interior designers for the reuse of a historic building should achieve a balance between the environmental, economic, and social needs of a society in a holistic way in order to provide a high quality of life for current and future generations.[18] Karen Hyllegard, Jennifer Ogle, and Brian Dunbar state that one definition of historic preservation directly connects to sustainability through "the use of processes or materials to sustain the existing form, integrity, and materials of a historic property."[19] They go on to mention a comment by Lisa Tucker, a prominent interior design educator, who states that there is a "lack of interior design research that simultaneously explores sustainability and historic preservation" and encourages "educators and practitioners to incorporate principles from both disciplines into the design process."[20]

Unfortunately, the sustainable benefits of working with existing building stock are not always effectively communicated to interior design students. Design professionals understand the importance of knowing how to work with existing buildings because these projects constitute the majority of their professional practice, but they may not make the connection between utilizing existing building stock and preservation. This could be in part because of the lack of historic preservation education at the undergraduate level along with not fully understanding the connection between interior design and preservation. A whitepaper prepared for a 2008 symposium on green building practices stated that "since most conflicts between green building and preservation standards can be resolved through creative design . . . schools should be altered to integrate these creative approaches. Instead of teaching future [designers] about how to create new green buildings, courses should emphasize how [designers] can successfully incorporate green building practices into historic buildings."[21]

Denise A. Guerin and Jo Ann Asher Thompson take this sentiment further by contending that interior design education must "implement evidence-based design criteria" in order to ensure that designers are creating a design solution of the highest quality. This serves to "prepare future designers to practice with the breadth and depth of knowledge required to solve complex interdisciplinary problems of human behavior and design."[22] Therefore, the integration of a project that involves historic preservation within the context of creating a sustainable design solution provides an opportunity for teaching interior design students about a multitude of issues at the same time for a deeper learning experience.

Once in professional practice, interior designers may not understand that existing resources can and should include the built environment as well as individual materials to achieve a sustainable design solution.[23] As mentioned above in the discussion of the three pillars of sustainability, there are many issues related to sustainable design beyond the environmental perspective so prevalent today, and as all aspects of sustainability are already being incorporated into the interior design undergraduate curriculum, their connection to historic preservation could easily be emphasized. Some of these include how buildings relate to the surrounding environment as well as their interior environment; the efficient utilization of interior spaces and resources; incorporation of energy-efficient lighting and other techniques such as daylighting; the environmental impact of finish selection with documentation supported by industry and practitioners; and the enhancement of collaboration skills.[24] Making the connection for students that what they are learning as sustainable design is also a part of the historic preservation ethic could make them more sensitive designers when working with existing building stock.

Since interior designers often work within existing structures and also focus on the three tenets of sustainable development throughout their designs it is evident from the literature review that it is a natural fit for them to specialize in rehabilitating historic buildings. Additionally, the specific guidelines for the rehabilitation and preservation of a building explicitly discuss issues pertaining to the design. Terminology and design techniques that are relevant to interior designers are found throughout resources available for historic preservation projects, including but not limited to the Secretary of the Interior's Standards for Rehabilitation,[25] the Secretary of the Interior's Standards for the Treatment of Historic Properties,[26] and *National Register Bulletin Number 15*.[27] Interior designers should understand the importance of these standards and how they help to determine if a project qualifies as certified rehabilitation for federal tax purposes. They have also been adopted by many historic districts and planning commissions across the country, as well as serve as guidelines for local officials in reviewing rehabilitation proposals. Not following these guidelines could result in the loss of state and federal tax credits and has the potential for the denial or delay of a proposed project. Although there is an obvious connection between interior design and historic preservation, not all interior design schools emphasize this.

Particular concern with the teaching of historic preservation in Oklahoma came from the Oklahoma State Historic Preservation Office (OSHPO). According to the 2010 document *Tomorrow's Legacy: Oklahoma's Statewide Preservation Plan,* one of the objectives was to "increase opportunities for college and university students to pursue historic preservation-related degrees and careers, and make information about appropriate preservation techniques and technology widely available."[28] But how does OSHPO go about meeting this goal with interior design students and how can educators help them achieve this objective? A true understanding of what students know and how they feel about historic preservation needed to be determined. Are any students actually working on projects that involve a historic building and/or the Secretary of the Interior's Standards of Rehabilitation? Do they know where to find that information? Are they even interested in the topic? Therefore, it is important to assess the level of current knowledge and interest in historic preservation that interior design students have before considering how a program can integrate historic preservation into its interior design curriculum.

Methodology

In order to attain this information, a survey was conducted and administered to all five universities in Oklahoma that had an undergraduate interior design program. These five universities range from community colleges to regional and state universities, as well as including both CIDA-accredited and non-CIDA-accredited schools. Quantitative research methods were employed for this study through the use of an online survey due to economic considerations and the need for rapid collection of the results. The data collected from this self-administered questionnaire were cross-sectional and analyzed using descriptive statistics. Four of the five universities responded to the researcher with their willingness to participate: Oklahoma State University, University of Central Oklahoma, University of Oklahoma, and Tulsa Community College. In order to keep student e-mail addresses confidential, directors of the selected interior design departments asked that the survey be e-mailed to them; they then e-mailed it to their undergraduate interior design students. From the estimates provided by each interior design department there was an approximate population of 350 students enrolled in their programs and surveys were distributed to each student because of the small population size. The survey was open from November 1 to November 17, 2010; a reminder e-mail was sent to each student approximately ten days after the first e-mail to increase the probability of participation.

This instrument was designed by the researcher to explore the main issues cited in the specific purpose of this study and was developed based on the review of the literature. OSHPO's architectural historian, Oklahoma City's historic preservation architect, and the University of Central Oklahoma's interior design director provided input to ensure content validity. To address face validity and determine if the language of the survey was understandable and if there were any flaws with the online delivery method, a pilot study was given to full-time faculty members in the Design Department at the University of Central Oklahoma. The twelve-question survey was organized into three sections. The first section asked questions relating to the demographics of the participants, such as grade level and which university they attended. The second section asked about the participant's knowledge of historic preservation terminology and involvement with preservation projects in school, and the third section assessed students' overall interest in the field of historic preservation. The questions in the instrument were multiple-choice, with a few questions allowing for further comment by the respondent. Responses were formatted as either a continuous scale ranking highest to lowest or as a categorical scale such as yes or no.

Study Results

Of the approximately 350 students e-mailed, 50 students responded to the online survey, for an overall response rate of 15 percent. Of these 50, 46 percent were from the University of Central Oklahoma, 36 percent were from Oklahoma State University, 16 percent were from Tulsa Community College, and 2 percent were from the University of Oklahoma. Of those who responded, 38 percent identified themselves as seniors, 20 percent as juniors, 26 percent as sophomores, and 12 percent as freshmen; 4 percent were identified as none/other. Results of the survey can be found in Table 14.1.

Table 14.1 Survey results from Oklahoma interior design students

Questions	Response in Percentage Yes	No	Not Sure
Have you taken a class at your college that discussed historic preservation? (For this survey, historic preservation means the process of design for the preservation, restoration, rehabilitation, and/or adaptive use of historic buildings.)	22	74	4
Have you been assigned a school project in an interior design class that involved a building that was 50 years or older?	44	50	6
Are you aware there are resources available for individuals working on historic preservation projects?	44	56	n/a
Have you taken any school-sponsored field trips to historic or rehabilitated buildings/neighborhoods?	40	60	n/a

Have you heard of any of these? (Check all that apply)	
The U.S. Department of the Interior	44
National Park Service	74
Technical Preservation Services	8
National Trust for Historic Preservation	54
Preservation Oklahoma	30
Oklahoma State Historic Preservation Office	24
No, I have not heard of any of these	18

	I know nothing about the topic	I am somewhat familiar with the topic	I have more than a basic understanding of the topic	I have extensive knowledge of the topic
How informed are you on the topic of historic preservation?	26	54	18	2

	No, I have never heard of that	No, - I've heard of it but don't know where to find that information	Yes, - if, so where would you find that information
If you were working in a project dealing with the historic preservation of an interior, would you know where to find The Standards of Rehabilitation?	64	30	6

	No role at all	Insignificant role	Significant role	Not sure how they play a role
At what level do you think interior designers play a role in historic preservation?	0	0	92	8

	Not interested at all	Somewhat interested	Very interested
How interested would you be to learn more about how historic preservation is related to the field of interior design?	2	34	64

After delving deeper into the results, the researcher discovered some inconsistent findings. When asked whether they had taken a class that discussed historic preservation, students from the same program and grade level reported both yes and no responses. It was also interesting that of those who reported they had not taken a class that discussed historic preservation, 35.1 percent said they knew nothing about the topic of historic preservation, 56.8 percent said they were somewhat familiar with the topic, and 8.1 percent said they had more than a basic understanding of historic preservation. Similarly, of those who did say they were somewhat familiar with historic preservation, although they had not taken a class that discussed historic preservation, 76.2 percent had never heard of the Secretary of the Interior's Standards for Rehabilitation, while 23.8 percent had heard of them but did not know where to locate that information. The individuals who responded "yes" to taking a class that discussed historic preservation also responded as being somewhat familiar with the topic (45.5 percent), or having more than a basic understanding (45.5 percent), with 9.1 percent having an extensive knowledge of the topic. For those students who responded "yes," 72.7 percent also reported being assigned a historic building for a project, with a majority indicating having been assigned a rehabilitation/adaptive reuse project; 54.5 percent had taken a field trip to a historic or rehabilitated building/neighborhood. Of those same students, 54.4 percent had heard of the Secretary of the Interior's Standards for Rehabilitation, while 18.2 percent felt they knew where to find them and 27.3 percent responded that they had never heard of them. Other interesting responses were recorded on the question related to taking field trips. For those who reported taking a field trip to a historic or rehabilitated building/neighborhood, 60 percent said they had never taken a class that discussed historic preservation.

The limitations of the study included time, reliance on department directors to e-mail the survey link to the students, and low response rate. The survey was conducted as part of a graduate research project; if it had been open for a longer period of time or at the beginning of the semester when students had more free time, there may have been a better response rate. Additionally, due to the low response rate it is impossible to generalize this information to other universities across the United States; however, this was intended as a starting point for the educators in Oklahoma, along with OSHPO, to determine if they needed to improve their teaching of historic preservation in the interior design classroom and to assess if these students were even interested in the field.

Integration into the Interior Design Curriculum

Overall, from the mixed results it appears that the issue of historic preservation is not emphasized, or at least not clearly explained to students. It is also possible that the topic is inconsistently taught because students from the same grade level and program are not responding the same way to whether or not they had a class that discussed the topic, had taken a field trip to a historic or rehabilitated building/neighborhood, or had been assigned a project that dealt with a historic building. It is also odd that students would have taken a field trip to a historic or rehabilitated building/neighborhood yet state this class never discussed historic preservation. Ultimately, although the results from this study indicated inconsistencies in exposure to and discussion of historic preservation, the large number of students who believe that interior designers play a role in preservation and indicated an interest in the subject is encouraging.

So, how do educators incorporate information and/or projects relating interior design to historic preservation into the design curriculum? As stated earlier, the national accrediting body of CIDA oversees the curriculum of interior design programs, so any additions to a design curriculum must consider the constraints of achieving or maintaining this accreditation. CIDA strives to ensure that interior design programs "prepare students for entry-level interior design practice and position them for future professional growth."[29] By necessity, a CIDA-accredited program must provide a broad overview of many different aspects of the interior design field to allow students to graduate within four years. Fortunately, this broad overview is often the method by which students are exposed to the principles behind historic preservation. Although each program accredited by CIDA must provide evidence of compliance with the required standards, it is left up to the individual program to determine overall content that fits into this frame of reference for the curriculum. Currently CIDA outlines sixteen standards, with fourteen of those related directly to student work. Working on a project that involves some aspect of historic preservation provides evidence of compliance with eight of those fourteen standards, so it is a natural fit in any accredited interior design program. For example, one logical way to incorporate more information on historic preservation is through the inclusion of sustainable design practices in the undergraduate curriculum, and evidence of the knowledge and application of sustainable strategies is required in several of the CIDA accreditation standards.[30]

In an effort to introduce interior design students to the principles of historic preservation as well as sustainability, a capstone course asked

14.1 "Old North." Photograph by the author (Settles)

students to adapt a historic building on a university campus into a community art center. The building is known as "Old North" (Figure 14.1) and was the first building constructed on the campus. The first incarnation of the building was completed in 1893, and served as classroom space for students attending this first institution of higher learning in the territory prior to statehood.

Interior design students were required to develop a new floor plan for the existing building of approximately 24,000 square feet. The final design was to include:

- Administrative spaces such as the offices and workstations necessary for the art center staff
- Public areas that consisted of a retail space, café, galleries for art, and a small theater, as well as appropriate restrooms for the building
- Educational and community meeting spaces such as classrooms, working studios, a conference room, and a ballroom for large gatherings
- An apartment for a visiting artist

- Maintenance areas such as gallery archives with conservation area, an office for the facilities manager, and a mechanical/electrical room

Project requirements consisted of specification books that provided purchasing information for finish and furniture selections, as well as a set of drawings that contained:

- Floor and furniture plans
- Reflected ceiling plan detailing the type and placement of lighting, sprinklers, and air supply and return registers
- Working drawings for custom-designed furniture pieces such as a reception desk, an entertainment center, and a conference table

Because the building is on the National Register of Historic Places, the students were also required to follow the Secretary of the Interior's Standards for Rehabilitation and Guidelines for Rehabilitating Historic Buildings as they developed their design for the areas of new construction, particularly Standards 9 and 10 that address new additions and new construction.[31] For example, new walls were added in such a way that the resulting spatial relationships honored the integrity of the structure and did not detract from the original architecture while being easily removable in the future, if necessary, to return the building to its original condition. Similarly, "distinctive features" such as original windows and doorways were retained to provide contemporary users with a direct link to the past.

This project provided students with practical experience in several aspects of sustainability and historic preservation. Along with selecting environmentally sustainable products and finishes for the building, students were able to incorporate other sustainable strategies such as the use of daylighting to reduce energy consumption, a benefit often present in historic buildings due to the necessity of abundant windows for natural lighting and ventilation, as well as strategies that addressed some of the issues inherent in creating an economically sustainable enterprise. They were also able to consider ways to create a socially sustainable space that would serve the cultural needs of the community through the inclusion of gallery spaces that could display a variety of artistic or historic artifacts important to those in the community. These same issues are also critical in the field of historic preservation; in the case of this project, sustainability has a direct connection to preservation as it involves the reuse of an existing historic building.

A portion of the final design submitted by a student follows. These renderings demonstrate the ability to incorporate contemporary aesthetics and functions seamlessly into a historic building, enhancing the appearance of both. For the reception area of the building (Figure 14.2), contemporary furnishings provide a minimalist yet visually interesting interior space within the historic shell of the building that allows the existing architectural features to stand out. These furnishings are appropriate for the contemporary audiences that will be utilizing the new community art center, while the simple shape of the pendant light fixtures is reminiscent of the style of fixtures that may have been in use during the early days of the building. The straight lines of a soffit over the seating area and the frames of a glazed partition for an adjacent conference room complement the lines of the windows providing natural lighting for the space.

Workstations designed for administrative staff (Figure 14.3) are located adjacent to a large bank of windows that supply abundant natural lighting, allowing the facility to reduce energy consumption while providing a nurturing environment for the employees through access to sunlight and natural views. Minimal profiles of upper storage elements allow daylight to penetrate deeper into the interior spaces of the building, reducing the need for artificial lighting in those areas. The placement of the various works of art forms a gallery-like atmosphere in the administrative area, inspiring employees with a display of artwork.

The placement of an informal seating area (Figure 14.4) on the upper level of the building creates a whimsical environment for patrons. The

14.2 Rendering of reception area for community art center. Rendering by Sam Ladwig

14.3 Rendering of workstations for administrative staff. Rendering by Sam Ladwig

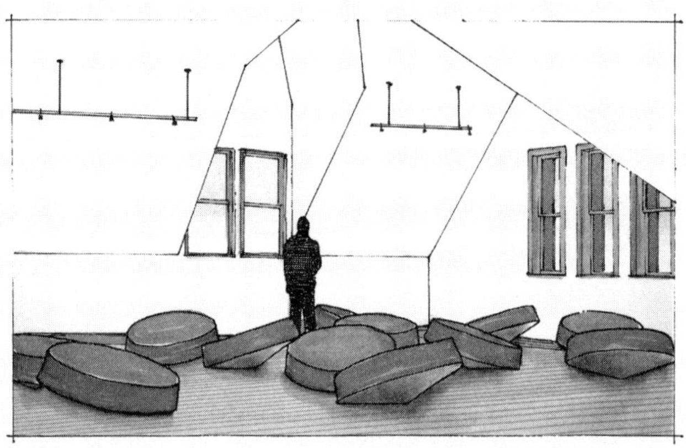

14.4 Rendering of informal seating area on upper level. Rendering by Sam Ladwig

angled lines of the low seating pieces mimic the angles of the dormers, while allowing visitors to appreciate the unique lines of the structure of the building. Though dynamic in nature due to interesting seating shapes, access to natural light, and views of the campus from the windows, the space remains a relaxing respite from other activities downstairs.

As is evident from the sample of the project provided above, the final design solution for this project produced a visually interesting, contemporary aesthetic within the historic shell of the Old North building. But the ultimate value of such projects comes in the wealth of skills the students gain through exposure to the challenges inherent in adapting a historic building for today's use. As interior design students are introduced to the principles behind historic preservation and sustainability within their undergraduate curriculum and are able to apply these principles to actual projects, they expand their knowledge base in both research techniques and practical experience. This practice also allows them to be more knowledgeable about what resources in the built environment are historically significant and thus need more sensitive consideration from designers.[32] This experience helps them determine the most appropriate application of finishes or historically relevant space planning more competently after exposure to and experience in these areas during their undergraduate degree program.

Conclusion

The definition of interior design emphasizes that there is a relationship between design and social responsibility. By breaking down the tenets of social responsibility into social, economic, and environmental aspects, a clear connection to sustainability becomes apparent. While both social responsibility and sustainability are typically taught in undergraduate interior design programs, historic preservation is often overlooked as a sustainable option. The survey administered to interior design students in four university programs in Oklahoma showed that students are often confused about historic preservation but an overwhelming number of them feel that interior designers play a significant role in preservation and are interested in learning more. A great way for instructors to teach historic preservation in a design studio is to create a project that involves the rehabilitation of a historic building. The studio can highlight the integration of interior design and historic preservation, while exposing students to the possibilities of what can be accomplished with a historic building. The general impression of many of today's students is that historic preservation consists of turning old homes into museums. Understanding that the adaptation of a historic building into a contemporary function is still considered preservation comes as a revelation—and one that sparks an interest in proceeding further, as seen in the results of the student survey discussed earlier. Unfortunately, if interior design students are not exposed to the opportunities of design professionals in the field of historic preservation during their undergraduate program, they may remain unaware of a potentially viable niche for future employment. According to the National Center for Education Statistics, in 2009–10 (the most recent year for which information is provided) only 7 percent of those who received a bachelor's degree in interior design went on to receive a master's degree in the field.[33] Undoubtedly, some interior design students who receive a bachelor's degree in that field go on to pursue an advanced degree in another discipline, but the majority go directly into professional practice where they are increasingly working with existing building stock, which may be historic and require a more sensitive approach to developing a designing solution. Having experience and practical skills in the strategies of sustainability and historic preservation in their undergraduate program better enables them to contribute to a project team working with a historic building. Historic preservation is undoubtedly a multifaceted field so in order for these students to gain a better understanding, faculty from many different disciplines must come together with Interior Design Departments to collaborate on various historic preservation project ideas that can utilize students from all types of backgrounds and majors. It would also be beneficial for students if there were a relationship between the Preservation and Design Departments on campus, allowing students to take preservation classes and earn credits toward their degree or possibly earn a minor in preservation. Many interior design faculty members do not specialize in historic preservation so it would be imperative that the knowledge provided to the student come from a preservationist expert. Topics such as building documentation, registering a historic property, and various preservation legal issues and economic issues are rarely discussed in the interior design curriculum and that is why a relationship between the two departments is so important. At the very least, if the departments could collaborate on preservation project ideas it would provide the students with valuable experience, which in turn, provides a potential market niche for professional practice and could represent a measureable advantage over other designers that is so critical in the difficult job market of today.

Notes

1. National Council for Interior Design Qualification, *Definition of Interior Design*, last modified 2004, http://www.ncidq.org (accessed 29 September 2012).

2. American Society of Interior Designers, *Health and Safety*, last modified 2010, http://www.asid.org (accessed 29 September 2012).

3. American Society of Interior Designers, *Health and Safety*.

4. International Interior Design Association, *Mission Statement on Sustainability*, last modified 2005, http://www.iida.org (accessed 29 September 2012).

5. International Interior Design Association, *Mission Statement on Sustainability.*

6. International Federation of Interior Architects/Designers, *Socially Responsible Design*, http://www.ifworld.org (accessed 29 September 2012).

7. Dianne Smith, *Interior Design as Social Design—What? When? And Why?* (Brisbane, Australia: Queensland University of Technology, 2006), 128–30.

8. Barbara Anderson, Peggy Honey, and Michael Dudek, "Interior Design's Social Compact: Key to the Quest for Professional Status," *Journal of Interior Design*, 32:2 (2007), 5–13.

9. Nadia V. Nieves and Catherine Anderson, "Transcending Global, Cultural and Disciplinary Boundaries: The Evolving Role of Interior Design," *Design Principles and Practices: An International Journal*, 4:4 (2010), 81–91.

10. David Philips, Oi-ling Siu, and Anthony Yeh, "The Impacts of Dwelling Conditions on Older Persons' Psychological Well-being in Hong Kong: The Mediating Role of Residential Satisfaction," *Social Science & Medicine*, 60 (2005), 2785–97.

11. Ayman Ahmed Ezzat Othman, "Corporate Social Responsibility of Architectural Design Firms Towards a Sustainable Built Environment in South Africa," *Architectural Engineering and Design Management*, 5 (2009), 36–45.

12. Othman, "Corporate Social Responsibility," 36–45.

13. Donovan D. Rypkema, "Economics, Sustainability, and Historic Preservation," paper presented at the National Trust Annual Conference, Portland, Oregon, October 2005.

14. Kaj Barlund, "Sustainable Development—Concept and Action," UNESCO, http://www.unesco.org/oes/nutshell/2004–2005/focus_sustainable_development.html (accessed 29 September 2012).

15. Pascal Bader, "Sustainability—From Principle to Practice," *Goethe-Institut*, http://www.goethe.de/ges/umw/dos/nac/den/en3106180.htm (accessed 29 September 2012).

16. Norman Tyler, *Historic Preservation: An Introduction to its History, Principles, and Practices* (New York: W. W. Norton & Co., 2009).

17. Beser Oktay Vehbi and Sebnem Onal Hoskra, "A Model for Measuring the Sustainability Level of Historic Urban Quarters," *European Planning Studies*, 17:5 (2009), 715–39.

18. Iman Raeisi, Alireza Kharazmi Nezhad, and Maryam Hafezifar, "Architectural Design Principles of Public Spaces Based on Social Sustainability Approach: A Case Study in Ardabil, Iran," *Design Principles and Practices: An International Journal*, 4:5 (2010), 99–113.

19. Karen Hyllengard, Jennifer Ogle, and Brian Dunbar, "Sustainability and Historic Preservation in Retail Design: Integrating Design into a Model of the REI Denver Decision-Making Process," *Journal of Interior Design*, 29:1/2 (2003), 33.

20. Hyllengard, Ogle, and Dunbar, "Sustainability and Historic Preservation," 33.

21. "Green Building Practices and the Secretary of the Interior's Standards for Historic Preservation," whitepaper presented at the Pocantico Symposium, "Sustainability and Historic Preservation—Making Policy," Pocantico Hills, New York, 2008.

22. Denise A. Guerin and Jo Ann Asher Thompson, "Interior Design Education in the 21st Century: An Educational Transformation," *Journal of Interior Design*, 30:2 (2004), 1–12.

23. Jack Pybum, "Historic Preservation in Architectural Education: Assessing the Past, Envisioning the Future," *Future Anterior*, 2:2 (2005), 44–51.

24. Cathy Steig, "The Sustainability Gap," *Journal of Interior Design*, 32:1 (2006), vii–xxi.

25. U.S. Department of the Interior, Secretary of the Interior's Standards of Rehabilitation, National Park Service, http://www.nps.gov/hps/tps/standguide/rehab/rehab_standards.htm (accessed 19 September 2012).

26. See Kay D. Weeks and Anne E. Grimmer, *The Secretary of the Interior's Standards for the Treatment of Historic Properties: With Guidelines for Preserving, Rehabilitation, Restoring & Reconstructing Historic Buildings* (Washington, D.C.: U.S. Department of the Interior, 1995).

27. National Park Service, *National Register Bulletin 15: How to Apply the National Register Criteria for Evaluation* (Washington, D.C.: U.S. Department of the Interior, 1995).

28. Oklahoma State Historic Preservation Office, *Tomorrow's Legacy: Oklahoma's Statewide Preservation Plan* (Oklahoma City: Oklahoma Historical Society, 2010), 41.

29. Council for Interior Design Accreditation, *Professional Standards*, last modified 2011, http://accredit-id.org/professional-standards (accessed 30 September 2012).

30. Council for Interior Design Accreditation, *Professional Standards.*

31. U.S. Department of the Interior, Secretary of the Interior's Standards of Rehabilitation.

32. Jeffery Ochsner and Gail Dubrow, "Architecture and Historic Preservation: Invigorating the Dialogue," *Journal of Architectural Education*, 47:4 (1994), 186.

33. U.S. Department of Education National Center for Education Statistics, *Bachelor's, Master's, and Doctor's Degrees Conferred by Degree-Granting Institutions, by Sex of Student and Discipline Division*, last modified 2009–10, http://nces.ed.gov/programs/digest/d11/tables/dt11_290.asp (accessed 30 September 2012).

15 The Critical Role of Preservation in Graduate Real Estate Curricula

Robert Benedict and Cari Goetcheus

Over the past two centuries the field of historic preservation has become its own distinct discipline with links to both older disciplines of history, architecture, and cultural studies and newer fields such as real estate, economics, and conservation, making preservation an endeavor that embraces a multidisciplinary approach.[1] Preservation curricula have long offered single courses in related fields to broaden the horizons of preservation students, yet a consistent curricula dilemma has been balancing the need to provide preservation-focused skill sets (i.e., preservation theory, historic style identification, preservation law, historic building materials, etc.) with rudimentary exposure to the variety of realms within which preservation resides (i.e., real estate development, public policy, land use planning, landscape architecture, etc.). The intent of this chapter is to study one of preservation's related disciplines—real estate development—and a perceived curricula gap that indicates for graduate students interested in adaptive reuse of historic properties and historic tax incentives that there is little historic preservation training currently offered in those programs. Prior to delving into the study results, it is first necessary to understand the evolution of real estate development graduate programs of study and a recent real estate practicum case study that directly led to this survey.

Evolution of Real Estate Development as a Graduate Program of Study

Creation of cities has occurred worldwide for millennia with entrepreneurs long playing a critical role in U.S. development. Although formal real estate courses were taught as early as the 1890s at Harvard and Columbia Universities, they lacked a structured content to create proficient real estate development professionals. As a result, there was an inconsistent familiarity with laws, customs, and pricing that often led to outright fraud and lack of confidence with brokers and developers.[2] In response to the lack of industry standards, unbridled developments, and odd, sometimes incompatible, juxtapositions of land uses in larger cities, by the 1920s a regulatory environment had arisen. As such, real estate practitioners began to be required to attain broad education and training.

Hence, by 1925 the University of Wisconsin's Richard Ely created a program in public land utility economics that eventually became a graduate program in real estate development. Under the leadership of the academic visionary James Graaskamp in the 1960s, the program became nationally renowned for its multifaceted ethical approach to real estate development. In addition to an increased focus on ethical standards, the University of Wisconsin graduate program in real estate also emphasized valuation and real estate finance core courses that ultimately influenced the foundation for the industry.[3] The Massachusetts Institute of Technology, New York University, Cornell University, and the University of Southern California soon followed suite with real estate graduate programs in the 1960s and 1970s. The trend broadened in the 1980s, 1990s, and the early 2000s with the emergence of development-oriented curricula via new programs at Texas A&M University, Johns Hopkins University, Clemson University, Arizona State University, and the University of Maryland.

As the advantages of embodied energy began to be appreciated in the 1970s, and the intelligent reuse of historic buildings was brought to the forefront, a 1980 seminal study by Richard G. Stein and Partners touted rehabilitation as an environmentally sensitive response to new construction.[4] Developers and preservationists discovered a mutual interest that influenced then emerging graduate programs in both disciplines. The use of historic tax incentives during the 1980s and subsequent decades also increased the awareness and viability of adaptive reuse development strategies. Graduate real estate courses, in such subjects as public-private partnerships and development process, began integrating aspects of the historic tax credit program into their syllabi, thereby raising student interest.

The expanding economy of the 1980s and 1990s demanded additional real estate professionals. Although many large real estate companies continued to mine master of business administration (MBA) programs for employees, those programs were traditional with an orientation toward finance issues and few courses in real estate. The increased complexity of the real estate industry, resulting from market segmentation and economic volatility coupled with a more-focused demand from practitioners, created a need for graduates with specialized real estate degrees and a broader skill set—hence the emergence of the master of real estate development degree. The increase in real estate development graduate programs responded to greater demand by companies looking to hire well-educated graduates with dual competencies in theory and practice.[5]

As real estate education evolved from the 1920s emphasis on purely financial reward, to 1960s enlightenment regarding the social impact of real estate development on communities, to 1990s increased market complexities, in 2008 Margo Weinstein and Elaine Worzala opted to research fourteen real estate graduate programs to determine "what elements make up a top graduate program in real estate that enhances practice."[6] From that survey of both new and well-established programs, eleven key elements were identified:

> strength of the graduate curriculum with core courses related to industry needs and job opportunities
>
> combination of theory and practice with case studies, simulation, and live projects
>
> faculty of scholars who understand the real estate business
>
> research and publication agenda by instructors to enhance the reputation of the program
>
> industry ties with support from active advisory boards, professionals, and companies
>
> participation of students and faculty at conferences and seminars
>
> mentors who provide a depth of understanding of the industry to the students
>
> career opportunities facilitated by the program
>
> university support and connections
>
> collaboration and alliances with other educational institutions
>
> core competencies to teach key skills and competencies to succeed in the industry[7]

The combination of these factors was identified as not only filling the increased demand for highly educated professionals in the real estate industry but also enhancing the reputations of the various programs. The mastery of a core curriculum in real estate consisting of courses that include real estate principles, development process, site planning, real estate finance, law, valuation, and construction management needs to be balanced with program administrators staying attuned to changing market needs of practitioners so that their graduates are marketable.

One of the biggest challenges faced by graduate programs in both real estate development and historic preservation is relevance of their curriculum to current market conditions. Graduate real estate programs are particularly challenged to meet the needs of an industry that has recently experienced profound changes, and has become more segmented with a broader demand for graduates who have skill sets ranging from complex financial modeling to asset management. To better prepare real estate development graduate students for this changing environment, many programs have begun to require completion of a core curriculum with areas of specialization focused on student interests.

Specialties have expanded over the past decade to include sustainability, green building practices, urban infill, mixed-use development, New Urbanist principles, asset management, and development finance. Adaptive reuse and historic rehabilitations have become increasingly popular topics as the traditional real estate discipline focus on greenfield and suburban development has been influenced by changing demographics and a greater demand for an urban lifestyle.

Many of the specialized graduate real estate programs have modified their curriculums to be more attuned to the demands of the employment market. In 2009, Charles C. Tu et al. explored stakeholder assessments of real estate programs engaged in traditional and multidisciplinary approaches.[8] A traditional approach is described as an MBA program with real estate concentrations, while a multidisciplinary approach, noted as master in real estate development (MRED), master of science in real estate (MSRE), and master of science in real estate development (MSRED), relies on an integration of related discipline coursework in areas such as construction management, architecture, and planning, with the intent to more clearly represent real-life practice. The multidisciplinary programs strive to not only fulfill the need for education in real estate finance, market analysis, and real estate development processes and valuations but also the current trends of sustainability and adaptive reuse.

Tu et al.'s study focused on the various elements of a successful real estate program, similar to Weinstein and Worzala, yet asked more detailed questions of faculty, students, alumni, and board members when they rated their respective programs. The key finding of the study was the need to revise existing programs and curricula to respond to the changing demands of real estate employers and market forces. To fulfill the need for real-time data, research, and connection to practitioners, and because there is no accreditation body devoted exclusively to real estate development programs, many programs have chosen to align themselves with professional advocacy organizations such as the Urban Land Institute, the American Real Estate Society, and the International Council of Shopping Centers.

Because of the interest in sustainability and adaptive reuse, real estate development graduate students and alumni have recognized the shared values they have with preservationists regarding the potential use of historic structures. Carl Elefante's 2007 proclamation in *Forum Journal* that the "greenest" building is one that has already been built has played a key role in elevating the interest of real estate development students to have a broader knowledge in this area.[9] The ability to rehabilitate a historic property for an adaptive reuse in a sensitive manner is derived from a clear understanding of community character and the complexities related to the disciplines of real estate and historic preservation.

In addition to the recent, shared theme of sustainability and green building, real estate developers and preservationists have both become proponents of economic incentives that foster a profitable model of development with historic rehabilitations.[10] It is widely accepted within both disciplines that the economics of historic rehabilitations is a limiting factor and even with different discipline theoretical approaches there are similarities that reinforce collaboration.[11]

Although real estate development graduates today are better prepared for complex development activities and increasingly complex financial and regulatory environments, because there are a limited number of programs across the United States there are only a small number of graduates who have benefited from this specialized education. As more graduates enter the real estate field with diversified interests, one of the greatest educational challenges will be to include additional disciplines in the curricula so as to provide a better understanding of the foundational attributes from both historic preservation and real estate development to foster increased collaboration.

To understand the possible difficulty in collaboration, it is necessary to explore the reality and stereotypes about the personalities within the real estate development field. The real estate industry has an entrepreneurial nature about it with practitioners willing to take substantial risk. The need to share a creative vision requires a self-confident individual who can demand exceptional performance from members of her or his development team. Yet it is a fine line for a developer to balance strong self-confidence and a positive ego, while allowing creativity to reign, which in many cases demands input from a variety of disciplines. As a result of the difficulty in balancing these aspects, a common stereotype of a developer is that of an overbearing egomaniac with unrealistic demands of the development team. Jon Hammer's 2003 *The Art of Ego Management* cites numerous biographies of successful developers William Zeckendorf, Paul Reichmann, and Donald Trump—all with unbridled egos.[12] Although a strong ego is often required to convey a strong belief in a risky development, if the ego is undisciplined it can unnecessarily restrain other members of the team from developing the needed "checks and balances" to counter irrational decisions. Team collaboration depends on the developer's willingness to hire independent and creative thinkers who provide creative services without being subjected to a narrowly focused vision. Often the developer's ego and ineffective collaboration is the result of unfamiliarity with the complexities of design issues or in the case of historic rehabilitations, the regulatory environment or the Secretary of the Interior's Standards for the Treatment of Historic Properties.

A successful paradigm for effective collaboration within the development team is the "cultivator" approach whereby a vision should be pursued for the common good with an interdisciplinary approach.[13] Richard Barrett's 1998 *Liberating the Corporate Soul: Building a Visionary Organization* advocates a similar approach with the individual rising above "self-interest to take on communal interests of well-being."[14] With an interdisciplinary curricula approach that increases the knowledge of preservation fundamentals, graduate students in real estate development will have a better understanding of the complexities of that field, engendering improved collaboration on historic rehabilitations and adaptive reuse projects.

In 2011, Joseph T. L. Ooi and Shi-Ming Yu surveyed real estate practitioners and stakeholders to identify key factors in the changing field of real estate development to assess how graduate real estate programs have responded to those changes. One of the three most important criteria identified was relevant coverage of a practical orientation. The ability to offer project-based approaches that simulate real-life practice has produced learning outcomes favored by students.[15] Ooi and Yu's research concluded that prospective real estate students are more interested in the practical application of new knowledge than in a theory and principles-based curriculum approach.[16] Of course, any special elective tracks should not only fulfill department and degree requirements, but should be compatible with the expertise of the faculty teaching courses and providing guidance to graduate students.[17]

In an attempt to do what Ooi and Yu's research indicates, a recent direction among many graduate real estate development programs is the addition of a practicum course. In lieu of a thesis, the practicum combines all of a program's previous coursework within the context of a capstone course. Practicum courses are usually structured in a team framework with the students completing a comprehensive development proposal on an actual site to gain a deeper understanding of the challenges of a "real" project strategy. It is within this team approach that graduate students experience how the developer, as a cultivator, can draw from an interdisciplinary approach to broaden the development vision.

Background on the Need to do a Survey

The impetus for this research arose from an assessment of the 2011 practicum in the Clemson University MRED program. Like other graduate real estate development programs, the purpose of Clemson's practicum is to demonstrate advanced skills via a semester-long project focused on the commercial development typology. As a capstone course, the practicum is a simulated development exercise that draws from all of the previous coursework and internship experiences over the two-year program. The practicum is completed during the final semester of the curriculum. The learning outcomes of such integrated capstone courses have been beneficial as a pedagogical strategy stressing participatory learning and creative problem solving.[18]

The Clemson practicum selects actual development sites and engages active participation from developers and related practitioners into the students' proposed developments. Although the students benefit from the insight and motivations of the developers, they are clearly instructed to create their own vision and development strategy for the site. It is a mutually beneficial arrangement as the students gain access to some of the leading developers in the Southeast, while the developers are provided with creative and professional site, market, and financial analyses. Many Clemson University MRED alumni during their exit surveys state that the practicum course was the most beneficial course of their graduate studies.

The Practicum Relationship with the Developer

The Clemson University MRED program reached an agreement with the developer Bob Hughes in the fall of 2010 to use the former South Carolina Department of Mental Health campus in Columbia as their 2011 practicum project. Hughes had recently entered into an option agreement for the purchase of the property. Prior to reaching an agreement with Hughes, the owner had retained the prominent architect and urban planner Andres Duany of Duany, Plater, Zyberk and Company (DPZ) to complete a redevelopment master plan for the site. Although Hughes, along with Cooper Cary Architects from Atlanta, later retained DPZ the students were invited to help create a new vision for the campus. Dramatically

15.1 Designed by Samuel Sloan, the Babcock Building was built in four phases from 1857 to 1885. Photograph by the author (Benedict)

different market conditions ultimately influenced Hughes's departure from the original DPZ master plan along with his desire to start with a clean slate for his development strategy.

The historically significant property consisted of a 165-acre, brick-walled campus with a complex circulation network lined by large trees that organized and connected numerous historic structures. Two iconic buildings on the site are well known: the Babcock Building (Figure 15.1) designed by Samuel Sloan and built in four phases (1857–85); and the original asylum building designed by Robert Mills and built in 1828.[19] Although the Mills building was excluded from the practicum project due to its continued use by the state, eight other historically and architecturally significant structures extant from the nineteenth and early twentieth centuries were included. Many of the historic structures are eligible for the National Register of Historic Places and capable of being adaptively reused for many purposes. Many other notable structures support the campus's architectural and historical integrity.

Aside from the noted structures, the campus design is also historically significant as a physical representation of the physician Thomas Story Kirkbride's influential theory on the "moral treatment" of patients regarding their mental health rejuvenation. Kirkbride's theories applied to hospital and grounds design before the Civil War, emphasizing parks and natural surroundings to both stimulate and calm patients' minds with natural beauty. As a result, the campus has a significant collection of mature hardwood trees of various exotic species, including a large Chinese tung nut tree, a Mediterranean cork oak, and the state record chaste tree. Magnolia trees line the main drive with many of them recognized as heritage trees. There are also many ornamental shrubs such as camellias and azaleas on the site.

Briefly used as a Civil War prison known as Camp Asylum, it housed captured Union officers prior to Sherman's invasion in 1865. The South Carolina Department of Natural Resources and the State Historic Preservation Office have been in negotiation with the current owner/developer regarding an archaeological survey to delineate the camp area.[20] Adjacent to the Babcock Building are several historic structures, including the 1918 male and female dining halls and the laundry building, which was built prior to 1888.[21] Lesser known due to their separation from the main campus, the historic bakery and mattress buildings are unprotected yet worthy of local historic landmark designation.[22]

Two additional structures that possess historic and architectural significance are the Williams and Ensor buildings. The Williams Building (Figure 15.2), formerly used for drug- and alcohol-addicted patients, is known for its monumentality with a red brick facade and imposing portico reminiscent of Classic Revival architecture. The Ensor Building, smaller in stature than the Williams Building, still possesses architectural significance as an excellent example of an early twentieth-century academic, research laboratory building.

Other notable buildings include the Chapel of Hope, built in 1959, and the physicians' cottages, a series of bungalows possessing distinctive craftsman elements. All of these buildings represent the expansion of the

15.2 The Williams Building was constructed in 1938. Photograph by the author (Benedict)

mental health facility into a self-sufficient campus from the late nineteenth century into the mid-twentieth century.

Class Structure and Course Challenges with the Subject Property

For the practicum, the students were divided into teams to complete a comprehensive development proposal. The course objectives required a thorough site conditions assessment, and market and financial analysis to prepare a master plan for a mixed-use, urban town center. The adaptive reuse of the historic buildings presented a unique challenge to the graduate real estate students. The Babcock Building, whose central portion had been listed on the National Register of Historic Places in 1981, posed the biggest challenge in some students' minds as they questioned the significance of the unlisted building wings that, ironically, were older than the central core.

The campus was considered endangered and local preservation leaders had long expressed concern about the future of its cultural resources. As the practicum project progressed through the spring semester of 2011, the graduate students completed a comprehensive assessment and proposal that their previous courses had enabled them to conduct, including in-depth market and financial analyses for a redevelopment plan. It became increasingly evident, however, that most of the students lacked a fundamental understanding of the architectural, landscape design, and historical significance of the property. Although their research revealed that the Babcock and Williams buildings and the campus entry gate were either locally designated historic landmarks or had been listed on the National Register of Historic Places, the students questioned why other, more utilitarian non-designated buildings, such as the 1917 dining hall and the physicians' cottages built in the 1920s, would be worthy of preservation. Similarly, the historic landscape elements of the campus were only considered by one of the four teams, which did ultimately integrate conservation of those elements into their final proposed development plans. The historic buildings included in the adaptive reuse plans presented unfamiliar challenges to the graduate real estate students such as repair or replacement of windows, removal of historic outbuildings, and even substantial exterior alterations like the removal of building wings. Although the development proposals included a comprehensive analysis of site conditions, zoning restrictions, in-depth market analysis, and highly detailed financial analysis including historic tax credits, without adequate historic preservation coursework, the students lacked the fundamental understanding of historic material assessments, the significance of local and National Register designations, and, to a lesser extent, the intricacies of historic tax credits to properly address all of the issues on the site. As a result, there was an overall lack of sensitivity to the historic elements within the redevelopment plans. Despite the challenges of their adaptive reuse proposals, the students were enthusiastic about the potential of the historic structures and the infill opportunities on the property, with many expressing a strong desire to be involved in similar projects in their professional career. The project was ambitious and rewarding for the students and the developer was extremely complimentary of the final proposals. A jury of local leaders and practitioners critiqued each team's proposal and concluded that the students had completed highly professional proposals with creative approaches that would be of great benefit. The only shortfall was the lack of preservation knowledge, which it is assumed would have led to more sensitive approaches for their adaptive reuse proposals. Although the students had been introduced to basic principles of historic preservation, historic tax credits, and related tax incentives through courses in real estate development process and public-private partnership, their knowledge was perfunctory. Additional readings were required for the practicum, and a doctoral student with professional experience in preservation was enlisted as a teaching assistant to assist the instructor of record, an assistant professor with a graduate degree and professional experience in historic preservation. The lack of previous courses in the MRED program placed the students at a disadvantage and despite the remedial coursework required while working on the project, the development proposals could have more strongly addressed adaptive reuse and historic rehabilitation work for the subject property.

Research Participants, Methods, and Questions

Upon completion of the real estate practicum, review of student course evaluations, and reflection by the authors on whether other real estate programs may be encountering similar experiences, the idea of surveying current students and alumni in both graduate real estate development and historic preservation programs evolved. The authors chose to survey the real estate development programs first, followed by the historic preservation programs. Hence, the hypothesis leading to the development of a survey was that there is a gap within the current curricula of graduate real estate programs regarding students who have an interest in historic preservation and adaptive reuse, with the perception that perhaps real estate development programs are not doing a good job in preparing students for historic projects they may encounter during their career. The emphasis on current students and alumni, rather than faculty or employers, was intentional for three purposes: to identify if future real estate development professionals have an interest in historic preservation, adaptive reuse projects, and the use of historic tax incentive mechanisms; to determine what kinds of education has occurred or does occur regarding historic preservation in real estate development programs; and to identify the kinds of typical historic preservation courses that may be of interest to real estate development graduate students. Based on the survey results there is an interest by the authors to further survey faculty and real estate professionals on these and related topics.

Although there are a variety of MS and MBA programs that have a concentration in real estate development that could have been included in this survey, the intent of this survey was to not only focus on programs that offer a master of real estate development *degree*, but programs that have similar mission statements and curricula that emphasize project-based coursework. As such, four programs were identified for survey: Arizona State University, Auburn University, Clemson University, and the University of Maryland. Once identified, program directors were contacted and invited to participate in the survey; all four program directors accepted the invitation. Via e-mail the program directors, or their designated administrators, then distributed to the program's respective current students and alumni information from the authors regarding

Table 15.1 **Real Estate Development Programs Surveyed**

	Students	Alumni
Arizona State University	40	240
Auburn University	29	0 (program started in 2011)
University of Maryland	90	150
Clemson University	20	96

Total Sample — 665

research intent and time commitment, as well as a URL link to the online survey. The program breakdown of students and alumni that were provided access to the survey are listed in Table 15.1.

The online survey, administered electronically via *Survey Monkey* during August 2012, consisted of thirteen closed-end questions with a combination of 5-point, Likert Scale rankings and yes/no/do not know answers. Questions 1–5 asked for foundational information such as discipline of study, whether the surveyed individuals pursued a joint degree or graduate certificate, why they had selected their graduate program, and if they had taken any preservation or design courses. Questions 6–13 asked about their perception of a relationship between the fields of real estate and historic preservation, whether their program of study adequately addressed preservation, if they felt specific courses in preservation would have been useful to their education, if they were interested in adaptive reuse projects or using historic tax incentives, whether they would be interested in an elective track in historic preservation or a certificate in historic preservation, and whether they felt working on a project with historic preservation students would have been useful to them. Although there was not any formal pre-testing of the survey questions, discussions with historic preservation and real estate program academic colleagues regarding the types of questions that would reveal the most information were undertaken.

Survey Findings

A total of 83 respondents completed the survey out of a pool of 665 potential current students and alumni across all 4 programs, resulting in a response rate of 12.5 percent. After confirming that survey respondents were either current students or alumni of a real estate development program (Question 1), answers to whether the respondents were pursuing joint degrees such as MRED/MHP (Question 2) and why they had selected their particular graduate program (Question 3) were revealed. None of the respondents were pursuing joint MRED/MHP degree although six respondents were pursuing joint degrees in real estate and planning or law. In Question 4 students revealed they selected their respective program primarily for the core curriculum (66 percent) and a desire to have an interdisciplinary curriculum (58 percent). This desire to learn from other disciplines is consistent with research findings related to an increased desire for additional coursework in historic preservation.[23] Question 5 confirmed that the respondents had mostly (85–88 percent) taken the same core courses in their graduate real estate curriculum with courses in principles, development process, finance, market analysis, and valuation.

Gauging the perspective of graduate real estate students toward whether there is a relationship between their discipline and historic preservation (Question 6), approximately 96.8 percent of respondents affirmed that relationship and 82.8 percent stated it would have been helpful to have taken fundamental preservation courses within their real estate curriculum (Question 8, part a). Two focal areas for real estate practitioners who undertake historic rehabilitation projects are knowledge of adaptive reuse and historic tax credits. Accordingly, respondents were asked whether they intended to be (or if an alumni, if they had been) involved in adaptive reuse projects with historic properties (Question 9, part a) and historic tax credits (Question 10, part a). Survey respondents revealed that 62.5 percent had a desire to be involved in the adaptive reuse of historic properties and 54 percent hoped to be (or had been if alumni) involved in historic tax credits. Respectively, 20 percent and 27 percent responded, "do not know."

To better evaluate courses that would appeal to graduate real estate students and alumni, respondents were asked to rank six fundamental preservation courses (Question 8, part b). The results, revealed in Figure 15.3, summarize the prioritized course rankings, with preservation economics and introduction to historic preservation being most desirable. This is consistent with a related question (Question 9, part b), where 80 percent of respondents stated it would be helpful (or would have been helpful with alumni) to have taken a course in historic preservation practices that focused on the adaptive reuse of historic properties.

The positive responses related to a desire for additional courses in historic preservation raise pedagogical questions as to what curricula framework would be appropriate. Two survey questions addressed whether the respondents would be willing to pursue an elective track (Question 11) or a certificate program in historic preservation within their graduate real estate curricula (Question 12). Figure 15.4 reveals there was a positive

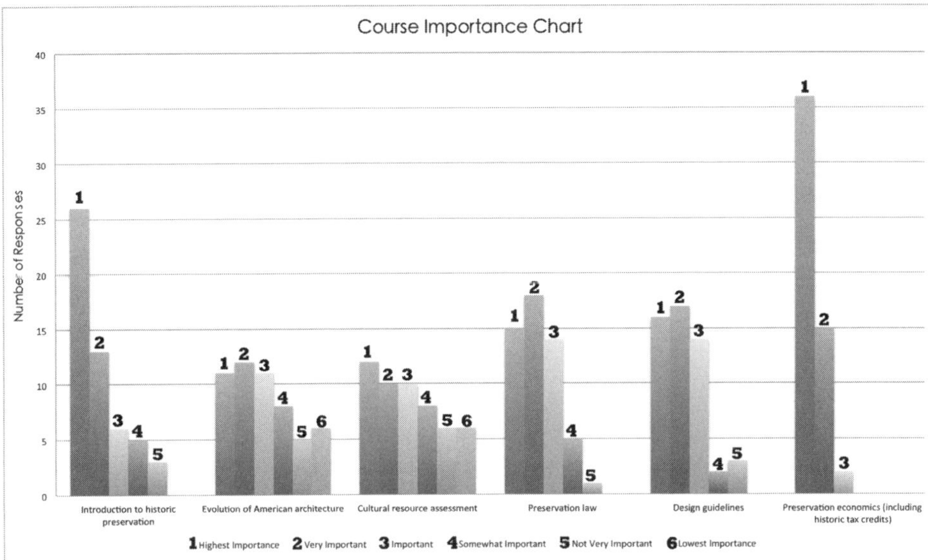

15.3 Survey respondents' desired preservation courses that could be offered in master of real estate development programs. Table by the author (Benedict)

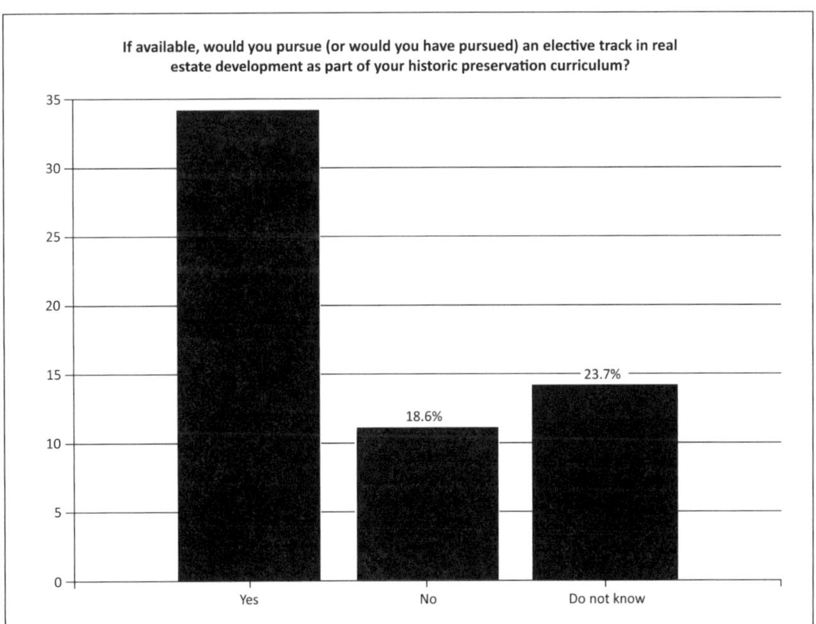

15.4 Survey respondents' interest in pursuing a preservation elective track in their graduate real estate development curriculum. Table by the author (Benedict)

response (57.6 percent) to pursuing an elective track while a certificate program was less appealing (47.5 percent). Historic preservation certificate programs typically require 9–15 credit hours and the respondents may have considered the drawback of an additional semester to fulfill those requirements. Elective tracks within many graduate real estate curricula, however, commonly do not demand additional course requirements.

Conclusion

This survey confirms the authors' hypothesis regarding a gap within the current curricula of graduate real estate programs for students who have an interest in historic preservation and adaptive reuse. Additionally, the authors' intent to identify interest by future real estate development professionals in historic preservation, adaptive reuse projects, and the use of historic tax incentive mechanisms; determine what kinds of education has occurred or does occur regarding historic preservation in real estate development programs; identify the kinds of historic preservation courses that may be of interest to real estate development students; and the notion that perhaps real estate development programs are not doing as good of a job as they could to prepare well-educated professionals that desire to work in the area of historic preservation were also confirmed.

Graduate real estate students value the interdisciplinary focus of their respective programs yet see a need for additional course offerings focused on preservation economics, historic designations/design guidelines, preservation law, cultural materials assessments, and best development practices for adaptive reuse projects. While in recent years graduate real estate programs have recognized the need to better integrate green building practices into their curricula, there has been little recognition of the need to integrate historic preservation knowledge into their course offerings. The only known real estate development program in the United States that offers an elective track in historic preservation is at the University of Utah. As one of their five focus areas (finance, transportation, sustainability, entrepreneurship, historic preservation), the historic preservation focus area requires 9 credit hours that specifically address preservation theory and principles. Completion of the coursework delivers a certificate of historic preservation to the graduate student.[24]

This research offers insight into graduate real estate students' desire for some education in historic preservation to enhance their potential for doing adaptive reuse project work, specific types of preservation courses that are considered value added in a graduate real estate program, and broadly how to bridge the gap between graduate real estate curricula and historic preservation. With increased collaboration between educators of graduate programs in both disciplines, students can be better prepared for this sector of real estate development.

Notes

1. Michael Tomlan, "Historic Preservation Education: Alongside Architecture in Academia," *Journal of Architectural Education*, 47:4 (1994), 187–91.
2. Michael Weiss, *The Rise of the Community Builders* (New York: Columbia University Press, 1987), 21.
3. University of Wisconsin School of Business, James A. Graaskamp Center for Real Estate Development, "Our History of Innovation," http://www.bus.wisc.edu/wcre/mba.asp.htm. Accessed 17 August 2012.
4. Richard Stein et al. *Handbook for Energy Use for Building Construction* (Champaign: Energy Resource Group of the Center for Advanced Computation at the University of Illinois at Urbana, 1980).
5. Louis A. Galuppo and Elaine Worzala, "A Study into the Important Elements of a Masters Degree in Real Estate," *Journal of Real Estate Practice and Education*, 7:1 (2004), 25–42.
6. Margo Weinstein and Elaine Worzala, "Graduate Real Estate Programs: An Analysis of the Past and Present and Trends for the Future," *Journal of Real Estate Literature*, 16:3 (2008), 387–413.
7. Weinstein and Worzala, "Graduate Real Estate Programs," 403–4.
8. Charles C. Tu, Margo Weinstein, Elaine Worzala, and Lauren Lukens, "Elements of Successful Graduate Real Estate Programs: Perceptions of the Stakeholders," *Journal of Real Estate Practice and Education*, 12:2 (2009), 105–21.
9. Carl Elefante, "The Greenest Building Is. . . . One That Is Already Built," *Forum Journal*, 21:4 (2007), 26–38.
10. Donovan Rypkema, *The Economics of Historic Preservation: A Community Leader's Guide*, Second Edition (Washington, DC: The National Trust for Historic Places, 2005), 28–29.
11. Jeremy Wells, "Historic Preservation: Challenges to Collaboration with Other Disciplines," *The Ethical Design of Places*, 40 (2009), 83–91.
12. Jon Hammer, "The Art of Ego Management," *Urban Land* (August 2003), 128.
13. Linda Groat and David Wang, *Architectural Research Methods* (New York: John Wiley and Sons, Inc., 2002).
14. Richard Barrett, *Liberating the Corporate Soul: Building a Visionary Organization* (Boston: Butterworth-Heinemann, 1998).
15. Jay Q. Butler, Karl L. Guntermann, and Mimi Wolverton, "Integrating the Real Estate Curriculum," *Journal of Real Estate Practice and Education*, 1:1 (1998), 51–66.
16. Joseph T. L. Ooi and Shi-Ming Yu, "Graduate Real Estate Education in Singapore: What Prospective Students Look For," *Journal of Real Estate Practice and Education*, 14:1 (2011), 35–45.
17. Kenneth C. Williamson III and David L. Bilbo, "A Road Map to an Effective Graduate Construction Education Program," *Journal of Construction Education*, 4:3 (1999), 260–77.
18. Edward M. Lonsdale, Kenneth C. Mylrea, and Martha W. Ostheimer, "Professional Preparation: A Course That Successfully Teaches Needed Skills Using Different Pedagogical Techniques," *Journal of Engineering Education*, 84:2 (1995), 187–91.
19. Historic Columbia Foundation, *Cultural Resource Management Assessment of the South Carolina Department of Mental Health Bull Street Campus* (Columbia, SC: Historic Columbia Foundation, 2005), 1–12.

20. Robert Hughes, interview by Robert Benedict, Columbia, SC, March 2011.

21. Sanborn Fire Insurance Company, 1888: 1910.

22. Historic Columbia Foundation, *Cultural Resource Management Assessment of the South Carolina Department of Mental Health Bull Street Campus,* 12.

23. Butler, Guntermann, and Wolverton, "Integrating the Real Estate Curriculum," 51–66.

24. University of Utah, "University of Utah Master of Real Estate Development," http://www.business.utah.edu/master-of-real-estate-development.htm. Accessed 1 September 2012.

16 Social Science Research Methodologies and Historic Preservation: Broadening the Possibilities for a Preservation Thesis

Jeremy C. Wells

Regardless of the type of major associated with a master's program, degree coursework typically terminates with some kind of capstone project or a thesis in order to demonstrate, in a holistic way, the mastery of particular subject matter.[1] Some programs require a thesis, project, or comprehensive exam, while others let students choose one of these options. Since the 1980s, there has been a trend in many academic degree programs to replace theses with capstone projects, due to problems with low completion rates for theses.[2] In general, however, there is a lack of research on the positive and negative aspects of the empirical research thesis, capstone project, or comprehensive examination in assessing student learning, and even less on how these activities relate to future professional endeavors. This chapter addresses the need for empirical theses in historic preservation degree programs and how a curriculum might accommodate this goal.

The thesis is nearly as old as the university itself, with origins in the medieval period as a requirement of graduate programs.[3] Over the centuries it has evolved from an articulated debate to a document that contributes to a discipline's knowledge through a rigorous research program. As it is envisioned today, a thesis provides an opportunity for a student to understand the process of research and its importance in empirical decision making. In social work, for instance, there appears to be a correlation between students who complete a thesis and the increased use of research findings in professional decision-making processes.[4] Conversely, students who do not undertake a rigorous research project in graduate school, such as a thesis, may therefore be unable to adequately understand research in general and therefore have limited abilities to interpret and understand original research as it applies to their professional work.

Theses have value that extend beyond the academic experience and enhance a discipline while providing experience applicable to a professional setting. Programs that emphasize the empirical thesis do so based on the expectation that the student will advance knowledge in a particular field through original research that questions existing paradigms and theories. In nursing research, for instance, there is evidence that students who produce theses do in fact publish their research and make a measurable impact on advancing their discipline.[5] John P. Carroll, Robert J. Cooper, and Karl V. Miller argue that contrary to the stereotype of the thesis as only being relevant in academic contexts, it instead presents "the most difficult task that [students] have ever undertaken, and following a difficult, challenging, and often tedious effort through to completion is an excellent way of learning perseverance. More than any other university educational experience, the thesis mimics the 'real world.'"[6]

Moreover, rather than being driven by relevance to professional practice, master's programs have dropped requirements for theses and substituted extra coursework in order to generate additional income, making a master's degree little more than an extended bachelor's program.[7] If an assumption can be made, therefore, that there is a benefit to a student completing a master's thesis, then what form should it take to offer maximum benefit to the student, the discipline, and professional practice? In order to answer this question, it is necessary to differentiate the empirical thesis from other kinds of capstone projects.

The Empirical Thesis as Opposed to a Literature Review, Policy Analysis, or Project

In 1930, Ernest Earl Lindsay and Ernest Otto Holland described a research thesis as "an original study contributing something to the total of human knowledge" while emphasizing the application of a rigorous research methodology toward a particular research question.[8] This essential definition remains unchanged today, but some master's programs allow a student to produce a "thesis" that is not empirically derived from research. These papers manifest instead as a literature review or policy analysis with limited capacity to contribute to human knowledge.[9] While these works may undoubtedly be useful in some contexts, they lack methodological rigor employing the collection and/or analysis of data to produce empirical findings within the framework of "original research" and as such, have limited utility in advancing the epistemological boundaries of a particular field.

The essential difference between a thesis and a project is that the former emphasizes generalizability or transferability to similar situations in an attempt to make original contributions to a field while the latter focuses on the analysis of an existing situation in an effort to provide a pragmatic solution.[10] A project uses the format of a professional report provided for a client as the model, often with a decreased emphasis on "academic" language and the use of a more accessible format, while the thesis is a scholarly research document typically formatted in a five-part format of introduction, literature review, methods, analysis, and conclusion, depending on the discipline, and contains more technical or discipline-specific language.

Within historic preservation, projects utilize an existing theoretical frame in an uncritical way. For instance, there is significant agreement on how a historic structure report, condition survey, preservation plan, or cultural landscape study is conducted. Students who do these types of reports as their capstone project collect data on a specific case using previous reports as templates, thereby perpetuating the way in which these reports are prepared. There is therefore no overt attempt to advance practice or contribute to the intellectual boundaries of a discipline. Moreover, projects are not driven by a research question or a hypothesis. All of these characteristics of projects are not meant to deprecate their value, for indeed, in a professional setting these reports are consistently produced and do add to an existing body of knowledge and have practical implications for conserving historic buildings, structures, or landscapes. But they do not teach students how to conduct or understand original research.

An empirical research thesis addresses a particular problem or issue in a discipline through theoretical and/or applied approaches, culminating in a unique contribution to a particular field area. A research question and/or a hypothesis are developed from this problem area. Unlike a project, there is an overt attempt to advance practice or contribute to the intellectual boundaries of a discipline.[11] While an empirical thesis can use a specific case or several cases in its research design, the overarching research question typically addresses a larger issue in the field that can be generalized or transferred to similar settings. Empirical theses utilize a well-defined research methodology and particular methods to collect and analyze data. In its most basic form, an empirical thesis asks a question and collects and analyzes data in order to provide an answer to that question.

Students who prepare an empirical thesis will learn how research is applied to a problem in a particular discipline in an effort to advance their profession. In architectural practice, for instance, there is a drive toward equipping students to understand "evidence-based design" through social science research, culminating in a research thesis applied to a particular design issue. Students who understand research in this way are more effective in designing places that are better for people when they begin their professional architectural practice.[12] In the field of psychology, students who understand research are able to apply their knowledge in professional careers in order to determine the quality of studies, to separate anecdotal from scientific information, to engage in critical thinking, and, in short, to "separate fact from fiction."[13]

What Is a "Historic Preservation" Thesis?

What is the discipline of historic preservation? Moreover, what are its boundaries? In other words, one needs to understand the boundaries of the discipline before making a determination whether or not a particular thesis topic is indeed a "preservation" thesis when advising students. There is not, unfortunately, a consensus on the nature of historic preservation as a discipline; some authors even disagree that it is a singular discipline at all.[14] Michael Tomlin, however, argues that historic preservation arose as a discrete discipline by the 1980s, representing "a full-time occupation that involved a commitment to a calling, formal organization, esoteric but useful knowledge acquired through intensive education and training, an orientation to service, and autonomy."[15] While preservation professionals employ a wide range of skills and expertise in areas such as materials conservation and preservation planning, most professionals specialize in a particular area of preservation practice, such as planning or historic site interpretation. Understanding the nature of these specializations is useful as an exercise for characterizing the field, but its primary value lies in helping students to understand potential topical areas for a thesis.

Historic preservation literature tends to segment preservation research and practice into existing disciplinary boundaries, such as the introductory texts that many students read by Norman Tyler, Ted Ligibel, and Ilene R. Tyler [16] and William J. Murtagh,[17] which define preservation through the activities of the architect, the planner, or the historian. There is evidence, however, to consider that the field has created its own, unique divisions as expressed through the actual jobs preservationists do. One way of categorizing these divisions is through an artificial device that articulates the inherent tension in historic preservation values as expressed through their theory and practice. In particular, there are two dichotomies that are most salient: a tension between community and expert values and a tension between age and design value. These values are graphically represented in Figure 16.1.

The dichotomy between community or sociocultural values and expert values is perhaps best represented through Laurajane Smith's work

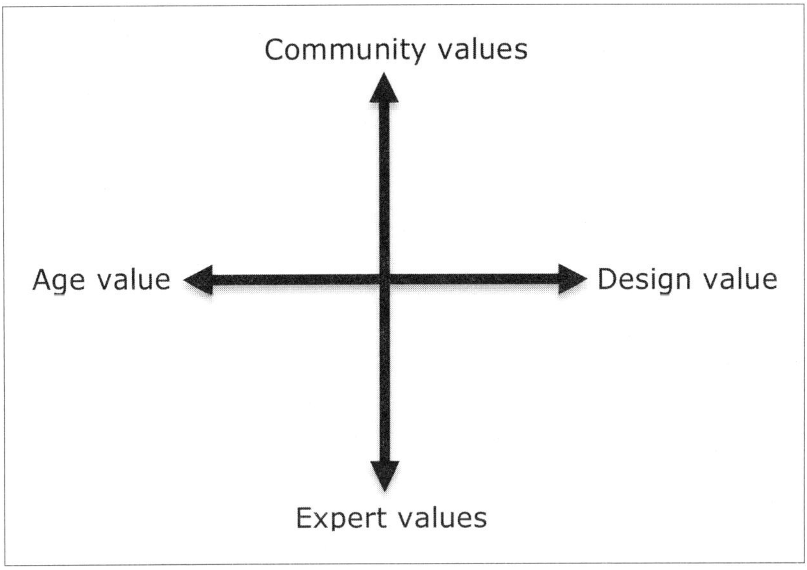

16.1 Defining the field through dichotomous values.

on the "Authorized Heritage Discourse" (AHD) in which "the proper care of heritage, and its associated values, lies with the experts, as it is only they who have the abilities, knowledge and understanding to identify the innate value and knowledge contained at and within historically important sites and places."[18] Other work by Randall Mason, Howard L. Green, and Emma Waterton, Laurajane Smith, and Gary Campbell[19] reinforces the idea that what may be valuable to a community is not necessarily valuable to a preservation expert who, through preservation doctrine, is obligated to privilege objective art/historical values in the assessment of significance. The other dichotomy that contrasts age value with design value derives from the nineteenth-century arguments between preservation and restoration epitomized by John Ruskin and Eugène-Emmanuel Viollet-le-Duc that are still with us today.[20]

Do these dichotomies work? A thought experiment is warranted to answer this question. In the former case, imagine a discussion on saving a historic building between a statewide preservation advocacy director and a preservation architect. Would they agree on all aspects of an intervention? Where would their values lie? Inevitably, the advocate would likely argue for greater retention of historic fabric while the architect would stress the programmatic requirements of the client in balance with preservation needs. Both perspectives have equal value, but the point is the difference in the perspectives. In the second case, imagine a discussion between a city preservation planner and an architectural historian on the value of a proposed historic district. The historian would point out the high-style buildings and possibly certain vernacular features, while the planner would be likely to focus on why this place has value to a community for shopping, recreating, or living—that is, its sense of place. Again, there is no ethical position on whether or not one set of values is more important than another; it simply shows that there are often opposed values in preservation practice.

The proof as to whether this values framework is functional becomes evident when placing the various types of preservation professionals who are in the field in areas that consider the interaction of these four, individual values. For instance, an executive director at a statewide preservation trust is driven by the need to preserve the age value of places, but is much more likely to be influenced by community values than expert values. A Main Street manager is even more likely to be driven by community values. A cultural resource manager (CRM), specializing in environmental review, is more likely to acknowledge design and political value within a regulatory framework, moving this position closer to expert and design values. An architectural materials conservator will be more likely to recognize expert values than community values, to consider the role of design intent in interventions, and to seek a balance between interventions and the retention of age value. Last, a historic site administrator would be the least likely to alter the historic fabric of buildings in recognition of art/historical and informational values.

When plotting these jobs on the values framework, a pattern emerges where half of the positions are inclined to value interventions while the other half of the jobs would be more inclined to value the retention of historic fabric, or the status quo. When drawn across the values framework, a 45-degree bisection is created to represent this idea. In looking at the way the jobs are arrayed across the framework, the last pattern to emerge is that each side of the rotated square that is created begs a label to describe the jobs that fall along a particular side. From the northeast quadrant, these labels are regulators, conservators, interpreters, and stewards based on the nature of the work performed. A list of these job titles, which is not meant to be all-inclusive, organized by these four specializations, is depicted in Table 16.1. The final values framework, referred to by the acronym RCIS for specializations in historic preservation is illustrated in Figure 16.2.

The assumption inherent in the RCIS model is that historic preservation *professions* in part define the *discipline,* but that they are not

Table 16.1 Preservation jobs by RCIS specialization category.

Regulators
Environmental Planner
Cultural Resources Specialist
Compliance Manager
Compliance Specialist
NEPA and Historic Preservation Specialist
Architectural Historian
Historic Preservation Specialist
Environmental Protection Specialist
Historic Preservation Planner
Cultural Resources Group Leader
Environmental Protection Specialist
Environmental Resources Specialist
Senior Scientist
Historic Preservation Officer
Tribal Historic Preservation Officer

Interpreters
Cultural Resources Program Manager
Natural and Historical Resources Instructor
History/Museum Program Coordinator
Historic Site Director
Project Director
Tour Director

Conservators
Preservation Architect
Landscape Architect
Historic Preservation Associate
Historic Architect
Architectural Materials Conservator
Exhibit Specialist

Stewards
Community Development Specialist
Downtown Manager
Main Street Director/Manager
Executive Director (of nonprofit)
Program Manager
Field Advocate
Heritage Tourism Specialist

equivalent. A discipline develops around a unique ontological and epistemological perspective on an object of study or practice, and uses existing or new methods in ways that are unique.[21] One could argue that the historic environment is the object of attention, the ontological orientation is centered on authenticity, and there is a unique body of knowledge on the identification and treatment of historic resources. In addition, local history research, as applied to understanding the objective significance of buildings and landscapes, is unique to historic preservation when compared to the other built environment disciplines. There is also an academic or scholarly side to historic preservation, such as heritage studies, which helps to define and expand the discipline's boundaries.

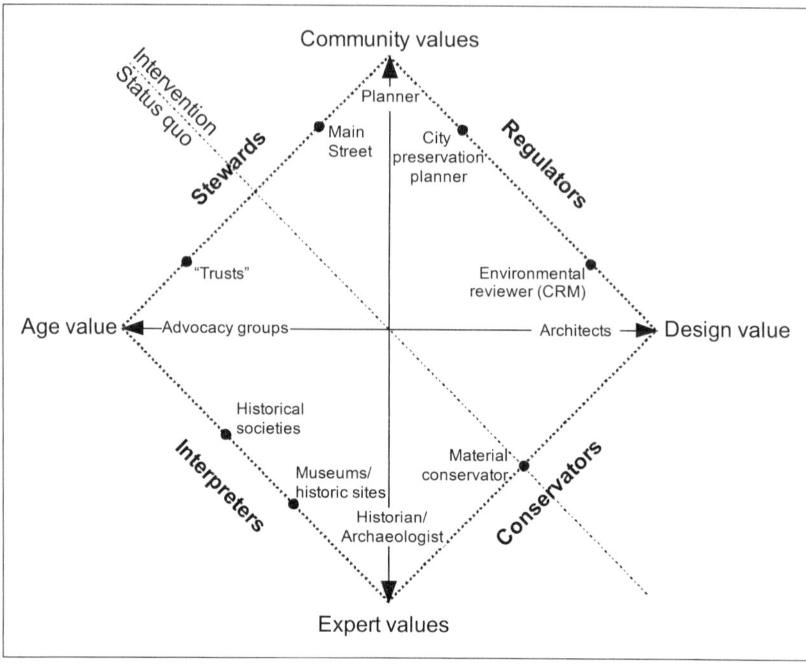

16.2 The Regulators, Conservators, Interpreters, and Stewards (RCIS) diagram.

Toward Evidence-Based Historic Preservation with the Empirical Thesis

The rationale for and benefits of historic preservation practice, according to Erica Avrami, Randall Mason, and Marta de la Torre, are "taken as a matter of faith" and not based on empirical evidence as far as decisions are concerned related to significance, interventions, and planning.[22] In the past fifteen years, there has been a remarkable critique against the rationalist/synoptic-based, doctrine-driven approach to historic preservation practice rooted in the values of nineteenth-century European, white aristocrats.[23] Whether this is called "values-based" conservation as opposed to "fabric-based conservation," "common sense" conservation based on "adaptive ethics" and "gentle decisions," or conservation where meaning is derived from contemporary "broad social processes,"[24] there is a consensus in moving away from traditional rationalist doctrine and basing more decisions on the values of stakeholders and empirical evidence obtained through the use of social science research methodologies in balance with expert/objective values.

But this change in value systems from experts to stakeholders is not a new idea: while historic preservation may be tardy in understanding broader human values, other built environment disciplines have addressed, if not necessarily embraced, this idea for some time. For instance, architecture began this debate in the 1970s starting with social scientists who had the idea that design should be, in part, driven by empirical evidence of how design benefits people in terms of physical and mental health. A number of architects then joined the movement for what is known today as "evidence-based design," which uses social science research methodologies to provide answers for design principles that are beneficial to human beings.[25] While it would be disingenuous to indicate the whole of architecture has accepted evidence-based design, it is ubiquitous in some areas, such as health care facilities, where the design of rooms has been correlated with reduced recuperation time for patients.[26] In a similar sense, these same kinds of social science research methodologies can provide empirical evidence to substantiate and adapt historic preservation practice to more effectively serve human needs.

With so much of historic preservation practice being based on doctrine, from the Secretary of the Interior's Standards to the Venice Charter, there is a great potential in the use of social science research methodologies to provide the kind of empirical evidence for these taken-for-granted aspects of historic preservation practice. If we accept that the conservation of the historic environment is ultimately to benefit *people* through the identification, interpretation, and treatment of historic objects, then the natural conclusion is that existing conservation doctrine is woefully inadequate in providing a basis for practice.[27] Generally speaking, areas that lack this kind of empirical evidence are related to the person/environment interaction and the perception, valuation, changes to historic resources, and assessment of authenticity, which begs a number of questions, such as:

- How do everyday people perceive/value the historic environment?
- What defines an "authentic" historic environment for those who inhabit and use these places?
- What are acceptable and unacceptable interventions from the perspective of stakeholders?
- What is the process whereby historical objects acquire cultural and/or social value?
- What kinds of physical and mental health benefits does the historic environment provide?

Other areas of potential research can be categorized using the RCIS organizational scheme, described previously. The regulators, conservators, interpreters, and stewards are areas with slightly different foci, and as such, will engender research questions specific to these practitioners.

Research Area: The Regulators

Practice as it relates to regulating the historic environment is driven by a need to understand community values and a greater acceptance of design interventions over the retention of the patina of place, or age value. Regulators are interested in understanding the needs and values of stakeholders. Questions that would provide empirical evidence for this area of practice include:

- How can law respond better to community values?
- What are pragmatic, cost-effective, and resource-efficient ways to gather community values to influence planning practice?
- How can design guidelines be better understood by a lay audience?
- How can design guidelines be crafted to incorporate stakeholders' values?

Research Area: The Conservators

This area of practice is influenced by expert/objective values and a greater acceptance of design interventions over the retention of the patina of place, or age value. Conservators are interested in understanding how interventions in the fabric of buildings, places, and landscapes can be balanced with the retention of authenticity. Questions that would provide empirical evidence for this area of practice include:

- To what degree can historic fabric be removed from a building while still being perceived as "authentic" by its users?
- How do people perceive the difference between "old," or original, fabric and new fabric?
- What sorts of material conservation treatments are preferred by people while still retaining perceived authenticity?
- What kind of interventions can be made on "historic" plant material while still retaining perceived authenticity?

Research Area: The Interpreters

The interpretation of the historic environment privileges expert/objective values while emphasizing the retention of historic fabric, patina, and age value. The interpreters are concerned with the informational value of the historic environment and effective ways to communicate this information and engage the public. Questions that would provide empirical evidence for this area of practice include:

- How do people engage with and become emotionally connected to the historic environment?
- To what degree do people need to become "performers" in the past and experience it vicariously?
- Are there differences, based on age, on how children and adults experience the historic environment and understand the past?
- How can historic house museums become more relevant to the public, especially as it relates to repeat visitation?

Research Area: The Stewards

Stewardship of the historic environment is closely linked with advocacy and a need to understand community values while emphasizing the retention of historic fabric, patina, and age value. Stewards are motivated by advocacy and education in an effort to conserve the historic environment for the public benefit. Questions that would provide empirical evidence for this area of practice include:

- How can preservation arguments be made using the language of stakeholders instead of experts?
- How can historic preservation be linked to the broader "conservation" movement in the eyes of the public?
- What are reasons the layperson would want to engage in historic preservation?
- How do laypeople perceive and understand the professional practice of historic preservation?

While these research questions are not meant to encompass every possible scenario, they do present a range of possible avenues of inquiry, any of which could be applied by a student to a particular thesis topic.

The RCIS categories offer a helpful way of describing practice so that a student can consider options for research that would have a larger and more relevant impact on the professional world. Students who approach research in this way are likely to transfer this expertise to their own professional practice. At a minimum, it would encourage empirically based problem solving by enabling burgeoning historic preservation professionals to be able to reference and understand existing research; ideally, such a professional would continue to engage in this kind of research for the benefit of the discipline and his or her clients.

Pragmatic Social Science Research Methodologies for the Empirical Thesis

In a typical historic preservation program in the United States that is a member of the National Council for Preservation Education (NCPE),[28] the only required research methodology that students must learn is the historical or interpretive methodology as applied to the documentation and recording of buildings. This methodology was borrowed from the discipline of history, especially as it applies to local history or public history research. Unless a student enters a program with a social science background or seeks courses outside of the normal curriculum, it is a fair assumption that a student will need to be taught how to conduct social science research before he or she is able to undertake an empirical thesis.

This requirement is a daunting challenge, as the potential number of social science research methodologies is large, ranging from ethnography and grounded theory to phenomenology and action research. In the social sciences, each discipline is normally expected to learn only one or two of these methodologies. For instance, anthropologists learn ethnography while sociologists learn grounded theory and survey research. Is it even possible to entertain the requirement that historic preservation students could learn the methodologies of anthropology, sociology, psychology, and humanistic geography? Realistically, the answer is no, this is simply not feasible. In addition, many quantitative social science research methodologies require a student to have a background in inferential, multivariate statistics, while many qualitative methodologies are time consuming in the data-gathering phase. The limitations of these methodologies are presented in Table 16.2.

What is possible, however, is that historic preservation students can be taught a range of *pragmatic* research methodologies. A pragmatic social science research methodology meets the following four requirements:

Table 16.2 Limitations of social science research methodologies.

Methodology	Limitations
Ethnography (incl. participant observation)	Time-consuming data gathering due to need to gain an *emic* perspective; difficult to collect sufficient data in a single semester.
Grounded theory	Time-consuming data gathering due to need to define a theory from the data; difficult to collect sufficient data in a single semester.
Phenomenology	Difficult for students to apply in a single semester because of the need to understand the structuralist philosophical basis for the lifeworld.
Ethnomethodology	Difficult to apply without a sociology background.
Action research	Too much time needed; difficult to complete in a single semester.
Experimental research	Difficult to apply without a science and statistics background.

1. It must be usable by a graduate student who may not have a significant social science background.
2. Data can be collected and analyzed in a single semester.
3. The methodology is able to answer a specific research question.
4. Reliability and validity are important, but "perfection" is not appropriate in this context.

A few social science research methodologies meet these requirements, including qualitative case studies using interview methods, survey (correlational) research, content analysis, photo sort operations commonly used in environmental behavior research, non-participant observation, and the rapid ethnographic assessment procedure.

The qualitative case study using interviews as a method is a well-established technique with a robust following. Robert Yin's *Case Study Research: Design and Methods* is perhaps one of the better guides for this methodology.[29] Guidance on effective interviewing is increasingly detailed and theoretical to the extent that interviewing is developing its own methodological approach. Herbert J. Rubin and Irene S. Rubin's *Qualitative Interviewing* epitomizes this perspective, in which the authors position qualitative interviewing within its own ontological orientation and a "responsive interviewing model."[30] During a qualitative interview, a student asks open-ended questions of an informant and then codes the resulting data into a thematic structure for analysis of meanings. The advantage to qualitative interviewing is that achieving the *emic* (internal) perspective of ethnography is not assumed, thereby reducing the amount of time required to gather the data. The downside to this approach, of course, is that significant meanings may be lost and the depth of understanding from the informant's perspective is compromised. If, however, the goal is to gather and analyze data in a single semester, these limitations can be accepted as long as the student acknowledges them.

Survey or correlational research has a long history in sociology. Usually associated with quantitative research, data are gathered via a survey instrument or questionnaire taken by the respondent or administered by the researcher. Responses consist of numerical variables that are conducive to statistical analysis. While multivariate inferential statistics are often employed, such as ANOVA, regression, and factor analysis, many research questions can be answered using simple descriptive statistics. Students, through the use of free and commercial software, can be taught how to utilize simple analyses, such as the t-test and chi-square, in describing the statistical relevance of their data. The major advantage to survey research is that the data can be gathered and analyzed fairly quickly within a single semester.

While content analysis does not directly involve human subject research, it uses written materials (e.g., books, newspapers), music, pictures, advertising, speeches, or artifacts as a proxy for human perception, values, and processes. The methodology can be quantitative, qualitative, or both. For instance, word frequency analysis indicates how often certain phrases appear in media to understand communicative values while this same media can also be analyzed in terms of patterns or themes, much as ethnography would do with a transcribed interview. As long as the analyzed media is reasonably comprehensive, a student should be able to gather and analyze data in a single semester.

Observation within an ethnographic context is the process whereby the researcher gathers data on the behavior of people that consists of a wide variety of verbal and nonverbal actions and phenomena. Participant observation requires that the student first immerse himself or herself in the cultural group under study by becoming an active, accepted, and contributing member of the group, thereby gaining an internal, or *emic,* perspective, which can be very time consuming. Nonparticipant observation gathers the same kind of data, but from the more detached frame of a covert observer where the people under study may not be aware of the researcher's presence. Non-participant observations can either be "structured" or "unstructured" in regard to how data are collected. With structured nonparticipant observation, the student creates a meaning framework prior to collecting the data and then develops a behavior schema to collect quantitative information about this behavior. A student using unstructured nonparticipant observation collects data first and then applies a behavior schema to it afterward.

To date, I have located only one social science research approach that has been specifically designed for assessing heritage values. In the 1990s, Setha Low adapted existing ethnographic methods for the purpose of assessing heritage values. Her "Rapid Ethnographic Assessment Procedure" (REAP) "help[s] conservation professionals and managers understand the complexity of social relations and cultural dynamics at play in the conservation planning and development of heritage sites."[31] While framed in ethnographic traditions, the REAP approach also includes other methodologies, including historical/interpretive ones. The methods utilized include physical traces mapping, behavioral mapping, transect walks, individual interviews, expert interviews, impromptu group interviews, focus groups, participant observation, and the use of historical and archival documents.

Helping Students with the Empirical Thesis Process

In order to encourage students to pursue empirical theses using social science research methodologies, more attention should be paid to giving students the skills to successfully complete the process. Oftentimes students are essentially left to their own devices when working on a thesis or choosing an advisor and a reader or readers, or perhaps they receive advice from a faculty member. Unless there is a specific research methods course or a seminar preparing students to work on a thesis,[32] students may have little or no idea how to structure a research proposal, conduct a literature review, and what the overall structure for a social science-based thesis is. While there are many useful books on preparing research proposals and a social science thesis, none focus on built environment research, much less the historic environment.[33] This leaves faculty as the sole source of information and guidance for this process.

Architecture and landscape architecture programs that emphasize environmental design and behavior research may offer a useful model in that many of these programs either provide the option for or require students to learn how to conduct social science research in preparation for the thesis. European heritage studies programs, because they are often affiliated with archaeology and anthropology programs, typically provide a research methods course in preparation for the thesis. These and other models from built environment programs may prove useful in informing curricular options for historic preservation programs.

At Roger Williams University, I teach a thesis preparatory seminar in the fall in order to ready students for their thesis in the spring. Students are encouraged to begin to think about a thesis topic and to investigate literature a year before their thesis is due. By the time they arrive in class for the fall semester, many students have settled on a broad topic area, which I help them refine throughout the course. The first focus is on completing a literature review. Using this foundation, my students then use Wayne C. Booth, Gregory G. Columb, and Joseph M. Williams's "three-step formula" for developing a research statement based on a topic, research question, and significance statement grounded in a problem area.[34] Typically, it takes students several weeks to work through various iterations of their research statement before they are ready to start preparing a research proposal.

The course also covers basic quantitative and qualitative research paradigms followed by specific research methodologies, including survey/correlational research, qualitative case study research, historical/interpretive research, content analysis, nonparticipant observation, and rapid ethnographic assessment procedures. Students have an opportunity in class to develop sample research designs based on different methodologies and to explore which methodologies may be a better fit given a particular research question. Throughout the entire class the need to develop a consistent research question that is narrow enough to be addressed in a single semester is emphasized; I present the thesis, therefore, as an answer to this question.

Overall, this process has worked well, but I have continually been unhappy with the research methodology texts that are available as most assume a specific disciplinary background of the student, such as anthropology, sociology, or psychology, or are written at too difficult a level to serve as introductory texts. Other issues include too much emphasis on quantitative or qualitative research rather than a balance between the two (again, issues rooted in particular disciplines for which the texts are targeted) and a lack of coverage of relevant, pragmatic research methodologies. John W. Creswell's *The Craft of Research* is perhaps the most useful, but its coverage of specific research methodologies is too brief and therefore needs to be supplemented with other sources.[35] Earl Babbie's *The Basics of Social Research* is written at a very accessible level, but overemphasizes quantitative research and is targeted at sociology students.[36]

Conclusion

As the conservation of the historic environment makes the kind of cultural turn that other disciplines have already taken, we need to recognize that students are the forefront of this shift in emphasis from expert values to social and cultural values. It therefore becomes increasingly important that students understand the empirical research process and the application of pragmatic quantitative and qualitative research methodologies if they are to be more effective professionals. While the immediate impact is the ability of students to contribute novel research to the discipline through thesis work, the skills that they learn are likely to be employed in professional contexts that will lead to better decision-making processes based on evidence rather than the doctrines that drive so much of contemporary preservation practice.

Although my own experience is anecdotal, I have found that my historic preservation students have the capacity to learn how to use pragmatic research methodologies to create empirical theses that address important questions in the field. The larger question is to what extent this should be encouraged in other programs that address the historic environment. If we, as a discipline, believe that historic preservation practice needs a stronger empirical basis for its actions and that better tools are needed to assess and understand stakeholder values, then we owe it to our students to equip them with the skills necessary to address this deficit.

Notes

1. This chapter uses the common terminology used in the United States for master's degree programs as well as professional practice.
2. Michael W. Singletary and James A. Crook, "Projects Replace Theses in Many Master's Programs," *Journalism Educator,* 40 (1986), 4–6.
3. See Arturo Arlo Norton, *Readings in the History of Education: Medieval Universities* (Cambridge, MA: Harvard University Press, 1909).
4. Kevin J. Corcoran, "Is There Educational Value in the Master's Thesis?" *Journal of Education for Social Work,* 20:3 (1984), 31.
5. Georgia Whitley, Lorys Oddi, and Deborah Terrell, "Factors Influencing the Publishing Efforts of Graduate Students in Nursing," *Journal of Nursing Education,* 37:4 (1998), 182–85.
6. John P. Carroll, Robert J. Cooper, and Karl V. Miller, "Non-thesis Master's Degree: Is It Good for the Student or the Profession?" *Wildlife Society Bulletin,* 26:4 (1998), 962.
7. Caroll, Cooper, and Miller, "Non-thesis Master's Degree," 961–63.
8. Ernest Earl Lindsay and Ernest Otto Holland, *College and University Administration* (New York: Macmillan Co., 1930), 221.
9. Corcoran, "Is There Educational Value?" 31.
10. William Gerald Webster, *Developing and Writing Your Thesis, Dissertation or Project: A Manual of Sound Advice about Conceptualizing, Organizing, Developing and Finalizing Your Terminal Graduate Research* (San Ramon, CA: Academic Scholarwrite, 1998), 41.
11. Yvonne N. Bui, *How to Write a Master's Thesis* (Thousand Oaks, CA: Sage, 2009); Frederick C. Lunenburg and Beverly J. Irby, *Writing a Successful Thesis or Dissertation: Tips and Strategies for Students in the Social and Behavioral Sciences* (Thousand Oaks,

CA: Corwin Press, 2008); R. Murray Thomas and Dale L. Brubaker, *Theses and Dissertations: A Guide to Planning, Research, and Writing* (Westport, CT: Bergin & Garvey, 2000).

12. D. Kirk Hamilton, "Design Based on Evidence," in *The Architecture Student's Handbook of Professional Practice* (Hoboken, NJ: John Wiley and Sons, 2009), 281–92.

13. Mark L. Mitchell and Janina M. Jolley, *Research Design Explained* (Belmont, CA: Wadsworth, 2013), 29.

14. Sharon Cather, "The Dilemma of Conservation Education," *Conservation, the GCI Newsletter,* 15:6 (2000), 9–12.

15. Michael Tomlan, "Historic Preservation Education: Alongside Architecture in Academia," *Journal of Architectural Education,* 47:4 (1994), 191.

16. Norman Tyler, Ted Ligibel, and Ilene R. Tyler, *Historic Preservation: An Introduction to Its History, Principles, and Practice* (New York: W. W. Norton Company, 2009).

17. William J. Murtagh, *Keeping Time: The History and Theory of Preservation in America* (New York: John Wiley & Sons, 2006).

18. Laurajane Smith, *The Uses of Heritage* (London: Taylor & Francis, 2006).

19. Randall Mason, "Fixing Historic Preservation: A Constructive Critique of 'Significance,'" *Places,* 16:1 (2003), 64–71; Howard L. Green, "The Social Construction of Historical Significance," in *Preservation of What, for Whom? A Critical Look at Historical Significance,* ed. Michael A. Tomlan (Ithaca, NY: National Council for Preservation Education, 1998); Emma Waterton, Laurajane Smith, and Gary Campbell, "The Utility of Discourse Analysis to Heritage Studies: The Burra Charter and Social Inclusion," *International Journal of Heritage Studies,* 12:4 (2006), 339–55.

20. See John Ruskin, *The Seven Lamps of Architecture* (London: Smith, Elder, and Co., 1849); and Eugène-Emmanuel Viollet-le-Duc, *The Foundations of Architecture* (New York: George Braziller, 1990).

21. Jack Amariglio, Stephen Resnick, and Richard Wolff, "Division and Difference in the 'Discipline' of Economics," *Critical Inquiry,* 17:1 (1990), 150.

22. Erica Avrami, Randall Mason, and Marta de la Torre, *Values and Heritage Conservation* (Los Angeles: Getty Conservation Institute, 2000), 10.

23. Avrami, Mason, and Torre, *Values and Heritage Conservation;* Mason, "Fixing Historic Preservation"; Green, "The Social Construction of Historical Significance"; Waterton, Smith, and Campbell, "The Utility of Discourse"; Randall Mason, "Theoretical and Practical Arguments for Values-centered Preservation," *CRM: The Journal of Heritage Stewardship,* 3 (2006), 21–48; Boguslaw Szmygin, "Classification of Historical Monuments," in *Values and Criteria in Heritage Conservation,* ed. A. Tomaszewski (Florence: Edizioni Polistampa, 2008), 153–58; Smith, *Uses of Heritage*; Salvador Muñoz Viñas, *Contemporary Theory of Conservation* (Amsterdam: Elsevier, 2005); Lisa Breglia, *Monumental Ambivalence: The Politics of Heritage* (Austin: University of Texas Press, 2006); Jeremy C. Wells, "Authenticity in More Than One Dimension: Re-evaluating a Core Premise of Historic Preservation," *Forum Journal,* 24:3 (2010), 36–40; John Pendlebury, *Conservation in the Age of Consensus* (London: Routledge, 2009); Jessica Williams, "Theories toward a Critical Practice," *Future Anterior,* 2:2 (2005), vii–ix; Silvio M. Zancheti and Jukka Jokilehto, "Values and Urban Conservation Planning: Some Reflections on Principles and Definitions," *Journal of Architectural Conservation,* 3:1 (1997), 37–51.

24. Mason, "Theoretical and Practical"; Muñoz Viñas, *Contemporary Theory of Conservation;* Green, "The Social Construction of Historical Significance."

25. D. Kirk Hamilton and David H. Watkins, *Evidence-based Design for Multiple Building Types* (Hoboken, NJ: John Wiley & Sons, 2009).

26. Rosalyn Cama, *Evidence-based Healthcare Design* (Hoboken, NJ: John Wiley & Sons, 2009).

27. Jeremy C. Wells, "The Plurality of Truth in Culture, Context, and Heritage: A (Mostly) Post-Structuralist Analysis of Urban Conservation Charters," *City and Time,* 3:1/2 (2007), 1–13.

28. In order to be a member of NCPE, member institutions need to present evidence that their students are taught how to document and record historic structures (see http://www.ncpe.us/about-ncpe/standards/#.UHB7Vvl27rM).

29. Robert K. Yin, *Case Study Research: Design and Methods* (Los Angeles: Sage, 2013).

30. Herbert J. Rubin and Irene S. Rubin, *Qualitative Interviewing: The Art of Hearing Data* (Los Angeles: Sage, 2012).

31. Setha M. Low, "Anthropological-ethnographic Methods for the Assessment of Cultural Values in Heritage Conservation," in *Assessing the Values of Cultural Heritage,* ed. M. L. de Torre (Los Angeles: Getty Conservation Institute, 2002), 31.

32. The graduate historic preservation curriculum at Roger Williams University includes a preparatory seminar for thesis research that has been effective in providing students with the skills to conduct social science research.

33. While there are no published "how to" guides for preparing a built environment thesis using social science research methodologies, there are many resources for using social science methods in built environment research such as Linda Groat and David Wang, *Architectural Research Methods* (New York: John Wiley & Sons, 2002), and John Zeisel, *Inquiry by Design: Environment/Behavior/Neuroscience in Architecture, Interiors, Landscape, and Planning* (New York: W. W. Norton & Company, 2006).

34. See Wayne C. Booth, Gregory G. Columb, and Joseph M. Williams, *The Craft of Research* (Chicago: University of Chicago Press, 2008).

35. See John W. Creswell, *Research Design: Qualitative, Quantitative, and Mixed Methods Approaches* (Thousand Oaks, CA: Sage, 2009).

36. Earl Babbie, *The Basics of Social Research* (5th Edition) (Belmont, CA: Wadsworth, 2011).

17 Learning Among Friends: Using Heritage-Based Educational Practices for Improving Preservation Law Pedagogy

Barry L. Stiefel and Gilbert S. Stiefel

The recognition of and appreciation for the diversity of philosophies and practices regarding heritage preservation is reflected in the 2008 International Council on Monuments and Sites (ICOMOS) Charter for the Interpretation and Presentation of Cultural Heritage Sites. One of the basic principles of this charter is *Inclusiveness* (Principle 6), which stipulates, "The Interpretation and Presentation of cultural heritage sites must be the result of meaningful collaboration between heritage professionals, host and associated communities, and other stakeholders." Underlying the principle of inclusion is the recognition and valuing of the contributions and participation of diverse cultural groups in the heritage preservation process—a process that is generally defined by laws and rules.

Lynne Armitage and Yung Yau have advocated for the integration and assimilation of conservation ideologies from places with different cultural backgrounds.[1] Meanwhile, Priya Jain and Goody Clancy have expressed concern that trained historic preservation professionals are sometimes perceived as "outsiders" whose perspective might lead to "the alienation of the people who lived in or actively used these [cultural] landscapes."[2] This situation is likely to be exacerbated in cases where professionals view themselves as imbued with the "correct" answer by virtue of their training.

Barry Stiefel and Gilbert Stiefel's "Learning Among Friends: Using Heritage-Based Educational Practices for Improving Preservation Law Pedagogy" was first published in *Preservation Education and Research*, 5 (2012), 75–86, and is republished here with the National Council of Preservation Education's generous permission. The authors are very grateful for the assistance provided by Orit Kent, senior research associate at the Mandel Center for Studies in Jewish Education at Brandeis University and Aviva Ben-Ur, associate professor in the Department of Judaic and Near Eastern Studies at University of Massachusetts, Amherst.

Principle 6 goes on to note, "The multidisciplinary expertise of scholars, community members, conservation experts, governmental authorities, site managers and interpreters, tourism operators, and other professionals should be integrated in the formulation of interpretation and presentation programmes" (Section 6.1). The diverse perspectives raised by this process often evolve into what has been defined as "ill-structured problems."[3] Ill-structured problems are those in which opposing or contradictory evidence, assumptions, or opinion exist and do not necessarily have one correct answer (as opposed to a math problem) but only better or worse solutions that involve a balancing of factors. Examples of realistic problems include poverty, pollution, and health care. Pedagogical procedures should reflect actual practice issues and methods.

The instructional methods most widely used at educational institutions in North America are products of Western European culture. While certainly effective, the question we propose is, does the way preservation education is taught in respect to the cultural heritage of minority groups provide the necessary *Weltanschauung* that sensitizes future professionals to the diversity of cultures and perspectives? Could preservation education be enhanced, and thus preservation practice, in order to make it a richer and more comprehensive experience if it were to consider other pedagogical alternatives? Preservation education must respond to the inherent sociocultural issues the country's demographic changes will make for the profession.

The arena in which we wish to address these issues is in the teaching of preservation law and legal practice for those studying to become professional consultants and administrators. The specific issue that we explore is whether the traditional guided-question approach of Socratic methodology, as developed by Harvard University's Christopher Columbus Langdell (1826–1906) in the late nineteenth century, is the best way to learn this material for professional preservation practice. The Socratic method is utilized in the teaching of law in universities across the country, although both law students and legal scholars have argued for its reform.[4] It is also used in the teaching of historic preservation law across the United States, including non-law degree–granting programs. For practical reasons should this be reconsidered for present and future students of historic preservation? Abdul Paliwala, a professor at the University of Warwick School of Law, argues that "unlike Socrates, Langdell's epistemology was not really a process of ethical self-discovery but technicist in argument to discover the structure of law . . . [Furthermore], pragmatists and realists suggested that the Case Method, by *concentrating* [author's emphasis] on the judicial decision, reified the decision and abstracted it away from the real life of the law."[5]

From our perspective, as teachers and academics of education and historic preservation, the emphasis of preservation legal education should be focused on "the real life of the law."[6] Paliwala's research explored how legal education might be enriched through the pedagogies of other cultures, using those of the Islamic Middle East and Confucian China as examples. While somewhat unorthodox, Paliwala's approach is not unique. Christine Zuni Cruz, a law professor at the University of New Mexico, studies the pedagogies and ethics of legal practice for indigenous peoples and teaches a course on the subject with an emphasis on the Navajo approach to law.[7]

In this chapter we illustrate another cultural-pedagogical alternative; the *havruta* methodology created by the Jewish people in rabbinical seminaries, called yeshivot (sing. yeshiva). Traditionally, students in these institutions of higher learning use this paradigm. Most generally, *havruta* is used to work through complex Jewish texts in teams of small student groups (see Figure 17.1). The texts are often legal but not exclusively.[8] The starting point is usually the Talmud and then later works and commentaries that continue to investigate features of the Talmudic text under study.[9] The *havruta* approach has been hailed as a model of success by a number of scholars.[10] The term comes from the Aramaic word for "friendship," and it requires the student to partner with another to learn a text

17.1 Postcard titled "Disputation," c. 1910, by Wilhelm Wachtel (1875–1942), depicting a Catholic monk and a Jewish scholar debating a religious text using the *havruta* method. From the William A. Rosenthall Judaica Collection, Special Collections, College of Charleston Library

by reading it, arguing over it, and trying to figure out what it means. While this pedagogy is traditionally used in the teaching of Jewish religious law, preservation law would be utilized as the content within the secular academic setting.

Havruta has been described as a form of collaborative learning and has been used in secular curricula in college-level English and American government classes, as well as in law school courses.[11] Our contemporary understanding of collaborative learning developed out of the work of Lev Vygotsky (1896–1934) and his Circle (1920–41). He believed that students are capable of performing at higher intellectual levels when asked to work in collaborative situations compared to working individually. He viewed group diversity in terms of knowledge and experience as contributing positively to the learning process.[12] Similarly, Jerome Bruner proposed that cooperative learning methods improve problem-solving strategies because the students are confronted with different interpretations of the given situation. The peer support system makes it possible for the learner to internalize both external knowledge and critical thinking skills, and to convert them into tools for intellectual functioning.[13]

More recent studies have affirmed that while collaborative learning approaches improve higher order or critical thinking about problems in a variety of content areas, these pedagogical methods do not diminish content knowledge. Daniel Marburger found in comparing student performance between cooperative versus traditional formats in an undergraduate economics class that even while no difference in multiple-choice exam performance between the two groups was discovered, cooperative learning did appear to have a significant positive effect on measures of the students' ability to analyze a case and apply their knowledge. He suggests that because multiple-choice exams "decompose" course content into smaller chunks, one may wonder whether previous empirical studies that disclosed no differences in test performance adequately distinguish between surface learning and deep learning.[14] These findings parallel those earlier reported by Anuradha Gokhale, who found that students in an electronics technology course who participated in collaborative learning performed significantly better on the critical-thinking test than students who studied individually. She also found that both groups did equally well on the drill-and-practice test.[15]

Like other collaborative learning approaches, an underlying concept of *havruta* is that knowledge is constructed rather than merely imparted. While *havruta* has also been described as fostering the development of higher order and critical thinking skills, it differs from other collaborative learning methodologies in two important aspects. The first is that the *havruta* methodology is intended to address the types of "ill-structured problems" involving differences in interpretation and perspective described earlier in this chapter. The second is that the partners remain the same during the course of a term. A study on *havruta* conducted at the University of Michigan also observed that "as a result of this prolonged partnership, students develop trust, which enables them to grapple more openly with the complexities they encounter in the text and in their discussions. The cooperative, trusting relationship between partners provides the framework within which students can evaluate their own epistemological assumptions and move to more advanced understandings about knowledge and knowing."[16]

A Brief History of Traditional Legal Education in the United States

The teaching of American law in institutions of higher education is almost as old as the United States, beginning with George Wythe (1726–1806) in 1779 at the College of William and Mary. It is perhaps fitting that he was the country's first law professor since he was a career lawyer, judge, and signer of the Declaration of Independence and the Virginia Constitution of 1776. Indeed, the academic teaching of law in the United States had commenced shortly after it started in Great Britain, beginning with Sir William Blackstone (1723–80) and his position in English common law at Oxford University in 1758. His publications were widely used in the teaching of law in Great Britain, its empire, and the United States well into the nineteenth century.[17] In 1784, the first American law school, Litchfield Law School, was established by Tapping Reeve (1744–1823) in Connecticut. This was a private institution. The pedagogy that professors like Wythe and the Litchfield Law School used was an analytical and systematized approach. During this time, and well into the nineteenth century, however, most practitioners of law received their legal education through an apprenticeship system of applied skills training.[18]

Despite the early start by William and Mary and Litchfield Law Schools, it was Harvard University's Law School that would rise to preeminence. Founded in 1817, it is the oldest continually operating law school in the United States. Between 1851 and 1854, Christopher Columbus Langdell attended Harvard Law School. Upon graduating, Langdell practiced law in New York City before returning to Harvard, where he took a professorship in 1870, soon becoming dean of the school. He remained in this post for the rest his career, until 1895. While a professor and dean, Langdell developed the method of learning appellate cases—

known as the case method—arguing that the study of law is an empirical "science." In this process, student learning is reinforced with the Socratic "question-and-answer technique"—the traditional law school "quiz." Because Harvard had one of the earliest successful programs and Langdell was notoriously effective as an administrator, his pedagogy spread to law schools across the country.[19] Langdell's students who took faculty positions at universities helped facilitate this proliferation.[20] Not until the mid-twentieth century was Langdell's pedagogy seriously scrutinized, resulting in the development of clinical legal education.[21] Today, the two are often conducted together within many law schools across the country. Barbara Blumenfeld describes the traditional American law school classroom:

> In the Socratic class room the professor asks questions about cases which the students should have read and briefed; the professor then presents hypotheticals that require students to apply the law to a new situation. While this to some extent develops the students' legal reasoning skills, there may remain the sense that the professor understands better than the students the reasoning involved in the hypothetical; the professor essentially directs the flow and direction of the conversation and of the reasoning, perhaps closing off some possibilities. The professor, through her questioning, leads the student toward an analysis or answer that the professor may have, or appear to have predetermined to be the best result of the discussion. Socratic method, because it is in essence a form of structured lecture, maintains a sense for students that there is a superior, if not correct, viewpoint held by the instructor.[22]

A Brief History of Traditional Preservation Law Education in the United States

The development of historic preservation law reflects a gradual evolution from the traditional government role in protecting property rights of individuals (a premise of property law) to its assertion of property rights on behalf of its populace, formally beginning with the Antiquities Act of 1906. While aspects of historic preservation law were embedded in and taught as part of property law, formal historic preservation legal education is a more recent phenomenon, beginning in 1971 with Cornell University's nascent curriculum. The course was developed by Ernest Roberts (1930–) at Cornell's Law School, which became part of the master of arts in historic preservation planning in 1974–75. This followed not long after the establishment of Columbia University's master of science in historic preservation, the first program in the country founded by James M. Fitch (1909–2000). During the 1960s, these institutions as well as the University of Virginia and University of California at Berkeley, had classes on the subject of historic preservation, with legal aspects as a point of discussion, such as the creation of historic districts and easements.[23]

Cornell Law School's Ernest Roberts received his LL.B. from Boston College in 1954. Meanwhile, the preservation education pioneer and attorney Robert Stipe (1929–2007), while on a Fulbright Fellowship at the University College of London, published an influential article in the July 1970 issue of *Preservation News* entitled "Preservation Lawyers—Unite." Stipe's experience in the United Kingdom must have moved him to have written such an article from the other side of the Atlantic. In response, *Duke University Law Journal* and the *Wake Forest University Law Review* published editions in 1971 and 1976, respectively, exclusively on preservation law.[24] At approximately the same time the National Trust for Historic Preservation (NTHP) also sponsored a conference on preservation law.[25] Circa 1970, at the time Roberts created his course and Stipe was engaged in his research in England, the National Historic Preservation Act of 1966 was only four years old. The "landmark" historic preservation case, *Penn Central Transportation Co. v. New York City,* would not be decided by the U.S. Supreme Court for another eight years. In the absence of these cornerstone cases and regulations, the material that was taught in the nascent classes on preservation law was quite different from what is taught today.

The first educators were lawyers by training. Indeed, in 1979 and 1983, respectively, the Preservation Law Institute and the American Law Institute–American Bar Association Committee on Continuing Professional Education also joined the bandwagon by running seminars and programs on historic preservation law.[26] As historic preservation programs proliferated across the country during the 1980s, 1990s, and 2000s, so did preservation legal education as part of the curriculum. Other than adding new material, as new court cases and legislation came about, the approach to preservation legal education has changed little over the years.

At present, there appears to be considerable variability in the instruction offered in preservation law to future professionals in the field. While several universities with law schools offer joint degrees in law and historic preservation—such as Boston University, Cornell University, Roger Williams University, and the University of Georgia—some other historic preservation programs require no specific coursework in preservation law. In these instances it is often subsumed as a topic under general courses such as preservation planning, economics, or theory. At those universities offering law courses within historic preservation or architecture programs, in some instances attorneys teach these courses, while non-attorney professionals teach these classes at others.

A New Approach to Historic Preservation Law Pedagogy

For attorneys, the goal of legal argument is to prevail. To accomplish this purpose, the use of the Socratic method may be well suited to "inculcate in students the habit of rigorous and critical analysis of the arguments that they hear, as well as the practice of assessing and revising their own ideas and approaches in light of new information or different reasoning . . . since developing the ability to present ideas forcefully and effectively . . . is integral to becoming a lawyer."[27] The objective for historic preservation professionals is to meet compliance requirements while balancing the needs of all stakeholders. Blumenfeld indicates that either methodology may foster the development of critical thinking skills in students. The benefit of *havruta* is that it brings in diverse perspectives for a "best" instead of an "only" solution.[28]

What should be the purpose of learning preservation law to a practitioner? In the opinion of others, as well as our own as instructors, learning the legal aspects of historic preservation is necessary so the practitioner and his or her client, agency, or organization can meet compliance standards.[29] Since during the majority of the time the use of preservation-related regulations involves compliance and adherence in deriving a best and inclusive decision rather than argumentation, how might the teaching of preservation law reflect this difference in purpose? Accessible data are not currently available on how the legal aspects of historic preservation are taught in the sixty-two programs (2012) listed by the National Council for Preservation Education (NCPE).[30] NCPE, the organization that has assumed the task of overseeing preservation education in the United States, has developed guidelines for minimum standards for degree-granting programs. *Standard 3.2.4. Legal Issues,* under section *Specialized Components,* is defined as the teaching of "Constitutional law, preservation case law, federal, state and local regulatory legislation and administration." Other than this, little else is mentioned by NCPE on this topic. The Lawyers' Committee for Cultural Heritage Preservation, "a nonprofit organization of lawyers, law students and interested members of the public who have joined together to promote the preservation and protection of cultural heritage resources in the United States and internationally through education and advocacy," was equally unhelpful, listing only twelve institutions offering courses in historic preservation law when there are actually many more.[31]

Furthermore, until recently, there has been little published by academic scholars on preservation education, let alone preservation law pedagogy. Books on historic preservation may briefly mention the beginnings of university-level preservation education, such as Fitch at Columbia University mentioned previously, but the focus is on curriculum materials (if on preservation education) and practice, site-specific case study histories, principles, and theory, as well as standards and techniques. Scholarly journals devoted specifically to historic preservation such as the *APT Bulletin: The Journal of Preservation Technology,* Columbia University's *Future Anterior,* and NCPE's *Preservation Education and Research* rarely publish articles on preservation law.[32] These publications focus on specific issues of preservation law but not pedagogical aspects. This is also the case for the various law reviews and reporters—one of the more important in regard to historic preservation law being the *Preservation Law Reporter* by the NTHP. Their scholarly emphasis has been on either the history and evolution of preservation or technical legal issues. *The Journal of Legal Education* also has not yet had an article devoted to historic preservation. Except in the early years of preservation education, during the 1970s, when a handful of academic articles identified the dearth of and dire need for teaching aspiring lawyers and practitioners preservation law, little else has been published on the delivery and effectiveness of this niche subject.[33]

From its origins as an interdisciplinary field, historic preservation has utilized pedagogical approaches derived from its allied areas of study. Michael Tomlan has mentioned that architecture-based courses in historic preservation were taught initially by "architectural historians, who were trained as architects,"[34] while content in such areas as history and American studies would be taught by members of those departments as the need arose. The teaching of preservation law was merely another subfield for the legal academic. As the field matures it has developed its own unique integrated perspective. It requires that practitioners understand and utilize principles of design as well as scientific and valid approaches to restoration of material integrity and to base these activities within normalized and legally prescribed boundaries in the context of a variety of inputs and perspectives.

So, how did we arrive at our new approach? During the 2004–5 winter break from doctoral studies, the first author, Barry Stiefel, enrolled at a yeshiva in Jerusalem, Israel. One afternoon, he was paired with a full-time student his age (mid-twenties) during an open study session. They turned to a random page in the Mishnah, a collection of oral laws that form part of the Talmud, and began studying regulations related to real property and land use.[35] His partner, or "havra-man," was out of his depth of understanding about the assignment. While his knowledge of Hebrew was far superior to Stiefel's—indeed, he translated much of the text into English with a keen understanding of the nuanced meanings of the language—his seminary-bound experience made it difficult for him to grasp the practical application of the land use ordinances. The first author, on the other hand, with his past experiences, had already learned about equivalent secular land use laws and had participated in their implementation.[36] Together, they struggled through the text, with each acquiring a greater understanding. Indeed, from this one afternoon, not only had the first author learned more about property law and land use, but he enjoyed it. What the first author found valuable about this learning method, in contrast to others, is that there was time and space to think and bounce ideas about the material through listening to and articulating with a partner. Most important, the partner was also in the same place of the process toward understanding of the material. A respectful, working relationship about learning had developed.

Jewish Pedagogy and *Havruta* Methodology

Jewish education regarding law is old. The most literal Hebrew word for "Jewish law" is *halacha;* however, a better way of understanding this term is as "the way" or "path," meaning that this is the manner by which things are to be done. These laws are derived from the Torah, which is composed of the Hebrew Bible, or Pentateuch, as well as the oral law, a literary corpus also known as the Talmud. Often all of these elements collectively are referred to as "the Law" within rabbinic literature. Learning of Jewish law is thousands of years old and took place in yeshivot. The eminent scholar Nathan Drazin summarized the fundamental differences between the philosophy of Jewish and Greco-Roman education, the forbearer of Western scholastic culture.

> The outstanding difference between Jewish and Greek and Roman education was, of course, in the matter of aims. In Sparta and for the early Athenians the chief aim of education was to make good citizens. Individual excellence was stressed in its relation to public usefulness . . . The goal of education for Socrates was the development of the power of thinking in order to enable man to arrive at fundamental universal moral principles. Other Greek philosophers held that since reflective reasoning was man's peculiar function, knowledge for its own sake was man's highest good . . . The chief aim of education in Rome was very much the same. The orator was considered the finest type of citizen. For the Jews, on the other hand, the religious motive was the dominating factor of education. All Jews were required to know the Law and to observe it in practice. Their education was hence thoroughly practical. It was integrated with all the activities of life. The development of the intellectual faculty was only a by-product of that education.[37]

To know and observe the law is the fundamental objective of Jewish education. The custom of learning with a partner also developed in yeshivot. Mention is made of the practice in early rabbinic literature;[38] however, there is disagreement among scholars on the exact age of *havruta* pedagogy.[39] In summary, the pedagogy requires students to study in groups and to present material to each other in a model of independence and interdependence.[40] The students usually recite the material aloud. Oral reading of Jewish text is an ancient custom in order to facilitate memorization. Listening and recitation of a law is a fundamental practice within *havruta* because repetition encourages exposure to multiple perspectives about a particular issue.[41] Following the oral reading students are encouraged to ask each other questions about the meanings and implications of what they have read. Depending on the course topic, student body, class time, or objective for assessment and grading, minor adjustments may be needed if utilized outside of a yeshiva. For instance, orientation to this method within a secular learning environment may include having learning sessions take place during class time so that the instructor can more readily monitor and provide feedback. Later, such discussions could be encouraged outside of the classroom environment as well. A comprehensive examination of this methodology can be found in Orit Kent's 2008 doctoral dissertation, *Interactive Text Study and the Co-Construction of Meaning: Havruta in the DeLeT Beit Midrash,* where multiple *havruta* study sessions between students are described.[42]

Paired study groups not only facilitated the understanding of text but also reduced the time demands on instructors (rabbis) in yeshivot. It is a philosophy for educating and not simply a set of instructional techniques. Pedagogical scholars agree that the method is innovative by also providing secondary cognitive and social benefits.[43] Of course, these benefits can vary depending on the experience and effectiveness of the instructor and the quality of the students. For instance, successful instructors have to offer upfront support, or guidance, for establishing an effective *havruta* learning environment. Students also have to be willing to participate and the methodology encourages this.

We wish to emphasize that like other collaborative learning approaches, *havruta* is not a pedagogical script but a setting of conditions that include instructions to students, physical setting, as well as monitoring, and regulation of this interaction in line with institutional constraints. These conditions are intended to facilitate particular types of interactions among the participants. It is important for instructors utilizing this approach to think of themselves not as expert transmitters of knowledge, but as designers of intellectual experiences for students that trigger specific learning mechanisms. As Pierre Dillenbourg notes, "this includes the activities/mechanisms performed individually, since individual cognition is not suppressed in peer interaction. But, in addition, the interaction among subjects generates extra activities (explanation, disagreement, mutual regulation, . . .) which trigger extra cognitive mechanisms (knowledge elicitation, internalization, reduced cognitive load, . . .)."[44]

Unlike some cooperative learning formats, *havruta* does not assign specific roles or portion out particular responsibilities to members, or produce a specific delineated product. The emphasis of *havruta* is on a continuous mutual effort to learn by solving problems together. This type of interdependent community, according to Jean MacGregor, possesses all the joys, tensions, and difficulties that attend communities. We note that these difficulties might include unequal contributions of effort and distributions of power or influence between partners.[45] This is where the instructor assists either in redirecting the group or, optimally, in providing the peers themselves with tools for self-regulation of their interaction.

Preservation Law as Taught at the Joint College of Charleston–Clemson University Program

For the preservation law class taught at the joint graduate program in historic preservation at the College of Charleston and Clemson University, each student follows the *havruta* methodology, defined in the syllabus as "involving the studying [of] text and laws with a partner, and entail[ing] intense debate." The students form their *havrot* groups on the first day of class, which are composed of two or three people, depending on the class size. A warning is given to the class that they should select partners wisely based on what they already know about one another in the program. A partner should be someone whom they can learn from and with since study and research take place both inside and outside of class throughout the semester. The best partners are those who can challenge each other the most in regard to inquiry and understanding. In this way both students push one another to grow intellectually. In summary, the pair of students is responsible for each other's learning (see Figure 17.2) while the professor supervises to assure quality control.

In the *havruta,* the students first review the assigned laws and associated readings outside of class together, such as the "takings" clause in the Fifth Amendment, the Antiquities Act, or the National Historic Preservation Act. The text of each law serves as the "halacha" and the associated readings as the Talmudic explanation, such as Section 106 of the National Historic Preservation Act and Thomas King's explanation of it in *Cultural*

17.2 The law class at the joint College of Charleston–Clemson University historic preservation graduate program. Photograph by Allisyn Miller, from the personal collection of Barry L. Stiefel

Resource Laws and Practice.[46] They are then to take some time to discuss what they have read so that all are on the same page. Following some comprehension of the law—more may be acquired with the next step—the students conduct some research in pairs and write about their findings and understanding of the law's significance from this experience.[47] Class begins with everyone coming together to share what they learned about the laws they studied in their *havruta.* Following each law, a brief lecture is given, called a *shiur* in the yeshiva environment, covering the highlights and lessons that everyone is to be aware of so that nothing is inadvertently left out. Some material that the students have studied is reviewed during the lecture; however, additional information is also incorporated. The new material is most frequently something significant that a pair or minority of students have discovered in their investigations that is worth sharing with everyone else. Within the class, students are also expected to ask questions about the material in order to facilitate intergroup learning.

Most of the time the class runs smoothly. One exception was in early February 2009, shortly after the Illinois Appellate Court decided *Hanna v. City of Chicago,* ruling on January 30 that Chicago's Landmark Ordinance was unconstitutional due to "vagueness." Students were concerned as to what this could mean or lead to—would local-level historic preservation be declared illegal in Illinois? What about elsewhere? Within the class, the legal aspects of the case were discussed vis-à-vis other material that had been covered, such as the U.S. Supreme Court's 1978 ruling upholding local historic preservation ordinances in *Penn Central Transportation Co. v. New York City.* While the matter of *Hanna v. City of Chicago* had yet to be redecided by the Circuit Court of Cook County—which happened March 6, 2009, since it had been sent back by the Appellate Court—by the end of class students had peace of mind through discussing the legal aspects with their *havruta* partner. *Hanna v. City of Chicago* would not be the end of local historic preservation protections in this country, let alone within the Chicago city limits. Legal precedents by higher courts ensured this and the students came to this understanding on their own. From the class's viewpoint of the most likely scenario, legal "vagueness" might be clarified by statutory interpretation, and at the time, an appeal was being made to the Supreme Court of Illinois. In the end, this did not happen either. The Circuit Court of Cook County "reversed and remanded" the former ruling of "vagueness" and historic preservation practice in Chicago returned to normal.[48]

Programmatic Benefits of Heritage-Based Educational Practices

Assuming that a practitioner's perspective is shaped by her or his educational experience, would it not be reasonable to consider the use of preservation education methodologies developed by other cultural traditions as a means of facilitating student awareness of minority heritage issues? Indeed, since "our knowledge cannot transcend our values and cultural concepts, rather it is grounded in them,"[49] we should try using this predicament to an advantage. Using *havruta,* or any other pedagogical method developed by a cultural group for that matter, can have a programmatic benefit within the heritage preservation field. Though not on the Intangible Heritage List, *havruta* is a social practice as defined by Article 2(c) of the 2003 UNESCO Convention for the Safeguarding of the Intangible Cultural Heritage. Using these pedagogies "ensure[s] respect for the intangible cultural heritage" and "raise[s] awareness at the local, national and international levels . . . ensuring mutual appreciation thereof." Considering the current state of world affairs, especially the Israeli-Palestinian conflict in the Middle East as well as the reemergence of anti-Semitism, exposure to a diversity of cultural traditions could have societal benefits by promoting tolerance through understanding of other people.[50]

Respecting other cultural traditions also has a place within legal practice and its implementation. Though not valid in American courts of law at the moment, from an ethical perspective the traditions related to the treatment of culturally important properties of ethnic minority groups needs to be touched on as something to be understood and respected by preservationists. The preservation law class would be the place to bring up such ethical issues for discussion, even if the coverage of cultural approaches must be selective due to the time constraints of a semester. In this way, historic preservation students can learn an additional ethical aspect related to sensitivity and compliance with cultural expectations and norms—an aspect that goes beyond the federal, state, and local laws and regulations.[51] Rules from particular ethnic and religious groups should also be respected.[52] For example, within the context of Judaism, the rabbis established guidelines for the proper treatment of synagogues and sites, which were recorded in the Talmud (c. 550 C.E.). These laws, taken from Rabbi Joseph Karo's (1488–1575) c. 1563 codification of Talmudic law, called the *Shulchan Aruch* (150:1–154:15), are the following:

- A synagogue should not be torn down or sold until a replacement for it has been built, unless it is in danger of collapsing, and parts of it may be taken down only on condition that it is rebuilt.
- Even a ruined synagogue must be treated respectfully, but it may be used for dignified purposes if this was stipulated when it was built.
- The materials of a ruined synagogue must not be used even to build a new one.
- The attic above a synagogue must not be used for disrespectful purposes; but if part of an existing building is made into a synagogue, the other parts of the building may continue to be used. These things do not apply to a place that is used for prayers only temporarily.
- A synagogue may be converted into a yeshiva, but not vice versa [since a yeshiva, a place of learning, is considered more sacred than a house of worship within the Jewish tradition].

In an ideal world these rules should be applied in addition to any other required building treatment, such as the Secretary of the Interior's Standards for the Treatment of Historic Properties. While the number of Jewish sacred properties within the United States is relatively small, exposure to cultural conventions of minority ethnic groups can push a professional to consider other ways of practicing, such as with Native American tribes and their traditional cultural properties.[53] Utilizing this ethical approach brings us back to Principle 6 on *Inclusiveness* of the 2008 ICOMOS *Charter for the Interpretation and Presentation of Cultural Heritage Sites,* discussed in the introduction of this chapter. In this way preservation legal education can take on an additional layer of significance and meaning.

Further Implications

Though more experimentation is warranted on practices for preservation legal education, students may find that methods developed by other cultures enable certain subjects to be learned more efficiently. *Havruta* is a methodology that has shown itself to be successful in other educational programs where there are issues to contend with for ill-structured problems, as shown in the studies surveyed. We can also recognize that the *havruta* way may not be for everyone considering how we are all different from each other. On the other hand, the use of alternative methods in instruction may attract a broader variety of students to participate in this process, promoting greater inclusiveness. What we have presented here is how it has been successful in our experience. Nonetheless, pedagogies by other ethnic groups—such as Islamic, Confucian, or Navajo—may be just as successful for learning law, as well as other preservation topics, as alternatives to Jewish *havruta.* Indeed, offering a sampling of ethnic pedagogies within a preservation curriculum, instead of just one or two, would bring a richer, more culturally diverse learning experience. Furthermore, heritage-based educational practices can have programmatic benefits for the preservation field by both putting social intangible heritage practices into use as well as exposing students to the "laws" of cultural minority groups.

Notes

1. See Lynne Armitage and Yung Yau, *Heritage Protection in the Built Environment in Hong Kong and Queensland: A Cross-Cultural Comparison* (ePublications@bond. http://epublications.bond.edu.au/era_ee/3, 2006).
2. See Australian Heritage Commission, *Ask First: A Guide to Respecting Indigenous Heritage Places and Values* (Canberra: Australian Heritage Commission, 2002).
3. Karen Kitchener, "Cognition, Metacognition, and Epistemic Cognition: A Three-Level Model of Cognitive Processing," *Human Development,* 26 (1983), 222–32.
4. Susan Williams, "Legal Education, Feminist Epistemology, and the Socratic Method," *Stanford Law Review,* 45:6 (1993), 1571–76.
5. Abdul Paliawala, *Reclaiming Ancient Pedagogies in the Information Age of Learning,* extract from the inaugural meeting of a new disciplinary interest group in Islamic Law (Scar Man House, University of Warwick, 2010), 1–9.
6. Paliawala, *Reclaiming Ancient Pedagogies.*

7. Christine Zuni Cruz, "Toward a Pedagogy and Ethic of Law/Lawyering for Indigenous Peoples," *North Dakota Law Review*, 82 (2006), 863–901.

8. See Orit Kent, *Interactive Text Study and the Co-Construction of Meaning: Havruta in the DeLeT Beit Midrash* (Ph.D. diss., Brandeis University, 2008).

9. The Talmud is a collection of writings constituting Jewish civil and religious law compiled during the early centuries of the Common Era.

10. See Aliza Segal, *Notes from ATID: Havruta Study: History, Benefits and Enhancements* (Jerusalem: Academy for Torah Initiatives and Directions, 2003).

11. Barbara Blumenfeld, "Can Havruta Style Learning Be a Best Practice in Law School?" *Willamette Journal of International Law and Dispute Resolution*, 18 (2010), 19; and Inger Bergom, Mary Wright, Marie Brown, and Michael Brooks, "Promoting College Student Development Through Collaborative Learning: A Case Study of Hevruta," *About Campus*, 15:6 (2011), 19–25.

12. See Lev Vygotskiĭ and Michael Cole, *Mind in Society: The Development of Higher Psychological Processes* (Cambridge, MA: Harvard University Press, 1978).

13. Jerome S. Bruner, "Vygotsky: An Historical and Conceptual Perspective," in *Culture, Communication, and Cognition: Vygotskian Perspectives,* ed. James V. Wertsch (Cambridge: Cambridge University Press, 1985), 21–34.

14. Daniel R. Marburger, "Comparing Student Performance Using Cooperative Learning," *International Review of Economics Education,* 4:1 (2005), 46–57.

15. Anuradha A. Gokhale, "Collaborative Learning Enhances Critical Thinking," *Journal of Technology Education,* 7:1 (1995), 22–30.

16. Bergom, Wright, Brown, and Brooks, "Promoting College Student Development," 21.

17. Steve Sheppard, *The History of Legal Education in the United States: Commentaries and Primary Sources* (Pasadena, CA: Salem Press, 1999), 7–13. Courses in Roman law and canon law, which are very different from common law, had been taught at Oxford and Cambridge universities since the twelfth century. Additionally, during the Middle Ages and into the seventeenth century, barristers acquired their educations through vocational exercises at Inns of Court.

18. Robert Bocking Stevens, *Law School: Legal Education in America from the 1850s to the 1980s* (Chapel Hill: University of North Carolina Press, 1983), 1–19.

19. Stevens, *Law School,* 51–72.

20. Sheppard, *The History of Legal Education,* 31–35.

21. Filippa Marullo Anzalone, "Education for the Law: Reflective Education for the Law," in *Handbook of Reflection and Reflective Inquiry: Mapping a Way of Knowing for Professional Reflective Inquiry,* ed. Nona Lyons (New York: Springer, 2010), 85–99. See also New York State Judicial Institute, "Introduction to Clinical Legal Education," in *Partners in Justice: A Colloquium on Developing Collaborations Among Courts, Law School Clinical Programs and the Practicing Bar,* 9 May 2005.

22. Blumenfeld, "Can Havruta Style Learning Be a Best Practice in Law School?" 54.

23. See Michael Tomlan, "Historic Preservation Education: Alongside Architecture in Academia," *Journal of Architectural Education*, 47:4 (May 1994), 187–96.

24. "Robert E. Stipe, 1929–2007," *Popular Government*, 73:2 (Winter 2008), 46–47; and Rufus L. Edmisten, "Tribute to Robert E. Stipe," *North Carolina Central Law Review*, 11 (1979–80), 201.

25. "Trust Sponsors 1st Conference on Preservation Law Problems," *Preservation News*, 11:6 (1 June 1971), 1–2.

26. See Gail Winson, *Historic Preservation Law: An Annotated Survey of Sources and Literature* (Littleton, CO: F. B. Rothman & Co., 1999).

27. Elizabeth Garrett, "The Socratic Method (Green Bag Article)," *The University of Chicago, The Law School*, 2011, http://www.law.uchicago.edu/socrates/soc_article.html (14 March 2011).

28. Blumenfeld, "Can Havruta Style Learning Be a Best Practice in Law School?" 50.

29. See Thomas F. King, *Cultural Resource Laws and Practice* (3rd Edition) (Lanham, MD: Altamira Press, 2008).

30. See Paul Kapp, *National Council for Preservation Education*, 2 February 2011 http://www.ncpe.us/ and et al. links (14 February 2011). The sixty-two programs counted included eleven undergraduate historic preservation programs, two undergraduate programs with certificates or emphasis in historic preservation, twenty-four graduate historic preservation degree programs, twenty-two graduate programs with certificates or emphasis in historic preservation, and three associate programs. Some programs, such as the College of Charleston with an undergraduate program in historic preservation and a joint graduate program with Clemson University, are listed more than once.

31. See The Lawyers' Committee for Cultural Heritage Preservation (2010), http://www.culturalheritagelaw.org/ and et al. links (17 April 2014). The twelve courses/programs listed were Southwestern Law School, University of Connecticut School of Law, University of Chicago Law School, Tulane University Law School, University of Maryland Historic Preservation Program, University of Boston Law School J.D./M.A. in Law and Preservation Studies, University of Missouri–Kansas City School of Law, Pace University School of Law, Charleston School of Law, University of Tennessee School of Law, Southern Methodist University Dedman School of Law, and Georgetown University Law School. Note that Cornell University, Roger Williams University, and the University of Georgia—institutions with joint law and historic preservation degree granting programs—are not listed.

32. In a survey of article titles by these journals since their founding, the *Bulletin of the Association for Preservation Technology/APT Bulletin: The Journal of Preservation Technology* (since 1969) has published less than a half dozen, *Future Anterior* (since 2004) has published zero on U.S. preservation law (there are several articles on Russian and Spanish heritage law), and *Preservation Education & Research* (since 2008), only a couple. None of these articles deal with pedagogical issues of preservation law.

33. Nicholas Robinson, "Historic Preservation Law: The Metes & Bounds of a New Field," *Pace Law Faculty Publications*, 381 (1981), 511–66.

34. Tomlan, "Historic Preservation Education," 188.

35. Tractate *Bava Batra*.

36. Barry Stiefel had a preservation planning internship at the city of Shaker Heights, Ohio, and an architectural historian position for a cultural resource management firm in Austin, Texas, in 2003–4, where he worked on projects related to some of the issues discussed in *Bava Batra*. Stiefel was also a doctoral student at Tulane University's historic preservation program at the time.

37. Nathan Drazin, *History of Jewish Education from 515 B.C.E. to 220 C.E.* (Baltimore: Johns Hopkins Press, 1940), 137–38.

38. See Babylonian Talmud, tractate *Berakhot* 63b.

39. The pedagogy used today can be verified to the early nineteenth-century yeshivot of Lithuania. The earliest of these was the yeshiva of Volozhin, now in Belarus, operating from 1803 to 1892. It is from this yeshiva that *pilpul* (complex analysis) and *peshat* (basic textual analysis) were developed. See Saul Stampfer, *ha-Yeshivah ha-Liṭa'it be-Hithavutah* (Jerusalem, Israel: Merkaz Zalman Shazar le-toldot Yiśra'el, 1995) on the Lithuanian origin. However, in Kent's *Interactive Text Study and the Co-Construction of Meaning* is a discussion (footnote 63 on pp. 24–25) with an exceptional critique of previous studies and lack of attention to other Jewish groups outside of Poland-Lithuania, opening the possibility for an older origin of *havruta*.

40. See Segal, *Notes from ATID*.

41. See Bergom, Wright, Brown, and Brooks, "Promoting College Student Development."

42. Transcribed *havruta* sessions are lengthy and are too large to produce in their entirety in this chapter.

43. See Segal, *Notes from ATID.*

44. Pierre Dillenbourg, *Collaborative Learning: Cognitive and Computational Approaches* (Amsterdam: Pergamon, 1999), 6.

45. See Jean MacGregor et al., *Strategies for Energizing Large Classes: From Small Groups to Learning Communities* (San Francisco: Jossey-Bass, 2000).

46. The associated readings used are mostly from King, *Cultural Resource Laws & Practice,* and Sherry Hutt, Caroline Blanco, and Ole Varmer, *Heritage Resources Law: Protecting the Archeological and Cultural Environment* (New York: Wiley, 1999).

47. Grading of students in most yeshiva environments is different from that in American universities. Therefore, this writing assignment was created as a modification of *havruta* methodology in order to better assess each student's understanding of the material.

48. *Hanna v. City of Chicago.* 2009. 907 NE 2d 390—Ill: Appellate Court, 1st Dist., 5th Div.

49. William, "Legal Education," 1572.

50. See Hillel Schenker and Ziad Abu Zayyad, *Islamophobia and Anti-Semitism* (Princeton, NJ: Markus Wiener Publishers, 2006).

51. The authors recognize that this can become a difficult ideal to live up to, such as if the cultural law of one group stipulates that the house of worship of another cannot be repaired or built higher than their own.

52. One could argue that there are exceptions, such as those provided by the American Indian Religious Freedom Act and the Native American Graves Protection and Repatriation Act, but these only give protection to federally recognized Native American tribes.

53. See Thomas F. King, *Places that Count: Traditional Cultural Properties in Cultural Resource Management* (Walnut Creek, CA: Altamira Press, 2003).

18 Conclusion: Common Problems and Potential Solutions

Jeremy C. Wells and Barry L. Stiefel

The "Preservation Education: Sharing Best Practices and Finding Common Ground" conference, on which this volume is based, offered a unique opportunity for educators from around the globe to concentrate on ways to assess and improve programs that focus on the historic environment and heritage. At the conclusion of the formal paper presentations, the participants assembled in a special session to discuss and refine concepts directly or tangentially raised in the presented papers, including some that were controversial. Through this process, the participants defined a common set of problems and potential solutions as well as a vision for the future of historic environment education. This chapter summarizes that discussion.

A Summary of Historic Environment Education

Participants presented on a wide variety of topics and issues, including the importance of the liberal arts, the relationship between undergraduate and graduate programs, job training, the failure and revival of crafts/trades education, pedagogical techniques, curriculum design, international perspectives, performance evaluation, and ethics. At first glance, while these appear to be separate topics with little relation to each other, many of the papers contained significant overlapping themes and content, which can be grouped into the following six categories, which were used by the participants to help organize their discussion:

defining the discipline

employment and relationship to job skills

communication, collaboration, and bridging across boundaries

ethics and quality issues

curriculum design

outcomes and assessment methods

Defining the Discipline

A consistent thread throughout the conference, including the discussion session, was a lack of agreement on defining the "discipline" in which historic environment practitioners and researchers engage their work. Some participants even questioned if it was appropriate to frame the work of practitioners and researchers in a separate historic environment discipline at all, suggesting that a specific endeavor must first originate in a non-conservation, parent discipline with the work then occurring in the historic environment. An example of this scenario is a licensed architect conducting a rehabilitation project on an historic house: the discipline is architecture while the domain of attention is the historic environment. In other words, in this point of view, the historic environment is where the work occurs, but the environment cannot be used itself to define a unique ontological or epistemological approach. This definition becomes problematic, however, with practitioners and researchers who have been educated and trained in aspects primarily identified with the historic environment, but not found in other disciplines, and therefore do not self-identify with any other discipline.

A related issue was a lack of consensus on terminology to describe the domains and activities of educators and practitioners of the historic environment. As clear ontological and epistemological boundaries for historic environment work and research along with consistent terminology are necessary for effective teaching (and are currently lacking), the conference participants thought that these issues should be considered fundamental pedagogical problems that therefore deserve more attention. Moreover, without agreement on the ontological and epistemological nature of work and research in the historic environment, it becomes difficult to define what "it" is, where "it" has been, and where "it" should be heading in the future.

Much like the multiple perspectives on the disciplinary nature of historic environment work, the participants acknowledged that there is confusion about what constitutes practice and research in the historic environment, given disparate national and cultural contexts—a troubling ambiguity that impacts teaching because it is not clear what students should be held accountable to learn. While acknowledging these national and cultural differences, participants believed that there was a potential for a shared, core set of principles, as well as an understanding of just what the historic environment is and how professionals ought to engage with it. This is an important, continuing topic of discussion that has broad impact on both practice and teaching, yet there are few, if any forums, for this kind of discussion to date within an educational context.

At a more specific level, descriptive terms for the activities of historic environment professionals and educators as well as terminology to describe aspects of the environment and its heritage objects are not consistent across disciplines, much less between countries. For instance, in the English-speaking world, the term for the field is "historic preservation" in the United States, "heritage conservation" in Canada, and the "heritage sector" in the United Kingdom. Descriptions of the natural- and human-modified environments are also quite varied, from "heritage townscapes" and "historic environment" in the United Kingdom to "cultural landscapes," which is favored in the United States. Non-English-speaking countries are equally varied; for instance, in Sweden, the term for an historic environment practitioner is an *antikvarie;* the English cognate is the pejorative term "antiquarian," which has a different meaning. Countries with Latin-derived languages use variations of the words "patrimony" and "culture" to describe the field.

In the United States, there is increasing discontent in continuing to use the phrase "historic preservation," not only for its grammatically incorrect construction and U.S.-centric usage, but also because in the public arena it conjures notions of preventing change and visions of embalming and preserving things in sealed jars.[1] The natural resource conservation movement has effectively latched onto the word "conservation," to such an extent that, in the United States, it is assumed to only apply to the natural, and not built, environment. This perspective may be changing, however, as more influential people in the field are advocating for a change. Donovan Rypkema, a widely acknowledged expert in the economics of building and place reuse, thinks that the United States should "join most of the rest of the world and be about heritage conservation, rather than historic preservation."[2] In 2012, the University of Southern California changed the name of its master's program from "historic preservation" to "heritage conservation" in order to remain "globally relevant."[3] Discussions about changing the name of the field from "historic preservation" to "heritage conservation" (or some other term) appear with increasing frequency in national conferences in the United States. There is, therefore, some evidence of convergence of terminology, although the conference participants agreed this will likely remain an issue for some time to come. Communication and collaboration among disparate educators will continue to be problematic until there is a common set of meanings that define historic environment research and practice.

Employment and Relationship to Job Skills

Traditionally, undergraduate education has focused on the liberal arts, but there is an increasing expectation today that students should be well prepared for specific career paths, engendering debate about the extent that these programs should be more vocational in nature. This argument also applies to undergraduate historic environment programs: should an emphasis be placed on liberal arts education versus the development of professional skills with the expectation that some skills will be learned on the job or through further, graduate-level education? An associated argument is if undergraduate degree programs should cater to specific job skills, especially when it is not clear to what extent historic environment employers value or do not value an undergraduate liberal arts education and if this background makes a more effective employee. Most positions that are not based in the trades require a graduate degree regardless, which reinforces the perspective that an undergraduate degree in the historic environment should focus more on the liberal arts and less on specific job skills. For graduate and vocational programs, however, students and employers expect there to be much more of a focus on the development of specific professional skills. There are few data from the employer's perspective, however, with the exception of vocations in traditional building crafts,[4] that have been used to develop curricula with the goal of equipping students with specific skill sets. Curriculum development, therefore, tends to be driven by the personal experience of educators who often have practitioner experience in the field prior to their academic engagement.

The qualifications of tomorrow's historic environment professionals, therefore, constitute an ongoing, open-ended question, but the participants believed that, regardless of specific employer requirements, there should always be an emphasis on problem solving in the teaching process and extensive fieldwork and collaboration along with service and experiential learning. This perspective is far from new, as experiential learning and fieldwork has always been central to educating students who will work in the historic environment. In the United States, for instance, Charles Peterson, who is widely acknowledged as a seminal figure in the history of historic preservation education, emphasized the need for students to be in the field, getting their hands dirty.[5] Most historic environment programs emphasize their experiential learning potential, as it tends to attract students interested in "real-world" experiences.

Communication, Collaboration, and Bridging across Boundaries

Problems with fragmentation and communication were prominent themes in the presented papers and pervaded much of the end-of-conference discussion. Due to small program sizes, historic environment educators tend to be isolated in their institution with few or no colleagues with whom to collaborate and brainstorm in order to improve pedagogical practices specific to the historic environment. There is simply a lack of opportunities to approach problems in a collaborative fashion with educators from different fields. Participants thought that this academic isolation leads to a perceived lack of relevance of preservation/conservation within the built environment disciplines in general and especially within the sustainability realm.

Outside of a few nationwide organizations that focus on conservation/preservation education, such as NCPE in the United States and Heritage Canada Foundation's National Roundtable on Heritage Education, educators from other countries, for the most part, have no ability to coordinate their efforts on a larger scale and learn about best practices in the field from international colleagues. The "Preservation Education Conference" offered the first opportunity that many of these educators to come together in the same room to discuss these issues, especially in an international context. Because of the rarified nature of this kind of communication, conference participants were quite interested in continuing the discussion using all means reasonably possible, especially those methods that could take advantage of Internet-based tools such as online forums, websites, and social media. Some participants called for an existing or new international nonprofit or nongovernmental organization to mediate and facilitate this exchange.

Potential academic collaborators exist in many other countries, offering an opportunity to learn from each other and share best practices, especially in terms of effective curriculum design. For instance, educators in the United States and Canada could look toward Europe and Latin America in their approach to "integrated conservation" as a potential solution to integrate sustainability, public health, and planning goals into conservation work. By pooling resources in this manner, there is also an opportunity to educate those empowered to make decisions that affect the historic environment, such as politicians and planners. All participants had a strong desire to learn about the variety of pedagogical, curriculum, and assessment techniques employed on an international basis and were interested in forming an international group of educators that would communicate on a regular basis via a web-based platform to share best practices and continue the discussion. Latin American, African, and

Asian representation, in particular, was encouraged as historic environment research and practice has tended to be dominated by North America, Europe, and Australia.

Partnerships could also be established between related fields and organizations. For instance, the real estate community could be tapped for educational programming and there is much to gain by engaging in a dialogue with existing organizations that overlap with conservation activity, such as the Society of Architectural Historians. Combining disciplines, where feasible, may also be an effective way to utilize limited resources and reach a larger audience. The potential for research collaboration exists for a broad variety of disciplines from architecture and planning to anthropology and law in a way that could effectively engage students and alumni. Most conference participants believed that the relevance of conserving the historic environment is much more likely to increase by involving related fields and organizations, but a minority were concerned that this kind of activity could lead to the dilution of the efforts of heritage conservation professionals and academics, and therefore should be approached cautiously.

A specific tool that would help foster communication and provide a bridge between different constituencies is a nonacademic, professional periodical that addresses historic preservation/heritage conservation practice, in either a national or an international context. This concern is perhaps most evident in the United States, where the consensus was that the NTHP's *Preservation Magazine* is not adequately addressing the relationship between professional practice and interested stakeholders. Instead, the magazine tends to focus on personal interest stories and historic homeowners and describes little in terms of professional practice. Some models to consider that seem to work well in the United Kingdom are the Institute of Historic Building Conservation's *Context* magazine and Historic Scotland's *Focus* magazine.

Last, while the concept of bridging arose in relationship to engaging across disciplines, organizations, and geography, conceptual divides were also discussed, primarily centering on linking the built and natural environments holistically; the mutually beneficial relationship between the practical and the academic; and approaching K–12, undergraduate, and graduate education in the historic environment as a continuum rather than as discrete, unrelated units. In terms of the latter theme, there was a great deal of discussion on how undergraduate programs in the historic environment should inform the graduate preservation program experience. It was not clear what differentiates the learning objectives and outcomes between undergraduate and graduate education, as the overlap between these kinds of programs can be substantial, and should therefore be addressed in the future.

Ethics and Quality Issues

Not surprisingly, there was concern that other disciplines, whose exclusive focus is not the historic environment, lack a conservation "attitude" to their endeavors, or fail to explicitly address the topic or do so in a tangential way, such as with the U.S. Green Building Council's LEED[6] standards and sustainability efforts. For instance, the conservation of the historic environment has, since its inception, focused on building and place reuse, the conservation of energy through maximizing the retention of existing building materials, sustaining environmentally friendly cultural building practices, and learning from passive climate control systems, yet other disciplines frequently fail to discuss these concepts in relationship to historic buildings and places, much less acknowledge that heritage conservators have a role to play in sustainability. While better communication and collaboration could go a long way in addressing this issue, more important, the participants thought that it was the role of historic environment educators to "inspire" and "challenge" other disciplines. Moreover, we should strive to practice what we teach, an activity acknowledged as sometimes lacking in our endeavors.

The conference participants stressed that all historic environment educators have an ethical obligation to communicate to their students, clients, and the public that work in the historic environment should embrace innovation, including the use of technology. While innovation can be described in terms of technological solutions, it can also be defined through methodological improvements, including the increased use of the social sciences in conservation practice. It is therefore the responsibility of educators to describe heritage conservation in progressive terms, an example of which is Silvio Zancheti's (see Chapter 6) framing of practice as the conservation of desirable meanings that present and future stakeholders have for an authentic historic environment, rather than the more simplistic and rationalist view of "managing change" to the fabric of place. Such an approach helps clarify that the conservation of the historic environment should focus on people as much as fabric and that authenticity can be understood as a concept independent of fabric through empirical means. By recognizing that meaning is separate from the heritage object, a number of dynamic, sustainable, and creative approaches can be utilized to preserve the authenticity of historic places, placing historic environment educators in the unique and progressive position of understanding how the human-influenced environment is perceived and should therefore be treated.

Innovation can also extend to assuring the quality of conservation practitioners. In most countries, any individual can call himself or herself a "historic preservationist," "preservation planner," "architectural materials conservator," or any number of job titles that address and interact with the historic environment, regardless of educational background, prior job experience, or ability, as the sector is usually not regulated, licensed, or certified by any governmental or nongovernmental body. As a result, some conference participants concluded that there is an ethical obligation to assure public and private entities as well as the general public that if someone practices as an architectural materials conservator, for instance, that he or she should be certified by some official body as to his or her capability. The certification of historic environment practitioners, however, is a controversial topic and one that was divisive among the conference participants. While there are no life/health/safety issues in most heritage conservation practices[7] (issues that drove the initial requirements to certify and license architects and engineers, for instance), there are relevant precedents, such as the certification programs of the American Institute of Certified Planners and the Institute of Historic Building Conservation (U.K.), that may be useful to study in order to provide better background on the advantages and disadvantages to this approach.

Curriculum Design

Curriculum design is an essential activity for educators and should reflect innovative approaches and have a strong relationship to practice and advancing theory. The field already has many diverse and rich programs, which is an asset that can assist in identifying best practices for the creation of new and the improvement of existing educational programs. Historic environment educators are particularly interested in the extent to which practitioners should be influencing curriculum design, including overall pedagogical approaches, the balance between the theoretical and the practical, and whether the curriculum should address a country-specific or an international market. While the conference papers addressed some of these issues, most remain open for significant discussion and research.

Conference participants discussed a variety of challenges related to curriculum design, especially in terms of time and resource limitations. For instance, there is wide agreement on the need to provide students with real-world opportunities through internships and experiential learning, as Anastasia L. Pratt (Chapter 11), Shelley-Anne Peleg (Chapter 9), and Robert W. Ogle (Chapter 4), discuss, but this requirement also means that traditional coursework needs to be reduced, sacrificing theoretical foundations in order to gain additional vocational/experiential opportunities. Obviously, both practical and theoretical perspectives are essential, but the balance between the two is largely a gray area, especially if the goal is to produce students with a minimal, expected level of proficiency. An example of an attempt to achieve this balance between the theoretical and the practical is with research design. Although sometimes viewed as unnecessary for practicing professionals, an understanding of empirical research is important to help these professionals to understand the sociocultural values associated with the historic environment in order to make more effective planning decisions, as Jeremy Wells (Chapter 16) advocates with his recommendations for student thesis research. There is a need for more scholarship, such as this example, which addresses the desired balance between the theoretical and the applied in heritage conservation pedagogy, given the large number of variables in program emphases and career outcomes.

While the development of a specific program's curriculum is of importance, so is understanding the relationship between the curricula of various types of related programs, which presents even greater challenges in terms of understanding how curricula ought to integrate. As the conference participants represented a wide variety of programs—vocational and professional programs were represented as well as diploma, certificate, associate, bachelor's, master's, and doctoral programs—this was a particularly important topic, with little consensus in terms of goals. While there are a wide variety of approaches between practical vocational/trades programs and more theoretical bachelor's and graduate degree programs, there is little agreement on how or in what ways they should integrate into a logical continuum, much less how they ought to differ from one another. The relationship between various types of historic environment degree and certificate programs also engendered much debate, but, again, little consensus. Agreement on how integration ought to be approached is an especially pertinent question for those institutions that offer undergraduate and graduate degrees that address the historic environment.

There was, however, broad agreement that curriculum design should continue to adapt to and incorporate evolving technology to help improve teaching and scholarship, but while recognizing that this change is desirable, participants complained that their institutions' bureaucratic environments often made change difficult, if not impossible, in some cases. Traditional disciplinary silos between departments not only make collaboration with other faculty and students difficult, but they also limit the potential to show students the interdisciplinary (or some would say transdisciplinary) nature of conservation. Historic environment and heritage programs in higher education also tend to be small, which limits available time and resources while making it difficult to alter the status quo. These challenges will likely remain significant in the future with little reason to expect significant improvements unless the higher education environment undertakes radical changes.

Outcomes and Assessment Methods

Most of the participants' home institutions failed to regularly assess the effectiveness of program curricula and the overall pedagogical approaches to instruction. The most effective way to address this situation is to change the overall institutional culture and realign expectations, although many felt powerless to effect such change, especially where there was a lack of resources and support. While there is significant scholarship on methods used to assess the curricula of higher education programs,[8] there is little guidance in terms of assessing the effectiveness of the curricula of historic environment programs, specifically. Some of the chapters in this volume help to bridge this gap, such as Robert Benedict and Cari Goetcheus's recommendations in terms of integrating preservation material into graduate real estate curricula (Chapter 15), Henry Russell and Philip Leverton's work on distance learning (Chapter 10), and Karla Nunes Penna and Elisabeth Taylor's assessment of training programs in Brazil (Chapter 7), but significantly more scholarship is needed to better understand what makes historic environment programs unique and how this information should impact the design of a program's curriculum. Such assessment methods should focus equally on students' as well as educators' performance.

In terms of specific assessment outcomes, there was a great deal of interest in pedagogical approaches to conservation instruction and which techniques were more effective than others. The contributions of Shelley-Anne Peleg (Chapter 9), Paul Hardin Kapp, Lauren Weiss Bricker, and Luis G. Hoyos (Chapter 12), and Fernando Diniz Moreira and Luiz Manuel do Eirado Amorim (Chapter 13) are examples of useful case studies that may help answer this question. The pedagogical heritage of different cultures may provide intriguing examples of improved methods, as these traditions have learning techniques that have been refined over hundreds of years, as Barry Stiefel and Gilbert Stiefel (Chapter 17) reveal in their challenge to the Socratic method for teaching preservation law. In their case study, collaborative, pair-based learning based on the Jewish *havruta* method may be more effective in helping students to understand divergent values and perspectives as well as appreciating problems more holistically. There are also many other case studies on pedagogical approaches in conservation referenced by these authors, but what is missing is a meta-analysis to help educators understand the best approaches and techniques and how these could be adapted for particular learning outcomes.

Ultimately, the assessment of a program's success should be dependent on the outcome of graduates and their overall career achievement. Most participants, however, indicated that their institution did not do a particularly good job tracking the success of graduates, at least in a formal way, although many program directors and coordinators were aware, to some degree, which students were establishing themselves on successful career paths. The participants stressed that this process should be more formalized and the information on where graduates find employment, how well their skills fit their job, and overall performance should provide a feedback loop into curriculum design. There was much less agreement, however, on how alumni could be tracked, the specific nature of the data gathered, and how the resulting information could influence an overall curriculum.

The Future

While predicting the future is always a risky endeavor, the educators assembled at the conference had a fairly clear vision of the future of historic environment education, with a primary focus on an unambiguous definition of the discipline and its activities. Within the larger sphere of higher education, theory is likely to continue to be deprecated in lieu of practical/hands-on/vocational approaches to curriculum development. Historic environment education is unlikely to be exempt from this trend, but in many ways, conservation/preservation education has always involved a significant amount of field experience and service learning; this foundation will likely expand to encompass greater opportunities. With an increasing international focus on conservation/preservation activities and a future that involves greater collaboration among educators from other countries, more field and service learning opportunities should be available to students. Greater collaboration may also catalyze communication between primary and secondary educators and among educators of certificate and degree programs at institutions of higher learning that is, for the most part, not taking place today. This bridge may then help in visualizing a complete conservation/preservation education continuum from primary to secondary education with an understanding that each level of education will be able to build on the previous level.

Although not entirely unexpected, the future of historic environment education engenders far more questions than answers, including politically sensitive issues such as certifying historic environment professionals and programs and the possibility that conservation/preservation programs will be made irrelevant by integrating them into existing built environment programs. Many of these issues have at their core questions of identity and defining practice and research within the historic environment. If conservation/preservation education leaders cannot agree on the ontological and epistemological domains of the discipline and its core endeavors, collaboration with other researchers and professionals will become increasingly problematic in the future. The first step, however, which the "Preservation Education" conference tried to address is to understand these issues in an effort for conservation/preservation educators across the globe to more purposefully forge a future for historic environment education.

Notes

1. Roberta Brandes Gratz, *The Battle for Gotham: New York in the Shadow of Robert Moses and Jane Jacobs* (New York: Nation Books, 2010), 60.

2. Donovan Rypkema, "Making Historic Preservation Relevant for the Next 50 Years," *Forum Journal*, 24:3 (2010), 18.

3. Kim A. O'Connell, "Field Survey: Where Are the Gaps in Preservation Education?" *Architect Magazine*, 11 (November 2012).

4. Examples of studies that address the necessary skills of heritage trades/craftspeople include National Heritage Training Group, *Traditional Building Craft Skills: Assessing the Need, Meeting the Challenge: Skills Needs Analysis of the Built Heritage Sector in Scotland* (London: National Heritage Training Group, 2007); and English Heritage, *Traditional Building Craft Skills: Skills Needs Analysis of the Built Heritage Sector* (London: English Heritage, 2013).

5. Charles E. Peterson, "The Role of the Architect in Historical Restorations," in *Preservation and Conservation: Principles and Practices: Proceedings of the North American International Regional Conference Williamsburg, Virginia, and Philadelphia, Pennsylvania, September 10–16, 1972*, ed. Sharon Timmons (Washington, DC: The Preservation Press, 1976), 1–12.

6. The Leadership in Energy and Environmental Design (LEED) program, which is administered by the U.S. Green Building Council, is "a green building tool that addresses the entire building lifecycle recognizing best-in-class building strategies"; see http://www.usgbc.org/leed.

7. It might be argued, however, that materials conservators ought to be certified in working with hazardous substances to protect themselves, their clients, and the public.

8. Examples of guidance for curriculum development include Robert R. Diamond, *Designing and Assessing Courses and Curricula: A Practical Guide* (San Francisco: Jossey-Bass, 1998); Harry Hubball and Helen Burt, "An Integrated Approach to Developing and Implementing Learning-Centred Curricula," *International Journal for Academic Development*, 9:1 (2004), 51–65; Peggy L. Maki, *Assessing for Learning: Building a Sustainable Commitment across the Institution* (Sterling, VA: Stylus, 2004); and Floyd G. Robinson, John A. Ross, and Floyd White, *Curriculum Development for Effective Instruction* (Toronto: OISE, 1985).

BIOGRAPHIES OF EDITORS AND CONTRIBUTORS

Barry L. Stiefel, Ph.D., is an assistant professor in the undergraduate historic preservation and community planning program at the College of Charleston as well as the joint College of Charleston/Clemson University graduate program in historic preservation. In 2011, Dr. Stiefel was awarded the College of Charleston's ExCEL (Excellence in Collegiate Education and Leadership) Award for Outstanding Faculty of the Year from the Graduate School. His research focuses on the preservation of Jewish heritage, from which he has published many articles. Stiefel has two published books, *Jewish Sanctuary in the Atlantic World: A Social and Architectural History* and *Jews and the Renaissance of Synagogue Architecture, 1450–1730*. Dr. Stiefel received his Ph.D. in historic preservation from Tulane University as well as a master of urban planning from the University of Michigan, a graduate certificate in historic preservation from Eastern Michigan University, and a B.S. in environmental policy from Michigan State University.

Jeremy C. Wells, Ph.D., is an assistant professor in the graduate historic preservation program at Roger Williams University, Rhode Island. His research addresses the sociocultural and experiential valuation of the historic environment and ways to assess these values, with a focus on phenomenology and mixed-methods, in order to inform planning practice for the historic environment. Wells is also involved in the Environmental Design Research Association (EDRA), where he created the Historic Environment Network that focuses on ways to integrate environmental design and behavior research into heritage conservation practice. He received his Ph.D. in environmental design and planning from Clemson University and also holds an M.S. in historic preservation from the University of Pennsylvania and a B.S. in historic preservation from Southeast Missouri State University.

Luiz Amorim has a bachelor degree in architecture and urbanism (1982, *Universidade Federal de Pernambuco,* Brazil) and a Ph.D. (1999, University College London). He held a private office between 1983 and 1988, but dedicated most of his time to teaching and researching, first at the Universidade Federal de Alagoas and later at the Universidade Federal de Pernambuco, where he remains to the present. His main field of research is urban and architectural morphology, with a particular interest in Space Syntax, but he has also published papers and books on modern and contemporary Brazilian architecture and heritage conservation. He was a visiting professor at the Taubman College of Architecture and Urban Planning—University of Michigan in 2004, a member of the Specialists Committee of Education of Architecture and Urbanism—Brazilian Ministry of Education and Sports between 1993 and 1994, and a member of various scientific committees in Brazil and abroad.

Robert Benedict, Ph.D., is the director of the master of real estate development program at Clemson University. Dr. Benedict received his master of business administration from the University of Georgia, a master of arts in historic preservation from Goucher College, and a Ph.D. in environmental design and planning from Clemson University. His research interests include historic district design guidelines, adaptive reuse of historic structures, and collaborative education in real estate and historic preservation. Prior to joining Clemson, Dr. Benedict was a real estate developer primarily focused on adaptive reuse and infill projects. He also was a historic preservation consultant specializing in preservation tax credits and National Register nominations. He also taught preservation economics at the University of Georgia and currently teaches development process, capstone, and preservation feasibility courses at Clemson University.

Lauren Weiss Bricker, Ph.D., is professor of architecture at California State Polytechnic University, Pomona, and director of the College of Environmental Design Archives-Special Collections. Dr. Bricker is past chair of the State Historical Resources Commission in California, and co-founder of the Commission's Committee on the Cultural Resources of the Modern Age. She is the author of *The Mediterranean House in America* (Abrams, 2008), and co-author of the catalogue *Steel and Shade: The Architecture of Donald Wexler*—which accompanied an exhibition of the same title (Palm Springs Museum of Art, 2011). She is cocurator of "Technology and Environment: The Southern California Postwar House," one in a series of exhibitions of the Getty's Pacific Standard Time Presents: Modern Architecture L.A. She is completing a manuscript for *Designing the Modern House* (W. W. Norton, 2014).

Regina Faden, Ph.D., joined Historic St. Mary's City (HSMC) as executive director in October 2008. Since her arrival, the museum has expanded it programmatic offerings, developed a new five-year strategic plan, realigned its marketing, and is leading an initiative to further develop the story of slavery at the museum. HSMC is affiliated with St. Mary's College of Maryland and partner in an undergraduate museum studies minor. Faden has helped museum staff develop museum studies courses and taught introduction to museum studies. From 2004 to 2008 Faden served as executive director of the Mark Twain Boyhood Home and Museum in Hannibal, Missouri. Since 1987, Faden has taught courses in American literature, rhetoric, business writing, museum studies, and American history at such schools as Boston College, Saint Louis University, University of Missouri-St. Louis, and St. Mary's College of Maryland.

Cari Goetcheus is an associate professor of historic preservation and landscape Architecture at the University of Georgia, College of Environment and Design, and director of the UGA-CED Cultural Landscape Laboratory. Prior to her academic career, Ms. Goetcheus worked in both the public and private sectors with firms known for their cultural landscape work. As a historical landscape architect with the National Park Service in Atlanta, Georgia, and Washington, D.C., Goetcheus worked with the cultural landscape inventory program. On a volunteer basis at the national level, Goetcheus was instrumental in developing the Historic American Landscape Survey program and its documentation guidelines. With twenty-five years of private, public, and academic experience in landscape architecture and preservation planning, Goetcheus's research interests include landscape preservation education, vernacular and ethnographic cultural landscapes, and the impact of African American culture on the landscapes of the Southeast.

Ingrid Holmberg has a bachelor's degree from the program in integrated conservation of built environments, University of Gothenburg (UG), and a doctoral degree in Conservation, UG, on a dissertation that explores ways in which the past participates in the social construction and imagery of a place (*On the Urban Surface: Historicization of Haga*). Her research is directed toward built environments as heritage, and in particular on the epistemological conditions for increased history of built environments, and on the societal processes that construct heritage. As part of the faculty she has for several years been manager of the integrated conservation of built environments program.

Luis Hoyos is a licensed architect and associate professor of architecture at the California State Polytechnic University in Pomona, where he teaches historic preservation and urban design. He serves as a member of the board of advisors of the National Trust for Historic Preservation and as a member of the Landmarks Committee of the National Park System Advisory Board. He is national co-chair for NPS of the just-released American Latino Heritage Theme Study. He was member and chair of the California State Historical Resources Commission and a member of the board of directors and chair of Preservation Advocacy at the Los Angeles Conservancy. As an architect he has received awards for the design of several historic building rehabilitations, including El Pueblo de Los Angeles, the Point Fermin Lighthouse, the Palmer Hotel, and the Cabrillo Beach Bathhouse.

Paul Hardin Kapp is associate professor of architecture, chair of the History and Preservation program at the School of Architecture, and associate director of the Collaborative for Cultural Heritage Management and Policy at the University of Illinois at Urbana-Champaign. He is also historic preservation architect and his work has earned awards from Preservation North Carolina, the Preservation Alliance of Virginia (now APVA), and the Association of General Contractors of East Tennessee. Prior to coming to Illinois, he was the historic architect and campus historic preservation manager for the University of North Carolina at Chapel Hill, where he also taught historic preservation in the Department of City and Regional Planning. He has served on the National Register advisory boards in Virginia and Illinois and is currently the chair of the National Council for Preservation Education. His most recently edited book, *SynergiCity: Reinventing the Postindustrial City* (University of Illinois Press, 2012), has won the 2013 Historic Preservation Award from the Center for Historic Preservation at the University of Mary Washington. In 2014, he will be a Fulbright Scholar at the University of Birmingham in the United Kingdom; he will continue his research on post-industrial historic preservation and urban regeneration.

Bosse Lagerqvist is, since summer 2012, head of the Department of Conservation at the University of Gothenburg (UG). He has a bachelor's degree from the program in integrated conservation of built environments, UG, and a doctoral degree in conservation, UG, on a dissertation on photogrammetry and information management. He has been part of the faculty at the Department of Conservation since the mid-1980s with a nine-year period as a director of studies. His research has over the years covered subjects such as recording methods, reuse of industrial heritage, and the maritime heritage including the heritage afloat. From January 2004 to December 2008 he combined the academic position with practice in industrial heritage development on a regional level. He is on the board of the Swedish Association of Industrial Heritage, and a member of the International Committee for the Conservation of the Industrial Heritage.

Philip Leverton obtained a degree in urban land economics at Sheffield Polytechnic, followed by postgraduate study in urban planning at City of Birmingham Polytechnic and research at the University of East Anglia. He spent nine years employed in local government in the United Kingdom, engaged with a range of planning, development, and conservation work while qualifying as a chartered surveyor and chartered town planner, before holding academic posts at Nottingham Trent University and the University of Glamorgan. Following further postgraduate work to obtain a master's degree in heritage management at the Ironbridge Institute, University of Birmingham, he was employed as project officer by The Waterways Trust before joining the College in 2004. Leverton's main research interests are influences on the evolution and regeneration of suburban and smaller urban areas, and the use of built and cultural heritage assets as a vehicle for regeneration.

Fernando Diniz Moreira is an associate professor at the Federal University of Pernambuco (UFPE) in Brazil. He holds a Ph.D. in architecture from the University of Pennsylvania (2004). He received his B.A. in architecture from the UFPE (1990) and a master's degree in city planning from the same university (1994). For more than two decades he has been teaching courses on theory and history of modern architecture, and on architectural conservation in varied schools. He co-founded the Center of Advanced Studies of the Integrated Conservation (CECI) and served as its general-director (2009–11). He is now federal counselor for the newly created Brazilian Council for Architecture and Urbanism (CAU-BR) (2012–14) His professional experience also included conservation plans for urban districts, convents, and other listed buildings. He has been participating in seminars and conferences worldwide and has been publishing about Brazilian modern architecture and urbanism in journals and books in more than ten countries.

Robert W. Ogle is director of historic preservation studies and administrative faculty for the Boston Architectural College (BAC), which offers graduate and undergraduate degrees plus a certificate in historic preservation. Prior to joining the BAC, he served as dean of career and technical education at Spoon River College and Lamar Community College. He also served as administrative director of the Center for Historic Architecture and Preservation and adjunct assistant professor in the graduate historic preservation program at the University of Kentucky. Mr. Ogle is a frequent speaker on the business and economics of historic preservation and consults on historic preservation pedagogy and curriculum development. He is currently pursuing a Ph.D. from Salve Regina University and has earned a master of historic preservation degree from the University of Kentucky, a certificate in historic preservation from Bucks County Community College, and a bachelor of science degree in finance and economics from Philadelphia University.

Shelley-Anne Peleg is the director of the International Conservation Center (in Acre, Israel), Citt'a di Roma, on behalf of the Israel Antiquities Authority. Her responsibilities include the development of the center as a leading practical conservation center in Israel and international academic relations. Within this framework, she is involved in national academic conservation programs, national practical conservation training programs, conferences on conservation of the built heritage, international conservation workshops, international and national student internships, and the development of a Cultural Heritage Library for Acre and Conservation Laboratories in Acre. She is an active member of the Israel National Commission to UNESCO—the committee of Conservation Training, a member of ICOMOS—Israel Scientific Committee for Conservation Training, and a member of the editorial board for the *Journal of Eastern Mediterranean Archeology and Heritage Studies,* published by Pennsylvania State University Press. Her academic research topics deal with the relationship between the local population, economic development, and conservation procedures within historic cities in Israel.

Karla Nunes Penna is an architect and urban planner, lecturer of the Centre for Advanced Studies in Integrated Conservation (CECI), and Ph.D. researcher of Curtin University's School of Education. She teaches courses on cultural heritage integrated into urban planning, management of conservation works, cultural heritage studies, and project management. She has been a heritage practitioner for fifteen years in Brazil, planning, coordinating, and implementing projects and public policies for preservation and conservation of cultural heritage in World Heritage Sites located in northeast Brazil. Much of her work is focused on developing strategic plans and initiatives to promote economic and social development, social inclusion, and carrying out the policies of preservation education programs in poor areas.

Anastasia L. Pratt is an assistant professor at SUNY Empire State College, where she coordinates the advanced certificate in public history and serves as faculty member for the Northeast Center and the master of arts in liberal studies program. Her research mainly focuses on the idea of "home" and explorations of that idea in buildings, images, literature, and popular culture. She is also very interested in the ways that virtual, distance, and open education learning tools can be used to enhance lifelong learning for adult students. Anastasia is the author of an Images of America book, *Clinton County,* and a forthcoming book focused on Clinton County's postcards.

Henry Russell studied for the Royal Institution of Chartered Surveyors diploma in building conservation at the College of Estate Management (CEM) in the mid-1990s and joined CEM as a course leader in 2001. He also contributes to CEM research projects and presentations at other institutions. Russell chairs the Gloucester Diocesan Advisory Committee for the Care of Churches and is a member of the Church Buildings Council. He is a member of the Education and Training Committee for the U.K. National Committee of the International Council on Monuments and Sites and a trustee of the Conference on Training in Architectural Conservation. He is also extensively involved in the work of leading U.K. professional bodies connected with heritage. Russell has provided parliamentary liaison support for the Heritage Alliance on the heritage aspects of proposed government legislation and policy guidance. He now chairs the Heritage Alliance's Spatial Planning Advocacy Group, which regularly liaises with English Heritage and government departments over changes to land use planning and heritage legislation.

Robert Russell, Ph.D., was for twenty years the Addlestone Professor in the Art History Department at the College of Charleston (S.C.). For a dozen of those years he directed the college's undergraduate program in historic preservation and community planning. In 2013, he moved to Newport, Rhode Island, to become the director of the program in cultural and historic preservation at Salve Regina University. An architectural historian by training, Russell has also become over the last decade an expert in issues of cemetery conservation and has restored monuments in many of the historic cemeteries and graveyards in and around Charleston.

Melissa Santana is an assistant professor of practice at Northern Arizona University. Her research emphasis is in historic preservation and its relationship to sustainable development, which includes social, environmental, and economic sustainability. Much of her research has focused on these concepts relating to Cuban architecture and the relationship between the United States and Cuba. Melissa's area of teaching includes building information modeling, design methodologies, the history of interior design, and senior capstone classes. Personal interests of hers include traveling as much as possible.

Valerie Settles is the director of the interior design program in the Department of Design at the University of Central Oklahoma. She holds master's degrees in both industrial engineering and interior design, and is currently completing a Ph.D. in human environmental sciences with an emphasis on interior design and historic preservation education. Her professional and teaching experience is in commercial interior design, materials and finishes, history of interior design, and interior design practice. She is an active member of the American Society of Interior Designers and the Interior Design Educator's Council.

Andréa Livi Smith, Ph.D., is an assistant professor of preservation planning and the director of the Center for Historic Preservation at the University of Mary Washington. Trained as an urban planner, preservationist, and architectural historian, Smith has focused her research on the intersection of urban design, transportation, and preservation. Among her other interests, Smith is active in pedagogical research and the integration of technology in the preservation classroom. More information regarding her ongoing endeavors can be found at http://andrealivismith.com.

Gilbert S. Stiefel, Ph.D., is an associate professor at Eastern Michigan University's Department of Special Education. He completed his doctorate in psychology at the University of Michigan in 1985. He specializes in the assessment of learning outcomes and has published several articles.

Elisabeth Taylor, Ph.D., is a senior lecturer at Curtin University's School of Education where she specializes in educational research with a particular focus on social and cultural aspects of education including girls' education, Aboriginal education, and education for sustainability. While she appreciates the value of quantitative approaches for appropriate research purposes, she prefers naturalistic research methodologies such as ethnography, phenomenology, and grounded theory approaches in her own work. Much of her research is embedded in critical constructivist and social constructionist research paradigms.

Ola Wetterberg has held the chair in conservation at University of Gothenburg (UG) since 2002, and was, unti 2012, head of the Department of Conservation. In 2013 he was appointed deputy dean at the Faculty of Science, UG. Previously he has held a position as expert at the National Heritage Board in Sweden. He has a bachelor's degree from the program in integrated conservation of built environments, UG, and a doctoral degree in architectural history, Chalmers University of Technology, Gothenburg, Sweden. His dissertation discussed how historical factors in building conservation and town planning were introduced in legislation and governmental organization during the first decades of the twentieth century in Sweden. His present research circles around the changing values and new uses of church heritage in contemporary society, and questions closely related to urban culture and heritage. He teaches history and theory of conservation, as well as conservation planning.

Silvio Mendes Zancheti, Ph.D., retired as Full Professor of the Graduated Program in Urban Development, the Federal University of Pernambuco (Recife, Brazil), where he worked for thirty years. Zancheti was the founding director of the Center of Advanced Studies in Integrated Conservation (CECI), as well as the coordinator of the UNESCO Chair in integrated conservation between 2001 and 2003. Zancheti has published intensively on heritage conservation theory, urban conservation, urban planning, architectural restoration, and urban history. He has also coordinated many urban plans including the Master Plan of Recife, the Master Plan of Olinda (World Heritage Site), and the Revitalization Plan of the Old Historic Center of Recife, as well as consulted to the World Bank, the Inter-American Development Bank, and UNESCO, among other accomplishments. Presently, he is a visiting professor at Mackenzie Presbyterian University.